T0134493

Human–Computer Interaction Series

Editors-in-Chief

Desney Tan
Microsoft Research, Redmond, WA, USA

Jean Vanderdonckt
Louvain School of Management, Université catholique de Louvain,
Louvain-La-Neuve, Belgium

The Human–Computer Interaction Series, launched in 2004, publishes books that advance the science and technology of developing systems which are effective and satisfying for people in a wide variety of contexts. Titles focus on theoretical perspectives (such as formal approaches drawn from a variety of behavioural sciences), practical approaches (such as techniques for effectively integrating user needs in system development), and social issues (such as the determinants of utility, usability and acceptability).

HCI is a multidisciplinary field and focuses on the human aspects in the development of computer technology. As technology becomes increasingly more pervasive the need to take a human-centred approach in the design and development of computer-based systems becomes ever more important.

Titles published within the Human–Computer Interaction Series are included in Thomson Reuters' Book Citation Index, The DBLP Computer Science Bibliography and The HCI Bibliography.

More information about this series at http://www.springer.com/series/6033

D. Scott McCrickard · Michael Jones ·
Timothy L. Stelter

Editors

HCI Outdoors: Theory, Design, Methods and Applications

 Springer

Editors
D. Scott McCrickard
Department of Computer Science
and Center for Human-Computer Interaction
Virginia Tech
Blacksburg, VA, USA

Michael Jones
Department of Computer Science
Brigham Young University
Provo, UT, USA

Timothy L. Stelter
Department of Computer Science
and Center for Human-Computer Interaction
Virginia Tech
Blacksburg, VA, USA

ISSN 1571-5035   ISSN 2524-4477 (electronic)
Human–Computer Interaction Series
ISBN 978-3-030-45291-9   ISBN 978-3-030-45289-6 (eBook)
https://doi.org/10.1007/978-3-030-45289-6

© Springer Nature Switzerland AG 2020
This work is subject to copyright. All rights are reserved by the Publisher, whether the whole or part of the material is concerned, specifically the rights of translation, reprinting, reuse of illustrations, recitation, broadcasting, reproduction on microfilms or in any other physical way, and transmission or information storage and retrieval, electronic adaptation, computer software, or by similar or dissimilar methodology now known or hereafter developed.
The use of general descriptive names, registered names, trademarks, service marks, etc. in this publication does not imply, even in the absence of a specific statement, that such names are exempt from the relevant protective laws and regulations and therefore free for general use.
The publisher, the authors and the editors are safe to assume that the advice and information in this book are believed to be true and accurate at the date of publication. Neither the publisher nor the authors or the editors give a warranty, expressed or implied, with respect to the material contained herein or for any errors or omissions that may have been made. The publisher remains neutral with regard to jurisdictional claims in published maps and institutional affiliations.

This Springer imprint is published by the registered company Springer Nature Switzerland AG
The registered company address is: Gewerbestrasse 11, 6330 Cham, Switzerland

Acknowledgements

A book cannot be written without contributions from a great many people. Certainly, all of the chapter authors went above and beyond in their writings, readings, and comments regarding this book. The participants at the many workshops relevant to this book, in particular, at the HCI Outdoors workshop at the ACM SIGCHI 2018, contributed greatly to the advancement of the core ideas of this book. Much thanks to the Fall 2019 students in CS 4784 HCI Capstone and CS 6724 Special Topics in HCI courses at Virginia Tech and in CS 656 Interactive Software Systems at Brigham Young U. (BYU) for their in-depth readings, insightful presentations and discussions, and cross-university feedback on chapters and organization. Financial support for the Tech on the Trail workshops was provided by Virginia Tech's Center for Human–Computer Interaction, Institute for Creativity, Arts, and Technology, and Department of Computer Science. M. Jones' involvement was supported by NSF grant IIS-1406578 and a travel grant from the BYU Computer Science Department.

Contents

Finding Human–Computer Interaction Outdoors

D. Scott McCrickard, Michael Jones, and Timothy L. Stelter

Abstract Human–computer interaction, as a discipline, has shifted from an examination of computers in controlled indoor environments to the study of technology use in a broader collection of settings, including the outdoors. This chapter seeks to explore the evolution of HCI outdoors as an area of study, seeking to identify the considerations that make it an important and unique domain. We begin by examining the tensions and opportunities that have long existed between technology and the outdoors, pointing to the unique position of HCI as a discipline for probing these issues. Using HCI as a lens, we then seek to understand what is meant by the outdoors, and how humans, computers, and their interaction together have evolved to a point that they can address issues of outdoor use. We introduce several seminal efforts related to the study of technology use in outdoor settings, including a collection of recent workshops and events that helped identify and bring together important ideas in the field. We conclude with a categorization and introduction of the chapters in this book on HCI outdoors. The chapters in this book present new theory, design, methods, and applications that will shape the emerging field of HCI outdoors.

1 Overview

As interactive computing pushes into outdoor activities, it is not clear what the role of this technology is or should be. It may seem odd to pair technology with the outdoors, as many look to the outdoors as a place to escape from technology. However, the benefits of using technology in outdoor situations hold promise for better experiences and better reflections after the experiences. People want to enjoy their outdoor experience, but to do so they may need information at the moment that

D. S. McCrickard (✉) · T. L. Stelter
Department of Computer Science and Center for Human Computer Interaction, Virginia Tech, Blacksburg, VA, USA
e-mail: mccricks@cs.vt.edu

M. Jones
Department of Computer Science, Brigham Young University, Provo, UT, USA

© Springer Nature Switzerland AG 2020
D. S. McCrickard et al. (eds.), *HCI Outdoors: Theory, Design, Methods and Applications*, Human–Computer Interaction Series,
https://doi.org/10.1007/978-3-030-45289-6_1

technology can provide. Or they may be unable to fully experience elements of the outdoors without technology. Or they may wish to capture aspects of the outdoor experience for scientific or personal advancement. Or technology may guide them to experience something positive but which they had not intended to experience. Technology can help us learn, calculate, remember, share, coordinate, work, play, and more. But, as both designers and users of technology, it is important that we seek to understand ways to use technology that meet our goals and desires outdoors.

This book explores how human–computer interaction (HCI) can help us understand, define, realize, and evaluate the emerging role of technology in the outdoors. In the 1970s and 1980s, the earliest years of HCI as a discipline, HCI methods largely focused on single users and desktop machines, using quantifiable performance metrics like learning time, completion time, and error rate as most popular ways to measure success—with its methods melded from cognitive science, psychology, and computer science. The 1990s and 2000s saw the growth of HCI, to include broader definitions of humans, computers, and interactions, along with a wider range of methodological disciplines such as ethnography, sociology, art, and engineering. Within the last two decades, HCI has cast a wide net, seeking to shift from desktop and laptop machines to include mobile and wearable devices, and from direct interactions to include indirect and sensed ones. This evolution of HCI as a discipline positions it as a lens through which to examine technology outdoors, a domain for which a traditional desktop-based direct interaction examination would not suffice.

An important early consideration for the editors was to identify what was meant by the outdoors. It is difficult to describe the true nature of outdoors, or even to outline what it is and is not, so we sought to establish a spectrum of factors for which our methods would be increasingly applicable. As a way to ground these ideas, consider a typical office park setting, such as the one where the first editor has an office. There is a large picture window at his office that looks over a sculpted lawn, a pond with a fountain, and paved walking trails. The trails lead to the Huckleberry Trail, a rails-to-trails multi-use path. This in turn leads to Pandapas Pond, an 8-acre day-use area that permits hunting, fishing, mountain biking, and horseback riding. The pond is part of the Washington-Jefferson U.S. National Forest, a vast minimally developed tract of land that spans several states. The Appalachian Trail, a U.S. National Scenic Trail that spans over 2000 miles across 14 states, cuts through the forest. The Appalachian Trail passes through some small towns and other semi-developed regions, but it also traverses near or through 20 National Wilderness Areas[1]

Each step in this narrative, from viewing a sculpted outdoor setting to traversing an untamed wilderness area, adds different opportunities, challenges, and drawbacks to appropriate use of technology in increasingly unwelcoming—and sometimes unwelcomed—environments. To some degree, this is because the design of many technologies has been targeted for more urban environments, both in the nature of the hardware and in the design of the technology. As examples, mobile phones tend

---

[1] The United States Congress established National Wilderness Areas with the passage of the Wilderness Act of 1964. Wilderness areas are protected tracts of wildlands where "man himself is a visitor but does not remain."

to be hard to read in direct sunlight, and wearable cameras exhaust their batteries after only a few hours. Potential users must either seek to suffice with inappropriate technologies or look to craft better ones.

Taking a step back, to many authors and artists, the outdoors is a place of solitude that should be devoid of technology—even among people who otherwise are tech-engaged or tech-knowledgeable. Eric Brende left a career in technology after completing his MIT degree to live devoid of most technologies, detailed in his book Better Off (Brende 2004). Bestselling books like Richard Louv's Last Child in the Woods notes the loss of exposure to nature for children and points to the "myopic focus on high technology as salvation" as a reason why young people lack this exposure (Louv 2008). Popular writers like Bill Bryson, when he encounters a hiker with a weather sensing station, laments "How I hate all of this technology on the trail" (Bryson 1998).

Yet, it is often technology that positions an outdoor experience as unique, special, memorable, and even possible. Mark Twain's Huck Finn had his raft that enabled him to travel the Mississippi River (Twain 1885), and Steinbeck's Joad family had a vehicle (and the knowledge to keep it working) (Steinbeck 1939). Sometimes, it's the lack of technology that makes an outdoor experience special, viz., walking the 2000-mile Appalachian Trail barefoot (Letcher and Letcher 2008), and sometimes it is an excess of technology (sacrificing convenience and practicality for data, knowledge, and understanding) as seen in Alan Dix's tech-enhanced walk around the perimeter of Wales (Asimakopoulos and Dix 2017; Dix and Ellis 2015). Scientists, environmentalists, educators, and search and rescue personnel all rely on technology in outdoor settings. Recreation activities become more accessible because of technology, including and especially for those with special needs, and the ability to reflect is enhanced. And technology provides avenues to learn skills that otherwise are hard to acquire, including skills related to navigation, health, and safety.

So how do we identify the appropriate situations for technology, and the appropriate ways to present information and engage with tech users in outdoor settings? HCI provides theories, methods, and assessment techniques that may prove helpful in addressing these problems, though it is not yet clear which best applies. HCI, only about 30 years old, is still a young discipline that has experienced significant change as new interactive technologies emerge. HCI has its roots and in its name the understanding of the opportunities, tensions, and interaction styles that occur when humans and computers come together. The discipline has evolved from focusing on controlled lab situations to include the examination of the wild. Miniaturization of technology and advances in power and network connectivity have made possible a broad array of functionality in outdoor settings. This book seeks to highlight emerging research that demonstrates ways that HCI can play a role in understanding ways that humans and technology interact in the outdoors.

2   Topical Scope

We describe the topical scope of the book using a broad HCI-based framework. The framework can be used to describe and discuss technology use in the outdoors. We intend for this framework to be a starting point and expect that it will evolve and perhaps, eventually, be completely replaced. As a lens, HCI foregrounds four elements of technology used outdoors: one or more humans, a computer system, human interaction with the computer system, and being outdoors. Table 1 contains a definition, categorization schemes, and several examples for each of these four concepts. The remainder of this section describes each concept as it relates to the broad space of HCI outdoors. The chapters in this book begin to populate this space and provide examples of different directions for research and practice involving HCI outdoors. (This section bolds references to chapter authors, with first initials provided to clarify ambiguity.)

2.1   Outdoors

In simplest terms, the outdoors is "a place or location away from the confines of a building."[2] This definition includes a wide variety of outdoor settings ranging

Table 1 Four elements of human–computer interaction outdoors along a selection of categories and examples elaborated in this section. The categories and examples here exemplify the broad base that exists and is emerging for the study and practice of HCI outdoors

Outdoors	Definition: an environment which is not indoors and lacks the controls and amenities of the indoors, for which factors like weather and lighting are of particular concern Categories: climate, degree of human development Examples: public urban spaces, groomed ski slopes, rain forests, deserts, long-distance hiking trails
Human(s)	Definition: individual or group for whom physical, mental, and interpersonal issues affect the situation and the technology use Categories: individual characteristics include age, gender, vision, memory, height, dexterity, disabilities; group characteristics include connectedness, communication, conflict Examples: children, people with autism, hikers, skiers, environmental engineers, citizen scientists, 5-person rescue team
Computer(s)	Definition: electronic system consisting of programmable hardware or software Categories: form factor, connectivity, sensors, input/output modalities Examples: smartphone, smartwatch, haptics, VR/AR headsets, the internet
Interaction	Definition: ways that humans and technology connect and communicate Categories: direct manipulation, commands, conversations, notifications Examples: typing, clicking, scrolling, learning, speech, gestures

---

[2]As defined in the online edition of the Merriam-Webster dictionary.

from city streets to remote wilderness. When presenting or planning work involving HCI outdoors, it may be useful to describe the outdoor setting in some detail. This can be done using existing schemes that classify the outdoors based on climate and on the degree of human development, which seem to have a significant impact on HCI outdoors. We describe two well-known classification systems: the recreational opportunity spectrum (ROS) for the degree of human development and the Koppen scale for climate. Alternative classification schemes exist for both climate and human development, as can be found in a climatology textbook (Rohli and Vega 2017) and other research involving the degree of human development (Hill et al. 2002). Classification schemes also exist for other properties of the outdoors such as plant cover or for bodies of water.

We focus on climate and human development as they seem to have a significant impact on HCI outdoors. Climate describes the range of weather conditions found at a location over a period of decades. Climate and weather impact how a user interacts with a device outdoors. On a cold day in an arctic climate, interacting with a smartphone touch screen is difficult because the user must take off their gloves to touch the screen and ungloved fingers can quickly become numb. However, on a warm day in a temperate oceanic climate, interacting with a touchscreen is simple.

Human development outdoors refers to elements of the built or cultivated environment. Human development dictates the power and network resources that will be available and often shapes social context. For example, primitive settings lack power outlets that are abundant in urban settings. Even in rural settings, access to networks may be limited compared to urban settings. Human development influences what is acceptable or even desirable in a given outdoor setting. For example, constantly checking email could be seen as intrusive in a wilderness region but as part of the routine in an urban area.

The Koppen scale classifies regions of land based on climate and consists of 26 climates organized into 5 primary groups (Rohli and Vega 2017): tropical, dry, temperate, continental, and polar. Within a primary group, climates are distinguished by monthly average rainfall and temperature over a period of decades. Primary groups are denoted by the letters A through E and subgroups are indicated using one or two additional letters. For example, the Koppen climate "Am" is a tropical (A) monsoon (m) climate, and climate "Dsa" is a continental climate (D) with dry (s), hot (a) summers. Climates and seasons play prominent roles in several chapters of this book. **Häkkillä's** chapter takes place in a cold subarctic climate (specifically in Koppen zone Dfc) in the winter, and **Anderson's** case study is set in spring in a semi-arid climate (in Koppen zone Bsk).

The recreational opportunity spectrum (ROS) categorizes outdoor settings based on the evidence of human impacts. Human impact is measured by the presence of built facilities (such as buildings and indoor plumbing), access methods (such as roads or trails), and the presence of other people (Clark and Stankey 1979; United States Department of Agriculture Forest Service 1986, 2011). While the ROS was developed by the United States Forest Service, it has been used in other areas of the world (Joyce and Sutton 2009; Paracchini et al. 2014). There are six top-level classes in the ROS: primitive, semi-primitive non-motorized, semi-primitive motorized, roaded natural, rural, and urban. Primitive settings normally lack built facilities, are not accessible by roads, and have few people present simultaneously. At the other end of the scale, urban settings have abundant complex facilities, are accessible by many well-maintained roads, and are often crowded with people. In this book, the degree of human development figures prominently in several chapters. For example, the chapters of **Balestrini** and **Aguiar** explore technology designed for urban environments, **Dix** and **Su** examine technology opportunities in rural environments, and **B. Jones'** studies technology supporting search and rescue in a primitive wilderness environment. **Alsaleem**'s sitski system has been used in several locations including testing at a ski resort in the Wasatch Mountains, Utah, USA. The ski resort is located in a high-altitude humid continental climate (zone Dfb) and was developed to become an urban setting in the ROS scheme.

2.2 Humans

The term human connotes many things, including abilities to think, reason, move, plan, communicate, and work together. In the short history of HCI, the concept of "human" has evolved considerably. The ACM SIGCHI Conference in the early 1980s primarily focused on single-user systems, in which a user in an office setting worked on focused, well-defined tasks with a clear end goal (e.g., remembering command names, editing text documents, navigating graphical interfaces). Measures of human performance focused on ways that people think, process, react to, and remember information, as well as on the physical work environment. The late 1980s and 1990s saw increased study of multi-tasking, ubiquitous computing, and computer-supported collaborative work (CSCW), examining how multiple people work together on many different tasks, using both computers in the traditional sense and technology on our persons and in our environment. During the 2000s, HCI has embraced a great many other fields, including art, architecture, geography, ethnography, sociology, and much more—each with its own ways of defining what it means to be human.

Core HCI textbooks and reference books focus on humans' abilities and characteristics, guiding designers to consider them in crafting and evaluating designs. In their widely used introductory textbook, Ben Shneiderman and his colleagues highlight the physical, cognitive, and perceptual abilities of humans, emphasizing the importance of considering cultural and international diversity, differences in personality, abilities and limitations due to age, and importance of considering users with disabilities (Shneiderman et al. 2016). Grudin notes the importance of considering perceptual, cognitive, social, and emotional characteristics of humans during design (Grudin 2017). Wickens et al. compare visual, auditory, and spatial factors for perception and attention in human performance (Wickens et al. 2015).

HCI practitioners and researchers employ user models to capture human characteristics viewed as most relevant to design. Generally, these user models are rooted in a data-centered understanding of the target user, toward ensuring that the design will meet the users' needs. For example, personas require designers to craft an archetype user that captures specific needs, based on the analysis of user data, then revisit the persona constantly during design to help guide decision-making (Cooper et al. 2004; Pruitt and Grudin 2003). Common user characteristics that are captured in personas and other user models include name, age, occupation, hobbies, relationships, and more. Increasingly, the discipline of HCI has examined humans not only as individuals but also as part of a group, such as a couple, family, team, or community. Factors of the group, such as connectedness, communication styles, and desire to cooperate or compete, must be considered when investigating and designing for the goals and needs of the people—not just as individuals but as a group.

In considering the human component of HCI outdoors, the chapters of this book represent many different ways to understand and design for humans. For example, the perceptual, mental model, attentional chapter by **B. Jones** and his colleagues focuses on distributed cognition, exploring how people bring their collective knowledge and skills to a search and rescue situation, and how technology can contribute to that knowing and doing. In contrast, the chapter by **Patrick** and his colleagues consider physical characteristics of users, considering how bone conduction devices can help people better use their auditory senses. The chapter by **Neustaedter** and his colleagues explores the connectedness of groups of humans (families), and the chapter by **Polys et al.** looks at how groups of people come together with technology in scientific inquiry. Some chapters focus on a particular subset of humans, such as the chapter by **Fails and M. Jones** that studies outdoor interfaces for children and the chapter by **Al Saleem** and his colleagues that describes a snow skiing interface to support people with disabilities. The careful consideration of what it means to be human helps craft technology solutions that meet real needs.

2.3 Computers

Describing the notion of a computer within HCI is a moving target. In HCI textbooks, the term "computer" is often paired with other terms—like "[computer] technology," "computer/electronic device," or "[computer] system"—and includes a focus on input and output devices like the keyboard, mouse, and digital display (Bryant et al. 2016; Carroll 2003, 2013; Dix et al. 2003). However, HCI paradigms that include indirect interaction de-emphasize traditional input and output devices, focusing on a richer collection of sensors, haptics, audio, and more. For example, the notion of the third paradigm (Harrison et al. 2007) and Weiser's concept of calm computing (Weiser 1991) both feature a tighter partnership between the computer and the human-centered actions that are important to its use.

In considering these different notions of a computer, we identify form factor, input/output modalities, sensors, and connectivity as particularly important for HCI outdoors. When using a computer outdoors, the form factor enables certain kinds of interaction possible but precludes others. A large interactive kiosk on a city street invites a group of people to interact but can not be (easily) deployed in a remote rainforest. On the other hand, a handheld smartphone can be used easily in temperate outdoor locations but not in cold climates while wearing gloves. Similarly, input/output modalities also determine what is possible or convenient when interacting with a computer outdoors. For example, handhelds and tablets are convenient on paved or even terrain, but they are challenging and dangerous on rough terrain. Sensors in the outdoors open a wide range of possibilities for direct and indirect interactions. Accelerometers and heart rate monitors in smartwatches allow devices to unobtrusively track steps taken, stairs climbed, and activity levels, while the user focuses on an outdoor activity. Connectivity cannot be taken for granted in the outdoors—both connectivity to global networks and connectivity to nearby devices. Connectivity to global networks has a significant impact on the outdoor experience. Walking through the woods while connected to a mobile data network with emergency help just tap away is different than walking through the woods while completely disconnected from outside networks.

Today, computers are highly modular in that they are coupled with a wide variety of sensors and network capabilities, appearing in many forms to address different needs. For example, a smartphone contains many sensors like GPS, accelerometer, gyroscope, biometric, ambient light, camera, microphone, and more; and usually includes both Wi-Fi and cellular communicators. And smartphones almost always have a small form factor that is comfortable to hold in one's hands.

In considering different roles for computing technology, this book examines an array of theorized, designed, and prototyped systems. Widely available handheld devices facilitate group tasks, as featured in the science-focused chapter by **Polys** and his colleagues, while the chapter by **Kiefer** looks at the design of augmented reality displays that track gaze. **Bartolome** focuses on a single app, Twitter, mainly used on mobile devices, while Dix explores how an array of apps on different devices collectively can gather information that can combine to reveal insights. Several chapters speculate on emerging and future tech use, such as **Anderson's** reimagining of body area networks for recreational hiking, **Kotut's** exploration of possible tech support for communities that exist on and around the trail, and **Cheverst's** examination of how technologies in mountaineering could enhance and eventually go beyond human mastery over nature. The chapter led by **Quitmeyer** pushes the boundaries of possible tech outdoor experiences by developing prototype tech devices that integrate with nature. **B. Jones'** chapter on wilderness search and rescue involves portable devices carried by team members and a desktop physical system with projected images at the command center in a parking lot, for which each device contributes to different levels of situational awareness. **Alsaleem's** tetraski is a kind of distributed system with physical input devices that are carried by both the tethered skier and the skier using the tetraski. The tethered skier's controller is a handheld device and the skier's controller is either a sip-puff tube or a joystick.

2.4 Interactions

The study of interaction in HCI examines the ways that humans and computers connect through the use of technology. In its earliest days, humans would craft their input to technology on cards or electronic tape or other media, which evolved into a specialized command language. The emergence of HCI as a discipline in the 1970s and 1980s corresponded with a more direct interaction between human and technology, with immediate feedback that led to richer connections and a much larger collection of tasks that could be accomplished. Increasingly thereafter, HCI broadened in its view of interaction, to include ways that technology blends into the tasks that people do in less visible ways.

Evidence-based knowledge can capture the physical and mental capabilities of a typical human-relevant in completing tech-related tasks, as seen in the relationship between distance, size, and time for hitting a target as captured in Fitts's law (Fitts 1954) and in timings for key presses and cognitive determinations in KLM and GOMS (Card et al. 1980). These are reflected in HCI guidance like Shneiderman's rules of thumb that provide interface design advice based on human abilities to recognize, remember, process information (Shneiderman ct al. 2016), and Dix's long-term memory networks and scripts that provide ways to represent knowledge connections that people form during decision-making (Dix et al. 2003).

Definitions and categorizations of interaction seek to differentiate ways that humans engage with their use of technology. For example, Preece, Rogers, and Sharp categorize interaction into five types: instructing, conversing, manipulating, exploring, and responding. Each type captures a different style, whether a command to accomplish a task or a dialogue between the human and computer or the exploration of a virtual space (Preece et al. 2019). Only one of the types—responding, a recent addition to a newer version of the textbook—is initiated by the technology to represent the tech-driven notifications and interruptions that often result from sensed information. Increasingly, it has proven important to consider not only direct, user-initiated interaction but also indirect interactions driven by sensors, cameras, biometric devices, geopositioning systems, and more. Numerous recent papers describe the notion of a third paradigm (Harrison et al. 2007) and a reconceptualization of interaction (Sellen et al. 2009) that encouraged researchers and practitioners to look beyond a human–machine coupling to consider the rich challenges and opportunities in the field of HCI through the notion of embodiment, focused on tight interconnections between humans, technology, and the places and situations in which interaction occurs through learning, speech, and gestures.

This expanding view of interaction melds with the vision of this book for HCI outdoors, reflected by the many chapters that feature interaction that goes beyond traditional interaction. For example, the chapter of **Fails and M. Jones** examines how technology augments outdoor experiences for children, keeping them safer and more informed. Several chapters examine emerging or understudied technologies, e.g., **Patrick** and his colleagues explore how emerging bone conduction devices can support multiple audio channels in noisy outdoor settings, while interactions in **Al Saleem's** chapter take place on the ski slope via the "sip and puff" input devices used by paraplegics. In their chapter, **Aguiar and Green** explore how a digital object can transform the way interpersonal interactions take place in an outdoor space. These and other chapters demonstrate the nontraditional ways that people interact with technology, and, in particular, the unique challenges that arise in settings when technology could prove annoying or even dangerous if designed poorly.

Bringing together the three pillars of HCI, it is important to consider humans and their challenges and opportunities in outdoor settings to understand how they want and need to interact with technology—or perhaps why they want to keep the technology in the background—to appropriately enrich their experience. Table 1 provides a roadmap to key factors to consider when exploring HCI situations in the outdoors, and in so doing it highlights avenues for future exploration and application. There is much to be learned in exploring different populations, technologies, and outdoor settings. The next section describes the evolution of the HCI outdoors research area, setting the stage for a description of the book chapters in the final section of this chapter.

3   The Emergence of HCI Outdoors

This section seeks to set the context for HCI outdoors by reviewing milestones in its emergence as an area of interest for researchers and practitioners, starting with some of the inspirational foundations from the 1990s and early 2000s, and then interconnecting and evolving through events and workshops in the 2010s. This book emerged as a core output from several of these workshops, collecting current work on HCI outdoors from participants in one or more of the workshops.

The early stages of the study of HCI explored people's interactions with computers in highly controlled indoor settings, but in 1991 Mark Weiser put forth a new vision of computing that he called "calm computing." In the last paragraph of "The Computer for the 21st Century" (Weiser 1991), Weiser wrote this about the potential of calm computing:

> There is more information available at our fingertips during a walk in the woods than in any computer system, yet people find a walk among trees relaxing and computers frustrating. Machines that fit the human environment, instead of forcing humans to enter theirs, will make using a computer as refreshing as taking a walk in the woods. [emphasis added]

Weiser seemed to be comparing his new vision for computing with a computer-free outdoor experience, with the assumption that "taking a walk in the woods" did not involve a computer and somehow was better for it. In the years since Weiser's vision was put forth, advances in computing technology have made it common to bring, or have available, highly connected computing devices when taking a walk in the woods. Because of this, Weiser's comment is even more apt. Researchers and practitioners in HCI must carefully consider whether a walk in the woods with a computer is as refreshing as a walk in the woods without a computer, or indeed whether that should even be a goal in pursuing HCI outdoors.

In a 2014 article in interactions magazine, Richard Coyne reflected on the merger of smartphones and nature outdoors (Coyne 2014). In the article, Coyne first lays out the case for nature as a restorative environment and then reviews potential pitfalls of bringing ubiquitous computing (which is not always calm computing) into that environment. But his point is not to leave the computing technology indoors, at home, while one is out in nature. Instead, he argues that smartphones and apps, "like a stunning new artwork," can "disrupt, and therefore reveal, aspects of our experience of the natural world." The editors of that issue wrote "we hope his story will lead to discussions about how HCI relates to nature" (Wakkary and Stolterman 2014).

HCI outdoors is not limited to pondering smartphone use in refreshing natural settings. Rogers' "research in the wild" methodology explores ways to take evaluation of interactive systems out of controlled laboratory settings (Rogers and Marshall 2017). A critical part of research in the wild is allowing people to interact with a system in their own environment and on their own terms. Many times, that environment is located outdoors. However, this outdoor setting is not necessarily in the woods or nature. Much of the research in the wild that takes place outdoors has been done on city sidewalks rather than forest paths.

Several workshops have been held to discuss perspectives and work related to HCI in the outdoors. These workshops include the NatureCHI series (Häkkilä et al. 2016, 2017) (as summarized in (Häkkilä et al. 2018)), Tech on the Trail (McCrickard et al. 2018; McCrickard 2017), UbiMount (Daiber et al. 2017; Daiber and Kosmalla 2016) at UbiComp, and an HCI Outdoors workshop (Jones et al. 2018) at CHI. Workshop attendees identified, discussed, and documented core HCI outdoors themes as they relate to many kinds of people, systems, interaction types, and outdoor settings. The editors of this book also participated in organizing some of these workshops. Early versions of many chapters appeared as position papers in the HCI outdoors workshop, and several workshop organizers and participants contributed chapters to this book.

The purpose of this book is to organize current theories, models, and systems related to HCI outdoors. By doing so, we hope to create a convenient place to find a wide range of current work and to accelerate progress in understanding HCI outdoors.

4 Overview of This Book

The 18 chapters in this book are organized into 5 parts, with each part representing a theme that the editors identified in prior literature or that emerged from outdoors-focused HCI workshops and other events. This section describes each of the parts and provides a brief overview of the chapters.

Part I: Rural Contexts The rural context is different from the urban context for which many interactive technologies were developed. These differences include differences in culture and infrastructure. The two chapters in this section reframe the rural from a pastoral fantasy where city dwellers go on vacation to a rural realism where people live. In the language of an American folk song, "the summer folks call it Paradise Mountain but we call it Poverty Hill" (The Kingston Trio 1964). The reality of rural life presents a unique set of opportunities and challenges for HCI outdoors that remain largely unexplored.

Dix uses a walk around Wales as a genesis for scholarship to reflect on interactive computing at the physical margins of Wales as well as the social and economic margins of society as seen in remote rural communities. Dix' walk raises questions about the role of the digital revolution in deepening social and economic divides between people at the margins.

Su's chapter explores infrastructure resources and social norms grounded in his experience in the rural West and Midwest of the United States. This chapter is written in an ethnographic style that "leaves the work open to new connections" and invites the reader to actively participate in finding meaning rather than presenting a pre-packaged set of themes and design implications.

Part II: Willed and the Wild The origin of the English word wilderness suggests that it is the place where wild things are located. In this context, the wild things are things that are "willed" in the sense that they act according to their own will rather than being controlled or domesticated by humans (Nash 2014). The wild side of HCI outdoors happens not just in primitive wilderness but also in urban settings—where study participants and other stakeholders act according to their own will, rather than being controlled or directed by a researcher. Chapters in Part II explore different perspectives of different types of research in wild settings.

Balestrini et al.'s chapter reflects on three case studies involving Rogers' research in the wild methodology in outdoor urban settings. In this methodology, the "wild" is the self-willed interaction of a passer-by with the system. The urban environment presents unique logistical challenges in deploying the system and unique challenges to sustainability in the sense of long-term deployment of a system.

Quitmeyer and Kelly move the creation of interactive media into the wilderness in order to drive the continued maturation of technological devices through exposure to a new environment. In this chapter, research in primitive wilderness involves scientific fieldwork sites as locations for developing new forms of behavioral media in the wild—with the belief that the wild setting will result in a very different design than would emerge from a controlled and domesticated setting. A unique feature of this chapter is that it involves tropical climates rather than continental or temperate climates found in many other chapters in this book.

Polys et al. describe a citizen-science application for use in wild forests in the Appalachian region of the United States. The application allows forest farmers to collect information about where forest and medicinal plants grow. That information can be used to manage plant resources in the wilderness without destroying the very characteristics that define the wilderness setting. The application was evaluated in the wild in two senses: first, it was used in wilderness forest areas and, second, users could use the system, however, they wanted. This chapter confronts not only logistical issues encountered when using mobile apps in primitive wilderness areas, but also encounters unique privacy issues related to tracking valuable plants on public land.

Part III: Groups and Communities Chapters in this section explore ways that technology can assist a collection of people toward a common goal or help them to feel more connected. In these chapters, the group might be a single family or an entire community of users. Each group and community brings a different set of goals and expectations to HCI outdoors.

The first chapter in this section is by Kotut and her colleagues, stemming from a series of workshop activities that leveraged expert knowledge to understand who is on outdoor trail settings. The activities sought to identify the people who used trails—whether for work, enjoyment, a sense of accomplishment, or something else—and then to cluster the people toward understanding the axes that define the trail users and the similarities and conflicts that arise between them.

The Neustaedter et al. chapter explores interactions between family members who wish to share an outdoor experience, but with one member unable to join in person. The shared experience is created by mobile phones that stream video and audio during bicycling and geocaching experiences, with the goal of providing a sense of presence and connectedness in the individual who was unable to attend. The authors crafted and deployed a prototype system, reporting on reactions on the quality of the experience and concerns regarding privacy.

B. Jones leads a chapter that examines how technology can assist in search and rescue situations in wilderness areas that lack networking, radio, and other tech-related support structures. The authors explore different roles, including victim, manager, field team, and management team, seeking to understand and support the needs and challenges of group communication. The authors note that technology can be invaluable at times, but it also must balance the desire for raised awareness with the need to complete a portion of the search task without interruption.

Part IV: Design for Outdoors Moving interaction to the outdoors creates a new set of design challenges and opportunities. Chapters in this section raise important questions about interaction outdoors and present design sensitivities or guidelines to consider when designing for outdoor use. Several forms of interaction are considered ranging from one person using a smartphone to several people interacting around a large installed structure.

Cheverst et al. reflect on design sensitivities suggested by different forms of "mastery over nature" that can be supported by technology in the context of mountaineering. This chapter discusses the social context of technology in mountaineering where the community's acceptance of a new technology can evolve over time and often involves nuanced rules. The chapter suggests ways that design of HCI for the outdoors might move beyond the trope of "mastery" over nature.

Fails and M. Jones explore the design of outdoor technologies for children. This chapter begins with the premise that children have different needs and goals than adults. Because of these different needs and goals, Fails and M. Jones present design considerations for outdoor technology for children. These considerations are drawn from the authors' prior work involving interaction design for children and studies of adults' perspective on hiking with children and technology use.

Aguiar and Green present the design of "communIT" a cyber-physical environment that addresses the decline use of public outdoor urban spaces due to an increase in virtual, rather than physical, interaction between people. The cyber-physical environment is a large-scale origami with lighting, displays, and audio that is approximately 9 feet long and 4.5 feet long and intended to increase social interaction in underused public outdoor spaces. This chapter is a focused study of a specific technology for social interaction in urban spaces.

Patrick et al. discuss situational awareness outdoors when using wearable auditory interfaces with a focus on bone conduction head-mounted devices. In the outdoors, traditional wearable auditory interfaces (such as headphones) can prevent people from hearing surrounding activities. These interfaces can be dangerous in some outdoor environments—such as during military operations. Patrick et al. consider how humans can receive auditory signals simultaneously through bone conduction and ear conduction. This chapter foregrounds human perception in the design of technology for outdoors.

Part V: Outdoor Recreation Outdoor recreation involves a person pursuing an activity other than work in the outdoors. The chapters in this section consider several different outdoor recreation activities and consider people with different skills, abilities, and goals. Users bring a unique set of intentions to outdoor recreation. Some intend to have a thrilling adventure; others intend to spend a few minutes at a roadside scenic viewpoint. Technology use during outdoor recreation can support or detract from many of these intentions, and the chapters in this section apply and extend HCI approaches to enable and enrich outdoor recreation experiences. Much work remains to be done to better understand HCI in the context of outdoor recreation.

Hakkilä and Colley describe four case studies involving the design, prototyping, and evaluation in the context of winter sports. They describe unique logistical challenges faced outdoors in the cold such as batteries draining faster and wires becoming brittle. This work involves supporting people who are already engaged in a physically active lifestyle outdoors and who have at least a moderate level of skill. HCI for outdoor winter sports remains largely unexplored, and many opportunities for research exist in this context.

Alsaleem et al. present a field study of a power-assisted ski chair for people with tetraplegia. Alsaleem et al.'s ski chair shares control between the skier and a control partner (ski instructor). More experienced skiers are given more control, while novice skiers are given less. The chapter presents the experiences of eight participants who used the ski chair while downhill skiing. Technology that supports recreation by individuals with tetraplegia, or other disabilities, may increase opportunities for participation for all users.

Anderson and M. Jones present a vision of HCI outdoors in which interactive computing fades into the background while enabling and enhancing a multi-day hike. In this vision, interactive computing is integrated into the equipment, clothing, and practices of a hiker. But computing always remains in the background until it is summoned by the hiker. Computing is meant to support rather than detract from the hiker's intent. Significant design and engineering effort are required to bring this vision to reality. Additionally, more work is needed to understand how interactive computing impacts the restorative nature of outdoor recreation.

Kiefer et al. present a novel approach to modeling gaze-guided narratives for tourists. A gaze-guided narrative is an explanation of a story connected to a specific place. As the tourist moves their gaze, the narrative adjusts the pacing and content of the narrative to dynamically tell a story. This chapter applies a formal modeling approach to specifying and eventually reasoning about a story graph used in a gaze-guided narrative. Gaze-guided narratives, and tools to support their creation, highlight the dynamic nature of some HCI outdoors activities.

Bartolome presents a study of tweets to investigate the culture of conservation around three-long-distance hiking trails in the United States. Groups of tweets related to each of the long-distance trails were analyzed to find topics, and a classifier was created to find tweets related to depreciative behavior on the trail. Her work suggests that a culture of conservation is not a priority in these communities' conversations on Twitter. While other chapters in this section focus on humans and computers interacting during outdoor recreation, this chapter considers interaction before, after, and during a hike along a trail. This research shows that more work is needed to discuss how HCI impacts and perhaps promotes sound conservation practices.

References

Asimakopoulos S, Dix A (2017) Walking: a grounded theory of social engagement and experience. Interact Comput 29(6):824–844

Brende E (2004) Better off: flipping the switch on technology. HarperCollins Publishers

Bryant RE, David Richard O, David Richard O (2016) Computer systems: a programmer's perspective, vol 2, 3 ed. Prentice Hall Upper Saddle River

Bryson B (1998) A walk in the woods: rediscovering America on the Appalachian trail. Broadway Books

Card SK, Moran TP, Newell A (1980) The keystroke-level model for user performance time with interactive systems. Commun ACM 23(7):396–410

Carroll JM (2003) HCI models, theories, and frameworks: toward a multidisciplinary science. Elsevier

Carroll JM (2013) Human computer interaction-brief intro. The encyclopedia of human-computer interaction, 2nd ed

Clark RN, Stankey GH (1979) The recreation opportunity spectrum: a framework for planning, management, and research. Technical Report PNW-98

Cooper A et al (2004) The inmates are running the asylum: why high-tech products drive us crazy and how to restore the sanity, vol 2. Sams Indianapolis

Coyne R (2014) Nature vs. smartphones. Interactions 21(5):24–31

Daiber F, Jones M, Wiehr F, Cheverst K, Kosmalla F, Häkkilä J (2017) UbiMount-2nd workshop on ubiquitous computing in the mountains. In: UbiComp/ISWC 2017-adjunct proceedings of the 2017 ACM international joint conference on pervasive and ubiquitous computing and proceedings of the 2017 ACM international symposium on wearable computers, pp 1022–1026

Daiber F, Kosmalla F (2016) UbiMount-ubiquitous computing in the mountains. In: UbiComp/ISWC 2016-adjunct proceedings of the 2016 ACM international joint conference on pervasive and ubiquitous computing and proceedings of the 2016 ACM international symposium on wearable computers, pp 1–5

Dix A, Ellis G (2015) The Alan walks Wales dataset: quantified self and open data. Open data as open educational resources, p 56

Dix A, Finlay J, Abowd GD, Beale R (2003) Human-computer interaction. Pearson Education

Fitts PM (1954) The information capacity of the human motor system in controlling the amplitude of movement. J Exp Psychol 47(6):381

Grudin J (2017) From tool to partner: the evolution of human-computer interaction. Synth Lect Hum Cent Interact 10(1):i–183

Häkkilä J, Bidwell NJ, Cheverst K, Colley A, Kosmalla F, Robinson S, Schöning J (2018) Reflections on the NatureCHI workshop series: unobtrusive user experiences with technology in nature. Internat J Mob Hum Comput Interact 10(3):1–9

Häkkilä J, Cheverst K, Schöning J, Bidwell NJ, Robinson S, Colley A (2016) NatureCHI-unobtrusive user experiences with technology in nature. In: Conference on human factors in computing systems-proceedings, pp 3574–3580

Häkkilä J, Colley A, Cheverst K, Robinson S, Schöning J, Bidwell NJ, Kosmalla F (2017) NatureCHI 2017-the 2nd workshop on unobtrusive user experiences with technology in nature. In: Proceedings of the 19th international conference on human-computer interaction with mobile devices and services, MobileHCI 2017

Harrison S, Tatar D, Sengers P (2007) The three paradigms of HCI. In: Proceedings of ALT.CHI

Hill MO, Roy DB, Thompson K (2002) Hemeroby, urbanity and ruderality: bioindicators of disturbance and human impact. J Appl Ecol 39(5):708–720

Jones MD, Anderson Z, Häkkilä J, Cheverst K, Daiber F (2018) HCI outdoors: understanding human-computer interaction in outdoor recreation. In: Extended abstracts of the CHI conference on human factors in computing systems, pp 1–8

Joyce K, Sutton S (2009) A method for automatic generation of the recreation opportunity spectrum in New Zealand. Appl Geogr APPL GEOGR 29:409–418

Letcher L, Letcher S (2008) The barefoot sisters southbound. Stackpole Books

Louv R (2008) Last child in the woods: saving our children from nature-deficit disorder. Algonquin Books

McCrickard DS, Horning MA, Harrison S, Harmon E, Dix A, Su NM, Stelter T (2018) Technology on the trail. In: Proceedings of the international ACM SIGGROUP conference on supporting group work, pp 365–368

McCrickard S (2017) Technology on the trail 2017 workshop

Nash R (2014) Wilderness and the American mind. Yale University Press

Paracchini ML, Zulian G, Kopperoinen L, Maes J, Schägner JP, Termansen M, Zandersen M, Perez-Soba M, Scholefield PA, Bidoglio G (2014) Mapping cultural ecosystem services: a framework to assess the potential for outdoor recreation across the EU. Ecol Ind 45(2014):371–385

Preece J, Sharp H, Rogers Y (2019) Interaction design: beyond human-computer interaction. Wiley

Pruitt J, Grudin J (2003) Personas: practice and theory. In: Proceedings of the 2003 conference on designing for user experiences, pp 1–15

Rogers Y, Marshall P (2017) Research in the wild. Morgan & Claypool Publishers

Rohli RV, Vega AJ (2017) Climatology, 4th ed. Jones & Bartlett Learning

Sellen A, Rogers Y, Harper R, Rodden T (2009) Reflecting human values in the digital age. Commun ACM 52(3):58–66

Shneiderman B, Plaisant C, Cohen M, Jacobs S, Elmqvist N, Diakopoulos N (2016) Designing the user interface: strategies for effective human-computer interaction. Pearson

Steinbeck J (1939) The grapes of wrath. Viking Press-James Lloyd

The Kingston Trio (1964) Poverty hill. Nick-Bob-John. Decca

Twain M (1885) Adventures of huckleberry Finn (Tom Sawyer's Comrade). Charles L. Webster and Company

United States Department of Agriculture Forest Service (1986) 1986 ROS Book

United States Department of Agriculture Forest Service (2011) ROS primer and field guide

Wakkary R, Stolterman E (2014) HCI and nature. Interactions 21(4):5

Weiser M (1991) The computer for the 21st century. Scientific American, pp 94–104

Wickens CD, Hollands JG, Banbury S, Parasuraman R (2015) Engineering psychology and human performance. Psychology Press

Rural Contexts

The Walk Exploring the Technical and Social Margins

Alan Dix

Abstract Walking has long been an instrument of political activism, such as the Jarrow March in Britain and the Salt March in India in the 1930s, and before that of war. It has been a spiritual practice, a source of literary inspiration and in some cases regarded as an art in itself. In the case of psychogeography, the act of walking is an integral part of academic and philosophical practice. However, it is fair to say that walking is not a typical part of HCI research methodology. From mid-April to the end of July 2013, I walked the perimeter of Wales, a distance of 1058 miles (1700 km). This was partly a personal journey encircling the country of my birth, not without overtones of pilgrimage, certainly a symbolic act, and maybe, depending on your definitions, art. It was also a research journey, seeking to understand the social and community issues of the 'margins' (literally and metaphorically) of a modern nation, including the impact or otherwise of information technology. This layering of aims and approaches could be regarded as post-modern, but I preferred the words of the Dean of Cardiff School of Art and Design, who described the methodology as mediaeval, and subsequently the blog about the walk was compared with the writing of Gerald of Wales written in 1188. In this chapter, I explore some of the things I have learnt from this perambulatory research; we will consider the design of mobile technology, the meaning of community and the role of the subjective in academic study. However, the 'results' of this are as much questions as answers. Remote rural communities in Wales, and across the world, often face a deepening of the existing social and economic divides, often fuelled by the digital revolution. Can appropriate design and policy counter the apparently inevitable technological entrenchment of existing power? Methodologically, is there a role for this level of slow-paced physicality and ethically is there a place for physical pain? Finally, a critical aspect of the walk was its permeability. I laid myself open to others as a living lab, and the data gathered was being made available to the entire research community. It started as my journey, but one of the first tangible outcomes was a digital exhibition by others, inspired by, but not 'about', the walk. Just as the act

A. Dix (✉)
Computational Foundry, Swansea University, Wales, UK
e-mail: alan@hcibook.com
URL: https://alanwalks.wales/

© Springer Nature Switzerland AG 2020
D. S. McCrickard et al. (eds.), *HCI Outdoors: Theory, Design, Methods and Applications*, Human–Computer Interaction Series,
https://doi.org/10.1007/978-3-030-45289-6_2

of walking collapses the distinction of places into a threaded narrative of journey, is there also a space for research that defies the discretisation of publications as metricised outputs, and dissolves the cabalistic divisions of disciplines and groups, a space for methods of work that link, join and lay themselves open to use by all?

1 Introduction

From mid-April to the end of July 2013, I walked the perimeter of Wales, a distance of 1058 miles (1700 km). This was partly a personal journey encircling the country of my birth, not without overtones of pilgrimage, certainly a symbolic act, and maybe, depending on your definitions, art. It was also a research journey, seeking to understand the social and community issues of the 'margins' (literally and metaphorically) of a modern nation, including the impact or otherwise of information technology.

In this chapter, I explore some of the things I learnt from this perambulatory research. We will consider the design of mobile technology, the meaning of community and the role of the subjective in academic study.

The chapter builds on a number of previous publications about the walk addressing issues from public policy (Morgan et al. 2014) to educational open data (Dix and Ellis 2015) and the nature of walking as a research instrument (Dix 2018b); however, the structure draws most strongly on the APCHI keynote which I gave soon after completing the walk in 2013 (Dix 2013b). Full details of publications and data arising from the walk can be found on the Alan Walks Wales website (Dix 2020).

2 A Brief History of Walking

Being bipedal is one of the defining features of humans compared with other animals, amongst other things giving us the freedom to use our hands to construct (leading to technology) and to gesture (leading to language). Our feet took us out of Africa and across the world from the lush lands of Persia and India to the only recently ice-gripped lands of Britain. For long periods of time, even animal transport was, in the large part, for the transport of goods, and it is only in the modern age that the wheel has superseded the foot for long-distance travel.

So, to a large extent the history of humanity is the history of walking.

2.1 Walking for War

Since the ages of the empires 6000 years ago, walking has been an instrument of war. Europe is crisscrossed by Roman roads built predominantly for the rapid movement of its Legions to control and subjugate an empire thousands of miles from end to end. This is a useful reminder too, that the technical development of transport is as much to do with the modification of the environment as it is with the development of machines to move through the environment; few cars can travel without roads. Whilst many animals accidentally create paths and tracks worn into the ground, we engineer these paths.

The histories of military campaigns are full of long marches: Napoleon's army lost in the snows of Russia, Mao's Long March. These become the subject of fable and folk tales, reflecting the close connections between narratives and journey that date back to the earliest times. Indeed, it is only in the late twentieth century that mechanical transport has taken over from the March for long-distance troop movements, and even then often to drop troops onto the ground for foot patrols.

2.2 Walking as Political Activism

More recently, as power structures have partially inverted, walking has been an instrument of political activism. At a small scale, the foot demonstration with banners and close-packed marchers is a common sight in modern states, albeit if these are sometimes crushed with more or less violence and sophistication. Protest walks can be used to highlight issues or to disrupt the fast flow of non-pedestrian traffic. In some cases, for example, the 'Marching Season' in Northern Ireland, it fulfils an older purpose of claiming land.

While the majority of walks of political activism are short, long-distance walks, by their rarity and by their scale, have created both immediate impact and a permanent place in the collective history. Notably in the 1930s, at opposite ends of the British Empire, Ghandi's Salt March in India protested against the draconian tax on salt, whilst the Jarrow March from Newcastle to London in the UK highlighted the poverty of the depression in the North of England. In the latter case, the walk was not just for its own impact, but because the walkers could not afford the one pound train fare to London to make their protest there. While the drone or inter-continental missile delivers the message of the powerful, the foot is the weapon of the poor.

2.3 Walking as Pilgrimage

Walking is often deeply connected with spirituality and across the world there are sites of pilgrimage, where it is not just the being at the place that is significant, but also the manner by which you get there. You may fly to Mecca but everyone walks seven times around the Kaaba; in Croagh Patrick in Ireland, climbing barefoot over the rough stones is part of the pilgrimage, bloody feet and all; and when Henry II did penance for the murder of Thomas Becket, he walked in sackcloth and ashes to Canterbury—the King just like a pauper.

2.4 Walking in the Humanities

Walking has also been traditionally associated with the arts and literature. In Australia, the songlines cut across the country, with stories of the dreamtimes attached to places along the way. Taking travel more generally, while the road movie is a recent genre, journey tales stretch back many millennia from the Exodus of the Israelites to Jason and the Argonauts in Greek mythology. In the Outer Hebrides, near the Isle of Tiree where I used to live, there are even special songs for 'waulking' the cloth, in early days literally treading on the wet cloth to set it.

Walking was critical in the European Romantic movement of the nineteenth century. Wordsworth is reputed to have walked 175,000 miles in his lifetime (Macfarlane 2013, p. 16), but also composed much of his poetry whilst pacing his study in Dove Cottage. His sister reported that his study was 12 paces across, and it is perhaps no surprise that his most common verse form was iambic pentameter, five 'iambs' each of two syllables, just like five left–right paces, with an extra pace at the end to breathe and turn—a perfect match between space and metre. Wordsworth was maybe more excessive, but not alone in his commitment to walking, which is a continual theme in nineteenth-century writing; Rouseau said *my mind only works with my legs*" (Rousseau (1782), quoted as in Macfarlane (2013, p. 27)).

More recently, psychogeography has adopted walking as a major facet of its methodology (Coverley 2010). This often involves deliberately arbitrary paths, for example, drawing a shape on a map and then trying to stick as close to it as possible. The idea here is that this avoids taking the obvious main routes and therefore immerses the walker in areas in a semi-random way, making each stand more starkly due to its unexpected juxtapositions.

The Wales walk is not so arbitrary, taking as route the existing borders and coasts of Wales, and yet there is an element of unchosenness, and there were certain areas, which you are forced to walk through, that you might otherwise avoid.

Psychogeography has been critiqued as being rich in methodology, but poor in results. The early idea was to try to understand the relationships between the physical geography of a neighbourhood or area in relation to its 'feel' and the impact on the psyche of visitor (and possibly inhabitant). Certainly from personal experience, it is challenging to turn the rich experience of the walk into lessons or results that can be useful more generally.

Psychogeography has also been predominantly interested in urban environments, but there are a number of writers, notably MacFarlane in his travel trilogy "The Wild Places", "Mountains of the Mind" and "The Old Ways", which are focused on the countryside and wilderness (Macfarlane 2008, 2010, 2013).

Given all of this, it is worth noting that today the rich walk for exercise or pleasure, and my own walk, albeit unusually long, was freely chosen. However, the vast majority of miles walked are not chosen: the refugee, the homeless, the worker who cannot afford bus fares or the old person in the countryside where there is no transport. Walking can be the weapon of the poor but is more often simply the lot of the poor.

2.5 Walking in HCI

While there was an extensive literature in these other areas, at the time of the walk there was relatively little within the HCI literature itself, the main exception being the use of walking as a means to elicit emotional impact of places (Bidwell and Browning 2006; Stanton Fraser et al. 2013) and the way walking fitted into everyday practices of rural life (Bidwell et al. 2013). However, in the intervening years, work on walking (Eslambolchilar et al. 2016; Posti et al. 2014), running (Curmi et al. 2013; Spillers and Asimakopoulos 2014) and other outdoor activities has grown dramatically as is evidenced by the chapters in this volume and the popularity of a number of workshops including NatureCHI (Häkkilä et al. 2016), CHI Outdoors (Jones et al. 2017), UbiMount (Daiber et al. 2017) and Technology on the Trail (McCrickard et al. 2018; Virginia Tech 2017).

3 Walking Wales

3.1 The Wales Coast Path

In May 2012, the Welsh Coast Path was opened. This is a mapped and way-marked route around the whole coast of Wales, a distance of 870 miles (1400 km). There were existing footpaths around sections of the coast, but this new national coast path linked them together as well as creating many miles of new footpath. This makes it the only country in world with a complete route around its coast. The coastline varies from sharp-edged cliffs to long dune-backed beaches, including some of the most remote rural areas of the country as well as passing through or near all the largest cities and towns. It is hoped that this new path will be a major stimulus to tourism and also be a symbolic part of the campaign to encourage exercise and physical well-being more generally in an increasingly obese nation.

3.2 Borderlands

In addition, there is an existing 180-mile (300 km) long-distance path along the route of Offa's Dyke the 9th Century border between Wales and England. These borderlands have always been contested and fought over leaving the detritus of war: Iron Age hill forts, Roman garrisons, Norman Castles and Offa's Dyke itself. The shifting line cuts north–south, in some places following the meandering edges of the Severn across its fertile flood plains; rather like modern oil-fuelled conflicts, there may have been less fighting if the land had been barren. Even in my own childhood, there were Welsh maps showing 13 counties in Wales and English maps showing 12. It was only during local government re-organisation in the early 1970s that the contested county, Monmouth, at the south of the borderlands, was, peacefully, ceded to Wales.

Together, the new Wales Coast Path and existing Offa's Dyke path mean that it is possible to traverse the entire periphery of the country.

In April 2012, I had been in Cardiff for a meeting and was driving back when I heard the news about the opening of the coast path. Instantly, I knew I had to walk it. Later, I realised that this expedition linked together many areas of my professional and personal life, but the instant response was more visceral, a knowing of the right thing to do.

I am not sure if the original conviction was in part a subconscious linking of these strands, or whether it was more that I creatively wove them together as I considered the idea. It is probably a combination of the two. However, if over the coming months there had been no merit in the initial idea and it had not made (some) sense under scrutiny, it would have died. It is so important to be open to these subconscious prompts and convictions, whether as the sublimation of our experience or the word of the divine, but the conscious deliberation and testing are also critical, which makes us human not mere animals.

In research, we often go to great lengths to describe our work as if it were the only and best thing to do, we have tables of criteria, and of course our own work, our own systems, have ticks in all the boxes. The truth is many of our choices are, while not utterly random, to a large extent arbitrary. There are many paths that we could take; some are clearly foolish and unlikely to yield knowledge, but among the rest there is rarely a single optimal thing to do next. If our research were really that linear, it would not be research. While most research choices are not as extreme as a 1000-mile walk, it is equally important to be honest about their reasons.

I started to walk in April 2013, nearly a year after the official opening. During that first year, there had been a small number of complete traversals of the Welsh perimeter following Wales Coast Path and Offa's Dyke. The first had been by Amy (Arry) Carmichael who ran (yes ran), the entire distance; 39 days, a marathon distance every day.

So, my walk was not the first, and certainly not the fastest, but I was undertaking it with an IT and community focus that was unique.

3.3   Vision

The vision that emerged for the walk falls into four interlinked facets:

Personal—I am Welsh, but hadn't lived in Wales for nearly 35 years, so the walk had elements of *homecoming*, in particular, it was planned to end in Cardiff, my hometown, on 28 July, my birthday. The act of *encircling* evokes a sense of *encompassing*, or even *repossessing*, as if in knowing the edges you know the whole. There is both a truth in this and also a fallacy. This is not so different from academic understanding; precise definitions are in a sense like borders: drawing a line around a topic or concept. As such they are at best misleading and at worst blind you with a false sense of understanding. However, in the act of defining, mentally walking the conceptual boundaries, you often learn things about the heart of the matter. There is also a sense of *pilgrimage*, perhaps more about roots and identity than spirituality, but the two are linked, childhood and church are inseparable, and just like the towns and cities, the majority of holy places in Wales are clustered around the coasts—the old paths of communication.

Practical—I aimed to understand the IT needs of walker and local communities along the way with an eye to doing something practical. On Tiree, I have been involved in a number of small projects to use IT in the community. One of these was a mobile heritage app, bringing the island's historic archive to life in the landscape … all with virtually no mobile signal! I also organise Tiree Tech Wave, a biannual hacker/maker event, once in the spring and once in the autumn. This is aimed partly at enriching the participants' creative engagement with technology, but also partly to bring technology to this remote community (Dostal and Dix 2011; Tiree Tech Wave 2013).

Philosophical—I have already mentioned some of the rich history and literature of walking. In my own work, I have reflected before on the rich understanding of *space* and over recent years issues of *physicality* have been central to a large part of my work (Dix 2000, 2009b; Dix et al. 2020; Ramduny-Ellis et al. 2010). This is partly because understanding human cognition can help design, but also has facets of a more philosophical enquiry. For the walk, issues of *identity* and *locality* were expected to be central, but also the way that the route of the walk moves through individual communities and localities, maybe threading together the disparate knots, or maybe simply acting as itinerant voyeur.

Research—The walk linked together a number of elements of my own *personal research agenda*, both the slightly more philosophical/cognitive understandings of space mentioned above and also the more technical issue relating to time and the user interface dating back over 25 years to my 1987 paper "The Myth of the Infinitely Fast Machine" (Dix 1987). As part of this, issues of intermittent and low bandwidth connectivity were expected to be particularly relevant. In addition to my personal research agenda, I offered myself to the community as a *living lab*: inviting other researchers to monitor me, wire me up or simply suggest concerns or issues to watch out for on the way. This included wearing biosensors, described below, using (or often failing to use) various mobile apps, and looking out for 'off-path destinations', that is, places to visit, eat or stay that were not immediately on the coast path.

4 No Hard Boundaries—Transdisciplinarity and Subjectivity

This sounds like a disparate set of goals and aims, and even more so since the walk also held an open agenda, looking for fresh questions and issues that arose on the way.

This is both a strength and a weakness.

In many ways, I took on too much, had too many expectations, and inevitably some aspects were less successful than others. However, this is also to be expected, the set of prior goals gave a prima facie reason for the walk, but one of the lessons of all field research and in particular 'research in the wild' is that it is rarely the initial objectives that turn out most significant. It is not that these initial goals are not important, they set an agenda and general outlook, and help clarify what is or is not likely to be a good data gathering approach. However, it is also important to hold these goals lightly, always ready to see the unexpected.

In addition to this tuned, yet open agenda, there is a more fundamental radical transdisciplinary approach to much of my work.

I make no hard boundaries between the personal and the philosophical, between research and practice. By this, I do not mean that distinctions do not need to be made as we reflect and report on work, but that the phenomena of the world do not fall into simple categories. In order to understand aspects of the word, we find it useful to make distinctions, to separate out certain kinds of phenomena and describe them in isolation, but this is an epistemological distinction not an ontological one.

Particularly problematic in the sciences is the role of the individual and the subjective. Interestingly, in philosophy, the role of the individual is less contested. Descartes *"I think therefore I am"* is a combination of subjective introspection and rational analysis, and the whole phenomenological movement is centred on the primacy of felt experience (Descartes 1637).

In the study of human consciousness, Searle distinguishes between *epistemic subjectivity* and *ontological subjectivity* (Searle 1997). Epistemic subjectivity concerns questions for which we may have an opinion, but where there exists some objective external answer; for example, "how high is the Eiffel Tower?". Ontological subjectivity is where the subjective experience is an essential part of the phenomena under study, for example, "is Paris romantic?". The latter may correlate with externally observable phenomena, such as brain scans, and may be influenced by objectively controllable influences, such as champagne intake, but the access to the 'romantic' feeling must always be through subjective assessment and experience.

Moreover, as we study phenomena, we inevitably bring our own biases and expectations, our knowledge and ignorance. In the hard sciences, the white lab coat in a sense embodies the idea that in some way all scientists are equal; whoever performs the experiment is immaterial to its results. This is the essence of repeatability. It is also the reason for the passive voice in scientific writing, "reagent X was added to Y and it was observed that Z".

However, even here things are problematic. In sunspot research, what counts as a single spot or group is hard to pin down; some people are better at identifying sunspots than others (Owens 2013). For this reason, the observer is also recorded and data is 'corrected' to take into account differences between observers; "It was observed that" is not necessarily an 'objective' statement.

Of course, this is even more relevant in human sciences. A Scottish Government survey was criticised because one of the questions concerned sexual orientation (The Scottish Government 2012; Wade 2013). The figure for non-heterosexual orientations was considered too low by some groups, who pointed out that a face-to-face survey in the family home would by its nature lead to under-reporting. In general, data gathered from people will undoubtedly depend on the skills, appearance and personality of the interviewer, and in many cases gender and ethnicity also.

When it comes to the interpretation and implications of raw data, these effects are even more extreme.

As an example, a piece of economic research examined emotional balance and happiness amongst different income groups in different countries and then correlated that with measures of the religiosity of individuals and of the nations as a whole (Gebauer et al. 2013). In general, richer people were happier than poorer people, but for those with strong religious faith the difference was far less (in a few cases even reversed). In general, those with faith were more balanced and happier and especially the poor were far happier if they had strong faith. However, the take-away message from the article was not that faith is good for you, but that religious faith was bad for the economy, because poor people with faith were not miserable enough and so would lack aspiration and not work as hard.

In general, the implications drawn, even from numerical results, depend on the expectations of the interpreter. Furthermore, not acknowledging this in the passive voice used in much of academic writing is at best disingenuous and misleading, and potentially deceitful.

This is not an argument to abandon the notion of objective knowledge, but more to accept that much of our work, by its nature, does not fall into the category of pure observer-independent effects. Rather than removing or ignoring the role of the researcher, we need to acknowledge and account for it, as is common and accepted practice in much of the social sciences and humanities.

All this said, an individual 1000 walk is probably a little extreme in terms of its subjective and personal nature than most work in HCI.

At a talk I gave at Cardiff Metropolitan University just before starting the walk, I had stated that the style of research was perhaps more in the style of nineteenth-century explorations. However, in her summing up after, the Dean of the Cardiff School of Art and Design suggested that it was more Mediaeval than Victorian. Later, someone commenting on my daily blogs compared them to the writings of Gerald of Wales, a twelfth-century writer (Gerald of Wales 1188), so the Dean clearly had a point. As she was a historian by background, this was intended as a positive remark, and I was very pleased with the notion, but I leave it to readers to make their own judgement.

5 Walking as Research

5.1 Slow Research

One of the most obvious features of walking as a research methodology is that it is slow. When I walk on the flat, say down a road, and I know where I am going, so don't have to think about the route, I walk approximately four miles an hour (6 km/h), compared with say 40 mph (65 km/h) driving down country roads, 70 mph (110 km/h) the maximum (legal) speed on a British motorway or 500 mph (800 km/h) in a plane.

In an age addicted to speed, walking is unconscionably slow, but the very slowness creates its own pace and forces you to notice things you might otherwise miss, and to experience places you might otherwise speed through. Combined with the systematic nature of the coastal path, this meant I saw things and areas I would have been unlikely to deliberately visit. This was particularly obvious in the Dee Estuary in the north-east of Wales, a very depressed and not at all pretty area, but one where I learnt such a lot.

In other areas, there has been an increasing appreciation of the value of 'slow'. This began with 'Slow Food' in Italy in 1986, but became more widespread with a broader 'slow movement' following Karl Honoré's "In Praise of Slow" (Honoré 2004). In the mid-2000s, I led a mini-project on "Slow Time" trying to help people become aware of the slower rhythms of life: milliHz (about 20 min), microHz (about 12 days) and nanoHz (30 years) (Dix and Phillips 2006). This was in turn inspired in part by Stuart Brandt's "How Buildings Learn", which explored the different timescales of domestic architecture (Brand 1997).

Although I had planned for this to be a 'slow' experience, in fact one of the pervading memories is of feeling rushed. My four mile an hour walking pace on flat roads that I know became two miles an hour on rough ground, where I needed to navigate and was taking hundreds of photographs a day. This was exactly the speed the Ramblers, those who walk regularly as a hobby, had told me to expect, but I had ignored this expert knowledge. Distances I had expected to take 4–5 h a day to walk were taking 8–10 h. As I had fixed the overall duration of the walk, I could not simply take more time, so for a long time the walk exhibited the same feelings of stress and time constraint as my normal academic life.

Slow is not simply a matter of walking.

It also hurts. Not all the time, and my feet were remarkably blister free, with just five sticking plasters used the entire journey. However, in the middle section especially, various long-term aches and pains emerged, and it took my feet approximately a month to recover after I finished. There are ethical issues here even when the task is freely chosen, but certainly you could not demand this kind of thing of a student. However, an element of discomfort and risk is common in many other areas of research from anthropology to vulcanology.

5.2   Waving Banners

One of the aims of the walk was to engage with local people and communities. The slow element was part of this, and one of the aspects compromised by the time constraints (not slow enough). However, this was also problematic due to my personality. Although I can talk endlessly, I find it very hard to start a conversation, especially with a stranger. During the walk, I wore a banner strapped to my rucksack. The banner meant that other people would initiate conversation, asking me about the banner. It also lent an element of 'officialness'; I was not simply sitting or walking, but someone on a mission.

The banner is an example of what I call 'personality prosthesis' (Dix 2018a).

You might have an artificial leg or arm fitted if you have had an accident, or simply wear glasses. Even if we have no impairment, we use various forms of physical prostheses to augment our bodies, using a forklift truck or block and tackle to lift weights too heavy for us, or car to move faster than our legs would carry us. We also use cognitive prostheses, a calculator to augment our mental arithmetic, or diary to help our memory. Although you might attend a gym or night classes to improve aspects of your physical or mental capabilities, there is no great shame in using these physical or cognitive prostheses.

However, when it comes to aspects of personality or cognitive style, people very rapidly fall into a language of moral failing, "if I were a more tidy person …", "if I were more organised …". Our underlying personality is not going to change easily, if at all (although maybe we can shape our character), so complaining about it is like an engineer saying "if only this steel were fifteen times stronger". As a designer faced with a material with limitations, we would work to achieve our aims *given* the limitations.

The banner was precisely that. If I were more extrovert, more gregarious, I would find it easy to strike up the conversations I wanted to. But I am not. The banner helped me to achieve the aims *given* who I am.

Never apologise for who you are, only for what you do.

5.3   The Best Technology

One of my aims was to investigate technology for the walker: what technology would make it easier/better for me as a walker, and for other walkers. I recall asking one walker, "what technology do you use?"; "a map", was his immediate answer.

Not everyone is like this, and an increasing number of people are using dedicated GPS devices or phone apps as their primary navigation. Indeed when I talked to Rosie Unsworth, who was walking the Wales Coast Path in the opposite direction, she told me that she had exclusively used her phone, in particular using (ViewRanger 2020), which enabled her to download all the OS maps for the path which would otherwise have been very voluminous.

I don't know the overall balance of technology use, as the nature of coast paths is that you only occasionally need any sort of navigation except when the path, for reasons of topography or legal access, has to branch inland. However, where I did observe others using navigation aids, it was exclusively a paper map or using maps and instructions in guidebooks.

This said, clearly the trend, especially among younger hikers, is to use more technology, as is clear in Ellie Harmon account of Pacific Crest Trail walkers (Harmon 2015). Although this is beginning to cause headaches for rescue services in the UK, who are increasingly being called out to help people who have only a GPS device or phone and have either dropped and broken it, or found its battery has run out.

In a 2013 survey in the White Mountain National Forest in the USA, less than a half of hikers had a compass with them, although 60% had some form of GPS (Mason et al. 2013). However, the paper notes that of the GPS users, the vast majority were using phone-based service that failed in the park, and that even dedicated GPS devices had black spots in the park.

To be honest, while I was wired up with biosensors (see next section) and had a 'Spot' device broadcasting my location to satellite to appear on a real-time map, I very rarely consulted navigation technology or other apps on the way. This was partly due to battery problems; my phone was most often in the rucksack charging on an external battery pack. It was also due to the difficulty of using the phone in slightly damp conditions. Some days, if I went into a cafe during the day or got to bed and breakfast at the end, it would be several minutes before the touch screen would respond to gestures, despite wiping both screen and fingers to dry them. There were also connectivity-related issues with many apps (see later).

After my camera, the most heavily used piece of technology that I had with me was an Olympus voice recorder. This had a number of advantages:

- *Physicality*—It had real buttons, and so it worked with damp fingers, and could be navigated by touch alone when cupped in one's fingers or held inside one's hood to protect it from rain.
- *Non-visual*—While there was an LCD screen, common functions could be operated without consulting this. I wear reading glasses and so using a screen involved getting glasses out, and trying to de-mist them, before being able to do anything. To be fair this is also a problem with maps.
- *On-the move*—The combination of the above, with the fact that, when the ground is not too rough, you can speak while talking, meant I did not have to stop to use it, important when timing got tight.

In fact, although I rarely saw people actively using technology for navigation, it is likely that many will have been carrying mobile phones, or consulted an online weather forecast before starting. Technology can be used in several ways during and around walking as an activity:

- *Actively used on the move*—navigation apps, infrequent Twitter, camera, voice recorder, wrist-watch-style heart rate devices (for consulting while moving), iPods and MP3 players.

- *Passively gathering/transmitting data*—SPOT and ViewRanger transmitted my location to online maps, biosensors, many now wear Nike Bands, or similar devices.
- *There for emergencies/occasional use*—mobile phone there in case of need, or maybe to be available to others if they need to contact you, the SPOT device had an SOS button, which would call emergency services if needed.
- *Used during breaks*—often this may be in places with better connectivity and under cover, for example, I used an iPad mini extensively for writing if I stopped in a cafe. People may use mobile Internet (where available) to book accommodation, or may use a rest gap to post statuses to social networks (signal allowing).
- *Used outwith the walk*—some technology is used before walking for planning, or afterwards for reminiscing, uploading photos, etc.

When I asked the question "what technology do you use?", and when I said that I rarely used technology, it was the first of these which was the focus of the negative response, but all of the above are important aspects of technology use.

5.4 Layers of Experience

Stavros Asimakopoulos analysed the extensive blogs generated through the walk and when he reported his results my initial response was disbelief. He told me that social issues dominated the blogs; however, I know that for virtually the whole time I was walking alone, sometimes meeting just a couple of people during the whole day. However, on reflection it was apparent that, just as in the case of the technology used, the moment of walking was only the centre of multiple spheres of activity: the stops made for food, overnight stays, family and friends that supported me, even you as the reader of this chapter (Fig. 1). Once this was apparent, I was able to list more than 20 different categories of social contacts, from other walkers to academic collaborators helping us build a rich picture of the human relationships during and surrounding the act of walking (Asimakopoulos and Dix 2017).

5.5 Data Gathered

I gathered a substantial amount of data, some for my own purposes, some more for others to use. Some of it is quantitative, some qualitative. The quantitative data was *implicitly* gathered, by automatic sensing, whereas the qualitative data involved some *explicit* conscious action and deliberation.

Location—There are GPX traces from multiple devices (Garmin stand-alone GPS, ViewRanger app on phone), and some GPS tags on images. This is real, messy data: sometimes batteries ran out, or I forgot to turn on the devices until a short way into the walk, or forgot to turn them off and so have extraneous data points while

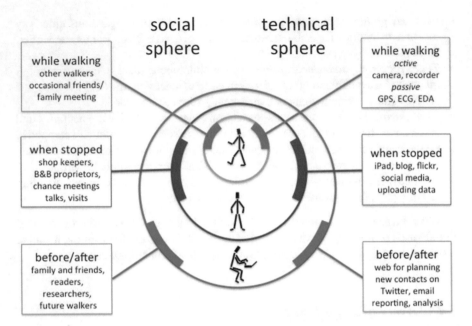

Fig. 1 Spheres of social connections and technology use (From Asimakopoulos and Dix (2017))

on public transport or driving. In addition, there are sporadic apparently random GPS signals, many miles off the actual position; I assume an artefact of the GPS location algorithms. Unfortunately, GPX files do not seem to include the accuracy figure generated by the GPS sensor. I intended to combine these into a definitive data source at some point, but there doesn't appear to be an off-the-shelf tool to do this. If combined there are lots of interesting issues to do with provenance (e.g. whether the data is from Garmin, ViewRanger or manual editing), and the notion of a track. The GPX format has either routes, which have points with no timing, or tracks, which have points with timing for every point, but a hand-edited track will have some points with no associated timestamp.

Bio-sensing—I wore a full ECG device (heart activity) and also an EDA monitor (skin conductivity). Both of these also include three-axis accelerometer data. The first of these is particularly voluminous sampling heart electrical activity at 64 Hz, giving rise to a 50 Mb binary file for a 2-day recording, which expands to 300 Mb in a more easily usable CSV format. The ECG data typically includes 2-day periods with overnight wearing in between to give rest heart rate and pattern. With around 60 days worth of recording, over 100 days this is believed to be the largest publically available longitudinal ECG dataset. The biodata can be cross-correlated with the GPX data and images (below) to be able to see what terrain gave rise to what kinds of heart activity.

Audio and images—As noted the camera and audio recorder were the most commonly used technology. There are typically 250 photos a day with 1 day having

643 photos. As well as simple things of interest, I also tried to photograph the path ahead when the terrain changed (e.g. grass to earth) and other things that I felt might be useful to help interpret the quantitative data as well as things relating to qualitative concerns such as signage or off-path destinations. Audio recording was more sporadic, but typically there are about a dozen audio logs per day, with a wide variety of topics. Again there is a lot of curatorial work to do; it would be good to transcribe the audio logs, and tagging 19,000 photographs is a major undertaking. There are substantial life-logging research challenges here.

Text—I have blogs of typically 2000–3000 words per day. Some were done straightaway, some as 'catch up' later. This is already more reflective, and mixes description of the walking itself, anecdotes about people met along the way, or things seen, childhood reminiscence and discussion of topics arising from any of these. Again there is a substantial process of semantically annotating this corpus of rich text and a major design challenge to find ways to extract 'threads' about various themes without losing the richness of integrated accounts.

Crucially, all of this data was made available to the research community to use. As noted there are various challenges arising and I am sure many that I have not thought of. As data provider there is a not insubstantial curatorial role in documenting the data so that others can use it independently, although I am also very pleased to work with others to interpret or enrich the data.

6 At the Margins

One of the core themes of the walks was 'the margins'. Walking the periphery of Wales is clearly traversing the physical margins of the country. This includes most of the major towns and cities of Wales, as they were typically close to the coast from the days when the sea was the easiest way to travel. However, it also passes through many of the most deprived ex-industrial areas of the North and remote rural areas of the West.

Often those at the physical margins, the remote rural areas, are also at the social and economic margins of society with a greater proportion of elderly and a lower average wage than the cities. However, in some ways, the physical margins of the walk highlight marginality in general whether you are in furthest edge of Wales, or the heart of London. This is very clearly also true in very different countries, such as in India where rural poverty is a major issue, but so also is the vast difference between rich and poor within the city.

Those at the physical margins and those at the social margins are also typically technologically disadvantaged. Free market telecoms infrastructure follows money, so those at the outer margins have poorer mobile coverage, poorer fixed Internet connections and, because they are also likely to be economically poor, old or low-quality devices.

In the UK, an increasing proportion of government services are provided through the Internet and commercially the cheapest way to get goods is often online. The poor and those in remote areas are likely therefore to be cut off from eGovernment and pay more for their goods. IT deepens the divide.

However, we can turn this round. Can we envisage IT that serves the margins? A growing number of researchers and designers are addressing just this question, led by pioneers such as Gary Marsden in Cape Town (Marsden 2008; Marsden et al. 2008). While IT development for the well-off will happen anyway due to commercial profit, IT for the margins needs those who care to act.

I visited Bangalore a few years ago as part of UKINIT exchange project. One of the things that struck me after that first visit to India was the commonality of issues between rural communities in India and rural communities back in the UK (Dix 2009a; Dix and Subramanian 2010).

Sometimes, there are lessons to be learnt from the UK's past as we went through industrialisation 150 years ago, and with hindsight maybe it is possible to ameliorate some of the problems left in the wake of the industrial revolution, for example, the breakdown of the sense of extended family and local roots.

Sometimes, there are positive examples from developed to developing economies.

One example is in the hand textile industry in India, which is suffering from factory competition. Textile production was the driving force of the industrial revolution, and, for reasons of control more than efficiency, weavers who used to work autonomously within their homes were forced into factories. However, the exception to this is Harris Tweed. Presumably, *because* of its remoteness, tweed continued to be woven by hand in the outer isles of Scotland. Now the brand 'Harris Tweed' is protected and can *only* be used for cloth woven in the weavers' own homes.

Lessons can also go in the other direction from developing to developed world.

Mitra's 'hole in the wall' project has achieved international acclaim (Mitra et al. 2005). However, Mitra later went to Newcastle in the UK and did similar work in the poor areas of that city. It was not identical, the British climate and urban vandalism would preclude an exact copy, but similar principles were applied.

At one of the Tiree Tech Wave events I organise, the youth worker from Tiree was giving a short talk about the particular problems of youth work on an island. One problem she mentioned was that, due to the distances and dispersed population, it was hard to communicate effectively. One of the attendees suggested (FrontlineSMS 2020), a system developed for NGOs in Africa. While the interface was not suitable, the youth worker was extremely enthusiastic about the underlying idea of using broadcast SMS messages and a dedicated portal, TireeConnect, was built which enabled her to send messages to SMS and social media from the same interface.

One of the ideas that has been on my mind since the early 1990s (pre-web) has been the demise of the village shop, and for that matter local shops in cities. I don't know if this has become a problem yet in other countries, but in the UK village shops and small shops in general get squeezed by larger supermarkets. They are not able to sell as cheaply and so those who can easily travel to large supermarkets do the majority of their shopping there only going to the village shop for 'emergency' items: a forgotten loaf of bread or bottle of milk. The village shop's sales drop, it is even harder to make a profit and many close.

As well as being sad for the shopkeepers, those who do not have cars, the elderly and the poor, suffer both before the shop closes from higher prices on already stretched incomes, and more so after when it can become exceedingly difficult to shop at all, with difficult and costly journeys by public transport … and of course buses in rural areas are infrequent when they run at all.

The question I have pondered for many years is whether IT could help, perhaps bring new forms of business (e.g. as email box for the elderly), to allow 'just in time' ordering, or be the drop-off point for other forms of postal deliveries (Dix 2008a, b; Dix and Subramanian 2010).

The solutions I considered 30 years ago are very different from those that might apply today, then it would have been dial-up connections but now broadband, then it would have taken radical changes to logistics, but now Internet shopping means that many delivery systems are already suited to small-run picking.

I never took the action 30 years ago that was needed to turn concept into reality, and it may well be that this is an idea that has passed its time. The crucial question is what are the similar issues today?

7 Community and Identity

One of my 'concerns' in walking was the local issues that matter to communities and indeed the whole nature of community 'at the margins'. Living in a small island and having lived in other rural areas in the UK, I have some idea of important issues, but areas differ and so I wanted to get some idea of the commonalities as well as differences between communities.

It maybe that I would learn nothing beyond whether the issues I was already aware of would apply more generally. However, my hope was that I would learn new things, not so much new answers, but new questions.

My first taste of this came in the first week of the walk.

7.1 An Interstitial Community

I was using my campervan as a base vehicle, and so it needed to be parked somewhere when I was using bed and breakfasts. As a first staging post, the van was parked in a small campsite near the heart of the old county town of Monmouth towards the southern end of the Welsh–English border. The van was at the campsite for 10 days, but I only slept there for two nights.

The campsite consisted of small holiday touring caravans, the sort that can be towed behind quite a small car. However, it was evident from the small 'gardens' with flowerpots and other things around many of them that they were sited semi-permanently. Many campsites offer 'season fees' that are a lot cheaper than the nightly fee, and I assume many of the caravans are parked for the entire season from April to October.

The small clubhouse had a bar and provided meals. It was itself run by one of the people staying in one of these small caravans. It was open five nights a week; the other two nights were when the proprietors went 'home'. However, the idea of 'home' was problematic; for 7 months of the year, they spent five nights of the week on the site. Other owners had similar patterns; one woman said she needed to go 'home' to do clothes washing as she had been several weeks on the site, but would be back after a couple of days.

The site was set within the middle of the local community of Monmouth and yet had an identity of its own, a community in the gaps.

In some ways, they have similarities to gypsy communities, except if this had been a gypsy encampment it would be rapidly broken up by the police and moved on.

However, unlike gypsies, these people had a parallel life somewhere else. In a way, they form a virtual community, like academic communities, or professional communities of interest, but differ in having a very well-defined physical location.

Certainly, this interstitial community, sitting between the cracks, challenges simple notions of locality and community, with multiple communities co-existing in the same locality and individuals belonging to multiple simultaneous 'local' communities. Demands of work are creating increasingly itinerant lifestyles for both city professionals (at the time of the walk I lived 350 miles from my place of work!) and migrant workers, so rather than being an extreme case, in some ways this small caravan community epitomises broader patterns of changing lifestyles.

7.2 Community and Cohesion

The north-east coast of Wales has some of the most depressed communities in the country. Rhyl functions as the dustbin of Liverpool. It is a run-down seaside town with a surfeit of old bed and breakfast accommodation. When families and individuals are too difficult to place in Liverpool (and there are some pretty rough areas of Liverpool), they are sent to Rhyl. Drug abuse and poverty are high, and it is the most depressed 'ward' (local authority unit) in Wales.

The reasons for Rhyl's problems are not hard to see. However, I was also struck by the way different communities facing hardship seem to cope differently.

Connagh's Quay is a small ex-industrial town on the Dee Estuary. The industries that gave employment to the area have all closed, and it is visibly run-down; even the pubs have closed, usually the last thing to survive in a British working-class area.

Further along the coast are other coastal villages that lost their industry. Penmaen-mawr used to have large limestone quarries. There is still some quarrying, but now using modern machinery and employing a tiny number of people. Furthermore, a road and railway cut the town from the sea destroying any potential for seaside tourism. There is a tiny area called the 'Promenade', barely 50 metres long, and reached through a tunnel under the railway and road. It has nothing going for it, and yet the promenade is one of the best kept that I saw in my travels, with a small beach cafe that has local heritage books to read while you eat. Local notices give a sense that there is a vibrant living community here.

Why does one community decay from within and another retain its heart? Is it the physical circumstances, the open sea lifting the spirits compared to the grey mud of an estuary? Is it simply distance from Liverpool? Or is it the difference between a past rooted in the ground beneath you, literally connecting you to your locality despite hardship, compared to the smell and filth of chemical production?

7.3 Language and Culture

In Wales, language, culture and national identity are intimately linked, even for those who do not themselves speak the language. In the UK, as in other areas of the world, regional languages are constantly under threat.

This has changed in my own lifetime. When I was a child Welsh, was not apparent with the exception of a Welsh version of the TV news (it was fun seeing the same images with different commentaries). However, following many years of campaigning by the non-violent language movement (and the activities of paramilitary groups, whose role is usually downplayed (Clews 2013)), there was a substantial change during the late 1970s and 1980s, with dual language signs, and most important S4C, the Welsh language TV station.

In contrast to the 1920s when children were punished for speaking Welsh in school (Lloyd 2016), now there are a large number of schools where the teaching is all done in Welsh, with substantial numbers of English-speaking parents sending their children as well as Welsh speakers. As I walked through the west of the country, people of all ages spoke Welsh as their main language and in Monmouth (in the east) I met an Englishman who had learnt to be a fluent Welsh speaker and later became the first person to address a local council meeting in Welsh.

However, in the last census the proportion of Welsh speakers in the core Welsh counties dropped slightly, after many years of increase (BBC 2012). One reason is incomers and retirees who can (if they don't learn the language) dilute the local language and culture, as well as price-out the young people from the housing market. Another is media. When S4C was founded, it was one Welsh channel with three other TV channels. Now it is one amongst hundreds of English language channels on satellite TV, with the majority of web materials also in English. This is of course a common story across the world, not least India with hundreds of languages under threat.

In principle, IT can help *long-tail* communities. The term 'long-tail' arose in the business community (Anderson 2006), but became one of the defining features of Web2.0 (O'Reilly 2005). Most traditional large businesses and early web sites focused on satisfying some broad interest shared by a large number of people, for example, people who like action movies, or the latest pop star. However, Web2.0 sites used the global reach of the Internet combined with web personalisation, to cater for smaller groups of people, for example, those interested in pet ferrets, or 1980s Newcastle-based Rock and Roll bands. In principle, this ought to also apply to minority-language groups, but this promise does not seem to be materialising. Can we help make this potential into reality?

One promising example of this happening is the translation of Code Club materials into Welsh (Code Club 2013; Coder Dojo Cymru 2013). For older children, programming language translation is probably not a big issue. However, for the youngest children, being able to not only read work cards, etc, in their own language, but also programme in Welsh not only reduces barriers, but also says that Welsh is a language of the future, not just the past.

Tourist towns often have maps: either paper maps to carry around or 'you are here' maps on boards. Some of these are 'standard' maps in terms of shape, but may have different things on them compared with route map: emphasising local businesses and accommodation, main shopping streets and historical attractions, but de-emphasising residential areas where tourists are not expected to go (and may not be wanted). Sometimes, they also differ in shape, maybe making the centre larger in a fish-eye effect, or drawn in semi-perspective, as if viewed from a hill rather than directly overhead.

Digital mapping has never been easier with Google Maps, OpenStreetMap, and in the UK, the Ordnance Survey making some of their mapping open data. However, the ease of using 'standard' maps runs the risk of replacing the more locally meaningful maps. As Barbara Bender said:

Post-Renaissance maps cover the surface of the world with an homogeneous Cartesian grip. (Bender 1996, p. 41)

In Cardigan in West Wales, a centenary was celebrated by knitting a giant cardigan (as in the kind to wear) that was a map of Cardigan. In the Dysynni Valley, I saw a 3D community map that was based on the 'standard' map (Whittle 1996) but made out of fabric and stitch, like the "Land of Counterpane" in Robert Lois Stephenson's "A Child's Garden of Verses" (Stevenson 1885).

Is it possible to retain the richness of local mapping in a digital age?

As an attempt to hold on to some of this richness, *Frasan*, the Tiree island mobile heritage app uses digitised versions of hand-drawn maps of Tiree for its 'zoomed out' view, only dropping into 'standard' maps when you zoom into detail (An Iodhlann 2013). It uses 'rubber sheeting' algorithms to map from the GPS coordinate system to locations on the map to plot the locations of archive items and the user's current location (Dix 2013a).

8 Health and Well-Being

When I started the walk, I had not walked any serious distance since I was 18 years old, and even then never day-on-day walking such as this. The fact that I was starting at such a low point will hopefully make the ECG data particularly interesting for health and well-being researchers.

In fact, walking for research is far from a stress-free contemplative experience! As well as spending eight to ten hours a day on my feet, I was writing approximately 2000 words a day and spending at least an hour 'tending technology' (charging devices, copying files from one device to another, etc.) and more when on Wi-Fi and uploading data. In addition, I had to either plan bed and breakfasts with virtually no Internet connectivity and/or plan public transport back and forth to campsites with, often, virtually non-existent rural bus services.

One consequence of this is that the ECG trace very clearly shows my heart rate soar at 5 am, at first light, when I start to stir and yet while still asleep begin to mull over the day ahead. Indeed, during this 'worry time' the heart rate peeked as high as when I was doing the most strenuous walking. No wonder people die at night!

Physically, after a few weeks, I was a mountain goat, becoming one of those really annoying people, who walk up steep hills effortlessly passing everyone on the way. However, another month in and long-term exhaustion and damage started to set in with various aches and pains and deep, deep tiredness. Happily, this too eventually passed, except for the soles of my feet, which took a month to recover after I finished.

I had expected that my legs would strengthen while walking, but that maybe my upper body would atrophy a little without similar exercise. I had intended to deliberately do exercises in the evenings, but never had time. When I got back I decided to try a few press-ups, and, to my astonishment, I could do 30 press-ups effortlessly when before the walk I could manage 10–20 with effort. In succeeding days, I found I could regularly do 50 press-ups at a time, and indeed have once done 100.

This is not upper body strength, but the fact that walking both strengthened my core muscles (stomach and back) and also improved general cardiovascular fitness. If you are strong enough to do one press up you are strong enough to do one hundred, it is getting oxygen and fuel to your muscles that is the limiting factor. This change in my metabolism has persisted and since the run I have regularly run the 35-mile Tiree Ultramarathon (Wright 2020).

Walking is in fact one of the best forms of exercise, with little risk of injury (well unless you walk 1000 miles at a go!), and many health benefits; even cancer recovery is significantly improved by walking.

In the UK, childhood and adult obesity is an increasing problem, as it is across much of the developed world. In the UK, the biggest problem is amongst the poor; calorie deficit is rarely a problem, just that the cheapest foods are 'junk foods', so a poor person's diet is usually a poor diet.

Sadly, while walking seems 'free', actually many are put off walking because of the need (in the British climate) for expensive rain gear, boots, etc.—fitness is big industry. I spoke to a taxi driver who was severely overweight, and loved walking, but couldn't as he was not able to find affordable rainwear in his size XXXL.

These equipment problems are compounded by expensive and infrequent public transport, which makes it hard to get out of the city unless you have a car. I recall when I was a child, I couldn't afford buses, and it could take an hour or two to get clear of the city before I walked in the countryside. I did it because (at that point!) I was already fit, but what about those who are taking their first tentative steps at exercise?

However, there are positive signs too. In Llanelli, where long-closed steelworks used to border the seacoast, the land has been reclaimed into nature reserves and waterside parkland. It is one of the poorer areas of South Wales, and yet there appears to be widespread pride in this urban-edge land that is designed for walking and cycling. As is common, the residential developments are 'executive', but the parkland is open to all.

9 Connectivity

I have been interested in timing issues in the user interface throughout virtually my entire academic career. In 1995 I wrote, what I believe to be the first journal paper on HCI issues for mobile systems (Dix 1995); the topic was not about screen size, but connectivity and disconnection.

At the time of the walk, I lived on an island with virtually no mobile signal and limited broadband, so I thought I was prepared for connectivity problems during the walk.

I was wrong.

It was far, far worse than I had imagined. For mobile signal, I rarely had more than two bars of GSM and often no signal at all, especially in places I stopped overnight. The best signal was on hilltops as they are more likely to be in line of sight of masts. This was compounded because Wi-Fi and wired Internet connectivity were equally difficult. In hotels and guesthouses, even when they had Wi-Fi, the technical setup was problematic (this is the same in the middle of cities also!); it is still remarkably difficult to simply set up a reliable Wi-Fi hotspot. Furthermore, the underlying Internet in outlying areas tends to be relatively low bandwidth, and, more critically, sporadic, with occasional drops for a few seconds or half minute.

The reasons for this are not hard to tell. First, the physical conditions are hard for both mobile and wired connectivity: long distances in sparsely populated areas with deep valleys and high hills. However, this is compounded by economic factors, basically signal follows money. If you look at mobile operators' coverage maps of the country, they at first appear to have relatively good coverage at the coast. However, if you look more deeply you realise, this is relatively good coverage just *off* the coast, mobile masts point to sea, not land.

The reason is simple, at sea are yachts, and yachting people tend to be well-off, whilst those living in remote coastal areas tend to be poorer.

9.1 Infrastructure or Privilege

When talking about the walk, I often ask the audience, "what was the greatest British Invention?" I get various answers, including the World Wide Web. The Radio Times have a list of "The 50 greatest British inventions" (Radio Times 2013) from telephone to television, hovercraft to hip replacement, photography to programmable computer; interestingly, the article is illustrated with an image of Tim Berners-Lee. The Daily Mail has a shorter list of ten inventions, which includes many of the same inventions as on the Radio Times list (Baylis and Membery 2011). However, it is the last item on the Daily Mail list, which does not exist at all on the larger Radio Times list, which gets my vote: the Penny Post.

In the early years of the nineteenth century, postage depended on the route and carriers taken and was often paid on arrival by the recipient. The fixed cost prepaid 'Penny Black' stamp changed this. There were already Penny Post systems in some cities, charging a single penny for delivery anywhere. Following proposals by Rowland Hill, this was extended to the entire country and later the Commonwealth (British Postal Museum & Archive 2013).

Hill fully understood the importance of this postal revolution for an informed and educated citizenry. In language, reminiscent of recent commentary on the web and the Open Data movement he writes:

> how much the religious, moral, and intellectual progress of the people, would be accelerated by the unobstructed circulation of letters and of the many cheap and excellent non-political publications of the present day, the Post Office assumes the new and important character of a powerful engine of civilization (Hill 1837)

Indeed within 20 years, the volume of post had quadrupled, easing not only the communication of ordinary people, but also business.

Now, the Internet has in many areas taken on the mantle of universal communication, not least in government services. However, this is predicated on universal access. Some years ago a small business won a case against the UK Inland Revenue, who were seeking to impose an Internet-only system for the payment of VAT (purchase tax). The business successfully claimed that lacking a computer, for religious reasons, it was unfairly discriminated against (Gledhill 1999). At an individual level, the UK's Universal Credit system is being introduced which brings all forms of welfare benefit into a single system. However, it too is to be an Internet-only system. Pilots for the scheme found that half of all claimants did not have home Internet and half lacked sufficient IT skills to use the system (Citizens Advice Bureau 2013; Sherman 2013). Given that those on welfare are disproportionally elderly, ill, disabled or poorly educated, this news is not altogether surprising; indeed, a report prior to the pilot suggested that only 8% of potential claimants had all the requisite skills (Citizens Advice Bureau 2013).

It is easy to think of web and Internet access as luxuries or optional, but it is clear that in so many ways it has become a necessary part of twenty-first-century citizenship. While I was walking a report was published that revealed that 50% of Welsh schools said that poor Internet speed was a major obstacle to education. This is a whole generation who are being brought up disadvantaged relative to those in more well-provided areas.

Of course, while this situation is problematic in Wales, similar patterns can be found across the world. In India, with high levels of illiteracy and poverty, no one assumes universal access to the Internet, but differential access to information and services will intensify existing socio-economic divisions within the country as well as between India and more wealthy parts of the world.

Connectivity problems do not just affect the poor and those directly lacking access. Current PC and phone operating systems and applications periodically update themselves. However, these software updates or not infrequently hundreds of Mbytes, or several Gigabytes in size. These can be impossible to instal over slow or intermittent networks. The un-updated PCs are then running older software with potential security flaws, fertile ground for malware to create bot farms to attack financial, government or military institutions.

9.2   Software Makes It Worse

However, on top of poor access to both mobile and fixed networks in rural areas, software makes things worse.

I had expected to heavily use Twitter during the walk, making semi-poetic tweets at beauty spots. Instead, I found mobile Twitter virtually unusable, typically freezing on a white screen with a blue top banner, not even getting so far as to say 'Twitter'. I believe there are three problems causing this:

1. While actual Tweets are just 140 characters, when delivered over the data API each one is wrapped in vast quantities of metadata in XML or JSON. The example feed in the developers' documentation (Twitter 2013) for accessing the timeline has one tweet with 74 lines of JSON taking 2 Kbytes and another with 108 lines taking 3 Kbytes. The sizes for XML format would be even larger.
2. The default download count for the timeline is 20 items, but it is clear that many apps access 50. A small number of large accesses is more efficient for the Twitter servers, but can lead to large results and hence very slow responses on mobile networks. At some point, these can become so slow that some part of the system times out.
3. The Twitter mobile app at the time appeared to be synchronous, downloading the timeline before showing the rest of the interface. This means that you cannot simply start the app and set a status.

Finally, if you are fortunate and patient enough to be able to set a status but in the meantime the network has dropped, several third-party apps and the Twitter mobile site simply lose the status. Happily, the Twitter app is slightly more resilient saving the un-sent status as a draft.

In contrast, email works slowly, but usably on just a few bars of GSM connectivity. Emails are much larger than tweets, but email is 1970s technology and so designed from the outset for slow and often intermittent (e.g. dial-up) networks.

Problems with software are not confined to mobile apps. Flickr uploader was particularly problematic when the Internet was at all intermittent. As noted, rural Internet often drops for a few seconds, even if it is otherwise able to provide usable bandwidth. I assume this is due to contention problems, or maybe parts of the network simply lose connectivity and have to re-establish handshakes. This would cause Flickr uploader to 'hang' in the middle of an upload. Even when the Internet returned the uploader remained frozen with some images uploaded and others not. Two things compound this:

1. It did not keep any track of what has been uploaded successfully, meaning you have to attempt to work out by looking at the web site which had and had not been successfully uploaded.
2. This comparison was made more difficult because the uploader did not add tags or add the images to sets until after they have all been uploaded. This meant that all the images that had been uploaded before the failure were uncategorized.

Note that these freezing problems are not confined to the rural margins of Wales or the remote islands of Scotland, but anywhere where networks become temporarily unreliable. During the walk, I took a short period of off-path when I went to Paris for the CHI conference. I was staying at the hotel attached to the Le Palais des Congrès, the largest conference venue in Paris. However, from about 7 to 9 am in the morning and pretty much all evening, the network behaved very similar to Tiree Internet on a bad day, just the pure volume of demand stressing the network leading to occasional 'outs', and, yes, Flickr uploader failed!

Both this and Twitter's behaviour are simply bad engineering, but bad engineering due to an implicit assumption that networks everywhere are the same as those found in Silicon Valley.

Software companies have understood the need for localisation, making interfaces more appropriate for individual contexts, in terms of language and (to a lesser extent) culture. However, this is not enough.

Software embodies technological and economic assumptions about context, which, when they fail, can effectively disenfranchise large swathes of the population.

These assumptions are very deeply entrenched, not just in app design, but in the underlying TCP protocols where 'slow start' behaves particularly badly with mobile or other 'gappy' networks.

9.3   Making a Difference?

There are various ways these problems could be addressed:

Public policy—It is not inevitable that rural and poorer areas are poorly provided. Some countries prioritise coverage over money when auctioning 4G space, or have had policies of subsidising broadband in outlying areas. However, this does need to be informed, for example, UK government is promoting 4G coverage as a panacea for improving rural broadband, but experience of 3G and 2G coverage makes this extremely unlikely to be effective.

Software design—Many of the problems mentioned for Twitter and Flickr are due to poor engineering and failing to take into account that network operations may be slow or fail. One simple approach is to design mobile apps as distributed systems rather than thin clients, effectively making intermittent access the default assumption, with better connectivity simply yielding better experience.

OS and platform design—Underlying operating systems and app platforms need to pass on information about connectivity up the stack to applications to enable them to modify behaviour. For example, the mobile phone knows the level of signal, but it is not easy for, say, a simple web app to access this. As well as coping with the presence of signal, it is also important to know whether bandwidth is metered as those on lower cost plans often have limited total download sizes or pay per megabyte.

Local webs—There are solutions for providing local web access even when there is little or no network connectivity, for example, 'Qraqrbox' uses a combination of cached web sites, local DNS redirection and solar power to provide micro-access points far form fixed infrastructure (Qraqrbox 2013). However, it is still more commonly the case that communicating between two computers in the same local area relies on 'tunnelling' through the telecoms operator's infrastructure to ISPs hundreds of miles away.

10 Research Looking Out

I have described how I offered myself as a living lab for others to give me instrumentation of various kinds. This worked more or less well in different cases.

Mobile-based applications suffered due to general problems with signal and battery power, and custom hardware struggled to survive days on end bumping around in a rucksack with constantly changing levels of temperature and humidity. These are classic problems when coming out of the lab into the field where the researcher is not on hand to tweak and nurse their technology.

On the other hand, the biosensors worked well providing a unique dataset and, despite a busier than expected walking schedule (due to overestimating my walking speed!), I was able to look out for evidence on a number of 'concerns' from others.

In HCI, we normally treat every enterprise as a one-off, with the researcher's individual (or a group's) goals investigated. In contrast to this solipsistic research model, I treated this expedition more like a deep space mission, supplying the launch vehicle (me!), but opening myself up to others' research agendas (and equipment).

This is not a common way to do research, and, not unexpectedly, not everything worked out as planned. However, I have learnt a lot about the reasons for this, and in general how to work in this more outward-facing mode of research. We are at a time when open access and open data are hot topics, but this kind of 'open research' is still uncommon.

Despite its difficulties, I believe more open 'research for others' is important if HCI is to develop as a discipline (Dix 2010). Whether it is experimental or qualitative work, we see large amounts of effort expended collecting data that is then discarded. Some disciplines now demand that raw data is published alongside experimental results, but this is rare in HCI, even in areas, such as Fitts' Law experiments, where there are few issues of anonymity or consent.

As noted, I have advocated previously that we should create more sharing points than the simple published paper, which does a bit of everything (often badly), instead allowing those with different expertises to apply them at appropriate stages of HCI research life cycle (Dix 2010).

As a personal step towards this, I am learning how to curate and document the data I gathered, quantitative and qualitative, so that it can be of use to others. In addition, I need to learn how to publicise the availability of this data. In HCI, we normally publicise the results of analysis of data, through conferences, and publications, but not the data itself, so this is also a new art for me.

As well 'outward-facing' work that I am directly involved with, I have seen a number of outcomes which are in a sense inspired by, or prompted by, the walk, but not 'my' outcomes.

While planning the walk, I found myself developing a new contact network of people interested in various issues connected with walking from health and well-being to tourism, arts, media studies and spatial cognition. This led me to introduce people who did not know of each other's work, but clearly have much in common. Only time will tell how productive these will be, but there is certainly the potential for some long-term outcomes, of which I will probably never be aware.

At a more concrete level, when I visited the University of Wales Trinity St David at Lampeter, the archivist at the Roderic Bowen Library and Archives produced an exhibition, especially for my visit. A table was spread out with documents, some dating back to the twelfth century, all opened on pages related to walking, maps of Wales and related topics. This exhibition was translated into an online form, an outcome 'due to' but not 'out of' my research (Roderic Bowen Library and Archives 2013).

11   'Take Aways' and the Future

This chapter covers a wide range of areas. The very idea of walking as research stretches the methodological boundaries of HCI. This is clearly not appropriate for all situations and to some extent as an experienced and successful researcher I have both the freedom to be more methodologically risky and also the experience to balance, mitigate and benefit from these risks.

From a design perspective, those at the margins whether geographic or social have different and special needs. There is often less money available so that appropriate design has to be smarter design. Often those already at the margins are further marginalised by digital technology; can it be designed to be part of the solution not the problem? This is made perhaps more critical because, in many parts of the world, a digital technology has shifted from being an optional tool for work or pleasure to being essential for full citizenship (Dix 2016).

I focused on connectivity as an issue as it is one I have studied for many years. It is safe to assume that, in the foreseeable future, those at the margins will always have poorer access to mobile and fixed Internet. This inevitably means that applications and services will be slower or in some way degraded, but crucially they should be designed so that this is a gradual degradation not leading to complete failure, as is evident in much commonly used software.

As well as being a societally important question, this is also an academically interesting one, with challenges for interaction design, software architecture and network infrastructure. It has been fascinating reading about how these issues arise in other parts of this book. My experience is that low bandwidth is less critical than intermittent service, but different areas and different parts of the world have different issues. In some places, cost is more of an issue, and in others digital literacy. If the core issue is cost, is this based on per megabyte data transfers or connection hours? Maybe it is common to have cheaper/faster periodic access with periods of total disconnection, in other areas permanent but low-grade access. Understanding these dimensions of connectivity is important if we are to be able to deliver appropriate guidance to designers and developers.

Moving back to HCI as a discipline, I am certain that academic maturity should involve more fine-grained use and reuse of each other's research data and materials. The World Wide Web was conceived as a way for physicists to share data from CERN, can we in HCI learn to use it in similar ways?

And finally, immediately following the walk I was often asked, "what next?" Seven years on I'm still not sure of the answer, but there will be something. Early in the walk I noticed people had started to talk to me as if I was one of the *kind of people who do things*. I found this strange as I always thought of other people as the *kind of people who do things*; I knew some of them, but that wasn't me. Only gradually did I realise (my goodness how late in life) that there is no *kind of people who do things*, just *people who do things*.

Acknowledgements Many people contributed to the planning, funding and execution of this expedition. Thanks particularly to my employers at the time Talis Education and the University of Birmingham for allowing me the time to do this. Also special thanks to those who supported the crowd-funding initiative and the dot.rural project at the University of Aberdeen (http://www. dotrural.ac.uk) for its support as part of its partner scheme. This paper is based on notes I wrote following a keynote talk I gave to APCHI 2013/India HCI 2013 in Bangalore, India on 27 September 2013 (Dix 2013).

References

Anderson C (2006) The Long tail: why the future of business is selling less of more. Hyperion, New York, NY. ISBN 1-4013-0237-8

An Iodhlann (2013) Frasan-Tiree mobile archive. http://frasan.co.uk. Accessed 27 Nov 2013

Asimakopoulos S, Dix A (2017) Walking: a grounded theory of social engagement and experience. Interact Comput. (in press, online 28 Aug 2017)

Baylis T, Membery Y (2011) The television to the railway steam locomotive: ten of the greatest British inventions. MailOnline. http://www.dailymail.co.uk/home/moslive/article-2034658/10-greatest-British-inventions-From-television-railway-steam-locomotive.html. Accessed 12 Sept 2011

BBC (2012) Census 2011: number of welsh speakers falling. BBC News. http://www.bbc.co.uk/news/uk-wales-20677528. Accessed 11 Dec 2012

Bender B (1996) Mapping Alteratve worlds. In: [14], pp 41–51

Bidwell N, Browning D (2006) Making there: methods to uncover egocentric experience in a dialogic of natural places. In: Kjeldskov J, Paay J (eds) Proceedings of the 18th Australia conference on computer-human interaction: design: activities, artefacts and environments (OZCHI '06). ACM, New York, NY, USA, pp 229–236. https://doi.org/10.1145/1228175.1228216

Bidwell N, Siya M, Marsden G, Tucker W, Tshemese M, Gaven N, Ntlangano S, Robinson S, Eglington K (2013) Walking and the social life of solar charging in rural Africa. ACM Trans Comput-Hum Interact 20(4):22:1–22:33

Brand S (1997) How buildings learn: what happens after they're built. Penguin. ISBN 0753800500

British Postal Museum & Archive (2013) Rowland Hill's postal reforms. http://www.postalheritage.org.uk/page/rowlandhill. Accessed 26 Nov 2013

Citizens Advice Bureau (2013) Universal Credit managing migration pilot baseline results summary. Report Released 10 July 2013. http://www.citizensadvice.org.uk/index/aboutus/publications/universal_credit_managing_migration.htm

Citizens Advice Bureau (2013) 22% don't have basic banking services needed to deal with Universal Credit. Press Release 6 Nov 2013. http://www.citizensadvice.org.uk/index/pressoffice/press_index/press_office20131105.htm

Clews R (2013) To dream of freedom: the story of mac and the free wales army. Y Lolfa. ISBN-10: 0862435862

Clifford S, King, A (eds) (1996) From place to place: maps and parish maps. Common Ground

Code Club (2013) https://www.codeclub.org.uk. Accessed 27 Nov 2013

Coder Dojo Cymru (2013) http://www.coderdojocymru.org/?page_id=2. Accessed 3 Dec 2013

Coverley M (2010) Psychogeography. Idea, Pocket Essentials. ISBN 1842433474

Curmi F, Ferrario M, Southern J, Whittle J (2013) HeartLink: open broadcast of live biometric data to social networks. In: Proceedings of the SIGCHI conference on human factors in computing systems (CHI '13). ACM, New York, NY, USA, pp 1749–1758. https://doi.org/10.1145/2470654.2466231

Daiber F, Jones M, Wiehr F, Cheverst K, Kosmalla F, Häkkilä J (2017) UbiMount: 2nd workshop on ubiquitous computing in the mountains. In: Proceedings of the 2017 ACM international joint conference on pervasive and ubiquitous computing and proceedings of the 2017 ACM international symposium on wearable computers (UbiComp '17). ACM, New York, NY, USA, pp 1022–1026. https://doi.org/10.1145/3123024.3124462

Descartes R (1637) A discourse on method. Project Gutenberg EBOOK, dated 2008. http://www.gutenberg.org/files/59/59-h/59-h.htm#part4. Accessed 27 Nov 2013

Dix A (1987) The myth of the infinitely fast machine. In: Diaper D, Winder R (eds) People and computers III-proceedings of HCI'87. Cambridge University Press, pp 215–228. http://alandix.com/academic/papers/hci87/

Dix A (1995) Cooperation without (reliable) communication: interfaces for mobile applications. Distrib Syst Eng 2(3):171–181. http://www.hcibook.com/alan/papers/DSE95/

Dix A (2000) Welsh mathematician walks in cyberspace (the cartography of cyberspace). (keynote) In: Proceedings of the third international conference on collaborative virtual environments-CVE2000. ACM Press, pp 3–7

Dix A, Phillips P (2006) SlowTime-LifeChimes. Art works. In: Proceedings of the first international symposium on culture, creativity and interaction design, CCID 2006. LeonardoNet Network, p 53

Dix A (2008a) The electronic village shop–enhancing local community through global network. Posted on 28 Feb 2008. http://alandix.com/blog/2008/02/28/the-electronic-village-shop-enhancing-local-community-through-global-network/

Dix A (2008b) The electronic village shop–update and kit. Posted on 2 Mar 2008. http://alandix.com/blog/2008/03/02/the-electronic-village-shop-update-and-kit/

Dix A (2009a) UK/India, a confluence of needs. UKINIT Newsletter. http://web.archive.org/web/20090408153309/, http://www.ukinit.org/ukinit-newsletter-march-2009. Accessed Mar 2009

Dix A (2009b) Paths and patches: patterns of geonosy and gnosis. In: Turner P, Turner S, Davenport E (eds) Chapter 1 in Exploration of space, technology, and spatiality: interdisciplinary perspectives. Information science reference, pp 1–16. ISBN 978-1-60566-020-2

Dix A (2010) Human-Computer Interaction: a stable discipline, a nascent science, and the growth of the long tail. Interact Comput 22(1):13–27. https://doi.org/10.1016/j.intcom.2009.11.007, http://www.hcibook.com/alan/papers/IwC-LongFsch-HCI-2010/

Dix A, Subramanian S (2010) IT for sustainable growth. J Technol Manag Grow Econ 1(1):35–54. http://alandix.com/academic/papers/IT-Sustainable-Growth-2010/

Dix A (2013a) Mental geography, wonky maps and a long way ahead. In: GeoHCI, workshop on geography and HCI, CHI 2013. http://alandix.com/academic/papers/GeoHCI2013/

Dix A (2013b) The Walk: exploring the technical and social margins. Keynote APCHI 2013/India HCI 2013, Bangalore India. https://www.alandix.com/academic/talks/APCHI-2013/. Accessed 27 Sept 2013

Dix A, Ellis G (2015) The Alan walks Wales dataset: quantified self and open data. In: Atenas J, Havemann L (eds) Open data as open educational resources: case studies of emerging practice. Open Knowledge, Open Education Working Group, London. https://doi.org/10.6084/m9.figshare.1590031

Dix A (2016) Human computer interaction, foundations and new paradigms. J Vis Lang Compu. Special issue in Honour of Stefano Levialdi 42:122–134. https://doi.org/10.1016/j.jvlc.2016.04.001

Dix A (2018a) Personality prostheses (Notes of TEDxNeathPortTalbot talk on 24 Nov 2018). Medium. https://medium.com/@alandix/personality-prostheses-54a3c7e0dca7

Dix A (2018b) Step by step research. Unpublished in into the wild: beyond the design research lab. Chamberlain A, Crabtree A (eds). Springer, pp 7–29. https://doi.org/10.1007/978-3-030-18020-1_2

Dix A (2020) Alan walks wales–academic writing. https://alanwalks.wales/writing/academic-writing/. Accessed 15 Feb 2020

Dix A, Gill S, Ramduny R, Hare J (2020) TouchIT. OUP. http://www.physicality.org/TouchIT/

Dostal J, Dix A (2011) Tiree tech wave. Interfaces, Summer 2011, pp 16–17. http://tireetechwave.org/events/ttw-1/interfaces-article/

Eslambolchilar P, Bødker M, Chamberlain A (2016) Ways of walking: understanding walking's implications for the design of handheld technology via a humanistic ethnographic approach. Hum Technol 12(1):5–30

FrontlineSMS (2020) Frontline story. https://www.frontlinesms.com/connect-with-us/our-story. Accessed 1 Feb 2020

Gebauer J, Nehrlich A, Sedikides C, Neberich W (2013) The psychological benefits of income are contingent on individual-level and culture-level religiosity. Soc Psychol Pers Sci 4(5):569–578. (Published online before print December 20, 2012), https://doi.org/10.1177/1948550612469819. http://eprints.soton.ac.uk/356074/ (see also my critique "the economics of misery " at http://ala ndix.com/blog/2013/08/28/the-economics-of-misery/)

Gerald of Wales (1188,1978) The journey through wales and the description of wales (Trans Thorpe L). Penguin. 1978/2004. 9780140443394. (orginally Itinerarium Kambriae, 1188) Full text at internet archive. http://www.archive.org/stream/itinerarythroug00girauoft/itinerarythroug00gira uoft_djvu.txt

Gledhill R (1999) Religious couple win fight to file VAT returns by post. The Times. http://www.thetimes.co.uk/tto/faith/article3900479.ece. Accessed 22 Oct 2013

Häkkilä J, Cheverst K, Schöning J, Bidwell N, Robinson S, Colley A (2016) NatureCHI: unobtrusive user experiences with technology in nature. In: Proceedings of the 2016 CHI conference extended abstracts on human factors in computing systems (CHI EA '16). ACM, New York, NY, USA, pp 3574–3580. https://doi.org/10.1145/2851581.2856495

Harmon E (2015) Computing as context: experiences of dis/connection beyond the moment of non/use. ProQuest LLC. 789 East Eisenhower Parkway, PO Box 1346, Ann Arbor, MI 48106

Hill R (1837) Post office reform: its importance and practicability. https://archive.org/details/cihm_2 1617

Honoré C (2004) In Praise of slow. HarperSanFrancisco. ISBN 006054578X

Jones M, Daiber F, Anderson Z, Seppi K (2017) SIG on interactive computing in outdoor recreation. In: Proceedings of the 2017 CHI conference extended abstracts on human factors in computing systems (CHI EA '17). ACM, New York, NY, USA, pp 1326–1329. https://doi.org/10.1145/302 7063.3049289

Lloyd G (2016) The welsh not or welsh note punishment system. Wrexham history. https://www.wrexham-history.com/the-welsh-not-or-welsh-note-punishment-system/. Accessed 8 Sept 2016

Macfarlane R (2008) The wild places. Granta Books. ISBN 1847080189

Macfarlane R (2010) Mountains of the mind: a history of a fascination. Granta Books. ISBN 1847080391

Macfarlane R (2013) The old ways: a journey on foot. Penguin. ISBN 0141030585

Marsden G (2008) Toward empowered design. IEEE Comput 41(6):42–47

Marsden G, Maunder A, Parker M (2008) People are people, but technology is not technology. Philos Trans R Soc A:1–10

Mason R, Suner S, Williams K (2013) An analysis of hiker preparedness: a survey of hiker habits in New Hampshire. Wilderness Environ Med 24(3):221–227. https://doi.org/10.1016/j.wem.2013. 02.002)

McCrickard D, Horning M, Steve Harrison S, Harmon E, Dix A, Su N, Stelter T (2018) Technology on the trail. In: (Workshop) in Proceedings of GROUP'18, 2018 ACM conference on supporting groupwork. ACM

Mitra S, Dangwal R, Chatterjee S, Jha S, Bisht R, Kapur P (2005) Acquisition of computer literacy on shared public computers: children and the 'Hole in the wall'. Aust J Educ Technol 21(3):407–426

Morgan A, Dix A, Phillips M, House C (2014) Blue sky thinking meets green field usability: can mobile internet software engineering bridge the rural divide? Local Econ 29(6–7):750–761. (Published online August 21, 2014). https://doi.org/10.1177/0269094214548399

O'Reilly T (2005) What is web 2.0: design patterns and business models for the next generation of software, O'Reilly Media, 30 Sept 2005. http://oreilly.com/pub/a/web2/archive/what-is-web-20.html. Accessed 1 Dec 2013

Owens B (2013) Spot of bother: have we been getting solar activity wrong? New Scientist, No. 2934, 14 Sept 2013, pp 36–39

Posti M, Schöning J, Häkkilä J (2014) Unexpected journeys with the HOBBIT: the design and evaluation of an asocial hiking app. In: Proceedings of the 2014 conference on designing interactive systems (DIS '14). ACM, New York, NY, USA, pp 637–646. http://doi.acm.org/10.1145/2598510.2598592

Qraqrbox (2013) https://www.qraqrbox.com/. Accessed 26 Nov 2013

Radio Times (2013) The 50 greatest British inventions. Radio Times. Published 8 Jan 2013. List at: http://www.radiotimes.com/news/2013-01-08/the-50-greatest-british-inventions. Full magazine download at: http://downloads.bbc.co.uk/tv/fiftygreatestinventions/50_greatest_inventions.pdf

Ramduny-Ellis D, Hare J, Dix A, Evans M, Gill S (2010) Physicality in design: an exploration. Design J 13(1):48–76. http://www.hcibook.com/alan/papers/Physicality-in-Design-DJ-2010/

Roderic Bowen Library and Archives (2013) Walking around wales: an exhibition to coincide with the visit of professor Alan Dix to the Roderic Bowen library and archives, June 2013. University of Wales Trinity St David. http://www.trinitysaintdavid.ac.uk/en/rbla/onlineexhibitions/walkin garoundwales/. Accessed 27 Nov 2013

Rousseau J (1782) The confessions of J. J. Rousseau, Book IX. (Project Gutenberg EBook, dated 2006). http://www.gutenberg.org/files/3913/3913-h/3913-h.htm#link9. Accessed 27 Nov 2013

The Scottish Government (2012) Scotland's people annual report: results from 2011 scottish household survey. 29 Aug 2012. ISBN 9781782560159. http://www.scotland.gov.uk/Publicati ons/2012/08/5277

Searle J (1997) The mystery of consciousness. Granta

Sherman J (2013) Half of benefit claimants lack skill to complete online forms. The Times, Wednesday 6 Nov 2013, p 6. (Report based on a Citizens Advice Bureau survey)

Spillers F, Asimakopoulos S (2014) Does social user experience improve motivation for runners? In: Marcus A (ed) Design, user experience, and usability. user experience design practice, LNCS 8520. Springer, pp 358–369. https://doi.org/10.1007/978-3-319-07638-6_35

Stanton Fraser D, Jay T, Eamonn O'Neill E, Penn A (2013) My neighbourhood: studying perceptions of urban space and neighbourhood with moblogging. Pervasive Mob Comput 9(5):722–737. https://doi.org/10.1016/j.pmcj.2012.07.002

Stevenson RL (1885) The land of counterpane. A child's garden of verses. Project Gutenberg ebook. http://www.gutenberg.org/files/25609/25609-h/25609-h.htm#THE_LAND_OF_C OUNTERPANE

Tiree Tech Wave (2013) http://tireetechwave.org/. Accessed 27 Nov 2013

Twitter (2013) GET statuses/home_timeline. Developers documentation. https://dev.twitter.com/ docs/api/1/get/statuses/home_timeline. Accessed 26 Nov 2013

ViewRanger (2020) http://www.viewranger.com. Accessed 1 Feb 2020

Virginia Tech (2017) What comes after CHI: technology on the trail. https://technologyonthetrail. wordpress.com/workshop. Accessed 2–3 Mar 2017

Wade M (2013) Fear of prejudice blamed as gay Scots fail to show in poll. The Times Scotland. 29 Aug 2013 (see note on 'Self-identified sexual orientation' in Appendix 2). http://www.thetimes. co.uk/tto/news/uk/scotland/article3854769.ece

Whittle J (1996) In Wiltshire and wales–the making of two maps–1986–1996. In [14], pp 77–81

Wright W (2020) Tiree Ultramarathon. Tiree Fitness. https://www.tireefitness.co.uk/tiree-ultram arathon/. Accessed 1 Feb 2020

Threats of the Rural: Writing and Designing with Affect

Norman Makoto Su

Abstract Drawing from the author's background and fieldwork in the rural West and Midwest, this chapter presents findings that are, at times, evasive and ambiguous. Stylistically, the writing foregrounds the unnamed and subliminal intensities that circulate in and out of the rural and onto the body. These rural affects give rise to our emotions shaped by social culture. This chapter is a provocation toward writing ethnographically inspired work in human–computer interaction (HCI). I suggest that the hallmarks of HCI research—deep analysis and clarity of argument—may unduly simplify the complexity of the rural, particularly its inhabitants. This chapter presents an alternative to normative modes of writing HCI, inviting multiple readings, interpretations, affects, and, indeed, "designs" from readers.

1 Front Matter

This chapter presents writings that draw from my experiences in the rural, both personal and professional (Hardy et al. 2019; Steup et al. 2019, 2018; Su and Cheon 2017). Each scene represents something about the various imminent forces—the tingling, indiscernible perceptions—that dance about in the rural. I, my body, felt these affects. Some scenes lie squarely in the rural. Some scenes lie at the juncture of the rural with other rurals, suburbans, urbans, and in-betweeners. All imply that the rural is always there, threatening to surge and explode. These scenes need not be read in one sitting, nor in the order presented.

N. M. Su (✉)
Luddy School of Informatics, Computing, and Engineering, Indiana University Bloomington, Bloomington, USA
e-mail: normsu@indiana.edu

© Springer Nature Switzerland AG 2020
D. S. McCrickard et al. (eds.), *HCI Outdoors: Theory, Design, Methods and Applications*, Human–Computer Interaction Series,
https://doi.org/10.1007/978-3-030-45289-6_3

I refer to myself as "he" to remove authorial authority.[1] "He" also highlights that these scenes are not the result of an intrepid "me" collecting the unvarnished truth.

2   San Martin: Rural South 101 of Silicon Valley

Crop of California Map (U.S. Geological Survey 2020)

To make that one-hour trip[2] (double that in rush hour) in California from San Jose (population ~1 million[3]) to San Martin (population ~7K[4]), he goes south, where highway 85 and 101 intersect. From there, 85 vanishes, four lanes dwindle down to two, and mountains, dry with yellow brush, run by the side, bobbing up and down. He thinks: *we're not in Silicon Valley anymore.*

After a long stretch of about eight miles, the lanes widen again. He drives past Morgan Hill to exit out of San Martin, making a sharp unprotected left turn at the end of the ramp.

---

[1]This is akin to a form of writing Søren Kierkegaard called "indirect communication." "Double reflection" is achieved via indirect communication which requires "a person [the reader] first grasp the relevant concepts (first reflection), but then go and think through what it would mean to apply these concepts to the person's own life (second reflection)" (Evans 2009, p. 35).

[2]~26 miles.

[3]2018 population estimated from 2010 census (U.S. Census Bureau 2020a).

[4]Latest figures are from 2010 census (U.S. Census Bureau 2020b).

He grew up in San Martin, a "rural unincorporated area" between Morgan Hill and Gilroy. Morgan Hill is known for its Mushroom Mardi Gras. Gilroy is known for its Garlic Festival; though now it is perhaps better known for its shopping outlets. When people unfamiliar with the South Santa Clara valley ask him where he's from, he replies with "one hour south of Silicon Valley or San Jose." The idea that San Martin is rural never crossed his mind. He never claimed to have grown up in "the country."

When someone says "rural," he thinks of the vast fields of corn, red barns, livestock, and small towns not too far from his current home in the Midwest.[5] This is a sort of romantic, packaged ruralism.[6] In fact, after living so many years in California, the idea of "rural California" seemed odd. How could a place less than an hour away from the valley that birthed the PC and teems with Prii (now Teslas) be rural?

3 Affective Infrastructures

His barn in San Martin, now a garage

---

[5] Bloomington, Indiana.

[6] There is substantial scholarship on the discursive function of terms such as country, rural, and nature. Bell (1994) speaks to how new, moneyed inhabitants, and long-time inhabitants of a village grasp at different notions of the country. In *Uncommon Ground*, we find a deliberate, often hidden, construction drawing from a romanticized nature of Yosemite Park (Olwig 1996) and Niagara Falls (Spirn 1996).

Infrastructures hint. They slyly suggest pathways. Roads don't always surprise us by making rides bumpy. Rather, cracks start weaving, becoming deeper in the asphalt. The lanes gradually fade. Five lanes (plus a carpool lane) slowly merge to four, then three, then—suddenly—you're on a two-lane highway. It's as if you've been driving with only one lane next to you the whole time. Their ordinariness[7] lulls you toward affects you embrace without thought.

Sometimes infrastructures jar. He drives by a neighborhood. The houses look expensive. The gardens are well manicured; the bricks are bright red; and the architecture seems to draw from Jefferson's Monticello. Then he makes a turn to the "wrong side" of town. A rush of fear, trepidation, and gloom envelops him. Buildings become derelict. Windows have security bars. He's only gone a few blocks and everything has changed. Things become more homemade—signs crudely painted, old shacks converted to restaurants that sell food, mom-and-pop shops.

In the rural, these affective infrastructures hit us harder. Class divisions, so tied to infrastructures, jut out in the rural.[8] He sees, feels, and hears the things that say who's well-off and who's not because they're right next to him.

This sudden uncertainty exposes judgment on infrastructures.[9] He is on the "wrong side" of town only because he is comfortable with the "right side" of town. He has the comfort of privilege, only to feel discomfort with squalor. He has judged this infrastructure as shitty because he is a product of other infrastructures.

4   A Dark Room for Rabbits

The whole family moved from San Jose to San Martin because his father dreamed of owning land. After, his dad always boasted of having a "one-acre property."

With that land, came animals. Their new neighbors had horses, pigs, and rabbits. During the summer, an awful stench of manure perfumed the hot dry air as the pigs sloshed around in the mud.

One childhood memory left an indelible impression. The neighbor's kids showed him a dark shed in the backyard. Inside, at chest level, were elongated huts with wire-mesh roofs sitting along both sides of a small path. Peering into the roofs, he saw rabbits furtively hopping about, munching bits of food. They looked oh-so-cute, but his neighbor explained—they'd be used for meat. His mother heard about the rabbits. She sighed,「かわいそう！」[10]

---

[7]Boring by nature, the use of infrastructures is transparent and taken for granted (Star 1999).

[8]In his ethnography of a village less than two hours from London, Bell (1994, p. 35) observes, "A number of residents suggested that class divisions were in fact stronger in country villages …than in the cities …poorer people find class differences stronger in the countryside".

[9]Star (1999) notes how infrastructures become apparent when they break down. I would also add that they become apparent when we *feel* unease.

[10]"Poor rabbits" in Japanese.

5   Life and Death

He's had four stray cats. The first was a mackerel tabby. She often rubbed up against his leg, meowing for food. She was affectionate but carried herself in a dignified manner.

She soon became pregnant. Her nipples were red, and her tummy swelled up. He vividly remembered when she gave birth. Frankly, she seemed confused. Her eyes went wide, and she ran about the backyard deck with her baby hanging out. The baby swung about, like a trailer loosely attached to a hitch.

The litter of babies was helpless. Squinty eyed—all the while hissing—they clumsily crawled around, nervously pawing in the air for milk from their mother. We started calling the mackerel tabby the "mother cat."

His family couldn't afford to take care of all the cats, so the kittens and the mother cat were sent to the shelter. He remembers turning around as he left the shelter and seeing the mother cat in a cage, meowing. His mom couldn't bear to look at her.

They kept one black kitten, a male. He later died after being run over by a car. His body was buried in the backyard. The dog would often sniff around the dirt there.

Later, after he left to college and work, they adopted another stray cat. She was not affectionate. She was wary. They'd see a splotch of white off in the distance. The mom worked hard to gain her trust, leaving scraps of food and wandering away to allow the cat to safely eat in solitude. She named her Shirochan.[11] Eventually, Shirochan trusted his mother enough to come by every morning for food. She warmed up to be being petted and even held—though, he thinks his mom enjoyed it most!

She got old. Her meowing, always a wheeze, became a whisper. An old ear injury suddenly came alive. As if covered in acid, everyday her ear dissolved, until bit-by-bit it nearly went to her head. She couldn't eat food well, chewing it gingerly, avoiding places where her teeth hurt. Eventually, she stopped coming by every morning. His mom would call for Shirochan, but to no avail. They knew she had probably gone off somewhere and died.

He thinks the cat's death hit his mom pretty hard. His mom explained, Shirochan was a *wild* cat. She had been in fights. She had seen a lot. She was street smart and survived. Yet, even with that tough exterior, she let them be her semi-family.

Lately, his mom has been taming another cat. Sometimes, she calls him Shirochan by mistake.

6   Posthuman Bodies

Cities subjugate humans, but moreso other beings. Trees are contorted with wire mesh to squeeze in dirt plots surrounded by sidewalks. Animals scavenge like thieves. Only at dusk do you see the glowing eyes of wolves on roads. Rat traps are smeared with peanut butter. Feral cats are ear tipped. Anti-roosting spikes adorn skyscrapers. We

---

[11] A affectionate nickname using the word for white, "shiro" (白), in Japanese.

rarely encounter animals except when they are expected—when they are leashed or deconstructed into pieces of meat, processed for sale. Of course, despite these attempts to reign in our non-human neighbors, many, like pigeons, adapt and thrive in urban landscapes.

In the country, we can't entirely avoid the trajectories of other beings. Roadkill lingers longer. A first timer can't get around that they've just killed an animal in the hunt, even if you call it "harvesting." Bugs buzz around, biting you. This isn't glamping.

7 Neighborly Hospitality

When their family first moved to San Martin, the neighbor next door gave them a carton of eggs, fresh from their chickens. They also gave them jam made from their apricot tree. It was a nice welcome. Both were delicious. Well, the eggs—they tasted the same as store bought, but they had beautiful, sunset yolks.

8 Horses for Meat

As children, they'd spy on the neighbor's yard through the knotholes of the fence. Their dog also spied with them.

The farthest edge of the backyard was only loosely fenced. The neighbors had a makeshift, wooden stable followed by a large, patchy dirt field. When you peered over the fence, the horse would gaily trot over. It readily took apples and carrots. Its long, grubby lips would reach over like hands. Lots of drool. He still remembers the horse merrily gnawing away.

Much later, they saw a large truck with a horse trailer come by on the side road by the backyard. He and his brother ran over to see strange men from the truck coax the horse to the trailer. The horse did not want to go. He later heard a rumor that the horse was to be slaughtered for dog food. What once was a neighbor was now fodder.

9 The Backyard Outdoors

His BB gun was a Red Ryder. With his brother, they picked off empty soda cans filled with water on wooden posts. The water gushing out proved they were sharpshooters. They'd occasionally pick more "natural" targets, like fallen walnuts from the tree. They were a harder to hit.

The NRA gun safety guidelines advised placing backing to catch missed shots. He was a methodical child and worried about shooting without the backing. But, they shot anyways. The original fencing in our backyard is leaning now, rotted away. But one can still see copper BBs stubbornly embedded in it.

A neighbor told them to be careful when shooting, lest those stray bullets nick someone's behind or, as the movie goes, pokes someone's eye out. They opted for safety glasses.

Once, someone's chicken escaped and ended up on the rooftop. He aimed high and shot at it with the BB gun. He wasn't sure if he hit it. Strangely enough, he and his brother couldn't find the chicken—maybe it ran off.

Even to this day, he feels guilty about shooting it. Guilty about not finding it.

10 Locating the Outdoors

What is the outdoors? Camping, hiking, and fishing are how we encounter the rough and tumble of the outdoors. A certain kind of cultural outdoors is wrapped up in RVs, tents, Thermoses, campfires, and s'mores. A brimming sense of freedom. A place where you can write your own *Travels with Charley*.

The backyard is a readily accessible microcosm of the outdoors. Between the backyard and the indoors is a glass door. The glass door gives us a glimpse of new possibilities and new constraints. You can see if it's worth going outside, if the weather suits.

Landscaping, gardening, patios, pools, flower beds, mulch, bird feeders, gopher traps, and more allow us to design the backyard. But things fail. Squirrels climb up bird feeders. Other things need upkeep. Mulch is overrun by weeds.

When we speak of the country or the outdoors, we probably all have it, even if it's just a flowerpot. Every home has an indoor and outdoor. Some of us dwell outdoors more, maintaining and shaping gardens. Some simply dabble, sitting on patio chairs, sipping mimosas, or drinking beers. Some outdoors feel cold and tidy. Others feel warm and disheveled.

11 Dark Skies

Tonight is the Perseid meteor shower. With nary a cloud in sight, it's promised to be a particularly good showing. His friend called, "Hey, can we go to your parents' to see it? Too much light pollution here to get a good view."

They set up a few lawn chairs in the front yard, got out some binoculars and telescopes, drank some hot cocoa, and were illuminated by a wonderful galactic viewing in the rural, pitch dark sky.

12   Like a Videogame

A short car ride away from his home is the "Coyote Valley Sporting Clays." It's loads of fun. Last time he took his Swiss friend there. He took him there to experience Americana.

He got a two-barreled shotgun, and his friend had a pump-action shotgun. Disks fly out, and they shoot. It's like a video game. You need a certain strategy—trace the path of the clay, get a little bit ahead of it, control your breathing, press the trigger, and hopefully the shotgun pellets hit and satisfyingly break apart the clay. If you miss, you only get one more shot to quickly hit the bird. Each station simulates a different animal. One drops a clay and it bounces along a hillside path, simulating a rabbit. Others mimic pigeons.

Once, when going up to the station, he lazily swung—not on purpose of course— the barrel toward his friend. "Whoa, watch where you're pointing that thing." He suddenly felt unnerved at the thought that he could kill someone instantly. He still thinks of that moment from time to time.

His shoulders were sore from the recoil for days after.

13   Just Accept It

Every time he goes home he expects it. Web pages load at a crawling pace, so much so that he notices the order in which text and images download and display, starting from the upper left. Sometimes the browser spits out a webpage from the modem, letting them know their connection was lost. The Internet is unstable,[12] like

---

[12] Internet stability is often more valued than mere access (Burrell 2018).

the pitted asphalt of country roads. It says to click a button to try and resolve the problem. He clicks once and, often, several times before it reconnects. Sometimes he just gets up and unplugs and replugs the modem. He complains to his parents that their Internet sucks but he knows it isn't their fault. They think it is plenty fast, but he can't work. Even with Zoom—the latest and coolest videoconferencing software— he grumpily turns off the video when joining remote meetings with colleagues. Too choppy and grainy.

He browses the slow Internet looking for faster internet. "Cable San Martin" or "Internet San Martin" yield few results. Every time he enters their home address, it says they don't have broadband access there.

One day, he goes to Charter's website and types in their address. It says there is a cable package. $45 for 100 Mbps. They are paying the same for 6 Mbps. He signs up, schedules a day for installation, but at the last step they say he needs to chat with customer support. They ask for his address again and they tell him sorry, we don't have service for your zip code. He was *so* excited, and now he is so disappointed. All the possibilities—zippy cloud backups, responsive websites stuffed with dynamic content, not having to tell the parents to stop watching videos so he could work— gone.

His dad shows him flyers from Viasat, exclaiming a "SERVICE ALERT" for "speeds (up to) 10x faster than typical DSL" at his address. The flyer has a photo of country homes with spacious land, lush trees, and cute sheds, all bathed in rays of sunlight. Presumably Viasat is this beacon of hope for the rural. He sees that it's for *satellite* service. $50 the first 3 months, but increases to $70 afterward. Sigh. What a rip off. He feels trapped and the companies know it too, the desperation in the air.

The other day he drove down the road off the highway to his home. At a four way intersection, hammered to a wooden post was a sign declaring, "Fast Internet (Viasat)." The internet companies certainly know how to reach their market population. They don't advertise "virtually." They know how to materialize affect. He fumes.

14 South Pride for the North?

When he interviewed, the university picked him up in a hired limousine. Apparently, these hired cars are commonly used for schlepping job interviewees as well as prom dates. At an intersection was a pickup truck with a huge confederate flag propped up in its bed. The flag flapped back and forth violently in the air. He tried to catch the driver's face but failed. He tried but couldn't imagine the same truck in California. It was like seeing something from the news, happening live in front of him. In the midst of small talk, he asked the driver about the confederate flag. The driver said, "There are a lot of stupid people here."

Later, his wife Googled Indiana's history. "It was part of the Union!"[13] He wondered if the people flying the flag knew that. But he later learned that Indiana has always been a state in flux, with one foot in the South and one in the North.

15 His Own Country

Photo by Kathryn E. Graber (used with permission)

The backyard is where the microcosm of the rural is constructed. It is a comfortable and convenient outdoors. Feel tired? Feel hot? Go back "inside." It's a way for suburbia to experience nature. Stray animals on the run.

The wildness of suburbia is made apparent through the neighborhood mailing list. Missing dogs. Found cats. Sightings of foxes.

An email is sent to the neighborhood mailing list with the subject header, "Chickens loose in street." A photo is attached showing a black and brown chicken at opposite ends running, in a blur against a static backdrop. Suburban cars, sidewalks, flowers, campaign signs, and trees are captured with crystal clarity. The chickens are the decisive moment, like the businessman of *Behind the Gare Saint-Lazare* caught in eternity galloping across a pool of water. He still gets giddy showing the email to everyone.

---

[13]The flag can just be a sign of white supremacy, not necessarily the strict historical meaning of aligning with the North or the South during the Civil War.

16 Unexpected Sights at Walmart

As he pushed his cart past racks of clothes in Walmart, he saw a lanky fellow with a white t-shirt tucked into blue jeans covering leather cowboy boots. The man had a white, bushy mustache, perfectly manicured. Along the man's hip was a leather holster brazenly holding a silver revolver. The revolver glinted in the fluorescent lights. He blinked a few times to make sure he wasn't dreaming. It was like a surreal scene from a movie featuring the actor Sam Elliot. He expected to see some unique characters at Walmart, but not a gun. People around didn't seem to care (or at least pretended not to care). You can carry a gun around in Indiana with a permit.

He's noticed that people wear camo to Walmart, to the grocery store, etc., much like folks in Silicon Valley, California wear yoga gear to Whole Foods.

17 The Gad-a-bout Newspaper

Shawn, a local bow hunter, recommended that he speak with Dr. Fred Philips, DVM (Doctor of Veterinary Medicine). He pointed out a local Indiana newspaper where Dr. Philips writes a column on trapping, *The Gad-a-bout* (what a name!). The byline is "Archery, camping, fishing, hunting, horses, humor, military, trapping, travel, events, opinions, etc." It encourages you to "Take One It's Free." It is full of advertisements—furniture shops, boat shops, farm equipment, fishing guides, gun repair, restaurants, and more. The column by Dr. Philips detailed the latest sales at a local fur sale.

- Thirty-two trappers selling 1,272 pelts to nine buyers for a total of $4,500.00
- Beaver XXL/XXXL had $20 offered / no sale
- Coyote Grease: $20.00
- Muskrats XL: $1.00–$4.00
- etc …

Dr. Philips ends with "Watch your top knot. Keep your eyes along the skyline."

He loves *The Gad-a-bout*. You can easily get lost in it. It provides a central peek into a part of Indiana he is not often exposed to. They have a nice website with all the previous issues in PDF.

Their Facebook presence is minimal. He felt a tinge of sadness reading a post by the editor:

> Well it's like this, I'm a writer who has little time to write. I'm 76, not getting any younger. It takes most of my time publishing The Gad-a-bout Newspaper and the rest delivering and preparing for the next one. All the things Facebook indicates I should do, I do in my paper. I have created 336 issues since 1990 and working on the 337th one this week, it will be printed on March 12th. I wanted to live long enough to create 500 issues, but to do that I have to publish for 14 more years and have little hope of being able to meet that goal.

He admires the editor's dedication.

His initial thought was "wow this newspaper is like Facebook." He did an about-face, rather—it is the other way around of course!

As he scrolls down, he sees other posts—about *Fox News*, about concerns with tearing down Christopher Columbus statues, about the second amendment.

This turns his stomach a bit, but one can admire while disagreeing, no?

18   Rural King

When friends and family from the West Coast come to visit, he takes them to Rural King. Where else can you instantly understand what "rural" is than in its eponymous store?

Go in and the smell of popcorn wafts. Scoop up the yellow-stained popcorn into the paper bag.

One section has sturdy, thick work boots.

Another has camo clothing, crossbows, and rifles.

Walking along, one can smell a musty amalgam of different livestock feed—chicken, rabbit, swine.

At the very back of the store a different kind of smell permeates—that of small livestock. In what essentially look like miniature horse troughs sit small chicks illuminated by heat lamps. You've got Barred Rock, Rhode Island Red, Ameraucana, all kinds of different chicks. Each trough is labeled with the chicken's statistics, like a baseball card. You also get a snapshot of what color the eggs will be. You've got the quintessential yellow chick. Ones with black and white stripes. Some of them at 99 cents a pop. There are a few rabbits there, too.

A large sign warns: "THE BABY BIRDS WILL GROW TO BE ADULT BIRDS." Presumably this is to warn city slickers that these animals are not just cute little pets.

Some of the chicks vigorously peck away at the feeder tray. Some are snuggling with their siblings, gently dozing.

The eye instinctively moves to the chicks that stay still. They look like loners. He bends down to get a closer look. Their beaks agape, eyes closed, one wonders how they died. Were they malnourished? Did the other chicks kill them? When will someone at the store come to clean away this sight?

A large cut-out board advertising a poultry feed brand shows a rooster saying "Best chick pic ever!" with a small chick. Their friend and his wife stick their faces through the holes and he snaps a photo. He chuckles at the double entendre, but wonders if it is sexist.

19   Bloomington Deer Collars

In Bloomington, the deer are not scared. They have full reign over their yards. They eat flowers, destroy gardens, and butt through fences.

They lay in their yard. When he comes out, they perk up and look at him. Sometimes, the younger ones run off, gracefully flying over fences. Most of the time, though, the older ones just look up, maybe grunt, but otherwise go about grazing or enjoying our manicured lawns.

The local biologists tag them, presumably to track their movements. There was talk of culling deer. They have an overpopulation of deer here. But the hipsters and animal lovers in Bloomington don't want to kill Bambi. It'll never happen.

20   A Child Among Children

He decided to take the Indiana Hunter Education class. It wasn't legally required, but he wanted to get a better grasp of what would be entailed. He drove on a backroad to a lodge. Inside, he felt sheepish—he saw mostly children. Well, he saw some adults, but they were the parents of the children taking the class. He was definitely the only Asian American there.

The instructor explained the parts of the gun to everyone. He spoke like a primary school teacher to his students. Many of the kids were already familiar with the information.

He scanned the room to see if there were other adult beginners like him. Nope, didn't look like it.

They gave everyone a nice booklet. He figured he could get what he needed from it. The class was too slow (for the kids' sake). At the break, he thanked the instructor and left.

21   Researching Gutting

Before the hunt, they had to consider the possibility they would actually harvest a deer. Where do they field dress it?

He did some research about field dressing a deer. The YouTube video was daunting. In the hot weather, you are in a race with time, and accidentally cutting the wrong organs could ruin the meat and make the work harder. If you don't dress quickly enough, the flies will take over the carcass, laying eggs, etc.

A deer is huge. The organs you pull out are massive, some looking like a pale white waterskin. He can't imagine the stench.

22 The Old Boys Club

He conducts an interview with Sam, a former employee at the Department of Natural Resources (DNR). He asks Sam whether being a biologist but not a long-time hunter was challenging at his workplace:

> Within Fish and Wildlife, there is definitely a culture of that. I would go a little bit further and say if you're an adult onset hunter, there is still bias against you. Even though I'd started deer hunting in 2010 [6 years ago] and turkey hunting in 2011, it was still like, "Oh, you're a new hunter and what could you possibly know? How can you teach hunting?"
>
> There are these confrontational type of questions that really showed the bias of, "Yeah, we want to teach people how to hunt, but even with our new hunters, we're not going to let them into our clique or our fold." So that's something that I'm facing professionally.
>
> I don't know if you could extend that to everyone or if that's just they don't like me …
>
> A lot of our staff, at least in Fish and Wildlife, this is the natural extension of their love for hunting, is they go into it professionally. For me, it will always be just one more outdoor recreational pursuit.

When Sam joined the DNR, he knew he wasn't part of the old boys club. It smarted. Those kids in the hunter ed class knew they were in the club.

23 Hunger Games

They signed up for a family archery workshop out in the Mt. Vernon Conservation Club. They went into a large cabin. There seemed to only be a few folks there already sitting, chatting, and laughing. The DNR officials seemed to know them already. When they came they greeted them warmly, but left. It seems like they were the only ones there for "official" business, for the class.

They went to a small area outside of the cabin set up for the archery practice. A makeshift target board propped up on the ground had a tarp, like an old blanket out to dry, behind it.

His wife was the better shot from the get-go. She was good at pulling the bright neon colored compound bow and getting the arrow to hit the target straight on. It was fun.

One of the officials told them that archery and bowhunting was especially popular with women. Women were inspired by the bow and arrow-wielding main character in *Hunger Games*, Katniss Everdeen.

24   A Mentor

They signed up for the Family Dove Hunt event. They took a rough, rocky road into the wildlife area, and found some laborers who directed them to a field full of knee-high grass off the main road.

They were the only ones driving a Subaru SUV. The rest had hulking, tough trucks. They all had their own guns and camo. Some came with families. Lots of kids.

They were the only absolute beginners. They were paired with John as their dove hunting mentor.

John gave him a 20-gauge shotgun, designed for youths. He also brought a bucket with a padded cushion seat to screw on the top. He had some extra lawn seats to sit on. John gave a quick lesson on holding, loading, and safely using the shotgun.

During the dove hunt, his wife didn't participate—she didn't want to kill an animal. John sympathized, saying that his own wife was hesitant but eventually warmed up to hunting, and now wants to do deer hunting.

He also told them that people often refuse to kill "beautiful" animals but are fine shooting "ugly" animals.

John worked as a biologist in private industry. It was a lot of hours, he made good money, and climbed the career ladder. But, he was tired of spending time indoors filling out forms.

He likes introducing people to hunting, especially adults who weren't exposed to this environment. He was a helper, like Mr. Rogers always talked about.

25   Not So Smart

Doves are not very smart. You shoot at them. They fly away. Five minutes past and the same birds are back where you shot them. They don't realize that someone is trying to kill them.

He also often heard that turkeys are dumb. Apparently, they have a pea-sized brain.

Hunters are always trying to get in the mindset of animals. They are centaurs. What is it like to be a duck or deer? Deer smell good but have bad eyesight. Ducks like seeing other ducks. Turkeys are the opposite of deer—they see well but have a laughably weak sense of smell.

26   Finishing Them Off

When you get a clean shot, everything is simple. But a few times when he went to get the dove, it was still alive. Its chest was raising and falling. The instructor said you twist the neck. It was easy to do, its neck bones cracked, like twisting and breaking a bunch of dried, hollow reeds.

One time, the instructor twisted the neck, inadvertently decapitating the head. Blood was spurting everywhere with gusto. This was unexpected. The dove's wings were flailing wildly.

With ducks, the injured ones—upon falling from the sky—will splash water everywhere as their wings beat violently against the surface of the pond. Doug, his hunting partner, went up to the ducks and shot them point blank. The water fell still. This disturbed him.

27 Peeling for Supermarket Meat

Processing doves is surprisingly easy. You make a small cut and just start peeling away the feathers. The bird is so delicate and light. Peeled feathers fly erratically like dandelion seeds in the wind. Some stick on his pant legs.

It's also surprising because the meat seems to simply "appear." You must, however, get past a moment of revulsion—the tentative first step where you first dig in and puncture the skin with your fingernails to pull away the skin with its feathers. It is a visceral feeling to transform an animal into a piece of meat that would feel natural plopped onto Styrofoam, shrink wrapped, labeled, and sitting in a supermarket. The surprise is that transformation—how readily his mind shifted to seeing the dove he killed as food.

Once you've peeled enough by hand, a sharp knife scrapes up and breaks the meat away from the muscle and bones.

The knife slips and he gets a pretty nasty gash. It's a dull pain. He's embarrassed, but they give him some gauze and tape to stop the bleeding. Looking at this finger now, it is smooth where the skin has healed.

28   Driving with Doug

At 9:30AM, he met Doug at Suzie's Diner in Solsberry, Indiana. He parked in a large, unpaved parking lot by the diner. The diner looked connected to a gas station. Doug came along with a large, powerful white pickup truck.

They'd go together to the draw. It's kind of like the lottery. The draw tells you where you'll hunt waterfowl. He recently looked up the diner on Google. It now says "recorded closed at this location." Apparently, it is now Sasha's Pancake House.

On the way to Linton, they drove by a gas station. The gas prices were *cheap*. "The gas here is always really cheap," Doug told him.

Doug also told him about his new boss at the DNR, some Purdue-educated guy. He didn't respect what Doug and the others knew about land management, like how to clear away invasive species.

As they neared the Goose Pond visitor center, Doug pulled his truck up on the side of State HWY 59, nearby the edge of the pond. They saw a few ducks and water chickens. He said, "This would be an easy place to hunt cause it's not too far from the parking lot." People don't want a long hike back while lugging their game. Pointing further down, past the pond, he explained, "There's a good place down there. Harder to get to though with all the water."

29   Improvising

They drove to a gravely parking lot to walk to the draw location. Doug gave him a pair of old waders (his son's) with boots attached to them. He knew they'd be too big for him, so he inserted some carpet scraps at the bottom so that they would fit.

Doug and Benny brought some cut oak from the surrounding area. They broke down the oak branches and stuck them in the grass to provide cover from ducks.

30   Becoming Nature

The water doesn't just appear. Patches in the Goose Pond dry up. They have a system now to pump water into areas to encourage ducks and other waterfowl to come. They don't need to rely on the rainfall anymore.

Neighboring farms help out too. They plant corn and other crops, harvest them, and leave some for animals. The crops are put in place before the floods.

31 Fucking Pricks Everywhere

The mud was a thick slurry. It was damn sticky. Each step he took off the mud, if he wasn't nimble, large strings of the wet slurry refused to let go. Sometimes his socks would come out of the boots.

Wading through the mud, his arms brushed prickly bushes and grasses. The hunters he tagged along with gave him a stool with legs that served as stakes you drove into the slurry. It wasn't the most comfortable stool, but it worked.

One time, he fell down in the mud onto his knees. Doug chuckled, "At least you didn't fall face flat into the mud!"

At home, he found his hiking pants and shirt infested with burs, those insect-like seeds called "beggar's ticks." For a few days after, he developed rashes everywhere on his arms. He slathered ice-cold aloe from the fridge onto his arms to soothe the itchiness.

32 Trumpeting Comfort

"Cognitive dissonance" is what pops into his mind.

In a momentary lull during the duck hunt, one of the rangers asked, "What do you all think of Trump?" They all agreed he was a bit of a loon, but, boy, they hated Hillary. Hillary was going to take their guns away. They didn't trust her.

He wondered how anyone could support Trump. The hunters he met were kind and generous with their time. They weren't like Trump. Yet, strewn about their homes were magazine articles trumpeting Trump.

In those conversations out in the marsh, he learned. People didn't necessarily like Trump. They knew Trump was mercurial, childish, and unqualified. They weren't idiots. They just hated Hillary. He would never vote for Trump, but he *understood* why sane others might.

33 Sunset

Duck hunting is allowed until sunset. Bob's smartphone tells them it is sunset. Hunting's over. They begin to pack up their gear for the day. Doug points out—the sun's still up! Do you want to stay an hour more? They all chuckle. It's the first time they've misjudged sunset. Those darned devices telling them when it is.

34 Target Bags

He stuffed the ducks whole into the reusable Target bags in the trunk of his car. They had some heft.

He arrived back home in the dead of night and called to his wife. "I've got some ducks I need to gut! Help!" Coming out to the carport, she wasn't happy he used those bags. She said they were ruined. They were permanently tainted by the ducks' death and blood.

Doug called him on the phone, "I forgot to tell you, don't get spooked by the water bugs on the birds. They often hitch rides on birds to go to different areas of Goose Pond."

The porch light wasn't bright enough. She held the flashlight for him while he gutted the duck under the carport. It wasn't as easy as peeling away doves. The ducks were larger and tougher to process. Something about their heft and size made their death more apparent. The loose duck feathers were buzzing all around them like a tornado, sticking to their clothes. It felt strange to be gutting ducks under the moonlight on the concrete.

35 Gamey

Teal is prized for its taste. Shovelers are the junkiest birds because they will eat anything. Ducks taste like what they eat.

Per Doug's advice, they brined the duck meat in salt for a couple of days to remove the blood. The internet warned not to overcook duck—keep it medium rare. They BBQ'd it on a gas grill with Aldi's steak seasoning and seasoning salt.

Still, it was too gamey. Maybe he needed a better recipe? Maybe he should've tried to cook it with the skin or fat? He longed for chicken. He was tempted not to eat it all but knew he had to. He felt a responsibility to eat what he killed.

John suggested cooking dove meat wrapped in bacon. When cooked in the cast iron it tasted good, better than the duck. His wife said, "I wouldn't classify it as good, but it was edible."

36 Retracing with the Help of His Google Friends

The outdoors is something he's researching. He was writing his fieldnotes like any good ethnographer would but wasn't able to keep track of where they went in that truck ride with Doug. On a whim, he opened Google Maps. Lo and behold Google had been diligently tracking him. The timeline beautifully showed the route—the U-turns taken, and the twisty, ad hoc route they traversed.

37 Old Tech at a Farm

Mike showed us an "Ohio Brooder." It is described in a 1942 circular by the Ohio Agricultural Experiment Station as a "type of brooder ...designed upon the basic principle that chicks ...can be depended upon to adapt themselves readily to their heat and air requirements when ample heat and air are provided." The boxes can adapt to different weather conditions—for example, by raising them to accommodate different or more mature chicks that are taller.

He marveled at the elegance of the design. It supported the agency of the chicks. Sure, it wasn't *the* most efficient way to raise chicks, but it was *an* efficient way that makes them happy!

38 Hospitality: Ladies First

The chicken farmers—a husband and wife—were *really* nice. He asked to use their bathroom before the interview. The toilet looked like it had been recently cleaned. The water had that distinctive blue color. The whole house was spotless. His research collaborator, Professor Dvorak, remarked, "I think they most definitely cleaned up the place for us." That was nice!

As they were leaving—despite their protestations—the couple insisted on giving them each a carton of eggs, fresh from their chickens. It was a sweet gesture, and he felt guilty for taking both their time and their eggs.

But the kindness of strangers is not uncommon in this rural context.

Professor Dvorak got in the driver's side of the car—naturally, to drive them back to the university. The wife remarked, "Oh she's driving? That's new." They smiled. He was taken aback by the comment.

39   Citizen of Starbucks International

He emailed back and forth to recruit a local bowhunter, Peter. They decided to meet in Martinsville. People at his university always talked about Martinsville's history with the KKK and racism. Vestiges of that past are no longer visible but serve to affect the entire city. No doubt the residents are aware of their city's lingering reputation. But, he isn't aware of their awareness.

He arranged to do the interview at Starbucks.

Starbucks sticks out like a sore thumb compared to the other restaurants in Martinsville. The "No. 1 Chinese Restaurant." The "Traderbaker Flea Market." Starbucks by contrast is bougie. Nonetheless, every time he passes by on the way to the Indy airport, he sees a long line of cars for the drive-thru snaking around that Starbucks. Go figure!

He met Peter at Starbucks, ordered his own latte, and asked him what he wanted, "my treat." Peter looked up and was overwhelmed by the coffee choices and lingo—tall, grande, flat white, etc. Scratching his head, Peter asked if they had hot chocolate.

He was bemused that Peter didn't know how to order at Starbucks.

Looking back, he wondered why he was bemused. He is ashamed. When he first started drinking coffee, he was confused by its choices. Of course, Starbucks is its own country with strange words like "Frappuccino" and "venti." He should look at his own consumerist-generation X commodification, having become a citizen of Starbucks International.

40   You Speak Good English

He met another bowhunter, Carl, at the local police station. They shook hands and exchanged pleasantries. Carl then remarked, "You speak really good English." Taken aback, he snidely replied, "Well I should, I was born and raised in California." During the interview, Carl also made allusions to Chinese bowhunters he was familiar with. Why bring that up? He's not Chinese.[14]

41   Ethnography in HCI

This chapter takes as inspiration Kathleen Stewart's *Ordinary Affects* (2007). It represents an attempt to employ a style of ethnographic writing not always encountered in the discipline of human–computer interaction (or anthropology). Ethnography, at its heart as well as etymologically, is the writing of culture. When we think of ethnography in HCI we often think of a certain structure to writing—introduction, related work, methodology (e.g., grounded theory), findings (the so-called thick

---

[14]The outdoors is frequently racialized as white (Finney 2014).

description (Geertz 1973)), and discussion (e.g., How does this transfer? What are the design implications? What are the sensitizing concepts? What are the theoretical claims?). At the risk of overgeneralizing, ethnographic styles of writing in HCI often predominately draw from the Chicago School. In the world of HCI, ethnography connotes certain legitimated repertoires of doing, reporting, and disseminating research.

Arguably, this dominant mode of writing, fruitful though it has been, ultimately is what Jansen (2016, p. 65) labels as "representational thinking and evaluative critique—reduction, demystification, totalisation."[15] To put in simpler terms, the Strunk and White ethnography must handhold the reader. It must collapse findings into "themes" and, further, the discussion must explicitly tie in with these themes. Or, it may map findings to all-encompassing theories that explain and predict. In *Writing culture: The poetics and politics of ethnography* (Clifford and Marcus 1986, p. 2), James Clifford similarly points out that despite its centrality, writing in ethnography has been bowdlerized by "the persistence of an ideology claiming transparency of representation and immediacy of experience." In other words, writing is rendered unproblematic.

I do not mean to disparage how we write ethnography in HCI. I also do not intend this chapter to bring innovative critiques on research at the crossroads of ethnography and HCI (Crabtree et al. 2009; Dourish 2006, 2014; Randall 2018). Rather, I seek to imagine an alternative "ethnographic" study in HCI, just as anthropologists have already reimagined what ethnographic writing should look like. This is a kind of writing that leads the reader but does not wholly foreclose interpretation. It leaves the work open to new connections, invites readers' active,[16] generative engagement, not just passive consumption.[17]

Stewart's approach harkens back, perhaps in ethnography's most raw form, to the making of texts. This tack makes transparent that the "self is an instrument of knowing" (Dourish 2014). A consequence of this viewpoint is that "data" from an ethnography consists not only what the researcher "observes," but also their own feelings and affect.

In *Ordinary Affects*, Stewart's subject is of everyday life in America. The book does not provide detailed instructions nor motivations for her "method" of writing. Her work blurs the boundaries between the social sciences, anthropology, and humanities. What is obvious is that her work deals with "affect." This affective turn has been talked about at length. Affect is "the feeling of having a feeling, a potential that emerges" (Rutherford 2016). Gould (2009, p. 19) defines affect's amorphous, visceral qualities—it is "nonconscious and unnamed, but nevertheless registered, experiences of bodily energy and intensity that arise in response to stimuli impinging on the body." Thus, affect gets at the opaqueness of feelings—its can't-quite-put-into-words force.

---

[15] A similar critique can be found in organizational studies: "Much of our writing is washed by a thick spray of claimed objectivity since artful delights and forms are seen by many …to interfere with the presentation of what is actually there in a given social world" (Maanen 1995).

[16] Reader reception theory makes a similar claim in the realm of literary theory (Su 2013).

[17] I am indebted for Ellie Harmon's feedback here, which I shamelessly quote verbatim.

Emotion then is a result of affect being reified, concretized into a nameable expression shaped (but not defined) by culture (Gould 2009, p. 20). The "affect is what makes you *feel* an emotion" (Gould 2009, p. 22). In spite of affect's causal role in expressing and identifying emotion, affect remains difficult to pinpoint. Moreover, affect and emotion are not so easily teased apart. By unpacking the film *Bend it Like Beckham*, Ahmed (2007) illustrates that the affect of happiness, particularly the happiness of multiculturalism, is often gendered. In that work, affect means almost the same as feeling. There is no one way to make the affective turn.

Here, I have adopted this dominant conception of affect as preceding feeling. Thus, affect attends to what leads us to feel and where that leading happens. This is one way understanding people in HCI can go beyond seeing and hearing what they do. Instead, it can begin to examine the subjective experiences of others and ourselves.

For me, there are two aspects that are most striking about Stewart's text—first, it reads like a collection of loosely tangled vignettes. Each is titled and differ in length (some are only a few sentences long). Some vignettes are explicitly linked to others. Some sound more "theoretical," talking about abstract concepts like the Scenes of Impact, Extreme Trajectories, and the Affective Subject, while others are more concrete and descriptive like a travelog. Overall, they are written in a blasé style that *feels* very different from traditional ethnographies in HCI. Stewart's work reads like something in between non-fiction and fiction.

Second, the writing is excruciatingly "tentative, speculative" (Jansen 2016, p. 70). It is an experiment to devise a new anthropological mode of writing (Jansen 2016, p. 63). To best depict affect, Stewart chooses to make the reader sweat. For the most part, the reader needs to digest and make sense of the vignettes themselves. There are no sections. No subsections. No thematic outline. No introductory paragraphs that signpost a quasi-theoretical framing of the ethnographic results. No figures. It deliberately avoids truth claims. This ethereal, yet nervous, quality of her writing is partially achieved through judicious use of words to convey affect: potentialities, trajectories, intensities, emergence, surges, immanent forces, pulsations, and the visceral. These words help us experience affect and its foreshadowing of the emotions we might feel.

Stewart's writing may frustrate the reader—it attempts to perform affect but nonetheless the reading experience never seems to sharply capture affect. It slips through the fingers. It is sly and sneaky, withering away just as it appears. It wallows in the "ambivalent and contradictory nature of our feelings," including their intertwining with our bodily senses and cultural surroundings (Gould 2009, p. 26).

Taken together, these two aspects attempt to "slow the quick jump to representational thinking and evaluative critique …by performing some of the intensity and texture that makes them habitable and animate" (Stewart 2008). In other words, Stewart wants us to dwell on the ethnographic writing without the writing dwelling for us.[18] Yes, the writing does perform, but only to give us a taste of the affect that so interested her (and us). It is a performance open to multiple interpretations.

I do not claim to have reached Stewart's heights, but I have endeavored to make this chapter one that "works best when you immerse yourself in it, when you let it affect you rather than trying to pin it down and force it to make sense" (Fannin et al. 2010).[19] Like Stewart (2007), I refer to myself in the third person. This choice gives the author less authority, less legitimacy, allowing the reader to reach their own affect with conviction—a sort of indirect communication that Kierkegaard employed.[20]

42 The Resonance of Multiple Ruralities

Michael Bell's (1994) beautiful ethnography of a country village, Childerley, warns us of pastoralism's allure:

> Pastoralism has been widely rejected by academics. In America, critics will pejoratively call pastoralism the "rural myth"…the "rural idyll." Rural sociologists have pointed out that pastoralism romanticizes the poverty of farm workers and peasants, turning them into "merrie rustics" and obscuring the extent to which the economic political forces of the city keep them impoverished. (p. 125)

Yet, Bell acknowledges his informants in Childerley would not agree with this assessment. It is still a "powerful idea" (p. 126) that the villagers employ to their advantage.

Childerley, as he discovers, is simmering with tensions. City people versus country people. Moneyed people versus poor people. Locals versus fly-ins. Those who have or lack country competence (Desmond 2008). A country village is not a monolithic entity.

Bell seeks a middle ground to theorize about nature and morality in Childerley. First, he proposes that we come to grips with the fact that: "It is deeply reassuring to find one's sense of order, one's categories of understanding, there in what one takes to be a different realm" (Bell 1994, p. 236). In other words, despite the paucity and imperfections of one's categories, "reducing" is something we are drawn to. In strange places, it comforts us and allows us to proceed.

Bell is not saying there is only one ideal for the country. Rather, people in the country seek to find different ways of living that *resonate* with each other, much like different bells in a tower, each with their own pitch, ring in consonance with each other.

This metaphor of Bell's bell reflects a wider move within rural sociology and geography away from traditional, obdurate distinctions between the urban and the rural often focused on their differing physical characteristics (Halfacree 1993; Lobao

---

[18] Stewart (2008, p. 72) finds sympathy with "weak" theories that "take on a life of their own as problems of thought …in contrast to a …theory that …dreams of a perfect parallelism between the analytic subject, her concept, and the world—a kind of razed earth for academic conversation."

[19] A student reported that this chapter's "writing grew on us, but like fungus."

[20] Kierkegaard's writing style has potential as a strategy for design (Su and Stolterman 2016).

1996). This is motivated by a desire to reject reducing the rural to simplified stereotypes—e.g., small, marginalized, and financially strapped (Bell 2007).

Instead, we see an increased set of bells being "rung." City people are adopting "rural" activities, particularly outdoor and nature activities, and symbols (e.g., camouflage clothing) (Lichter and Brown 2011), thereby invigorating businesses in rural counties (Flachs and Abel 2019). Farming is no longer a small enterprise endemic to the country but, rather, now part of a global, corporate agriculture (Hess 2009). Rural and urban areas have integrated "migrants" from one another (Salamon 2007; Smith et al. 2001), leading to both tension and appropriation (Lichter and Brown 2011). Scholars have argued that rural studies must examine particular conditions in particular settings (Hoggart 1990).

This cultural turn (Woods 2012) highlights the increasing intersection of rural geography, sociology, environment, and other disciplines (Woods 2009). Scholars now focus on how rural people perform and enact rurality (Woods 2010). For instance, they now emphasize their social interactions in communities, participation in loosely defined social movements, values, and management of rural identity (Woods 2003). These enactments of rurality are not merely in interactions or speech but also in the embodied practices such as those in agriculture, farmers' markets, and agrotourism (Carolan 2008).

This chapter highlights the affects of different ruralities which swirl around each other. I would add that our bodies *feel* these ruralities everywhere, this resonance that Bell speaks of. But, more significantly, my writings highlight points in time when *my* affects have collided. This resonance is constantly teetering from consonance to dissonance. My bodily experiences are a mish-mash of multiple geographies of suburbans, urbans, and rurals. We want to reduce. I'm always marveling at similarities despite differences and differences despite similarities. They bump against each other, threatening an explosion of energy that reverberates. Taking Bell's metaphor, these affects may be harmonious or dissonant, or, more likely, something in between.

The affective textures in my scenes are designs that invite one to flex their emotive muscles. I have conveyed how rural forces are felt, influenced by the urban, suburban, and rural histories ingrained in my own body. Moments will occur when the reader's feelings resonate with mine. In other moments, the reader will feel a discordant chord. Like any design, my scenes—my texts[21]—are to be at once discussed and judged. At times, I was able to reflect on my own "emotional habitus."[22] Such writing thus offers the potential to reorient away from taken for granted attitudes and ways of feeling the rural. Yet, in many cases, I was a slave of emotions underlying my well-worn assumptions of the rural. It is my hope that the comfort or discomfort from reading designs like the scenes of this chapter give rise to other designs of variegated forms, mired in affect.

Acknowledgements I am grateful to Leslie S. Liu and Amanda Lazar for many enjoyable discussions and suggestions on this chapter. Ellie Harmon's incisive comments helped this work

---

[21] A parallel approach with images in HCI are pictorials (Blevis 2014).

[22] "A template for what and how to feel." (Gould 2009, p. 34).

meaningfully speak to a greater audience. I owe a debt to Scott McCrickard for so graciously cultivating a community of scholars passionate about the outdoors and HCI. My wonderful collaborators Majdah Alshehri, EunJeong Cheon, Lynn Dombrowski, and Rosemary Steup provided constructive critiques. Special thanks to Lilly Irani for pointing me toward affect theory. Colleen Jankovic deftly copyedited this chapter. Lastly, I am grateful to Michael Jones, Tim Stelter, and their students for their willingness to provide feedback by exposing their own affect. This work was supported in part by the National Science Foundation through CAREER grant IIS-1845964.

References

Ahmed S (2007) Multiculturalism and the promise of happiness. New Form 63:121–138

Bell MM (2007) The two-ness of rural life and the ends of rural scholarship. J Rural Stud 23(4):402–415. https://doi.org/10.1016/j.jrurstud.2007.03.003

Bell MM (1994) Childerley: nature and morality in a country village. University of Chicago Press, Chicago, IL

Blevis E (2014) Stillness and motion, meaning and form. In: Proceedings of the SIGCHI conference on designing interactive systems (DIS '14). ACM, New York, NY, pp 493–502. https://doi.org/10.1145/2598510.2602963

Burrell J (2018) Thinking relationally about digital inequality in rural regions of the U.S. First Monday, 23, 6. https://doi.org/10.5210/fm.v23i6.8376

Carolan MS (2008) More-than-Representational knowledge/s of the countryside: how we think as bodies. Sociol Rural 48(4):408–422. https://doi.org/10.1111/j.1467-9523.2008.00458.x

Clifford J, Marcus GE (1986) Writing culture: the poetics and politics of ethnography. University of California Press, Berkeley, CA

Crabtree A, Rodden T, Tolmie P, Button G (2009) Ethnography considered harmful. In: Proceedings of the SIGCHI conference on human factors in computing systems (CHI '09). ACM, New York, NY, pp 879-888. https://doi.org/10.1145/1518701.1518835

Desmond M (2008) On the fireline: living and dying with wildland firefighters. University of Chicago Press, Chicago, IL

Dourish P (2006) Implications for design. In: Proceedings of the SIGCHI conference on human factors in computing systems (CHI '06). ACM, New York, NY, pp 541–550. https://doi.org/10.1145/1124772.1124855

Dourish P (2014) Reading and interpreting ethnography. In: Olson JS, Kellogg WA (eds) Ways of knowing in HCI. Springer, New York, NY, pp 1–23. https://doi.org/10.1007/978-1-4939-0378-8_1

Evans CS (2009) Kierkegaard: an introduction. Cambridge University Press, New York, NY

Fannin M, Jackson M, Crang P, Katz C, Larsen S, Tolia-Kelly DP, Stewart K (2010) Author meets critics: a set of reviews and a response. Soc Cult Geogr 11(8):921–931. https://doi.org/10.1080/14649365.2010.529659

Finney C (2014) Black faces, white spaces: reimagining the relationship of African Americans to the great outdoors. University of North Carolina Press, Chapel Hill, NC

Flachs A, Abel M (2019) An emerging geography of the agrarian question: spatial analysis as a tool for identifying the new American Agrarianism. Rural Soc 84(2):191–225. https://doi.org/10.1111/ruso.12250

Geertz C (1973) Deep play: notes on the balinese cockfight. In: The interpretation of cultures. Basic Books, New York, NY, pp 413–453

Gould DB (2009) Moving politics: emotion and act up's fight against aids. University of Chicago Press, Chicago, IL

Halfacree KH (1993) Locality and social representation: space, discourse and alternative definitions of the rural. J Rural Stud 9(1):23–37. https://doi.org/10.1016/0743-0167(93)90003-3

Hardy J, Phelan C, Vigil-Hayes M, Su NM, Wyche S, Sengers P (2019) Designing from the rural. ACM Interactions, 37–41 July/August. https://doi.org/10.1145/3328487

Hess DJ (2009) Localist movements in a global economy: sustainability, justice, and urban development in the United States. Urban and industrial environments. MIT Press, Cambridge, MA

Hoggart K (1990) Let's do away with rural. J Rural Stud 6(3):245–257. https://doi.org/10.1016/0743-0167(90)90079-N

Jansen S (2016) Ethnography and the choices posed by the 'affective turn'. In: Frykman J, Frykman MP (eds) Sensitive Objects: Affect and Material Culture. Nordic Academic Press, Lund, Sweden, pp 55–77. https://doi.org/10.21525/kriterium.6

Lichter DT, Brown DL (2011) Rural America in an Urban society: changing spatial and social boundaries. Ann Rev Soc 37(1): 565–592. https://doi.org/10.1146/annurev-soc-081309-150208

Lobao L (1996) A sociology of the periphery versus a peripheral sociology: rural sociology and the dimension of space1. Rural Soc 61(1):77–102. https://doi.org/10.1111/j.1549-0831.1996.tb00611.x

Olwig KR (1996) Reinventing common nature: Yosemite and Mount Rushmore—A Meandering tale of a double nature. In: Cronon, W (ed) Uncommon ground: rethinking the human place in nature. Norton, New York, NY, pp 379–408

Randall D (2018) Investigation and design. In: Wulf V, Pipek V, Randall D, Rohde M, Schmidt K, Stevens G (eds) Socio-Informatics: a practice-based perspective on the design and use of IT artifacts (1st ed). Oxford University Press, Oxford, UK, pp 221–241

Rutherford D (2016) Affect theory and the empirical. Ann Rev Anthropol 45(1): 285–300. https://doi.org/10.1146/annurev-anthro-102215-095843

Salamon S (2007) Suburbanization of the heartland newcomers to old towns. University of Chicago Press, Chicago, IL

Smith MD, Krannich RS, Hunter LM (2001) Growth, decline, stability, and disruption: a longitudinal analysis of social well-being in four Western rural communities. Rural Soc 66(3):425–450. https://doi.org/10.1111/j.1549-0831.2001.tb00075.x

Spirn AW (1996) Constructing nature: the legacy of Frederick Law Olmsted. In: Cronon W (ed) Uncommon ground: rethinking the human place in nature. Norton, New York, NY, pp 91–113

Star SL (1999) The Ethnography of Infrastructure. Am Behav Sci 43(3):377–391. https://doi.org/10.1177/00027649921955326

Steup R, Dombrowski L, Su NM (2019) Feeding the world with data: visions of data-driven farming. In: Proceedings of the SIGCHI conference on designing interactive systems (DIS '19). ACM, New York, NY, 1503–1515. https://doi.org/10.1145/3322276.3322382

Steup R, Santhanam A, Logan M, Dombrowski L, Su NM (2018) Growing tiny publics: small farmers' social movement strategies. Proceedings of the ACM on human-computer interaction, 2(CSCW):165:1–165:24. https://doi.org/10.1145/3274434

Stewart K (2007) Ordinary affects. Duke University Press, Durham, NC

Stewart K (2008) Weak theory in an unfinished world. J Folk Res 45(1):71–82

Su NM (2013) The social life of tunes: representing the aesthetics of reception. In: ECSCW 2013: proceedings of the 13th European conference on computer supported cooperative work, 21–25 Sept 2013. Paphos, Cyprus. Bertelsen OW, Ciolfi L, Grasso MA, Papadopoulos GA (eds). Springer, London, UK, pp 207–228. https://doi.org/10.1007/978-1-4471-5346-7_11

Su NM, Cheon EJ (2017) Reconsidering nature: the dialectics of fair chase in the practices of American midwest hunters. In: Proceedings of the SIGCHI conference on human factors in computing systems (CHI '17). ACM, New York, NY, pp 6089–6100. https://doi.org/10.1145/3025453.3025966

Su NM, Stolterman E (2016) A design approach for authenticity and technology. In: Proceedings of the SIGCHI conference on designing interactive systems (DIS '16). ACM, New York, NY pp 643–655. https://doi.org/10.1145/2901790.2901869

US Census Bureau (2020a) US Census Bureau QuickFacts: San Jose city, California; United States. https://www.census.gov/quickfacts/fact/table/sanjosecitycalifornia,US/PST045218. Accessed 13 Feb 2020

US Census Bureau (2020b) US Census Bureau QuickFacts: San Martin CDP, California. https://www.census.gov/quickfacts/sanmartincdpcalifornia. Accessed 6 Jan 2020

US Geological Survey (2020) The national map small scale. https://nationalmap.gov/small_scale/printable/reference.html#California. Accessed 13 Feb 2020

Van Maanen J (1995) Style as theory. Organ Sci 6(1):133–143

Woods M (2003) Deconstructing rural protest: the emergence of a new social movement. J Rural Stud 19(3):309–325. https://doi.org/10.1016/S0743-0167(03)00008-1

Woods M (2010) Performing rurality and practising rural geography, performing rurality and practising rural geography. Prog Hum Geogr 34(6):835–846. https://doi.org/10.1177/0309132509357356

Woods M (2012) Rural geography III: Rural futures and the future of rural geography. Progr Hum Geograph 36(1):125–134. https://doi.org/10.1177/0309132510393135

Woods M (2009) Rural geography: blurring boundaries and making connections. Prog Hum Geograph 33(6):849–858. https://doi.org/10.1177/0309132508105001

Willed and the Wild

Moving HCI Outdoors: Lessons Learned from Conducting Research in the Wild

Mara Balestrini, Sarah Gallacher, and Yvonne Rogers

Abstract Researchers are increasingly adopting 'research in the wild' approaches to design and evaluate prototypes in public spaces and to understand how city dwellers interact with them. Although 'in the wild' studies can provide more ecologically valid findings compared with typical performance measures collected in the lab, there are challenges associated with designing for and deploying in emergent contexts. A huge amount of work is involved, especially navigating the range of pragmatic and logistical concerns that inevitably arise. It is messy, expensive, time consuming, and unpredictable where often things don't go according to plan. However, such practicalities are rarely discussed in published studies. The importance of the 'behind the scenes' work in making research in the wild happen should not be underestimated. In this chapter, we focus on three case studies where technology prototypes were evaluated in the wild. These are discussed in terms of: technology and design, space and place, social factors, and sustainability. Finally, we provide a set of practical recommendations for researchers and practitioners in the field.

1 Introduction

Research in the wild (RITW) is considered as an umbrella term to refer to how, what, and where research is conducted in naturalistic settings (Rogers and Marshall 2017). An underlying goal is to understand how technology (custom built and off-the-shelf) is and can be used in the everyday/real world, in order to gain new insights

M. Balestrini (✉)
Ideas for Change, Barcelona, Spain
e-mail: marabalestrini@ideasforchange.com

S. Gallacher
Arup, London, UK
e-mail: sarah.gallacher@arup.com

Y. Rogers
University College London, London, UK
e-mail: y.rogers@ucl.ac.uk

© Springer Nature Switzerland AG 2020
D. S. McCrickard et al. (eds.), *HCI Outdoors: Theory, Design, Methods and Applications*, Human–Computer Interaction Series,
https://doi.org/10.1007/978-3-030-45289-6_4

about: how to engage people/communities in various activities, how people's lives are impacted by a specific technology, and what people do when encountering a new technology in a given setting. The output from such research is used to develop new understandings, theories, or concepts about human behaviour in the real world.

RITW is increasingly conducted outdoors, especially in urban settings, with the aim of investigating how they may support and extend a range of user experiences, including playfulness (Müller et al. 2009), reflection (Johnson et al. 2012), and social interactions (Brignull and Rogers 2003; Fischer and Hornecker 2012). Problems addressed are equally diverse, including loneliness amongst city inhabitants, impact of tourism on the environment, and discerning what divides and concerns a community (Koeman et al. 2015). However, designing technology to address these problems in urban contexts is complex in ways that cannot be predicted or controlled for. There are many aspects that need to be taken into account. Sometimes, the problems being addressed are referred to as being 'wicked' (Nelson and Stolterman 2003); by this is meant the many perspectives of the stakeholders involved are difficult to take into account.

A main benefit of using RITW outdoors is the opportunity to gather valuable insights on how passers-by notice and interact with public or civic situated technologies, and the extent to which they are willing to engage with them, integrating them into their own routines in meaningful ways, either opportunistically or in the long term. However, conducting in-the-wild studies is not straight forward. There are many challenges associated with deploying novel prototypes in outdoor settings, including engaging with pre-existing communities, and possibly affecting people's lifestyles and routines (Rogers and Marshall 2017). Such concerns and observations are rarely described in the literature but are arguably as important to understand and learn from when designing and deploying technologies in the wild. Different settings, especially when moving from indoors to outdoors, create different challenges, meaning that technologies have to be designed and adapted for the different settings (Harris et al. 2004).

We have conducted many in the wild studies over the last 10–15 years. As part of the Interdisciplinary Collaborative Research Institute (ICRI) on Connected Cities, we have focussed on how to design novel urban technologies for engaging communities, fostering social interactions, and collecting environmental data (see cities.io). Many of the findings have been published in research journals and conferences. Here we summarise lessons learnt from three of these, which involved facilitating different user experiences in outdoors settings: one involving social interaction and humour (JokeBox), another eliciting public people's responses to an urban event (VoxBox) and the third involving collecting environmental data as a way of assessing the health of an urban park (Urban Bat Monitoring). The three case studies revealed many unexpected challenges, including difficulties associated with collaborating with pre-existing communities that lack technical skills and have their own expectations with regards to the technologies, to technical hindrances such as lack of connectivity or access to power in outdoor settings. We conclude with a set of lessons learned to consider about the hidden aspects of conducting research in the wild.

2 Background

A number of in-the-wild studies have revealed various social phenomena that emerge when situating novel technology in the wild. For example, Müller et al. found out that many public displays fail to sufficiently attract attention from passers-by due to 'display blindness' (Müller et al. 2009), a phenomenon that happens because people expect displays to show uninteresting content (e.g. ads). However, social activity around the display can play a key role in fostering initial engagement. The honey-pot effect refers to the phenomenon by which the physical presence of others interacting with the display can draw attention and encourage others to engage, too Brignull and Rogers (2003). Peltonen et al. found that people can learn how to interact with a device by observing others who are doing it, often leading to 'chains of interaction' (Peltonen et al. 2008). Other factors that have been found to play an important role when deploying such technologies include understanding the relative contribution of the built environment in a deployment context (Fischer and Hornecker 2012), the important role played by 'champions' and 'comperes' who can draw people to interact with public displays (O'Hara et al. 2008) and the affordance of the materials used (Liu et al. 2018).

There are many ways of conducting research in the wild. An initial challenge is to decide what can be realistically discovered or demonstrated, which methods to use to achieve this and what to expect when using them. Sometimes, it might involve deploying many prototypes in people's homes to observe the varied adoptions and appropriations of many people rather than a few (Balestrini et al. 2015; Houben et al. 2019; Houben et al. 2016). Other times, it entails months of community-building and different stakeholder engagement in order to build up trust and commitment before studying the outcome of an intervention (e.g. changing habits to enable communities to reduce their energy or increase their exercise). Still, other times, it can involve running a longitudinal study across geographical boundaries to determine how new tools encourage participation in different cultures, such as citizen science projects (Balestrini et al. 2018).

A goal of much research in the wild is to make an impact and where possible to leave a technology in situ for a community to take it over and appropriate in a manner that is useful in the long term, and of perceived benefit to the community. However, communities who have been the benefactor of research technologies have revealed the difficulties that can emerge after their project has finished and the researchers have left the field. The tensions that have been reported mainly focus on the needs to manage expectations, the struggle for maintenance and appropriation of technology prototypes by the community (Taylor et al. 2013). In addition, the role of the researcher who is required to manage design process tensions has been questioned (Adams et al. 2013; Balestrini et al. 2014). Adams et al. (2013) have discussed some of these hurdles using a fashion metaphor that illustrates how communities expect 'ready-to-wear' technologies while researchers aim to design innovative 'catwalk' prototypes that are not necessarily built to be used beyond the research intervention.

In addition, there are a lot of practical concerns that will determine what can be achieved, such as how much funding is available, the time of year, logistics and gaining the trust of and acceptance in a community in order to get people on board to see the potential value of a proposed technology. Another practical problem that researchers face is how best to capture as much of people's behaviours as they approach, use, and walk away from a public installation or technology. It is one thing to put cameras in the corners and ceiling of a lab and let them run. It is another to work out a 'mobile' way of recording multiple people moving around in a large outdoor area without arousing suspicion.

The research that is reported from in-the-wild studies often focusses on the motivation behind the design of the technology, and the resultant insights about how they are approached, used, adopted, and impacted a community. What is often missing from these is the work that is needed to make the technology work (cf. Bowers (1994), Jackson et al. (2017)). Here, we present three case studies that reveal the challenges encountered before, during, and after deployments of technologies outdoors. We outline a number of practical challenges that can arise which can determine the extent to which a project succeeds, organised around four main themes: technology and design, space and place, social factors, and sustainability—here referred to as durable and resilient in a way that the beneficiary community can use it in the long term. Finally, we outline some seemingly commonsensical, but often overlooked logistical challenges that arise during the 'hidden practice' of conducting in the wild research.

2.1   Case Study 1: The Jokebox

In many urban settings, people do not interact with others that they do not know and yet they are often in close proximity in the same spaces. Our research was concerned with whether technology can be designed to break this deadlock. The Jokebox (see Fig. 1) was designed as a prototype technology to address this challenge; the aim was to facilitate eye contact in order to foster shared encounters among strangers in public spaces (Balestrini et al. 2016). It was intended to attract strangers passing by and provide an opportunity for them to engage with it, and in doing so trigger an interaction with each other. The prototype was designed as a stand-alone physical installation comprising two boxes (with arcade push buttons and portable speakers embedded at the top) that were at waist height and a few feet apart. Each box can detect people walking nearby within 2 m and invites them to interact with the Jokebox by playing an audio instruction. The Jokebox explains that it will play a joke when the two buttons on the top of each box are pressed at the same time. However, it

Fig. 1 The Jokebox deployed in a public square in London

requires that two people do this. The goal was to encourage people to listen together, look at each other and maybe even laugh or talk.

Methods used

The Jokebox was deployed in seven outdoor settings in two cities in Mexico and the UK: two parks and university campuses, one shopping mall, a pedestrian area, and a bus stop. These disparate locations were chosen based on their potential to attract different types of people and encourage different kinds of social interactions. The main finding from the studies was that by encouraging people to make eye contact and by using audible jokes, users engaged in a process of face-to-face interaction that often led to further conversation. We also found how the context of deployment and the role of local characters and emergent champions to draw others to interact were critical to the success of the installation but varied across the different locations.

The study was conducted over 14 months using two different approaches. The first one deployed a high fidelity prototype comprising a number of features that had previously been tested and implemented in the lab. This approach proved to be too constraining, however; only a number of pre-coded features in emergent contexts were ever tested. The second approach adopted a more agile approach by using a Wizard of Oz method, which enabled tweaks to be made on the fly and a wider number of features to be tested when deployed in the wild.

We followed a rapid ethnography approach to evaluate how passers-by interacted with the Jokebox. The device was installed five times at each location during two-hour slots, for a total of ten hours at each place. Each deployment was video-recorded, accounting for over 40 h of footage. Moreover, two observers collected qualitative data in a covert manner during each deployment, sometimes mixing among participants to hear their conversations. Field notes and photos were also taken. In order to control for returning participants, the same observers were assigned to the same locations throughout the deployments. We analysed the video footage using an interaction analysis approach (Heath et al. 2010), which has been used to evaluate social interactions in natural environments. The interactions with the Jokebox and social interactions derived from these behaviours were used to index the video sequences and the most relevant sequences were transcribed and triangulated using the data provided in field notes.

Lessons Learnt

Technology and design: *robust prototype versus agile method.* Following a 'technology probe' approach, the first prototype of the Jokebox was designed and tested in the lab (cf. Hutchinson et al. (2003)). The various interface features were adjusted according to the feedback provided by users during the lab trials to improve the user experience. When the prototype was deployed in the public spaces, however, a number of technical problems became apparent that had not arisen in the lab. For example, the range defined for the sensors that were used to detect passers-by had to be constantly adapted to the deployment setting. At the bus stop, the sensors were found to be too sensitive, triggering audible content as cars drove by and people walked nearby. In the large outdoor park, the opposite was found: they were not responsive enough to passers-by walking past. The audio levels at which the instruction and jokes were played had to be adjusted as well, as different outdoor and indoor settings produced different background noises that made the Jokebox's content either inaudible or too loud. It was also found that different audiences found the types of jokes more or less funny that could be changed more readily using a Wizard of Oz approach than with a fixed high fidelity prototype.

Adopting an agile design approach in the wild, therefore, proved to be more effective insofar as interface and system changes could be made relatively easily in situ compared with developing a robust prototype in the lab, that was much more difficult to adapt, after it had been installed outdoors. In particular, it enabled the input (in this case movement detection sensors) to be adapted to the outdoor setting more easily as well as adjustments to the output (in this case the volume of the audio and the type of content) in order to deliver a user experience that was tailored to each situation. It was found, for example, that triggering a simple *'Hello!'* was significantly more effective in attracting people than using the instruction *'If you want to hear a joke press both buttons at the same time'*. While it is important to deploy robust and stable prototypes in the wild, the use of agile methods and adaptable features in the wild can be a more effective approach to understanding how to design technologies for a variety of outdoor uses that can respond to emergent contexts.

Space and place: *assessing the impact of the system.* Each context and setting was found to trigger different types of activities, human behaviours, and social norms. While the Jokebox resulted in many people using it in parks, squares, and the shopping mall, it did not always produce enjoyable user experiences at the bus stop. It was observed how some people wanted to have a moment of quietness when they were waiting for a bus rather than have to hear the Jokebox speaking—which occurred every time someone walked through the bus stop. If other people interacted with it, the jokes were equally disruptive to those wanting to just sit. For some bus commuters, it became too annoying, even to the extent of them choosing to move to another bus stop. Hence, it is important to consider how deploying technologies in such outdoors spaces can impact upon the lives and routines of those who have used the space a priori to the installation.

Social factors: *local characters as champions.* At the park, the bus stop, the mall, and one of the public squares, the Jokebox attracted some local people who acted as champions enticing others to interact with the system (O'Hara et al. 2008). However, it was noticed that particular kinds of individuals, like street musicians or food sellers sometimes appropriated the Jokebox opportunistically. They found a strategic space next to the Jokebox where to display what they were offering, hoping to attract potential customers. While sometimes they actually attracted passers-by to the Jokebox, in other cases their behaviour deterred participation from people who walked by and on seeing them, preferred to avoid them. Public places are complex; space is contested, and social practices can at times blend or compete. When deciding where to deploy technologies it is important to be mindful of the presence of local characters and decide whether to foster opportunistic appropriation or avoid it.

Sustainability: *leaving it to run by itself.* In three of the deployment settings, local characters or operations managers (e.g. at the mall) thought that the Jokebox had enabled interactions that were beneficial for the place, for people, and for themselves and some asked to keep it there. However, it was not designed to be handed over to others but required maintenance by people with technical skills. This can create a dilemma—when a novel technology prototype introduces new practices and behaviours that people become attached to. If it is possible to leave the technology there then plans need to be set in place with those who manage the deployment sites or think of ways in which research prototypes could be handed over to communities (cf. Balestrini et al. (2014), Taylor et al. (2013)) if they are perceived as having the potential to deliver benefits in a given context.

2.2 Case Study 2: The Voxbox

The aim of VoxBox (see Fig. 2) again was to attract passers-by, but this time to give their opinions about an event they were attending. It was designed to be physically attractive and create a more enjoyable and engaging experience when giving responses to questions (Golsteijn et al. 2015). The interface was highly visible taking on the form of a playful 'physical questionnaire' that enabled respondents to answer questions through using a range of physical interaction mechanisms (in the form of physical buttons, sliders, dials). In addition to gathering opinions, VoxBox also visualised the passers-by's answers in real time on LED displays to allow participants to compare how their views related to others. It also incorporated a physical progress chute at the side where a ball dropped down to show how many of the questions had been completed.

Fig. 2 VoxBox system. Front and back

VoxBox was designed to get a sense of the 'feel-good factor' of the events and questions were developed in collaboration with event organisers. The questions included closed questions and focused on demographics (using push buttons); the user's current mood (using sliders); the user's connection to the crowd (through rotary knobs); and the event (through spinners). The final module uses a phone handset to ask one open question out of a set of five. The answer was then spoken into the handset and recorded.

Deployment

VoxBox was initially deployed at outdoor 'Fan events' held in two London Parks as part of The Tour de France (an annual European cycle race) when it passed through. The first Fan Park event where VoxBox was deployed was in a city centre park, close to the action of the Tour de France cycle race. The event was well attended by approximately 20,000 people throughout the day. The second Fan Park was held in a business area away from the city centre a week later (when the tour had moved on and there were no British cyclists in winning contention). This event was not as well attended with approximately only 1,000 people visiting. At both events, the VoxBox was in high demand and encouraged interaction and much relevant feedback was obtained from a broad demographic including young and old, groups of people, couples and individuals, disabled and able-bodied.

Lessons Learnt

Technology and design: *user volumes and throughput.* The significant difference in attendance at the two outdoor events highlighted a need to consider varying levels of high and low use when designing interactive installations for public environments. The VoxBox was specifically designed to accept feedback from one person or group of people at a time, and on average it took three minutes to complete. This meant that there was a maximum throughput of users and a limit to the number of people giving feedback that could be received during the course of an event. At the second event where user volumes were low most people could walk up and use VoxBox immediately. However, during the first event the large number of people and demand meant that there were often queues to use VoxBox and in some cases people decided to leave the queue before it was their turn. To be able to handle higher user volumes and demand would require designing the VoxBox interface to enable multiple people to interact with different elements at the same time. Indeed, this kind of parallel multi-user interaction approach was adopted in the design of the Sens-Us installation (Golsteijn et al. 2016), where instead of having one box, five separate stand-alone devices were designed, each having different question types. They were also located in different places meaning that five individuals or groups of people could interact with Sens-Us at the same time.

Space and place: *space and environmental constraints.* When VoxBox was deployed at the Fan Parks, it was allocated to a site within the event space. There was limited control over this and therefore the researchers had to adapt to the available space on arrival. At the first deployment, the site was between two large tents and as such made it difficult to position VoxBox in a way that would entice people to walk around to the back of it to see the visualisations appearing on that side. At the second deployment, a corner plot was provided allowing it to be positioned in a way that could be easily approached from the front or back. Other environmental factors such as the popularity of neighbouring stalls, the audiences they attracted or the noise levels and smells that they generated also were found to affect who was drawn to it.

Social factors: *managing user and stakeholder expectations.* With the popularity of interactive exhibits in museums and galleries around the world, the general public can have high expectations when approaching and using an interactive prototype in the wild. However, there is a big difference between high fidelity, polished end products that are installed in museums and the research prototypes that are deployed in the wild. Typically, such prototypes can suffer from regular malfunctions, greater wear and tear and simply being bashed about by users, especially children. They can be easily broken in ways that participants invited to test them in labs would not do. It is important to think of what might break a priori and how it can be fixed there and then.

Sustainability: *leaving it to run by itself.* Voxbox was very successful and well received. The result was that the research team become inundated with requests for customising a Voxbox for their own use. For example, we were approached by many marketing companies, airlines, councils, and theatres, to name a few—all asking how they could get their own VoxBox or to hire the original. We were able to do this for some of the requests but many had to be turned down, because of the labour costs, materials needed to adapt VoxBox, and the time required. Knowing how to manage these expectations and having a sustainability or scalability plan is important so as not to disappoint people or miss opportunities for further deployments.

2.3   Case Study 3: Urban Bat Monitoring

The third case study is quite different than the other two, involving designing an outdoor monitoring system that could help researchers and ecologists working in urban settings, by providing them with a new way of monitoring the environment. In particular, the Urban Bat Monitoring project investigated how Internet of Things technologies coupled with Machine Learning techniques could improve bat monitoring across large urban spaces and engage the public in nature conservation (Kaninsky et al. 2018). Bats are considered an important species for helping with environmental monitoring. They are often described as 'indicator' species as their presence is a positive sign of a healthy surrounding environment. As such, many ongoing bat monitoring schemes across urban spaces contract ecologists to carry out surveys over a few nights, several times per year. However, current survey methods are very labour intensive and only provide a small snapshot of bat activity levels during the survey nights. Instead, a new sensing system was developed that could provide a more continual and granular way of monitoring bat calls throughout the night while also reducing the manual and tedious work required of ecologists.

Deployment
Technologists and ecologists co-designed and developed 15 smart bat monitors called Echo Boxes (see Fig. 3). Each Echo Box captures full-spectrum audio and processes the audio using on-board deep machine learning algorithms to identify if bats are present and what species they are. This processing happens in a matter of seconds on board the sensor device itself and then sends small results packets across the network to cloud storage in near real time.

Fifteen Echo Boxes were installed across different habitats in a large London park in May 2017 that have been constantly collecting data on bat activity since. Hence, they were designed to be a long-term fixture, providing the ecologists with a continuous stream of bat call data. This includes detecting an average of 5000 bat

Fig. 3 The EchoBox bat sensor; and deployed on a lamp post in a London park with signage

calls per night during warmer months and classifying up to five different bat species in the park. The data is displayed online for all to see (batslondon.com) and shows live updates during the night. This has provided an unprecedented level of data for ecology monitoring that not only shows how to use IoT to improve upon manual data collection, but also gives an extremely detailed view of bat abundance and the health of the surrounding environment over time and space. The network of Echo Boxes was initially only intended to be deployed for three months but they have now become a permanent feature on the park due to requests from ecologists and park stakeholders. Compared with Voxbox, it was more feasible to have in place a sustainability plan following the deployment.

Lessons Learnt

Technology and design: *presenting complex data to the public.* The audio data from the bat calls was transformed into spectrogram images that show the amplitude of sounds across different frequencies over time. While ecology experts are familiar with spectrograms it requires considerable training to understand and make inferences from them. In addition to the public website, a challenge was to develop a public installation on the park that could convey bat calls to the general public with no training. From the bat call data collected, it was clear that the range of calls captured by the 15 sensors in one night could differ by an order of magnitude, with one of the sensors being particularly active (thousands of calls per night), while others would only capture dozens, hundreds or no calls. The approach adopted was to represent the bat calls data as an interactive visualisation overlaid on a map of the park showing where the sensors were placed (Johnson et al. 2012). A slider was also provided to enable users to find out about the variation of bat calls during different periods of time. Using this, the general public could obtain a bird's eye view of which bats were calling and how many bats there were in the park each night. A study of how the indoors installation was used found that many people who had interacted with it then returned to the park to look for the Echo Box sensing boxes on the lamp posts. This form of indoor-outdoor connection was considered key to its success; enabling initial interest in what was being presented on a display to be extended further outside rather than stopping after members of the public had moved on from the installation.

Space and place: *understand what is possible and available in the wild setting.* When things fail or go wrong outdoors, researchers do not always have the tools and resources available to them that they might do in a lab or indoor setting. Therefore, it is important to consider how to recover devices from failure and debug issues when they are deployed in the real-world location. This is particularly important if the device is being deployed in less accessible locations as in the case of the Echo Boxes which were installed on lamp posts at heights of greater than 4 meters. Once installed, only approved engineers could ascend to the heights required to physically reach the boxes using cherry pickers or specialist ladder and harness systems, which incurs additional financial cost. Therefore, once the boxes were installed on lamp posts it was undesirable for researchers to require physical access to them again.

As one researcher commented 'we might as well be sending them to the moon'. In such cases, several measures can be put in place so that the sensing devices can be accessed remotely, and all maintenance and software updates performed without needing a physical connection to the device. Additionally, when recovering or debugging the prototype in the lab before deployment, researchers should try to perform all necessary operations using only the tools and options that would be available to them when the device is deployed in the wild. For example, if the device will not be physically accessible researchers should refrain from plugging USB cables into serial ports to interact with the device, or pushing hardware reset buttons to power cycle the device, or any other option that would not be available to them once the prototype is deployed on site.

Social Factors: *socio-political frictions of experimentation in public*. When conducting research in the wild, a highly experimental activity is often taking place in the public realm and hence methods, procedures, and possibly also data are often on display in ways that they would not be in a lab environment. Additionally, devices and systems under test are in prototypical form, with iterations of improvements and optimisations still being carried out during the experiment lifetime. This can make stakeholders nervous and keen to get a feel for the user experience or data provided by the installation before publicly promoting it. For example, park stakeholders were anxious that bat data visible through the public website would show little to no bat activity, suggesting an unhealthy park. Preliminary data from the Echo Boxes, that was not shared publicly, proved to stakeholders that this was not the case. On finding this out, the park managers were happy then to embrace the system and actively promote the public website and data, even working with researchers to develop additional interactive installations to give park visitors further means of exploring the bat data

However, it is also important to exercise appropriate controls over publicly visible aspects of the wild deployments in order to manage expectations and retain credibility as researchers. The network of Echo Boxes was highly experimental with unknowns about how the hardware, software, and machine learning algorithms would function once deployed. Researchers intended to monitor all aspects to better understand and improve them during the course of the deployment, meaning that the prototypes deployed at the start of the experiment were not yet optimal or fully validated. Prior to the public launch of the accompanying website, researchers were faced with a dilemma. The yet unvalidated machine learning algorithms were sometimes producing unexpected results such as bat calls being detected during the daytime, or rare species being detected that were highly unlikely to inhabit the park. For example, like in the case of the JokeBox where sensors were accidentally triggered by unexpected events, the noise made by a certain kind of bicycle whizzing past could sometimes be mistaken for a bat call. Further investigation of the algorithms was required to validate the results being produced, but in the meantime the researchers faced a dilemma: should they share the unvalidated and questionable results publicly on the visualisation website? Although disclaimers could have been attributed to the yet unvalidated results, the researchers felt that it would not be enough to overcome potential damage to the credibility of the early system or their own credibility within research fields. As such, questionable results were initially filtered from the public website until validation and optimization activities could be completed.

Sustainability: *not leaving the wild*. The network of Echo Boxes was initially intended to be deployed in the park for three months. However, at the time of writing they have remained installed and operational for two years and counting. The continuous data streams on bat activity levels are unprecedented and have proven so valuable for researchers, ecologists, and park stakeholders alike that further investments have been made to maintain the deployment for the long term. It has now become a real-world testbed where researchers and ecologists can continue to test, improve, and verify bat detection algorithms. Equally for park stakeholders, it remains a flagship example of their smart park vision and a unique selling point to attract visitors and interest. To reach this agreeable situation it was essential to have clear understandings of responsibilities between involved parties, for example, with park stakeholders agreeing to invest in the ongoing maintenance of the installed hardware on their park infrastructure, and researchers agreeing to invest in further research and development using the installed hardware. While all sides continue to get a valuable return on investment it is likely the agreements and deployment will remain.

3 The Logistical Challenges of Conducting Research in the Wild

Rogers and Marshall (2017) discuss at a general level some of the practical challenges of conducting RITW. These included managing expectations, dealing with the unexpected, identifying and resolving tensions, and overcoming the novelty effect. Here, we add a further set of logistical challenges that need to be considered—which became apparent and at times sticking points—when conducting the three case studies. Being prepared for all eventualities by running through in advance what could possibly go wrong or what might not be available (that is normally taken for granted indoors) can help with enabling the project to work. These are:

Technology and design
Being able to transport and carry the prototype to the outdoors site It is important to give some thought a priori to how the prototype will be transported. If it is large, can it be broken down easily and put into a taxi? If using own transport is there parking nearby? Is permission needed to get onto the site?

Connecting to power and connectivity outdoors It helps to consider in advance where the prototype will be placed outdoors and whether there is nearby power and connectivity. This determines the communication method needed to design for (e.g. WiFi, Bluetooth) and whether the design requires its own battery supply or not. Having ready access to power is simply taken for granted when indoors. However, being outdoors is another matter. Power sockets don't grow on trees! Connecting to a power source outdoors, therefore, can be challenging. Similarly, WiFi maybe patchy or not available. Hence, being prepared for all eventualities can help overcome potential disasters, such as bringing extra power extension cables and a 3G/4G dongle in case the WiFi network on site is not reliable. If the deployment is long term, it is important to train other stakeholders in basic maintenance, especially those who will be on site.

Space and place
Adapting to the vagaries of outdoor elements Being outdoors means being prepared for the elements, i.e. sunlight (that can cause overheating), rain (that can cause the prototype to trip if water gets in), wind, and sunlight (making it difficult to read a screen). One minute it can be sunny, the next raining. Ambient noise, easy access, and how near a footpath, can also affect who walks past and who will stop. Visiting the site at different times of the day can help to get a better understanding of how environmental and social variables may change throughout the day.

Having an accessible location and providing clear signposting Ensuring beforehand that someone who has authority over the location will be there on site and contactable is important—especially if it requires access. Placing posters, signs, or other information to let people know about the project lets the public find out more about the project as the researchers may not be around or when it is considered undesirable for them to encourage participation or intervene.

Social factors
Investigating the setting prior to the deployment Public settings are characterised by emergent behaviour and varied audiences. The installation of an interactive device in a public setting is likely to trigger different forms of appropriation, either opportunistic or not, by local characters, champions, or comperes. It is important to investigate the setting prior to deploying any technology in order to identify local characters and visitors' routines and think of how they may interact with the device or have an impact on how others may—or may not—interact with it.

Coming to terms with others needs and expectations Additionally, stakeholders that work at the given space (e.g. park) or visit it frequently (e.g. bus stop) are likely to have specific expectations regarding the technology and how it may affect their routines. It is important to discuss such expectations and think through the ethical considerations of deploying technologies that may have a negative impact on other people's routines (i.e. causing anxiety or annoyance), a priori in order to avoid frictions, or undesired consequences.

Sustainability
Being prepared for damages and asking others to help out People may use a prototype in way not foreseen especially when deployed outdoors. For example, we witnessed children using considerable force when pressing buttons and using sliders both on Jokebox and on VoxBox—that caused them to break. It is important to have spare parts at hand if things get broken or damaged. The responsibility for taking care of

the prototype (especially when the researchers are not there) needs to be shared so that those who manage the deployment setting can do basic repairs.

Planning for afterwards It is important to talk about future plans throughout the project and who will fund and maintain it. After seeing how successful (or not) the prototype is, stakeholders may have changed their views. If further deployments are requested by stakeholders, an agreement needs to be worked up for a future deployment agenda that suits all parties (as happened in the bat monitoring project).

4 Conclusion

Deploying technology prototypes outdoors can provide new insights into how people use, integrate, and appropriate (if at all) them in their everyday lives. Nevertheless, working in emergent contexts is often challenging, with researchers becoming 'boundary creatures' (Adams et al. 2013) having to negotiate tensions and manage unexpected hurdles. Our experiences of designing and deploying novel technologies outdoors have shown how the unexpected happens. The bottom line is to be flexible and agile, capable of dealing with disappointment, and firefighting on the fly. By being more aware and prepared for handling the diversity of logistics, contingencies, and practicalities that need and can arise, researchers can make working in the wild work for all concerned.

References

Adams A, Fitzgerald E, Priestnall G (2013) Of catwalk technologies and boundary creatures. TOCHI 20(3):15:1–15:34

Balestrini M, Bird J, Marshall P, Zaro A, Rogers Y (April 2014) Understanding sustained community engagement: a case study in heritage preservation in rural Argentina. In: Proceedings of the CHI'14. ACM, pp 2675–2684

Balestrini M, Diez T, Marshall P, Gluhak A, Rogers Y (2015) IoT community technologies: leaving users to their own devices or orchestration of engagement? EAI End Trans Internet Things 1(1)

Balestrini M, Diez T, Pólvora A, Nascimento S (2018) Mapping participatory sensing and community-led environmental monitoring initiatives, EUR 29095 EN. Publications Office of the European Union, Luxembourg. ISBN 978-92-79-79348-6, https://doi.org/10.2760/38330, JRC110750

Balestrini M, Marshall P, Cornejo R, Bird J, Tentori M, Rogers Y (2016) Jokebox: coordinating shared encounters in public space. In: Proceedings of the CSCW'16. ACM, pp 38–49

Bowers J (October 1994). The work to make a network work: studying CSCW in action. In: Proceedings of the CSCW'94. ACM, pp 287–298

Brignull H, Rogers Y (2003) Enticing people to interact with large public displays in public spaces. In: Proceedings of the INTERACT'03, Zurich, pp 17–24

Fischer PT, Hornecker E (2012) Urban HCI: spatial aspects in the design of shared encounters for media facades. In: Proceedings of the CHI'12. ACM, pp 307–316

Golsteijn C, Gallacher S, Koeman L, Wall L, Andberg S, Rogers Y, Capra L (January 2015) VoxBox: a tangible machine that gathers opinions from the public at events. In: Proceedings of the TEI'15. ACM, pp 201–208

Golsteijn C, Gallacher S, Capra L, Rogers Y (June 2016) Sens-Us: designing innovative civic technology for the public good. In: Proceedings of the DIS'16. ACM, pp 39–49

Harris E, Fitzpatrick G, Rogers Y, Price S, Phelps T, Randell C (January 2004) From snark to park: lessons learnt moving pervasive experiences from indoors to outdoors. In: Proceedings of the AUIC '04, Australia, pp 39–48

Heath C, Hindmarsh J, Luff P (2010) Video in qualitative research. Sage

Houben S, Rogers Y, Capra L, Gallacher S, Nunez N, Nisi V, Gavrilov D (July 2019) Roam-IO: engaging with people tracking data through an interactive physical data installation. To appear in Proceedings of the DIS'19. ACM

Houben S, Golsteijn C, Gallacher S, Johnson R, Bakker S, Marquardt N, Capra L, Rogers Y (May 2016) Physikit: data engagement through physical ambient visualizations in the home. In: Proceedings of the CHI'16. ACM, pp 1608–1619

Hutchinson H, Mackay W, Westerlund B, Bederson BB, Druin A, Plaisant C, Beaudouin-Lafon M, Conversy S, Evans H, Hansen H, Roussel N (April 2003) Technology probes: inspiring design for and with families. In: Proceedings of the CHI'03. ACM, pp 17–24

Jackson G, Gallacher S, Wilson D, McCann JA (November 2017) Tales from the wild: lessons learned from creating a living lab. In: Proceedings of the FAILSAFE'17. ACM, pp 62–68

Johnson R, Rogers Y, van der Linden J, Bianchi-Berthouze N (2012) Being in the thick of in-the-wild studies: the challenges and insights of researcher participation. In: Proceedings of the CHI'12. ACM, pp 1135–1144

Kaninsky M, Gallacher S, Rogers Y (June 2018) Confronting people's fears about bats: combining multi-modal and environmentally sensed data to promote curiosity and discovery. In: Proceedings of the DIS'18. ACM, pp 931–943

Koeman L, Kalnikaite V, Rogers Y (2015) "Everyone Is Talking about It!": a distributed approach to urban voting technology and visualisations. In: Proceedings of the CHI'15. ACM, 3127–3136

Liu C, Bengler B, Di Cuia D, Seaborn K, Nunes Vilaza G, Gallacher S, Capra L, Rogers Y (June 2018) Pinsight: a novel way of creating and sharing digital content Through'Things' in the wild. In: Proceedings of the 2018 on designing interactive systems conference 2018. ACM, pp 1169–1181

Müller J, Wilmsmann D, Exeler J, Buzeck M, Schmidt A, Jay T, Krueger A (2009) Display blindness: the effect of expectations on attention towards digital signage. In: Proceedings of the pervasive 2009, pp 1–8

Nelson HG, Stolterman E (2003) The design way: intentional change in an unpredictable world: foundations and fundamentals of design competence. Educational Technology

O'Hara K, Glancey M, Robertshaw S (2008) Collective play in an urban screen game. In: Proceedings of the CSCW'08. ACM, pp 67–75

Peltonen P, Kurvinen E, Salovaara A, Jacucci G, Ilmonen T, Evans J, Oulasvirta A, Saarikko P (2008) It's Mine, Don't Touch!: interactions at a large multi-touch display in a city center. In: Proceedings of the CHI '08. ACM, pp 1285–1294

Rogers Y, Marshall P (2017) Research in the wild. Synth Lect Hum Cent Inform 10(3):i-97

Taylor N, Cheverst K, Wright P, Olivier P (2013) Leaving the wild: lessons from community technology handovers. In: Proceedings of the CHI'13. ACM, pp 1549–1558

Wild Birthplaces of Behavioral Media

Andrew Quitmeyer and Kitty Kelly

Abstract Interactive digital technology provides an unprecedented new way to communicate through rich behaviors that sense and react to the world. Our most complex designs still pale in comparison to the richness of the behaviors of the simplest living creatures. We do not yet know the key techniques and aesthetics involved in arranging these configurations of creatures, environments, and computers to be able to truly harness this new behavioral medium. Just like living creatures, the behaviors of our technological devices are shaped by the context in which they develop. We need to expose our technology to a vast array of new situations, experiences, and contexts in order to mature programmable technology beyond its status as a simple tool into a ripe new medium. Naturalists studying animal behavior conduct their work in uncontrolled, wilderness field sites because it is only there that you can observe the full range of a creature's behaviors that have evolved to fit the specific milieu. Likewise, contemporary Human–Computer Interaction researchers are conducting studies "in the wild" where technologies are experienced in situ. This chapter explores using different sites of scientific field work (expeditions, field courses, and field stations) as fertile areas for developing interactive media.

1 Introduction: Creatures and Computers

1.1 Behaviors Are Unique

This chapter concerns itself with two very special things that exist in our world: creatures and computers. Both are able to sense and record events happening around them in their environments. Both are able to deliver new stimuli back to the world.

A. Quitmeyer · K. Kelly (✉)
Digital Naturalism Laboratories, Gamboa, Panama
e-mail: kitty@dinalab.net

A. Quitmeyer
e-mail: andy@dinalab.net

© Springer Nature Switzerland AG 2020
D. S. McCrickard et al. (eds.), *HCI Outdoors: Theory, Design, Methods and Applications*, Human–Computer Interaction Series,
https://doi.org/10.1007/978-3-030-45289-6_5

Both are able to join these senses and actions via some internal system of rules or processes.

Such networks of sensing and acting are called "behaviors," and, until recently, the ability to enact intricate behaviors distinguished living creatures from the rest of the material universe. Now, though, this ability to sense and react to the world is shared by both natural living creatures and digital computers. Programmable materials provide a new medium for communicating in the very format of life itself and allow us to explore new ways of understanding and interacting with the rest of the living world.

1.2   Behaviors Are Shaped by Their Environments

Just like living creatures, the behaviors of our technological devices are shaped by the context in which they develop. A creature's actions precipitate from intermingling natural forces, and a computer's functions are developed by human social forces.

Both types of behavior, digital or natural, acquire idiosyncrasies formed by their environments. A male bowerbird cannot build its courtship nest without twigs from the nearby forest, and it never would have evolved this behavior at all in a non-forest environment. Similarly, the basic functions of human-based dating apps (like "swiping" in Tinder) would not function, nor would even be developed, outside of the pre-existing environment of human-made infrastructure (GPS, telecommunications, mobile SDKs) enabling its abilities.

The manner in which these processes are created, however, is quite different. Organismal behaviors grow to fill niches in environments over millions of years. Digital behaviors have to be crafted to fit into new contexts. Natural behaviors are open-ended in purpose, while digital ones are purpose-built toward specific agendas. Animal behaviors are very old. Computer behaviors are extremely new.

Thus, this new, behavioral medium is still immature. Our most complex designs still pale in comparison to the richness of the behaviors of the simplest living creatures. We do not yet know the key techniques and aesthetics involved in arranging these configurations of creatures, environments, and computers to be able to truly harness the new behavioral medium. The way to foster advances in any media form comes from immense amounts of experimentation. We need to expose our technology to a vast array of new situations, experiences, and contexts in order to mature programmable technology beyond its status as a simple tool into a ripe new medium.

Most of our technology, however, is constrained in focus, implementation, and development for human-centric activities and environments. To the naturalist Lorenz, "one can only get to know…animals by letting them move about freely" (Lorenz 1952). Perhaps the same is true of the capabilities of our technology.

Like an animal caged in a zoo, limiting the context in which we develop novel technologies to one specific environment limits the overall expressiveness of the behaviors that could develop. Instead, we propose to push our technology into dynamic ecosystems flooded with sophisticated behaviors. The natural, uncontrolled world is an endless network of commingling behaviors. Developing interactive tools that can participate in these behavioral ecosystems will not only help us solve mysteries about the dynamic actions of the creatures within, but also push our devices to develop more intricate, robust behavioral abilities. Nature is the mother of the most incredible systems ever created, and the wilderness will provide a fertile ground for developing our own technology.

1.3   Research Goals: Developing Behavioral Media in the Wild

Our research in the field of "Digital Naturalism" originally focused on developing a framework to help designers create interactive tools that serve field biologists studying animal behavior (Quitmeyer 2015). The work established a series of guidelines in technology development that aimed to preserve the values of foundational naturalists while supporting contemporary research (Quitmeyer 2017). The resulting four guidelines are Technological Agency, Contextual Crafting, Behavioral Immersion, and Open-Endedness. Respectively, these urge designers to make tools understandable and manipulable; build these tools in close proximity to the wilderness; viscerally engage the human and non-human participants; and design tools that promote open-ended discovery.

Such design work can cut both ways, however. Pushing a nascent medium into new challenges and locations feeds back into the development of the medium as a whole. One's tools reflect where they are born. Experimenting with our technologies in wild, new contexts helps us uncover their unique affordances. Scientific field sites are hot spots of uncontrolled dynamic interaction with environmental factors and living creatures. Thus, they are ripe for exploration as sites to innovate and develop new, interactive media.

2   Target: Maturing the Behavioral Medium

Digital interactive technology is still in its infancy as a medium. Janet Murray, a seminal digital media researcher, poses that the duty of designers is to mature novel technologies into rich, new modes of communication. According to her, the way to accomplish this task is by eschewing the conventions of prior communication forms and wildly experimenting with the unique characteristics of the medium in new ways (Murray 2003).

2.1   Film's Parallel

In her quest to develop the digital medium in general, Murray models her approach
on the historical evolution of another relatively new medium, film. She states:

> The key to [cinema's] development was seizing on the unique physical properties of film: the
> way the camera could be moved; the way the lens could open, close, and change focus; the
> way the celluloid processed light; the way the strips of film could be cut up and reassembled.
> By aggressively exploring and exploiting these physical properties, filmmakers changed a
> mere recording technology into an expressive medium (Murray 1997).

Early films simply copied the conventions of preceding media such as theater.
Actors stood in a single plane in front of a stationary camera, emulating the setup
of the theater and the audience. It took decades of directed experimentation with
filmmaking tools to push the boundaries of the camera's capabilities and to discover
the "cinematic grammar" that gives movies their unique abilities. Film pioneers
developed the medium even further when they moved the filmmaking process entirely
out of the studio altogether.

2.1.1   Wild Behavior's Influence on Film as a Medium

Looking back at Murray's cinematic analogy, we can learn more about how the
medium's experimental context can also drive the medium's evolution. Through
collective experimentation with a new technology (sequential photography), filmmakers developed specific terminologies, methods, and heuristics which pushed
forward both the science and the medium (Fig. 1).

Interacting with wild behaviors is responsible for the birth of the medium of film
in the first place. Driven by an urge to understand some of the rapid and complex
behaviors of animal movements, Étienne-Jules Marey began experimenting with

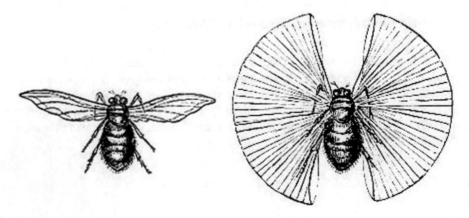

Fig. 1 Étienne-Jules Marey: study of insect wing movements (Marey 1874)

sequential photographic techniques in the mid 1800s. These ethological tools helped illuminate the previously hidden behaviors such as the figure-8 pattern of bee's wings in flight, or the graceful descent of a landing bird (Marey 1874).

More famously in the United States, Eadweard Muybridge created early motion picture methods to study the behavior of horses' gaits. These early photographic experiments for understanding animal behaviors were then developed into the new recording format of "motion pictures" by the end of the 1800s. As cinematic pioneers engineered new techniques for creating and sharing human-centric dramas, documentarian-naturalists utilized the growing framework of this new medium to study animals while helping to drive film's maturity themselves.

Jean Painlevé conducted early experiments combining both studio and on-location filming in the early 1900s. Using "continuity editing" styles established by D.W. Griffith, Painlevé successfully blended disparate footage and created drama within animal spectacles capable of drawing humans into the narrative (Painleve 1950). To fit the needs of naturalists like Jacques Cousteau filming underwater life, camera technology had to be refined to be self-contained and watertight (Cousteau 1964). As this genre developed, naturalists established their own techniques, such as Attenborough's often-emulated narration style, and his back-and-forth movement from disembodied voice to in-scene interaction. Most recently, the continual push for knowledge and understanding from series like the BBC's *Planet Earth* or *Life* has contributed intricate new compositing effects used to study the development of entire landscapes of life over several years (BBC 2011).

The development of nature-based filmmakers shows this back-and-forth development of an ethological tool blossoming into a new medium, which in turn provides a new means of exploring and sharing animal behavior. This type of directed technological experimentation with the unique challenges of natural environments birthed film-specific grammars and techniques that developed the rest of the medium as a whole.

2.2 Developing Interactive, Behavioral Tools in Nature

Pushing these film tools into the challenging world of wild animal behavior thus greatly aided the development of the filmic medium. Similarly, we can utilize the natural world once again as a breeding ground for the development of interactive, behavioral media.

3 Approach: Pushing Technological Development into the Wild

Digital technology has a tendency to overpower the context of both its use and development (Agre 1997). Its fragility and power requirements cause most interactive technology to be created and used in similar, rigidly controlled environments, like climate-controlled electronics laboratories. A homogenous environment, however, can make development stagnate. Instead, both field biologists and some HCI practitioners advocate for exploring and analyzing new behaviors and interactions in wild, untamed spaces.

3.1 The Naturalist's Argument for Research in the Wild

Scientific work has traditionally navigated a tension between the lab and the field. Rigorous control of the environment and experimentation in the lab could yield consistent results, but it also cuts off access to animals' higher, more complex behaviors. Uexküll's phenomenalistic ethology also promoted this idea. Parikka describes that while Uexküll noted "the importance of the physiology of an animal in a materialist vein," these structures are active only in their associated milieus (Lorenz 1952, 98). Lorenz provided an apt example of these contextually unveiled performances during his studies of a unique variety of aqueous shrew: "Another surprising detail which I only noticed when I saw my shrews in the water was that they have a fringe of stiff, erectile hairs on the outer side of their fifth toes and on the underside of their tails. These form collapsible oars and a collapsible rudder" (Lorenz 1952, 98). Divorced from their natural environment, Lorenz would have had a harder time discovering the normally invisible and unique behavior of the shrew's hairs, which are only activated in their complementary setting.

The ethologist Lehrman further remarks on the importance of context for behavioral research. He notes:

> When we watch animals at different levels on the evolutionary scale, as when Seitz watches fishes [or] when Dr. Tinbergen watches gulls…the observer can get a feeling of what is going to happen next…on the one hand [this is] compounded in… the intellectual experience of relationships that are involved… and on the other hand, of building yourself into the situation (Lehrman 1955).

Tinbergen also describes how the unique characteristics of a specific place can have great impacts on behavior. He says, "Ethological evidence is mounting which shows that different species, even in roughly comparable situations, learn different things, and that different responses of the same animal are changed by different aspects of the environment" (Tinbergen 1974, 150).

3.2 HCI "In the Wild" in the Wild

The historical push for conducting research in natural wilderness is mirrored by a recent drive in some branches of Human–Computer Interaction (HCI) for conducting studies "in the wild." Yvonne Rogers describes in "Interaction Design Gone Wild" that some researchers "are decamping from their usability labs and moving into the wild-carrying out in situ user studies, sampling experiences, and probing people in their homes and on the streets" (Rogers 2011). In the world of HCI, this term "in the wild" seeks to acknowledge the embeddedness of interactive devices in everyday life (Chamberlain et al. 2012; Crabtree et al. 2013). Thus, like the Naturalists before them, the researchers bringing HCI "into the wild" attempt to deal with the ineffable challenges of complex, embedded systems by studying them in situ.

A couple key differences do, however, arrive in the HCI concept of research "in the wild" and the digital naturalism ambition described in this paper. First, human–computer interaction is inherently anthropocentric. Its key concern is "how people react, change and integrate [interactive electronics] into their everyday lives" (Rogers 2011), and the "wild" areas often refer to houses, shopping centers, public transit hubs, and other human-oriented spaces.

The second difference between our approaches is that digital naturalism pushes for not only *testing* but also *developing* technology in situated, uncontrolled places. This work builds upon the "in the wild" narrative, arguing that context matters not only to the *use* of novel tools, but that environmental factors affect these tools from their very conception. Tinbergen in his "Four Questions" says that the goal of understanding behavioral systems lies in exploring both the proximate causes of specific interactions as well as their evolutionary history (Tinbergen 1963). As designers, we can view the development of new, rich behavioral systems in a similar manner. Tools should be designed, built, and studied in the contextual environment of their eventual use. In the same way that natural ecosystems permit the full expression of natural behaviors, they can also promote the expressiveness of synthetic behaviors. Instead of keeping the design of our technology trapped in numbing laboratories, exposing interactive technologies from their earliest development to rich environments can help us explore all the behavioral possibilities of this new medium. What better place to conduct such designs than biological field sites themselves?

4 Examples: Three Formats of Field Sites as HCI Studios

When looking for ways that digital technology could better serve the needs of animal behavior scientists (Quitmeyer 2017), we were also able to isolate sites with great potential for developing the behavioral abilities of interactive technology in the wild. These sites of innovation emulate research sites typical to many field biologists. The common structures enabling biological field research, such as expeditions, field courses, and field stations, can also function as unique formats for developing and experimenting with interactive technology.

Many other initiatives and projects similarly promote scientific field sites as places for media innovation and development. Marko Peljan's "Makrolab" was a mobile workspace designed to bring artists and scientists to novel places of exploration (Birringer 1998). Jacobs and Zoran explored digital crafts via a mobile prototyping truck that connects with traditional craftspersons in hunter-gatherer tribes in the Kalahari (Jacobs and Zoran 2015). Earth Co-Lab offers artist and interaction designers residencies at scientific field stations (Khan 2017), and the Finnish Bioart Society offers a residency at an "artistic laboratory and platform for art, science and society in Katajanokka, Helsinki" ("Bioart Society" n.d.). In fact, several of these groups have actually joined together in a European Union "Creative Europe" program of "Feral Labs," creating a network of camps pursuing field work in art-technology-science ("Feral Labs Network" 2020).

These structures all seek to move the site of developing behavioral media out of traditional laboratories and into spaces of rich, uncontrolled, wild interactions. The following describes the format and examples of three forms of biological research sites which have been transformed into places of outdoor media experimentation.

4.1   Expeditions

The basic model we have pursued as a site of experimental interactive innovation is based off a field biologist's research expedition. In their work, these scientists often journey into natural areas, collect data or perform experiments, and journey back out. Expeditions can take the form of simple day trips, or they can be conducted as week-long voyages. Emulating a research trip into the wilderness exposes oneself and one's technology to a discrete experience with wild behaviors and challenges for interaction.

4.1.1   Hiking Hacks

a. *Format*

"Hiking Hacks" were the first trips we organized to explore the concept of moving the interactive technology laboratory into the wild. We would collect a group of designers and tag along on a biological field expedition in places like Panama, Madagascar, or the USA. During the expedition, we would carry tools necessary for designing interactive technology, and we would work to construct our own laboratories for prototyping behavioral instruments.

Fig. 2 Party boat with light, sound, and vibrational stimuli presented to a semi-aquatic stream environment

A typical Hiking Hack[1] starts with a journey in, where the designers openly explore the new environment, become familiar with the scientific processes and devices being used, and quickly prototype simple interactive tools. Next, the team sets up basecamp, and along with it, ephemeral laboratories (generally out of foraged materials like fallen branches) for conducting experiments and developing more sophisticated interactive devices. After days of iteratively refining and testing experimental media forms, the team packs up camp, and researchers document and reflect on their projects and experiences on the journey home.

b. *Example Projects*

Example exploratory projects include the "party boat" exercise, which became a staple of later outdoor workshops. This concept was based on the scientist participants' official "playback" probes, which sought to see which animals nearby would respond to a specific sound played in the forest. The "party boat" generalizes this practice in a fun, simultaneous exploration of the digital assets available and the surrounding ecosystem. Participants have a limited timeframe to quickly put together a device creating as many different stimuli as possible (e.g. sound, motion, vibration, light, smell). The device is then placed into different areas of the nearby habitat and observed to see what responds. An ideal party boat can be programmed to cycle and change patterns over time to see what types of creatures respond to the changing, multimodal stimuli. For instance, observing the flashing, buzzing device one night in the forest, let us immediately see that some moths only flew by at particular colors of the LED, and the fishing spiders on rocks nearby noticed certain vibrations on the water (Fig. 2).

An example of a larger, core Hiking Hack project is the development of a modular ant sensor. While accompanying a myrmecological expedition in remote Madagascar, one of the key projects became finding a way to inexpensively monitor ant traffic

[1]Previously published research about these "Hiking Hacks" includes more detailed models for planning activities and events, lists of essential gear, hierarchy of needs for wilderness workshops, and designs for portable studios (Quitmeyer 2018b).

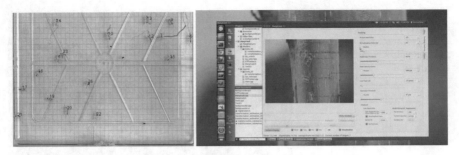

Fig. 3 Lab (functional) versus Field (failure) use cases of our Manytrack Ant-Tracking Software

along entirely arbitrary geometrical forms of the forest (such as a branching tree). Much previous work had been done writing computer vision tracking software for monitoring small insects in the controlled environment of robotics laboratories. Over several years of development though, little progress had been made in tackling the intricacies of finding ways to sense some of the smallest animals across multiple three-dimensional surfaces. This inspired a driving challenge on this Hiking Hack (Fig. 3).

The prototype developed in the forest took only four days to make and consisted of a series of sanded-edge fiber optics connected to photosensors and an Arduino. It could sense the movement of large insect traffic, such as beetles, but unfortunately not the small local ants. It did not completely solve the initial challenge of tracking the ants, but building the device on-location inspired research into another crucial aspect which may have gone overlooked: how to display and interpret such data if these sensors existed? One quick, successful solution was the creation of a tongue display made by embedding electrodes into a leaf and insulating it with honeybee wax collected nearby. The display helped the researcher embody the sensory data flowing from various parts of the tree in an ambient fashion as small stimulating shocks to the tongue. This permitted one's other senses (such as sight) unencumbered access to study other parts of the ecosystem (Quitmeyer et al. 2015) (Fig. 4).

The work spawning from this project, hatched in the cloud forest of Madagascar, has continued developing for many years. While the problem is not yet solved, it has fostered much research into alternative sensors, such as a DIY version of Graphene Putty called "Goophene" capable of sensing heartbeats, inertial movement, and larger insects (Quitmeyer 2018a). It also fostered continued inspiration in other human–computer interaction design. For example, Perner-Wilson took her experience with edge-lit fiber optic experiments in the jungle to collaborative projects at her e-textile tailor shop in Berlin, where she created glowing costumes and even helped develop a new type of connector for working with edge-lit optical fiber and digital controllers (Perner-Wilson and Satomi n.d.).

These first Hiking Hacks gave an initial taste of the vast potential for exploring the behavioral medium in wilderness areas rife with stimuli. They also spurred development of basic infrastructure to foster further work. After observing the field biologists' customized backpacks, Perner-Wilson and Quitmeyer began side research

Fig. 4 Initial fiber optic prototype ant sensor and tongue display

into a "Wearable Studio Practice" to develop tools and protocols (Quitmeyer and Perner-Wilson 2015; Perner-Wilson n.d.) that let designers remain in wild areas while doing things like soldering and programming. Like Cousteau's inventions for filming and remaining underwater, infrastructure such as Perner-Wilson's custom backpacks that turn into electronics studios enable researchers and designers to quickly set up workspaces in remote areas. This "wearable studio" gear became key infrastructure for leading larger and longer initiatives in wilderness interaction design.

4.2 Field Courses

Field biologists require specialized, contextually particular skills, which is the reason this discipline traditionally runs field courses. These courses offer unique training in wilderness conditions to ensure a researcher is adequately prepared for the challenges of their own field site. For behavioral media experimentation, the structure of a field course offers a chance to expose a specific set of technologies or techniques to the unknowable inspirations of natural environments. They generally differ from the model of the previously discussed "expedition," in that they tend to be physically static.

4.2.1 Master of Advanced Interaction- Valldaura Field Course

For the 2018 Master's students of interaction design at the Institute of Advanced Architecture Catalonia, our research was tapped to lead a field course to explore new ways of sensing. With collaborator Hannah Perner-Wilson, we crafted a series of outdoor exercises to promote the students' discovery and awareness of potential sites of novel interaction and behaviors surrounding them in the natural world. The course took place over a week in the Valldaura Mountains overlooking Barcelona.

At the beginning of the course, the students were instructed in the basics of electronic interaction design (such as making simple circuits, sensors, and actuators), but they were challenged to forage for natural materials which had to be incorporated into their behavioral apparatuses. An example would be a student's adoption of a dangling, copper-covered pinecone as a basic tilt sensor, or the use of a spittle-bug's bubbling expulsions to close a switch and trigger the light of an LED. As the course developed, the participants continued to develop more sophisticated and embodied sets of sensation that necessarily incorporated natural materials. Importantly, to maintain the participants' ecological focus throughout their process, they were also charged with an additional duty throughout the course: they had to develop their tools within their own outdoor studio (Fig. 5).

The first two days of the course were spent in mobile, outdoor studio facilities designed by Perner-Wilson and Quitmeyer from the Hiking Hacks, in order to connect the participants with many of the key affordances of designing electronics in harsh environments. After this point, however, the students were challenged to construct their own studios from foraged materials. Working in studios immersed in nature gave students continued experience building and interacting with the natural materials

Fig. 5 Wilderness workshop in the Valldaura countryside

surrounding them. The end effect was that it not only inspired and mutated their original designs: it gave them the tacit knowledge of working with nearby materials and creatures to iterate and refine their original prototypes.

4.2.2 Digital Naturalism Conference

a. *Format*

The goal of the Digital Naturalism Conference (Dinacon) is to recreate the experience of a university field course. The first Dinacon ran as an 8-week long, outdoor conference on a small island in Thailand. The second took place over 31 days at a jungle research station in Gamboa, Panama. In both conferences, hundreds of people applied from 6 continents; 100 actually attended; participants came in and out for durations of 5–21 days; and an average of 30 participants were present at any given time (Fig. 6).

The first Dinacon housed participants in a large campground and cabins situated between rainforest and the sea. Research facilities included electronics prototyping stations, industrial design, sewing, microscopy, and theatrical performances. With the Earth Co-Lab non-profit organization (Khan 2017), we also rented a 30-m commercial diving yacht, which we retrofitted into a floating makerspace complete with modular workbenches and biological flow tanks for studying ocean organisms.

The second Dinacon aimed to directly emulate the famous field courses hosted by the Smithsonian Tropical Research Institute in Gamboa, Panama. Participants camped in the forest or stayed in dorms at an eco-lodge, and worked exploring historic biological field sites and at the newly founded Digital Naturalism Laboratories.

Dinacon also sought to abstractly emulate the sharing and peer-review process governing scientific work. The conference only has three rules for participation (Quitmeyer and Khan 2018):

Fig. 6 Map of the facilities of **a** Dinacon 2018 in Koh Lon, Thailand and **b** Dinacon 2019 in Gamboa, Panama

1. Participants have to make *something*
2. They must openly document and share their project
3. They must have at least two other participants review their project.

These basic rules enabled participants to freely explore and develop their own technological projects without the worry of being confined to the protocols of one particular field or another. The minimalist structure also ensured that all participants would come away from this experience with a freshly documented project, reviewed, and ready to be shared back with the world (Fig. 7).

b. ***Example Projects***

Example projects include multiple open-source synthesizers that create musical samples from the natural environment. Some art-science projects studied hermit crab behavior by having the crabs create art with light-up LED backpacks and long-exposure photography. The difficulties discussed among scientists and designer participants about canopy research in jungles led one roboticist, Michael Candy, to create a functional tree climbing robot that could quickly set up remote cameras for

Fig. 7 Candy's tree climbing canopy observation drone

Fig. 8 Hoogendijk and Neilson's 360 camera trap observing Gill's behavioral treadmill assay

forest observation. This functional device was built in only three days, but because of its development in situ, it underwent several iterations. Though its design was based off existing industrial window cleaning robots that use fans or vacuums to attach to buildings, Candy discovered that when climbing the natural, irregular surface of a rainforest tree, much more wind-force was needed to attach to the surfaces. However, this amount of pressure inhibited vertical movement, and thus he was inspired to create a new undulating motor drive from a series of wire brushes that allowed the robot to successfully climb to the peaks (Fig. 8).

Two participants took advantage of broken equipment and repaired a non-functioning 360-degree camera to become Arduino-controllable. This allowed them to re-invent the traditional camera trap free from the directional bias of their limited fields-of-view. They combined this prototype to help monitor another project by neuroscientist Jon Gill. Gill took tools he traditionally used in controlled laboratories, such as the canonical mouse-wheel treadmill, and adapted it for use with wild animals to lead a new type of research into cross-examining the behaviors of wild and captive animals. Both projects' developments and research have continued past the first and second Dinacons. Gill continued his research in wild behavioral lab tools at the second Dinacon in Panama, creating and testing a new generation of prototypes. Hoogendijk wrote and defended her Master's thesis on the 360 camera trap and developed further prototypes of the "Panatrap" with Quitmeyer under a Conservation X Labs research grant (Quitmeyer and Hoogendijk 2019).

Full, open-source documentation of all the Dinacon projects is available on the conference website (www.dinacon.org) or in the free books compiling the experiences (Quitmeyer and Khan 2018).

4.3   Field Stations

For biologists, field stations are the most permanent structures that allow access to investigate wilderness areas. Some scientific field stations are single outposts with the bare essentials for survival and tools. Others are massive networks of cutting-edge facilities housing hundreds of researchers at a time. The key similarity of these field stations is the proximity of their facilities to natural areas.

4.3.1   Boat Lab

The "Building Open Art and Technology" (BOAT) Lab was an endeavor to establish a DIY community science makerspace in a small village on the Philippine island of Negros (Quitmeyer and Zero1 n.d.). The town, Banilad, was home to a marine protected area covering a coral reef. The lack of municipal sanitation, oversight of park rangers, and local interest left this marine protected area in poor condition (polluted, broken, and poached) (Fig. 9).

To foster more interest in this natural feature, and therefore strive to protect it, we came together with the community to build a modular, floating laboratory for art and science (Quitmeyer 2016). Floating over the reef, the vessel had electronics and scientific workstations and allowed participants to build devices for interacting with the nearby reef. Projects included: building an open-source submarine drone; weather station; automated water quality monitoring station; and a theatrical performance staged on the water. The participants even built a programmable LED frame that could display live data and a waterfall projection screen to show footage captured by the submarine drone.

Fig. 9 The BOAT Lab off Banilad village in the Philippines

4.3.2   Dinalab

Our latest endeavor attempts to directly emulate one of the world's oldest and most prestigious field stations, the Smithsonian Tropical Research Institute (STRI) in Panama.

STRI was started in 1923 as a small field station on Barro Colorado Island (BCI) using the flooding from the recently built Panama Canal as a large-scale experiment. Since then, it has grown into one of the world's premier scientific research station clusters and attracts over 900 yearly scientists from across the globe ("Oral History Interview with Bennett and Bennett" 1975). STRI's research sites like BCI and "Pipeline Road" are some of the most scientifically studied areas on Earth ("Smithsonian Tropical Research Institute" n.d.).

a. *Format*

In a preliminary attempt to capture the dynamism and resources of such an established field station, our research team purchased a canal building directly in Gamboa, near STRI itself. This house is currently being built into "Digital Naturalism Laboratories" (DINALAB). It aims to function as a miniature version of STRI, but it focuses its research into the development of behavioral media for exploring the natural world (Quitmeyer n.d.). It houses facilities for engineering, design, and rapid prototyping next door to the incredible natural testing ground of the Soberanía National Rain Forest. It also provides scientists and designers with access to deeper jungle with a 4 × 4 "Dinatruck" and mountain bikes. The deployable outdoor backpacks used in the Hiking Hacks are available for checkout for setting up remote labs in the jungle during day trips (Fig. 10).

DINALAB runs a series of open labs giving free consulting and tool access to nearby scientists and community members. This new laboratory also provides a residency program for designers to develop innovative behavioral tools with access to the scientific and natural resources nearby.

b. *Examples*

Most of 2019 was spent renovating the Dinalab building into a functional fabrication lab in preparation for its grand opening during Dinacon 2. It hosted over 112 Dinacon participants plus five residents developing art-science-tech projects throughout the year. Though its work has just begun, many interesting discoveries and encounters have already happened. For instance, one researcher used a Raspberry Pi and 360-degree microphone (made waterproof) to set up a fully functional Virtual Reality Audio livestream from the jungle. Though the device was rigorously tested against the vagaries of the weather, it failed two months after deployment when it was found that the leaf-cutter ants had chewed through the electronics cables. Another prototype is already underway, but this demonstrates the importance of in situ development to help prepare for the unexpected.

Hosting technological development nearby field work has also spawned many fruitful collaborations. For instance, STRI biologist Jay Falk was conducting field

Fig. 10 Sights and Features of Dinalab—Rainforest/Backyard experimental area, Art-Science Gallery, residents conducting field work with portable studios nearby, animal monitoring equipment (humming bird heart-rate sensor development), and electronics laboratories

work with hummingbirds and found that the vital characteristics, such as heart rate, of many of the species he worked with were not yet described. Luckily, the developer of the Open-Source heart-rate monitor, Joel Murphy, was visiting Dinalab, and the two were able to successfully modify Murphy's human-based monitors for use with hummingbirds. More interactive art-science-tech projects and situations will soon be available for documentation and analysis as Dinalab enters its operational first year.

5 Conclusion

Working outdoors in biological field sites exposes both ourselves and our practice to the dynamic, behavioral conversations constantly happening around us. Moving the development of interactive technology out of the laboratory and into the wilderness also transports our designs outside the realm of purely anthropocentric interactions. One participant's takeaway from a Hiking Hack was that "Maybe being indoors, it is easier to explore our own minds, but being outdoors places you into conflicting minds." Laboratory development can be invaluable for refining a singular concept, but before we commit to a single vision of this powerful new medium, we first need to discover all its possibilities. Our Digital Naturalism work will continue with more Hiking Hacks, field conferences, and exploring this idea of in situ HCI development and testing in even longer formats at our field station in Panama. For other researchers and practitioners also seeking to explore the behavioral new medium, our main advice is to take any project you are doing, and just try to build some part of it outside. You notice things that surprise you as you build and test your projects in nature and will gain insights into the massive networks of behaviors surrounding you. Creating interactive technology in the wild will foster the development of a rich new medium for communicating with not only ourselves, but with the entire natural world.

References

Agre P (1997) Toward a critical technical practice: lessons learned in trying to reform AI. Social Science, Technical Systems, and Cooperative .... http://books.google.com/books?hl=en&lr=&id=xxhMzog9MkQC&oi=fnd&pg=PA131&dq=Toward+a+Critical+Technical+Practice+:+Lessons+Learned+in+Trying+to+Reform+AI&ots=pF6rY5JxQR&sig=ytKBLmgsB11CDEwmqD3TgLZfvfU

BBC (2011) Life on location–time warp. UK. http://www.bbc.co.uk/programmes/p005hh0x

"Bioart Society" (n.d.) https://bioartsociety.fi/about. Accessed 12 May 2019

Birringer JH (1998) Makrolab: a heterotopia. PAJ J Perform Art 20(3):66–75

Chamberlain A, Crabtree A, Rodden T, Jones M, Rogers Y (2012) Research in the wild. In: Proceedings of the designing interactive systems conference on-DIS' 12. ACM Press, New York, New York, USA, p 795. https://doi.org/10.1145/2317956.2318078

Cousteau J (1964) World without sun. http://www.youtube.com/watch?v=6cIjgL2lkwA

Crabtree A, Chamberlain A, Grinter RE, Jones M, Rodden T, Rogers Y (eds) (2013) Introduction to the special issue of 'The Turn to The Wild'. ACM Trans Comput Hum Interact 20(3):1–4. https://doi.org/10.1145/2491500.2491501

"Feral Labs Network" (2020) https://www.ferallabs.net/

Jacobs J, Zoran A (2015) Hybrid practice in the kalahari: design collaboration through digital tools and hunter gatherer craft. In: The 33th international conference on human factors in computing systems (CHI' 15). ACM

Khan T (2017) 'Expeditions,' earth colab. http://earthcolab.com/expeditions/

Lehrman DS (1955) The perception of animal behavior. In: Group processes: transactions of the first conference, pp 259–67

Lorenz K (1952) King Solomon's ring: new light on animal ways. Psychology Press. http://books.google.com/books?id=M6tqEYDh2CgC&pgis=1

Marey E-J (1874) Animal mechanism: a treatise on terrestrial and Aërial locomotion. D. Appleton, 549 and 541 Broadway. http://books.google.com/books?id=hdc4AAAAMAAJ&pgis=1

Murray JH (1997) Hamlet on the holodeck: the future of narrative in cyberspace. http://books. google.com/books?hl=en&lr=&id=bzmSLtnMZJsC&oi=fnd&pg=PR9& amp;dq=Hamlet+on+the+Holodeck&ots=L2kHRYDdrD&sig=HijTas-bgOXfxC3u 0jLDsH3Cu98

Murray JH (2003) Inventing the medium. In: Wardrip-Fruin N, Montfort N (eds) The new media reader. MIT Press, p 823. http://books.google.com/books?hl=en&lr=&id=DQYXoRx9CcEC& pgis=1

Oral History Interview with Bennett CF Jr, Bennett AC (1975) http://siarchives.si.edu/collections/ siris_arc_217731

Painleve J (1950) Science is fiction: the films of Jean Painleve. http://www.imdb.com/title/tt1801 090/?ref_=fn_al_tt_1

Perner-Wilson H (n.d.) Wearable studio practice (2016) http://www.plusea.at/?category_name=a-wearable-studio-practice. Accessed 5 Jan 2017

Perner-Wilson H, Satomi M (n.d.) Bumblebee breakout-KOBAKANT. https://www.kobakant.at/ DIY/?p=7166. Accessed 12 May 2019

Quitmeyer A (n.d.) Digital naturalism laboratories–institute for interactive jungle crafts. http:// www.dinalab.net/. Accessed 11 May 2019

Quitmeyer, A (2016) Waterspace. https://www.scribd.com/document/313378537/Waterspace

Quitmeyer A (2017) Digital naturalist design guidelines: theory, investigation, development, and evaluation of a computational media framework to support ethological exploration. In: C and C 2017-Proceedings of the 2017 ACM SIGCHI conference on creativity and cognition, pp 184–196. https://doi.org/10.1145/3059454.3059462

Quitmeyer, A (2018a) Goophene: hypersensitive graphene sensors. https://www.instructables.com/ id/Goophene-Hypersensitive-Graphene-Sensors/

Quitmeyer A (2018b) Hiking hacks. In: Proceedings of the 2018 on designing interactive systems conference 2018-DIS'18. ACM Press, New York, New York, USA, pp 945–56. https://doi.org/ 10.1145/3196709.3196748

Quitmeyer A, Hoogendijk D (2019) Panatrap–digital naturalism laboratories. https://www.dinalab. net/category/projects/panatrap/

Quitmeyer AJ (2015) Digital naturalism: designing a digital media framework to support ethological exploration. PhD Thesis-Georgia Institute of Technology

Quitmeyer A, Khan T (2018) Proceedings of the first digital naturalism conference. In, 340. Phuket. https://www.scribd.com/document/388308632/Proceedings-of-the-First-Digital-Natura lism-Conference#from_embed%23p38

Quitmeyer A, Perner-Wilson H (2015) Digital naturalism 'Portable Studio Design'. http://andy.dor kfort.com/andy/digitalnatural/2015/06/11/portable-studio-design/

Quitmeyer A, Perner-Wilson H, Fisher B (2015) Hacking the wild: madagascar

Quitmeyer A, Zero1 (n.d.) 'Waterspace,' American arts incubator. http://americanartsincubator.org/ exchanges/philippines-2016. Accessed 17 Sept 2017

Rogers Y (2011) Interaction design gone wild: striving for wild theory. Interactions 18(4):58–62. https://doi.org/10.1145/1978822.1978834

"Smithsonian Tropical Research Institute" (n.d.) http://stri.si.edu/english/about_stri/index.php. Accessed 13 Oct 2014

Tinbergen N (1963) On aims and methods of ethology. Z Tierpsychol Beih 20:410–433

Tinbergen N (1974) The animal in its world (Explorations of an Ethologist, 1932–1972): field studies. Harvard University Press. http://books.google.com/books?id=cUzO7MNzIKkC&pgis=1

PlantShoe: Botanical Detectives

Nicholas Polys, Peter Sforza, and John Munsell

Abstract This chapter discusses the design and deployment of a citizen science application to inventory iconic medicinal non-timber forest products in the wild, such as black cohosh, ramps, and Bloodroot. The application is called PlantShoe (a pun on 'Gumshoe') and is used on mobile devices to collect data in the field about forest medicinal plants and their growing conditions. The users' data is fed into a database, which they can manage, study, and share. Plantshoe data is a part of a larger regional community and consortium which is collecting information about the ecology and distribution of medicinal forest plants. Such analyses can help forest farmers and wild stewards in their processes of site selection and management of these valuable botanicals. We describe our usability engineering in the development of the PlantShoe application and enumerate key design tradeoffs we encountered. Thus, the design decisions and results of PlantShoe provide rich material for the design of future technology on the trail.

1 Introduction

Outside the home, and just beyond town, lies another great paradox: the wild. Since the earliest days of our consciousness, and certainly our writing, we have wrestled with the notion of *the wild* as something else: an unknown place that is revered with mystery and wonder, and with danger and fear. It is a dynamic that is framed in myths

N. Polys (✉)
Advanced Research Computing, Virginia Tech, Blacksburg, VA, USA
e-mail: npolys@vt.edu

P. Sforza
Center for Geospatial Information Technology, Virginia Tech, Blacksburg, VA, USA
e-mail: sforza@vt.edu

J. Munsell
Department of Forest Resources and Environmental Conservation, Virginia Tech, Blacksburg, VA, USA
e-mail: jfmunsel@vt.edu

© Springer Nature Switzerland AG 2020
D. S. McCrickard et al. (eds.), *HCI Outdoors: Theory, Design, Methods and Applications*, Human–Computer Interaction Series,
https://doi.org/10.1007/978-3-030-45289-6_6

and stories from around the world: seekers can find everything in the wilderness from adulthood to healing, and even redemption. The notion of the wild and wilderness has been the focus of reflection and literature since the earliest days of communication and reflection, from nonfiction reflections on our interactions with the wild (e.g., Nash 1967; Strayed 2103) to fictional imaginings of adventures tailored for the young and old (e.g., London 1903; Sendek 1963).

It is only in contrast to the wild that civilization can be conceived. Indeed, it has been argued that the entire human enterprise of crafting technology and artifacts is for the sole purpose of controlling the wild—or at least keeping it at bay long enough to get our offspring to maturity. Since its invention, technology has served humankind to 'move the needle' and even 'change the equation' when it comes to mitigating, exploiting, and subduing the wild. Whether for survival, comfort, or wealth: as a species, we are intimately dependent on our natural resources and the balance of our civilization with the wild. When we design Human–Computer Interactions for the wild, we must consider the impacts of the technology on the user experience of the wild: Does it get in the way? Is it safe? Does it disturb the environment or other people? The notion of "in-the-wild" research in Human–Computer Interaction has been explored with regard to questions like these that go beyond the sort of things that can be studied in a lab setting (Crabtree et al. 2013).

In the Appalachian Mountains of the United States, wilderness is not just a characteristic of the region's ecology, but a long-standing part of its culture. Harvesting forest medicinal and edible plants is part of a multigenerational economic tradition. There are numerous forest botanicals with medicinal and nutritional properties, and long-standing markets, such as black cohosh, goldenseal, bloodroot, Ginseng, and ramps. These species thrive under the forest canopy in a biodiverse environment, and wild-growing plants are regularly harvested to supply an ever-growing nutraceutical market (Kruger et al.). Increasing the intentional farming of marketable species and the management of existing wild populations is a priority among a growing base of stakeholders.

An important question is how we use human–computer interaction (HCI) to build technologies that help us study the habitats where these plants grow, and to translate these findings to new, beginning, and seasoned forest farmers. The PlantShoe application was developed for anyone who wants to securely document plant population locations and growing conditions and thereby contribute to advances in how we conserve non-timber forest products through cultivation. Those who would like to tend planted and wild stand crops using forest farming methods will benefit from the information provided by the PlantShoe application.

Appalachia is vastly forested and wild-ness is central to its forest-dependent economy. As human–computer interaction (HCI) designers and tool producers, how do we balance the introduction of technology into the wild of Appalachian forest medicinal and edible products without spoiling the essential quality—the 'wild-ness'—we are seeking to study? This chapter details our approach to technology on the trail and our findings from designing and deploying the PlantShoe Botanical Detectives application for field use. The design choices and feedback from users provides insight into this and similar applications for the wild.

A USDA Extension Innovation Grant funded the PlantShoe project to improve the conservation and cultivation of non-timber forest products as part of the Appalachian Forest Plant Inventory Citizen Science (AF-PICS) program. Mountain medicinals and edibles are a latent economic value for the Appalachian region and a strong element for small farm diversification and land productivity under the forest canopy. Our innovation was to build a mobile application that could collect data about wild populations to better understand their growing conditions and to give better site suitability assessments for new forest farmers.

The goal of the PlantShoe application is to empower natural observers with a tool that helps them document trips, forest sites, and plant growing conditions so they can share that data securely with scientists. To address this, PlantShoe is a mobile phone-based citizen science application that is location-aware and built to record, survey, and census various plant populations in the wild. Upon returning to the networked world, users can upload their observations to their accounts, allowing them to review, edit, and analyze their collected trips. Users can also generate reports or their trips including GIS maps and local information about soil types [SSURGO], soil productivity [Schaetzl], forest canopy (classification from the 2011 Land Cover Database [Homer]), slope, elevation, and aspect of their plots.

This chapter outlines our approach and method of building technology to be used in the wild. This opportunity presents several design and engineering challenges. The PlantShoe application starts with data collected from citizens and scientists in the field using only their mobile phones. The application supports the structured capture of form data, images, and even audio, to catalog and GPS-locate plant populations. While we expected our users to be enthusiastic in their sampling for science, we did not want the tool to be intrusive to the natural experience (distracting, frustrating, taking too long to complete). HCI in the wild must consider the function and the context of the tool. In addition, features for technology on the trail must be designed to operate within realistic power and networking constraints. We also must tackle the real requirements of user safety and data privacy.

2 Background

Forest Farming is an agroforestry practice that cultivates medicinal, edible, decorative, and handicraft crops under a forest canopy that is modified or maintained to provide shade levels and habitat which favor growth and enhance production (Chamberlain et al. 2009). Consumer demand for sustainable herbal products with known plant origin and quality, along with new FDA regulations concerning product sourcing and manufacturing has prompted manufacturers to seek and pay premium prices for forest farmed raw material. However, information about where and how to farm marketable medicinal forest plants is underdeveloped. At the same time, a changing climate is altering site conditions and habitat for many plant species

(Iverson et al. 2008). Appalachian forest owners that aspire to begin or improve medicinal plant cultivation on their property need to know where to establish and manage resilient stands of salable species.

We will develop and deliver an internet-based geodesign application to Appalachian forest owners that will improve the precision of forest farming sites and the selection of non-timber forest products (NTFPs). Markets for NTFPs continue to grow. For instance, herbal supplement markets that depend on NTFPs currently exceed one billion dollars annually in the United States and are rising (Vaughan et al. 2013), and herbal dietary supplements sales have been on the increase annually for over a decade (Smith et al. 2017). Interest in edible forest products also is mounting, including ramps, mushrooms, and syrups. Appalachia is iconic in the world of NTFP trade. The region is home to habitat for more than 15 farmable woodland plants and full of ethnobotanical connections to herbal and edible woodland plants and fungi dating back generations (Trozzo et al. 2019). Industry efforts are underway to develop long-term arrangements with local forest farmers that supply verified forest-grown material using organic techniques, best handling and post-harvest processing, and value-added practices.

Geodesign is an important component of future geospatial technology, made possible in part through advances in computing and information sciences. The dynamics of land use decision-making are changing with the variety and complexity of available information, requiring new modes of interaction and engagement. The concept of geodesign as a collaborative framework emphasizes geography as a common denominator in multidisciplinary engagement and research. It addresses some of the major limitations of design and planning through software and compu-tational infrastructure that enable the modeling and simulation of alternative design proposals. Geodesign also brings new concepts and vocabulary to computer science by enriching holistic, exploratory thinking to improve land use design and planning precision. The success of the geodesign approach in supporting decision-making depends on the interactive fusion of multiple data sources, and their integration into various growing and climate models.

Citizen science brings forward the proposition that a wider community of people can conduct the valuable scientific observation. Grass-roots surveys, such as the Audubon Society's annual bird count (in its third decade: birdcount.org), have given rise to a strong community movement and institutional support. Much of this is due to advances in technical (software to support online and standard methods for data collection; for example, (Lukyanenko 2011)) and social trends, including increased education and interest as well as advances in virtual training and communication. While a multitude of biological monitoring citizen science programs currently exist (see USDA Forest Service Citizen Science Programs), forest monitoring is noted as an under-utilized opportunity for public engagement (Daume et al. 2014). Citizen Science 2.0 refers to adopting the Web 2.0 model, which puts a primacy on dynamic, user-generated content, and social media and data sharing (see Fig. 1).

With hundreds of millions of mobile phones armed with sensors, memory, and networking, the opportunities for citizen science continue to grow. Much more than just monitoring presence, data can be collected across a wide swath of space and

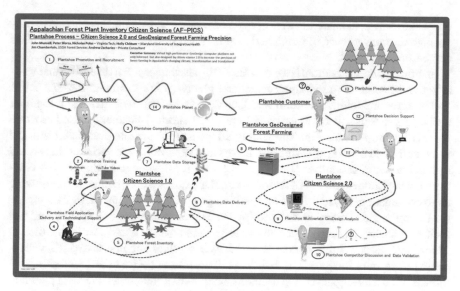

Fig. 1 PlantShoe Citizen Science supporting forest farming geodesign

time, including ground-truth context, condition, and other key ecological and habitat parameters. From video training for invasive plant ID on smartphones [Starr et al.] to public engagement [Varner et al.], mobile citizen science has been used to assess plant diversity in Spain [Garcia et al.], to catalog invasives [Gallo et al.], and to document trail conditions by a photo [Sang & Shelby].

3 PlantShoe Background and Goals

This project seeks to increase the precision and resilience of forest farming by improving decision support at a relatively low cost across a broad physiographic area for several marketable native plants. It will help forest farmers rapidly respond to market opportunities and better prepare to sustainably manage their site and plant species in light of environmental change. This project brings new innovation to the rapidly growing fields of geodesign computer visualization and citizen science 2.0 to improve forest monitoring protocols and to build a geodesign decision support system to increase forest farming precision and outcomes.

The data collected by the PlantShoe Botanical Detectives will provide new data points about the habitat and conditions where these plants thrive. By analyzing this data in the context of other GIS layers, we can better understand the growing conditions that support these plant populations and thus pursue conservation through cultivation. Through technology on the trail and citizen science, we hope to increase our ecological understanding and propagation of these valuable species. It is only through the convergence of multiple disciplines and new innovations that such ideas can become manifest.

In prior work, the authors have created Web-based geospatial databases and visualization systems for agricultural users and planning. For example, the SANREM global agroclimatology [sanrem] and GeoVine [geovine]) websites bring together GIS layers such as soil and slope with decades of historical weather data and growing models for crop simulation. The widely adopted GeoVine site crunches historical weather data to feed the growing simulators and suggests grape varieties that would fit local growing conditions [Radics et al.]. Our prior work finds that the 3D environment supports modeling of factors like solar exposure and temperature, allowing us to document geospatial locations and integrate them with other GIS data layers, for example, the GeoSpy and SpeedSpy Web3D interface lets users query and test their broadband connectivity on the road (Sharakhov 2012 and 2013a, b), the 3D Blacksburg Project built standards-based web services for interactive 3D visualization of terrain, imagery, and buildings [Tilden et al.; Kim et al.], and other 3D models of Blacksburg have been used for collaborative and immersive town planning (Polys et al. 2018). For natural resources management and agriculture, the team has also explored the power of data fusion and 3D visualization using *fusality* to document and communicate facts about local watersheds and forests (Polys et al. 2016), and we used local drone-based Lidar to create 3D models of Catawba Sustainability Center property, together with the US Forest Services' tree growth simulator, to project 3D growth of different planting scenarios into the future (Wang et al. 2017).

These applications demonstrate the potential of Web-based GIS platforms to deliver new data-driven capabilities and experiences for many different types of stakeholders including designers, scientists, engineers, landowners, the government, and the public. In addition to solving practical planning problems with such interactive 3D visualization platforms, we have found that technology can increase people's awareness and affect toward the wild. In a recent experiment using 3D Blacksburg and Stroubles Creek data (Polys et al. 2017), we compared the efficacy of adding a game-based element to the interactive 3D visualization interface. We found that the game-based condition yielded significantly more spatial knowledge about the creek's location (underground across campus) and significantly higher self-ratings of knowledge about and affect toward the creek.

We used citizen science and geodesign to increase the precision of site and species selection for forest farming systems in the Appalachian Mountains. Precision agriculture is a rapidly advancing field, which uses computer technologies such as guidance systems and data mapping with GPS and field sensors and robotics to improve the efficiency and profitability of farms. It helps farmers improve the precision and efficiency of their farming activities by providing accurate pictures of the different resources and conditions on their land and tradeoffs between site-specific operations.

The goals of the project are to:

1. Develop a geodesign application that improves farming precision of four medicinal/edible plants native to the Appalachian Mountains: black cohosh, goldenseal, bloodroot, and ramps
2. Launch the Appalachian Forest Plant Inventory Citizen Scientists (AF-PICS) program to help gather the data needed to build a forest farming geodesign application
3. Translate project findings across the Cooperative Extension System and beyond.

To accomplish these goals, we have formed a broad multidisciplinary partnership consisting of Virginia Tech and Maryland University of Integrative Health, four non-governmental organizations covering southern and northern Appalachia (Appalachian Sustainable Development; Blue Ridge Woodland Growers; Rural Action; United Plant Savers), and the USDA Forest Service Southern Research Station. Together, the non-governmental organization partners maintain 1100 + person Appalachian non-timber forest product network with emphasis on medicinal plants: The Appalachian Beginning Forest Farmers Coalition (ABFFC). Virginia Tech leads eXtension's forest farming community of practice, but all project partners maintain community membership. The PlantShoe project brought together several areas of expertise; Forestry (Munsell), Geospatial Informatics (Sforza), and Computer Science and Human–Computer Interaction (Polys).

4 PlantShoe Application Design

In designing and developing PlantShoe, we undertook the scenario-based design usability engineering approach of Rosson and Carroll (2002), with an emphasis on user experience (Hartson and Pyla 2012). Scenario-based design centers the crafting of an application on a narrative that includes stakeholders, goals, and activities. From this narrative, features emerge for activity design, information design, and interaction design, leading to prototyping and system development in support of deployment and testing. The design features can be formulated as tradeoffs, which are then resolved by theory, guidelines, or new usability studies.

The primary stakeholders are, of course, the end-users of the application. We consider a range of possible users and motivations in generating the application scenarios. First-order stakeholders are the citizen scientists themselves. We expect a mix of naturalists, scientists, and forest farmers to be end-users of our application. Second-order stakeholders include consumers of medicinal plants, who wish to have an adequate and reliable supply.

We considered users with different backgrounds and motivations in our scenario-based design. Given the mission of the project, we centered on two crucial types of users: the individual hiker (amateur naturalist) and the landowner. We believe that these types capture key features of our potential users in terms of (a) their motivation, and (b) their access and likelihood to document the wild. Sample scenarios are:

Mabel, an outdoor enthusiast, enjoys hiking and getting into the woods. She often brings a pack with water and snacks. She keeps her phone, wallet, and keys in this pack for safety, bringing the phone out from time to time to take scenic pictures. She knows a few plant names, but not many, and while she wishes to learn more, she is hesitant to install yet another app on her phone with a field guide. When she hears that medicinal plants grow in the local area, she attends a local workshop about wild foraging and discovers the PlantShoe project. She thinks she could contribute to science during her hikes, and considers it a challenge to find and document a few plots this season.

Ida, a farmer looking to diversify production of a family woodlot's production. Knowing there are wild populations of medicinal and edible plants in the region, she sets out to find some and grow them on her property. Using the regional forest farmers network and community, she hopes to collect enough information to build a viable production of non-timber forest products under the canopy. She installs PlantShoe; while visiting the Website, clicks the perimeter of her timber lot on the map interface to get a report on site suitability and possible species affinities.

These users *may* have some knowledge of botany and ecology, but it should not be assumed. Indeed, our application is meant to collect scientific data to build growing models of different species. To maximize the likelihood of receiving reliable data, a key element of our system design must include accessible instructional material. The website and application 'on-ramp' must, therefore, include links to resources about the plant species, including videos and factsheets. The mobile application should also have such information resources 'on-board' so that users can reference soil types, hill slope, canopy density, and other variables accurately while in the field. The field survey protocol should also be as efficient as possible so that users do not need to spend too much time documenting a site.

Building on this design rationale, the system should support a structured data entry that is easy to use under various lighting conditions in the field. We adopt, for example, the typical approaches, such as larger fonts, high contrast between figure and ground, good layouts that provide good Gestalt [GG]. Such a requirement also leads us to prefer the multiple-choice patterns, unless the input data type is truly unstructured. Because we have the capability of multimedia sensors onboard the mobile device, we can enable the semi-structured capture of imagery, photos, audio, and even video as part of the site documentation. The amount of multimedia captured has direct implications for implications user experience, from time to power to upload; in this section, we describe these tradeoffs we encountered and how we resolved them over two iterations to full deployment.

There are other important design elements illuminated by our scenario-based design. Since we are dealing with a combination of GPS locations and items of value on private and public land, it was essential that we define and promote a responsible Privacy Policy. We devised three tiers of data access that are detailed below: researcher, participant, and public. Each level's responsibility and privileges must be detailed and presented to the user upon install, sign-up, or use. Another design element stems from legal implications supported by the scenario narratives: while users may have outdoor experience, we cannot assume this. Indeed, when producing a mobile application for the wild, 'Safety is a Number One Priority.' PlantShoe provides a safety checklist on the website and in the app to prepare users logistically before they go into the field. In addition, we don't want our app to put users into dangerous or compromising situations. The field collection protocol and mobile application design must balance best-case scientific scenarios with the real constraints of safety in *The Wild*. These constraints become important elements in our interaction design and in version 1 (detailed below). Finally, indemnity information must also be reviewed by users before the installation of the mobile app.

The remainder of this section describes core decisions that were made in each phase of our scenario-based design process. Activity design identifies the key high-level activities that need to be accomplished. Information design focuses on the ways that information is presented to the user. Interaction design considers how users interact with the information.

Activity design. To accommodate the diverse but sometimes non-technical skill sets of our target users, there are several redundant ways that users may engage with the PlantShoe application: centrally from the mobile data collection app but also from the website and its resources and site reporting. While we present principal elements of the whole system, we will focus on the design of the mobile application for data collection in the field.

The first thing PlantShoe seeks to do in activating the PlantShoe software application is to open the site survey tool on their device, review app information, and (upon first use) accept the liability terms and conditions of use and data use and security terms intellectual property statement. The field survey tool provides directions for plot establishment, collecting field data in two phases: minimal and expanded. The minimum amount required to submit a PlantShoe plot to the AF-PICS program includes plot location, location contingency, assessment, photograph capture, and audio description. Additional information that will be useful for characterizing the habitat includes forest slope position, forest floor, and soil sampling, and forest canopy density. This extra data capture, while difficult and time-consuming, can increase a PlantShoe's score in the AF-PICS Competition. By separating the different levels of information request into separate activities,

Information design. Both the app and the website include visual resources and references about the different plant species, about soil types, slope positions, and forest canopy references. While in the field, users can also access informational figures and images during the field survey protocol. Both the Web and the mobile App version are designed with Gestalt principles for quick identification and visual indexing into species-specific resources. On the website, there are hyperlinks to several resources, including official and community factsheets. For the mobile version, we need to have some set of references on board for users to access when they have no live network connection. Given the size of the mobile screen and the non-technical nature of many of our users, we choose not to use a visual index showing all species at once; rather, we must list the species in text, and provide a button for more information. In this case, the image and identification guidelines are shown on one screen (Fig. 2).

Through the Website, users can access reports of their trips in an interactive Web map. The map interface provides both satellite imagery and road map as base layer views. In addition, new plots can be queried for species site suitability. Based on the

Fig. 2 Mobile app version
of PlantShoe provides a
single layer of information
tailored for a user who may
have minimal technical skills

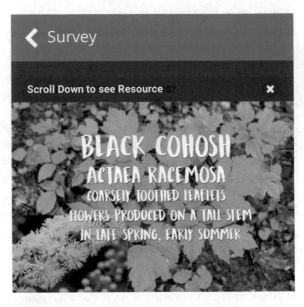

known GIS layers in the online PlantShoe system, several graphs and visualizations can be generated and viewed online.

Interaction design. The activity design provides a structure that points to certain elements for the design of user interactions with our mobile application. We began by thinking about the maximum amount and variety of data we could collect with a mobile device, and what scientific value it might have after processing. For example, GPS data and ground truth about slope, soil, and canopy is directly valuable to our existing models. However, we also investigated the feasibility of several modalities and pipelines further out on the research spectrum. Our choices in using familiar interaction styles that were matched to the platform of the user's device shorten the learning curve, thus supporting more user interactions.

Fig. 3 A photosphere (inside-out) capture from the field (left) and Outside-in X3D photogrammetry result with a photosphere (right); our capture results can be run on any Web browser, VR Goggles, or CAVE projection

We considered several possible multimedia capture workflows for the mobile application that could merge ground truth measurement with the ecological parameters and habitat of a wild plant population. *Video* is captured with in-device cameras, capturing near-HD first-person perspectives of locations under a variety of lighting conditions. *Photos* capture important aspects of the area, including pictures of the plot from several angles (the classical documentation approach where the user directs the image toward the interesting features), an outside-in photo protocol such as structure from motion (sfM) that uses multiple pictures to generate a 3D model of the objects in the plot, and an inside-out photo protocol uses 360-degree panorama stitching together multiple photos to create a 3D photosphere (see Fig. 3). *Audio* supports recording notes about the plot and area. All of these features are augmented with structured form entry using familiar radio buttons, checkboxes, text, and undo/redo.

Prototyping and evaluation. The first version of the system supported the standalone Website and PlantShoe app that each allowed users to collect and review information. The information was stored on a server, uploaded when connectivity was available.

Version 1. This first version of PlantShoe was evaluated with several users in the Appalachian Beginning Forest Farmers Coalition (ABFFC) to elicit feedback. We cataloged known plant populations in several states using the app, finding several important constraints and usability issues. Our first evaluation of video capture was not positive. We could not distinguish any scientific benefit of the captured product for such large cost: from a battery to the variety of optics, and the memory and upload cost required to take video documentation of the site out of consideration. The workflow for on-site documentation was complex and cumbersome for users. Audio, however, has less overhead and was a good fit for recording observations. Symbolic (text) entry is time-consuming and error-prone, making a simple audio recording of observations attractive. We added a simple recording feature that allowed users to start, pause, stop, re-record, and save their audio notes for each plot. Users would be trained on what features to note about plant health, slope, soil, canopy, etc.

In early field tests, we also prototyped the photo capture activity as either: (a) an orbital (*outside-in*) image series to generate a 3D point cloud of the stand through photogrammetry or, (b) Google street view app to generate a 360-degree photosphere

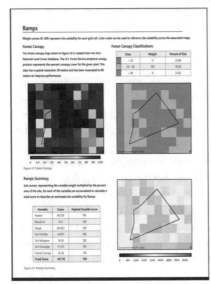

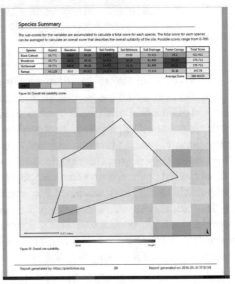

Fig. 4 An early example of the site sustainability report: **a** Site query-by-plot Web-based map interface (top). **b** Sample pages from the report generated by user-submitted data. 60 x 60 meter cells are shown here; new data and processing allow us to deliver PlantShoe data in 10 x 10 meter cells

(*inside-out*) of the stand's forest context. One hand, a good capture could produce reasonable results for both sfM and photospheres (Fig. 3); however, the skill required to produce such a capture is high, requiring the user to achieve a correct series of picture positions and orientations. Consistency of the capture is a problem and the success rate for our focused testers was well below 50% (Fig. 4).

The *inside-out* image capture used the Google StreetView app to collect multiple photos and stitch them together into a spherical 360-degree panorama with an equirectangular image projection. This process creates a photosphere that can be used in Web3D or Virtual Reality to generate an interactive, photo-realistic perspective from that point of view. The typical capture process assumes that the camera position does not significantly change throughout the image series. In practice, however, this puts the user in the middle of the plot, possibly damaging the plants. Because we are interested in a non-destructive sampling of our wild plots, this was not an attractive option. The *outside-in* image capture requires at least two orbits around the plot and photos at 23-degree angles (minimum) in order to generate a reasonable 3D reconstruction later. There are additional challenges for photogrammetry of natural objects, and that is their natural motion (from the wind) displaces their position over short time periods.

In addition to requiring much physical contortion and compromise, both of these mobile image capture workflows can take well over 6 min, requiring the user to capture from 27 to 56 images from specific angles around the site. The effort required for both *outside-in* and *inside-out* photo captures was significant. With current mobile cameras, we faced the facts of destructive sampling of the plot and the large size of the photo collection upload. In addition, the immediate scientific value of the data product was not clear or compelling enough to warrant this effort. In the end, we did not include either in the production PlantShoe mobile data application (Version 2). Instead, we provided users the ability to capture photos for the app in a less structured way, as is more typical of outdoor tourism and sought to capture canopy closure, soil type, and plant condition through structured forms and onboard visual references.

Version 2. We refined the field collection protocol based on the prototype feedback. In addition to the changes mentioned above, we improved the contrast of our image supplementary material (for sunny conditions) and published the app for public download. Users could download the App from the iStore and from Google Play. Upon installation, a user account is created in the PlantShoe backend where trip data and plot observations will be uploaded and stored. By Version 2, we had our workflow and data packages specified and had implemented the local save of each collection (in the field) and the subsequent (network-dependent) upload to the PlantShoe system. The released Plantshoe App presented safety information as the first button and then the main page integrated a link to each survey activity (Fig. 7).

We also implemented a Leaderboard for the AF-PICS Competition, where detectives could keep track of their trips and compete for a free registration to a Forest Farming Conference in Kingsport, Tennessee the next year. Response to the Leaderboard and the 'gamification' of PlantShoe was generally positive; we observe that it can incentivize users to participate more. In our experience, it seemed to only be a motivator for the top users: many users were casual participants and did not see themselves as competitors, rather as scientists or hobbyists. Their use (and re-use) was more determined by how usable the app was to accomplish the data collection in the field. We feel that gamification's best potential could be achieved with further community partnerships and promotions.

The PlantShoe app debuted at the United Plant Savers 2017 Ginseng Conference in Charleston, WV (https://unitedplantsavers.org/). With the release and promotional material, we also created a training video, which was shown and then added to the Website. The video was also added to the Forest Farming YouTube channel (https://www.youtube.com/user/exforestfarming), where a number of informational videos are available. The PlantShoe video explained the project and field protocol, including the photo capture and audio notes features.

In PlantShoe, privacy was a major concern since many of these species have significant market value and are precious enough to make secrecy the default behavior.

Our users are protective of their wild plots for reasons of both economy and conservation. Therefore, it was essential to be transparent about the levels of data access and security among other users and the researchers. We paid special attention to our declaration and practice of privacy. We crafted privacy measures to combat possible illegal harvesting of plants and to protect reporters. To release a production application through a State University with Federal money required that we specify and publish our Privacy Policy and disclose the levels of data access. Some key elements include an agreement to Virginia Tech Policy 700 Acceptable Use of Information Systems at Virginia Tech, encrypted exchange over https (encrypted passwords and cookies), declaring what information we will collect (app: GPS and field data collection; Website: Google Analytics data), and supported access to data for PlantShoe users, researchers and administrators, and the general public.

Site sustainability report. The GIS data layers used in the Website site suitability analysis were generated for the Appalachian mountain region and published on the www.plantshoe.org website. Through an online 2D map interface, users can zoom in to the meter level and draw plot areas, thereby providing a query to the system, which will generate a PDF a site report for download.

For the report results, we adopted a common color map vocabulary from cartography that drove the presentation of results to users. The site report Web interface is shown in (Fig. 9a). The geospatial database includes a large set of data attributes, specifically aspect, elevation, slope, soil fertility, soil moisture, soil drainage, and forest canopy. Users can select their query plots in an interactive GIS map interface. This spatial query is then evaluated by the backend and the system then generates a PDF site report showing a large set of graphs and information detailing suitability scores for black cohosh, goldenseal, ramps, and bloodroot. In the near time (2–3 min), a pdf report is prepared and ready for download by the user (Fig. 9b).

5   Initial User Reactions

On average there are currently 10 users per day (982 in the 2019 season) using the interactive tools and looking at the PDF resources. Some of those users run polygons queries and get reports; for example, there were 15 reports run in the period Jan 1–June 2, 2019; there were 54 site reports generated in 2018. The Web interface and geodesign report includes SSURGO soil data [DG] across Appalachia.

A broader study of user feedback is planned, but here are three quotes from the open-ended feedback form for PlantShoe users:

> It's fun to be part of a large project and with Plant Shoe, it's easy. With this on the back of my mind while I'm hiking or rambling about in the woods, it's a great way to keep a useful eye out and easily contribute useful data.

> I have 47 acres of mixed hardwoods with some conifer in the eastern panhandle of West Virginia. I have been using the Plant Shoe app for a couple of years now when I go walk my property. What I like about apps like Plant Shoe is that they give me more appreciation for

my land, in a fun way. I end up paying more attention to the plants, topography, and sounds. Plus I get to contribute to regional conservation science.

I had the opportunity to test the PlantShoe siting tool on my 290 acre family farm in West Virginia. I was specifically interested in locating potential hot spots for ramps on this property. I was very impressed with the accuracy of the data produced as it corresponded correctly with actual ramp patches on the property. This is an extremely useful tool for individuals like me that want to explore the potential of underutilized farm and forest land.

These positive testimonials help our confidence that the tool can work and be beneficial for our target audience. However, we have very little negative feedback, presumably since if users hit a breakdown they just quit the app and never used it again. However, it can be noted that one younger user (18) commented on the look and feel of the PlantShoe phone app and quickly stated about its graphic design, "Boomer." At least two lessons can be gleaned from: consider multiple generations' esthetics and always include artists in your multidisciplinary teams.

6 Conclusions and Future Work

Research in the outdoors presents unique challenges to designing new, usable, and safe technology. In our case, we are working with a known form factor and a familiar device, but in an unfamiliar location for which the device is not designed nor well suited. The mobile phones of today have reasonable battery power for a day hike, but of course, it drains faster when using multimedia and networking. Searching for networks is especially expensive. Such operational constraints of power and network are very real on the trail and forced some design choices for us. There were also safety and liability concerns, as well as privacy issues.

Each data capture requirement and modality imposes additional overhead on the user, who is meanwhile attending to the physical (rather than digital) surroundings. Getting a user all the way to clicking the button to open an in-field survey is a challenge itself, but getting them to complete the survey is another. Each step in the protocol must be motivated by scientific relevance and then tested in the field, preferably with novice users under supervision. While image capture and technology is viable for trained naturalists and researchers, it still remains questionably viable for most hikers and landowners.

The true power of mobile citizens and the flora census will come when our scientific methods, technology, and data validity all align. Indeed, with new generations of citizens and scientists out on the trail and exploring The Wild, we have a great opportunity. PlantShoe was designed as a tool to increase the monitoring, modeling, and cultivation of our native NTFPs. From better batteries and wireless networks to new sensors and acquisition platforms such as mobile cameras and drones, the quality, velocity, and volume of data will grow. We can see many paths to this potential: many rich directions for future research and applications of the NeXtension tool.

First and foremost, technology continues to miniaturize; meanwhile, wireless coverage is increasing. With this trend, we expect to see more technology on the trail.

If designed to be 'transparent to the user,' such technology may be a great benefit. If it asks of the user too much attentional resources, they may annoy the user, or even put the user in danger. For us working toward the goal of scientific validity, we expect that with better instruments, we may measure new things. With the increased variety and resolution of sensors and more computing power and memory on mobile devices, we *could* improve our environmental monitoring, modeling, and management. This future requires further informatics innovation: to improve the reach and validity of citizen science with monitoring of populations and better models to support each species' reproductive conditions.

In order to take advantage of these new mobile sensors and computing platforms for citizen science, we will need to design our interfaces to live in the space between vernacular use and trained protocol. Indeed, the learnability of data capture protocols will be crucial to their success. Thus, we can identify two immediate research opportunities: the effectiveness of different training approaches, and the effectiveness of additional on-site prompts and support, such as is possible with Augmented Reality. Designers would do well to focus on safe, efficient workflows and the use of multimedia cues to improve the validity of data capture from the field.

In addition, as photogrammetry methods and algorithms continue to improve, and we can have higher confidence in the derived digital products: our 3D reconstructions and computation of leaf area, for example. Similarly, with new mobile wide-field and depth cameras and machine learning, we may derive more accurate measures of forest canopy closure, tree density, and even the diameter at breast height (DBH) of nearby trees. We see great potential for citizen science applications like PlantShoe to link geographically and temporally dispersed observations and thus improve our understanding of flora in the wild and their growth dynamics.

The compounding, viral properties of social media, and the cooperative citizen science approach have fertile HCI research potential toward maximizing the validity and statistical power of Wild observations. This approach will leverage a broader variety of the larger population but also study the dynamics of communication and data sharing among communities. We believe that technology and digital tools with positive physical feedback loops can help users pay more attention to the natural world; they can also provide new opportunities for learning and reflection on the trail. Using public and shared data, we can consider a new way of engaging with the wild: not just sustainably, but regeneratively: not as a novelty or a fringe movement but a fact and fabric of our computing culture.

Acknowledgments Funding for PlanShoe was provided in part by eXtension Foundation and USDA NIFA. Thanks to Virginia Tech Advanced Research Computing and the Center for Geospatial Information Technology for their continued support.

References

Abowd GD, Mynatt ED, Rodden T (2002) The human experience [of ubiquitous computing]. IEEE Pervasive Comput 1(1):48–57

Chamberlain JL, Mitchell D, Brigham T, Hobby T, Zabek L, Davis J (2009) Forest farming practices. In: Garrett (ed) North American agroforesty: an integrated science and practice, 2nd ed, pp 219–255

Crabtree A, Chamberlain A, Grinter RE, Jones M, Rodden T, Rogers Y (2013) Introduction to the special issue of "The Turn to the Wild". ACM Trans Comput Hum Interact (TOCHI) 20(3)

Daume S, Albert M, von Gadow K (2014) Assessing citizen science opportunities in forest monitoring using probabilistic topic modelling. Forest Ecosyst 1:11. https://doi.org/10.1186/s40663-014-0011-6

Dourish P (2001) Where the action is. MIT Press, Cambridge

Gallo T, Waitt D (2011) Creating a successful citizen science model to detect and report invasive species. Bioscience 61(6):459–465. https://doi.org/10.1525/bio.2011.61.6.8

García MB, Silva JL, Tejero P, Pardo I, Gómez D (2019) Tracking the long-term dynamics of plant diversity in Northeast Spain with a network of volunteers and rangers. Reg Environ Change 19(2):391–401

Geovine Website (2020) https://geovine.org/vineyards/. Accessed 20 Jan 2020

Gilliam FS (2007) The ecological significance of the herbaceous layer in temperate forest ecosystems. BioScience 57(10):845–858. https://doi.org/10.1641/b571007

Handfield R, Walton SV, Sroufe R, Melnyk S (2002) Applying environmental criteria to supplier assessment: a study in the application of the Analytical Hierarchy Process. Eur J Oper Res 141:70–87. https://doi.org/10.1016/S0377-2217(01)00261-2

Hartson R, Pyla PS (2012) The UX Book: process and guidelines for ensuring a quality user experience. Elsevier

Havens K, Vitt P, Masi S (2012) Citizen science on a local scale: the Plants of Concern program. Front Ecol Environ 10(6):321–3

Homer CG, Dewitz JA, Yang L, Jin S, Danielson P, Xian G, Coulston J, Herold ND, Wickham JD, Megown K (2015) Completion of the 2011 National Land Cover Database for the conterminous United States-Representing a decade of land cover change information. Photogramm Eng Remote Sens 81(5):345–354

Iverson LR, Prasad AM, Matthews SN, Peters M (2008) Estimating potential habitat for 134 eastern US tree species under six climate scenarios. For Ecol Manag 254:390–406

Kim J-S, Polys N, Sforza P (2015) Preparing and evaluating geospatial data models using X3D encodings for web 3D geovisualization services. In: Proceedings of the 20th international conference on 3D web technology (Web3D '15). ACM, New York, NY, USA, pp 55–63. http://dx.doi.org/10.1145/2775292.2775304

Kruger SL, Munsell JF, Chamberlain JL, Davis JM, Huish RD (2020) Projecting medicinal plant trade volume and value in deciduous forests of the Eastern United States. Forests 11(74):1–20

Lukyanenko R, Parsons J, Wiersma YF (2011) Citizen science 2.0: data management principles to harness the power of the crowd. Lect Notes Comput Sci 6629:465–473

Munsell JF, Davis JM, Chamberlain JL (2013) Forest farming. In: Gold M, Cernusca M, Hall M (eds) Training manual for applied agroforestry practices. University of Missouri Center for Agroforestry, 165p

Polys N, Newcomb C, Schenk T, Skuzinski T, Dunay D (2018) The value of 3D models and immersive technology in planning urban density. In: Proceedings of the 23rd international ACM conference on 3D web technology (Web3D '18). ACM, New York, NY, USA, 4 pages. Article 13. https://doi.org/10.1145/3208806.3208824

Polys N, Hotter J, Purcell L, Lanier M, Wolf J, Hession C, Sforza P, Ivory J (2017) Finding frogs: using game-based learning to increase environmental awareness. In: Proceedings of the 22nd international conference on 3D web technology (Web3D '17). ACM, New York, NY, USA

Polys S, Hession M (2016) Extensible experiences: fusality for stream and field. In: Proceedings of the 21th international conference on 3D web technology (Web3D '16). ACM, New York, NY, USA

Radics P, Sforza P, Farrell B, Newman J, Polys N, Mosaavi A, Sutherland B, Wang H, Roghair L, Pierson M, Bock M (2015) Vineyard site assessment and simulation of grape varieties in the Eastern U.S. In: The 4th annual extreme science engineering discovery environment conference 2015 (XSEDE'15), St. Louis, MO

Rosson MB, Carroll JM (2002) Usability engineering: scenario-based development of human-computer interaction. Morgan Kaufmann

Kim S-O, Shelby B (2005) Developing standards for trail conditions using image capture technology. Leisure Sci 27(3):279–295. https://doi.org/10.1080/01490400590930691

Sanrem Global AgroClimatology website (2020) http://arcgis-research.gis.vt.edu/cgit/global/index. html. Accessed 20 Jan 2020

Schaetzl RJ, Krist FJ Jr, Miller BA (2012) A taxonomically based ordinal estimate of soil productivity for landscape-scale analyses. Soil Sci, 177

Smith T, Kawa K, Eck V, Morton C, Stredney R (2017) Herbal supplement sales in US increase 7.7% in 2016. Mark Rep (115). http://cms.herbalgram.org/herbalgram/issue115/hg115-herbma rketrpt.html. Accessed Nov 2017

Sharakhov N, Polys N, Sforza P (2013a) SpeedSpy: a mobile Web3D platform for visualizing broadband data. In: Proceedings of the 18th international conference on 3D web technology (Web3D '13). ACM, New York, NY, USA, p 208

Sharakhov N, Polys N, Sforza P (2013b) GeoSpy: a Web3D platform for geospatial visualization. In: Proceedings of the 1st ACM SIGSPATIAL international workshop on MapInteraction (MapInteract '13). ACM, New York, NY, USA, pp 30–35

Soil Survey Staff, Natural Resources Conservation Service, United States Department of Agriculture. Web Soil Survey. Soil Survey Geographic (SSURGO) Database for all available counties in Virginia. http://websoilsurvey.nrcs.usda.gov/

Starr J, Schweik CM, Bush N, Fletcher L, Finn J, Fish J et al (2014) Lights, camera…citizen science: assessing the effectiveness of smartphone-based video training in invasive plant identification. PLoS ONE 9(11):e111433. https://doi.org/10.1371/journal.pone.0111433

Suchman LA (1987) Plans and situated actions: the problem of human-machine communication. Cambridge University Press

Tilden D, Singh A, Polys NF, Sforza P (2011) Multimedia mashups for mirror worlds. In: Web3D '11 proceedings of the 16th international conference on 3D web technology, Paris. ACM

Vaughan RC, Munsell JF, Chamberlain JL (2013) Opportunities for enhancing non-timber forest products management in the United States. J For 111(1):26–33

Varner J (2014) Scientific outreach: toward effective public engagement with biological science. Bioscience 64(4):333–40

Weiser M (1993) Ubiquitous computing. Computer (10):71–72. https://doi.org/10.1145/1718918. 1718946

Groups and Communities

Opportunities in Conflict on the Trail

Lindah Kotut, Michael Horning, and D. Scott McCrickard

Abstract People spend time on trails for a great many reasons. Often their reasons overlap—sometimes in positive ways but occasionally in conflict. Although there have been studies of individuals and unique groups that utilize the trail, there is a need first to first understand trail users. These users span different groups that use the trail, and the communities that inhabit the region surrounding the trail. It is importanat to the understand the group–community interaction especially in the presence of technology. In this chapter, we methodically consider these groups and communities, and identify relationships and tensions that emerge from their interactions with each other. We argue that exploring tensions provide a space to identify design opportunities to mitigate conflicts and improve the sense of community on the trail.

1 Introduction

The trail provides an interesting context by which to consider people (who are the trail users?), technology (what do they take with them on the trail?), together with the attitudes toward the usage of said technologies and whether it is viewed negatively (Bryson 1998) or positively (Fondren 2016). We contend in this chapter, that understanding trail users and their dynamics, particularly the tensions between different hiker groups, helps with understanding how these groups interact with technology. This understanding will in turn help in directing analysis and presenting design guid-

L. Kotut (✉) · D. S. McCrickard
Department of Computer Science, Virginia Tech, Blacksburg, USA
e-mail: lkotut@vt.edu

D. S. McCrickard
e-mail: mccricks@vt.edu

M. Horning
Department of Communication, Blacksburg, USA
e-mail: mhorning@vt.edu

L. Kotut · M. Horning · D. S. McCrickard
Center for Human Computer Interaction, Virginia Tech, Blacksburg, VA, USA

© Springer Nature Switzerland AG 2020
D. S. McCrickard et al. (eds.), *HCI Outdoors: Theory, Design, Methods and Applications*, Human–Computer Interaction Series,
https://doi.org/10.1007/978-3-030-45289-6_7

ance and/or opportunities for encouraging community, toward diffusing inter-group conflict.

Examples of overlap and conflict are exemplified in the goals of day hikers and long-distance hikers. Both benefit from well-maintained paths, shelters, water sources, and restroom facilities (Appalachian Trail Conservancy 2018). They also benefit from applications developed to lead them to these needed resources. But these hikers may differ in their ability to plan for when they arrive at a point (relevant in the nature of campsite reservation systems), and their need to resupply along the trail (e.g., highly portable food versus bulky luxury food).

Identifying the types of users and understanding both similar and differing goals of being on the and trails, needs while on the trail their are crucial to be able to design technology that is both useful to the trail users while also mitigating the tension that would otherwise emerge from designing for groups with discrete needs.

To achieve these goals, we involved stakeholders and researchers who work at the intersection of technology on the outdoors to be able to:

- Identify who the trail users are, their goals and needs on the trail
- Understand the tensions and conflicts emerging from the interactions of the different trail users
- Distinguish between groups (transient users) and community (permanent inhabitants) of the trail
- Identify opportunities for technology design for this space

This chapter highlights three exercises that we conducted with trail users, trail stakeholders, and researchers in the trail space over a period of 1 year, as a means to meet the goals outlined above, and to improve our understanding of trail needs. By involving stakeholder participants, we were able to identify trail users in the first exercise. The second exercise involved grouping the identified trail users according to similar goals to identify common needs and also tensions and conflicts that emerge from conflicting needs. We then selected groups from that exercise to delve deeper into their activities as part of the third exercise. These exercises provided us with an opportunity to discuss the technological impact on the individual, group, or community on the trail, which we discuss in later sections.

2   Background

The outdoor space and how people interact with it has been defined by researchers in different ways. Recent research and workshops have directly participated or indirectly contributed to the creation of this design/information space. We focus on those work in this section, introduce the "trail" information space, and discussing the trail users by introducing, together with the role that technology plays (if at all) in their trail use.

2.1 The Outdoors

Rural areas often have vast wilderness spaces for hiking and other outdoor activities that have long been touted as an enriching, and worthy of preservation and even cultivation (Hardy et al. 2019; Nash 2014). However, not everyone has the same objectives when using wilderness spaces. Reasons have ranged from going to the trail as a means of "escape" (Mills and Butler 2005), in search for individual meaning (Berg 2015), coping with war losses (Shaffer 2004), responding to life crises (Strayed 2012), or as a sense of adventure (Bryson 1998). The revealed motivations have implications on the differing goals even among people who are identified as part of the same collection of people, which undermines any sweeping assumptions that are made about the outdoor space: who uses trails, what technology they use, and their attitudes toward the usage of said technologies.

Recent workshops focusing on Human–Computer Interaction have further highlighted the importance of the outdoor space and have spanned the discussion of the rural space in broad terms (Hardy et al. 2018), to more narrowly defining the aspects of the outdoors to identify both challenges and opportunities for designing for the outdoors (Jones et al. 2018), or focusing directly on a theme applied to a section of the outdoors such as technology on the trail (McCrickard et al. 2018).

As we elaborate further in later sections, many participants in these workshops contributed to this work, either by participating directly in the affinity diagramming sessions (Kotut et al. 2018a, b) or indirectly in the creation of this design and information space (Hardy et al. 2018; Jones et al. 2018).

2.2 The Trail

Our main focus in this chapter is the trail—as part of our *Technology on the Trail* initiative (McCrickard 2017), where we consider technology use and non-use involving different activities on the trail (Druin et al. 2017). These activities broadly involve technology that support *preparation* for the trail, aid the trail *experience* and facilitate post-trail *reflection* (Stelter and McCrickard 2017).

There are different trail users and identifying their needs and technology use is an important first step (Goldenberg et al. 2008). Fields (2017) leveraged the use of cultural probes to understand the technology needs of these trail users, to provide "harmonious" technology–nature design recommendations. Kondur (2018) expounded on the technology aspect by clustering trail users based on their technology use. To add richness to the clusters identified, Kondur then crafted personas that helped to reflect some of the differences among hikers in the identified clusters, such as the fact that, while younger trail users embrace technology, they yet lack financial resources to support their preferences.

Focusing on the larger trail community and especially considering the Triple Crown trails (Appalachian Trail, Continental Divide Trail, and the Pacific Crest

Trail), Bartolome (2018) leveraged Twitter data and topic modeling in an effort to identify topics that describe the distinct communities representing the three Triple Crown trails. Bartolome's work also considered depreciative trail behaviors to further understand cultural differences between trails and the larger hiker attitudes toward trail health, together with the tensions that arise in the case of conflicting trail ethos.

Similar overlap and conflict occurring across different types of trail users sharing the same trail space have been identified: hunters, for example, apply different ethos behind their choice of weapons depanding on the prey, and tension arise from the differing choices and conflicting ethos (Su and Cheon 2017). Tension can extend to preferences that preside over the choice of technology to use while on the trail (Ande et al. 2017), such as hikers who exercise preferring the use of headphones contrast to naturalists who study plant propagation on the trail.

These works show that the presence of groups with differing goals, practicing different ethos concerning trail use, and who have different reasons for using technology may be a source of tension or conflict on the trail. Our work considers the boundaries between groups and choices toward identifying opportunities for design in a manner that addresses these tensions.

2.3 Trail Users

In defining trail users, we consider the terminology of use. Which would best describe these users? And how do we differentiate between transient users such as thru-hikers, and permanent inhabitants of the trail environs such as farmers?

Differences between these terms have been long debated. Grudin's classic paper (Grudin 1994) does not explicitly define these terms, but it does refer to *groups* as a subset of an organization that tends to be small and task-focused while referring to *communities* as larger and loosely connected around ideas and themes (e.g., the CSCW community). Ospina differentiates groups as having a sense of belonging and shared purpose, while communities may share the belonging but may differ in their practices and values (Ospina 2017). We can also look to social media and "communities in cyberspace" (Wellman and Gulia 1999) for a distinction between these terms: a Facebook group is an invitation-based collection of people that share specific interests or backgrounds, while a Facebook community is open to anyone with an expressed interest in a topic. Once you are in a Facebook group, you have a great deal of power to post, comment, and invite others, while a Facebook community has a leadership structure that controls information flow.

Groups then, tend to be small, focused, and somewhat exclusive, with membership centered on some sort of common criteria such as thru-hiking or search and rescue work. Members of a group tend to have some familiarity with each other either in person or by the compatibility of goals. *Communities* on the other hand, would generally be larger and center on common beliefs, concerns, or behaviors (e.g., the Appalachian Trail Community that span across hikers of different types and distance, trail maintenance workers, foragers, scientists, etc.), or a shared space that is defined by a physical or natural border (Hoggett 1997), such as farmers or locals.

Given these definitions, we identify two distinct trail users: *Groups* to refer to transient or temporal users who are either passing-through or using the trail temporarily and *Communities* to refer to trail users who inhabit the trail or surrounding areas on a permanent basis, whose identities can also be inferred from physical or natural borders. The interaction between these distinct populations further provide insights into tensions that may emerge from differing ethos in the use of the trail, or differing attitudes around the use of technology on the trail. For instance, due to their transient nature, *Groups* tend to interact frequently with other *Communities* and *Groups*, and therefore have a better understanding of the overall culture, while at the same time, are more likely to cause tension especially in cases where trail etiquette and ethos are in opposition (e.g., improper food storage by hikers, and a proportional increase in bear–human conflict).

3   Our Approach

The role of technology enhances the personal experience on the trail, such as the use of fitbits and headphones (Ande et al. 2017), citizen scientist water quality monitoring, and logistical planning of trail practicalities (e.g., campsite reservations) (Kotut et al. 2020). However, tension can exist in the roles of groups or communities in outdoor settings. Hunters, for example, agree on the ethos of "fair chase" (Su and Cheon 2017), but different types of hunters differ on how they interpret this notion depending on their attitude toward the role of weapon technology (crossbows versus bows, rifles versus bows) in hunting.

By using participants who span trail stakeholders, trail users, and trail researchers, we endeavored to first curate an exhaustive list of trail users (Sect. 4), and then (1) identifying select groups that would most benefit from technology and (2) discussing tensions and conflicts that emerge from their interaction with technology (Sect. 5). Finally, using a minimal pair of definitions distinguishing between transient trail users (*Groups*) and those who permanently inhabit the trail or areas surrounding it (*Communities*), we sought to examine how the select trail-related collections of people differed in their goals and approaches, building upon previous inguiries (Kotut et al. 2018a, b) used to identify different facets of roles and goals for technology on the trail (Sect. 6).

4   Who's on the Trail

As an initial approach, we first wanted to identify the various users of a trail and then cluster these users into subgroups (e.g., day hikers, thru-hikers, etc.) so that later analyses could explore the goals, tensions, and commonalities among these

Fig. 1 Affinity
Diagramming/Cluster
Labeling Session

trail users. We describe the exercises to identify the trail users below and expound on the emerging groups and the design opportunities these groups present in this, and subsequent sections.

4.1 Identifying Trail Users

We organized an initial workshop activity and asked an estimated 25 participants that spanned trail users, trail stakeholders, and researchers on different aspects of the outdoors, to first identify types of trail users on Post-It notes, then to cluster them in subgroups of their choosing. Clustered subgroups were generated by participants who identified 132 unique types of trail users (excluding exact duplicates, while retaining singular/plural differences like scout and scouts). Participants spent a great deal of time crafting the notes, leaving little time for clustering—but at the same time, established the opportunity for the follow-up activity described here.

Our follow-up activity shifted the focus from people to their goals. We assembled a group of nine people, two professors and seven graduate students, to participate in a second affinity diagramming session (Fig. 1). The aim of this second session was first to cluster the trail users identified in the first workshop, and then to apply selective coding (Corbin and Strauss 1990) to identify axes of interest that would help to order and differentiate cluster items.

4.2 Who's on the Trail Findings

In discussing the rationale for note axis placement during the affinity diagramming session, it was clear that some of the notes did not fit the clusters they were placed in. This was made evident when participants considered all the clusters and the emergent patterns on holistic viewing. Mismatched notes were then moved around to a group with closer affinity and at the end of this exercise, seven clusters of different sizes emerged, with a consensus that cluster overlap yet remained.

Emergent Clusters

Part of the affinity diagramming exercise was to consider cluster naming, based on the commonality of each note in a given cluster. The cluster name should best describe all the notes in each cluster. Some clusters were easy to label, while the ones identified to have overlaps were more difficult to label. Seven initial clusters emerged and were named: *Management/Maintenance (Job), Passive/Active/ Thrill-Seeking Recreation, Socialize, Gatherers, Discovery/Research, Recreation, Exercise,* and *Discovery/Learning (Organization)*.

It was clear both from observing the cluster labeling exercise and the resulting discussion that the clusters with multiple labels had a lot of overlap and could be further refined. There was consensus on clusters labeled with mononyms as being satisfactorily descriptive. The remaining clusters would benefit from further fine-tuning. Out of this refinement exercise, 12 clusters emerged in total. New clusters tended to be a split of the original title and placed close to the parent cluster, the distance between clusters being arbitrary. The final clusters were labeled: *Volunteer, Job, Thrill-Seeking Recreation, Anti-Society Sentiment, Mental Health, Family Connection, Ad-Hoc Socializing, Formal Socializing, Active Recreation, Sight-seeing, Training,* and *Passive Recreation*.

The clustering exercises also made evident the order/hierarchy of hikers within a cluster: The likelihood of having single hikers, hikers with dogs or machines (e.g., bicycles, ATVs) in a specific group, easy to determine.

Axes of Interest

We then considered the relationships between clusters by contemplating possible axes placement with which the clusters would fit. We describe these axes below.

Anti-social Versus Extremely Social axis quickly emerged, as it naturally followed two general intentions: Broadly, tasks to complete in isolation on the trail versus people to meet while hiking on the trail. The "*Gatherers*" (e.g., mushroom gatherers) group was placed toward the *Anti-social* extreme on the axis, while families and dog walkers groups were placed toward the *Extremely Social* end.

Opportunists Versus Intentionalists axis also had a general consensus; one participant posited that it was because the axis was naturally goal oriented—the two labels forming the extreme end of the axes. *Sightseers, Time-killers* and *Picnickers* were considered **Opportunists**, while *thru-hikers, spelunkers* and *Birdwatchers* were considered **Intentionalists**. "**Accidental**" was a midpoint axis label that was suggested to represent spontaneous hikers—the Ad Hoc Socializing cluster that contained *Dog Walkers*, for example, fit this categorization.

Monetary Versus Altruistic axis emerged when considering monetary gains, or lack thereof. Users on the **Monetary** end of the scale were considered hikers who would not be on the trail if there was no incentive. Those grouped under the "job" affinity: *Trail Markers, Forest Rangers*, etc., were considered toward the **Monetary** end, while "Volunteer" hikers: *Trail Angels, firemen,* and *National Park Service (NPS) Volunteers* were placed toward the **Altruistic** end.

Mental Versus Physical axis considered internal (invisible) gains, and was made up of hikers positioned explicitly under the "**Mental**" affinity that included *Solo Day-Hikers, Nature Lovers, Thinkers* and *Rehab*, compared to external (**Physical**) goals (those with identifiable/visible results), for example: *Trail Markers, Loggers* and *Herbalists*.

Other Axes: *Experiential versus Task Oriented* was discussed as a potential axis but was ultimately rejected based on the fact that it was too connected: an experiential goal could turn into a task-oriented goal. Other axes considered but not discussed included: *Active versus Passive, Random versus Non-Random*, and *Good versus Evil*.

5   Inter-Group Tensions

Given our understanding of the people on the trail from the initial exercise, together with their clusters as determined by the affinity diagramming session, we wanted to have a fine-grained understanding of the groups. To achieve this, we used the trail user groups from the first workshop session as seeds in a second workshop to identify (1) those groups that would most benefit from technology and (2) groups that revealed tensions and conflict. In this section, we highlight interesting groups that emerged from the second workshop exercise and further, how different tensions surfaced. We then discuss design opportunities proffered by the tensions we identified.

5.1   Opportunity in Conflict

We engaged ten participants who are involved in research surrounding technology and the trail, during a GROUP[1] workshop session focused on discussing Technology on the Trail (McCrickard et al. 2018). We divided the participants into two equal teams (*blue team* and *yellow team*). We then had each group consider 35 unique hiker groups from the original workshop session (Table 1). We first approached the question of what technology design opportunities could be found in these groups and goals, by considering the question of benefit: which groups benefit from technology, and which do not? Each participant in the team was given eight votes: four (indicated with green dots) used to signify groups they judged to benefit from technology, the remaining four (red dots) to signify a detriment. Figure 2 highlights a selection of the groups and the votes for/against them.

---

[1] https://group.acm.org.

Table 1 35 unique groups were curated from previously identified hiker roles and used to determine technological benefits for each. Contentious and/or interesting groups are in bold, and we further discuss them below ([1]Mental/Physical, [2]Search and Rescue)

Activists	Guide-Book Authors	Park Rangers	S & R[2] Workers
Bikers/Activists	Herbalists	Plant Foragers	Section Hikers
Bird Watchers	Historians	Prof/Army Training	**Solo Hikers**
Boy/Girl Scouts	Hunters	Pet Owners	Sponsored Hikers
Day Hikers	Locals	Picnickers	**Tourists**
Exercisers	Loggers	Property Owners	Thru-Hikers
Families	Maintenance Workers	Recreational	Trail Angels
Farmers	**M/P[1] Rehab**	Retirees	
Fishermen	Horse-Back Riders	**Scientists**	

Fig. 2 Selection of trail users from the workshop session: *Tourists, Mental/Physical Rehab, Families* and *Solo Hikers*. These groups of hikers were considered contentious either because of the vote discrepancy between the two groups of participants (Comparing votes between the *Yellow* team versus *Blue* team) or based on explicit identification of a group being contention based on workshop participants discussion

5.2 Technology Opportunity Results

Figure 2 provides a glimpse of how each team voted across the hiker groups for the most contentious user groups. Two groups particularly stood out from this exercise based on the vote discrepancy across teams: *Mental and Physical Rehab*, received four red votes from the *yellow* team, signifying detriment from technology, and received no votes from the *blue* team. We also labeled *Solo Hikers* group as contentious for it received three green votes from the *blue* team with no votes from the *yellow* team.

After the clustering and voting exercise, the two participant teams were tasked with selecting a group of hikers considered to be interesting or contentious based on voting decisions. All participants would then discuss these groups to identify and understand inter-group tensions and possible design opportunities. Hiker groups were considered based on various subjective factors: how they were organized in clusters, how the participant teams voted for them, and how groups were selected by each team for further discussion. The selected groups were connected with interesting characteristics and underlying issues that led to the choices. We describe these connections below.

5.2.1 (Un)Clear Hiking Goals

Clarity, or lack thereof of group goals while on the trail was important. The *Families* group was selected by both teams as interesting not only in how to design for them, but also in how the group sparked debate on the difference between interacting with technology in contrast to with people on the trail, especially when the hiking goal is not clear. This discussion was also true of *Tourists* group, which received the most votes across the two teams and further prompted a debate on the definition of 'tourist.' For these groups, often there are conflicting goals within the families or tourists, and often the goals are more ephemeral and not tied to reaching a destination, collecting artifacts, or completing a task.

5.2.2 (Im)Practicality

When discussing the usefulness and practicality of technology on the trail, *Search & Rescue* group was voted for the group most likely to benefit—notably because of direct association of the service with technology. This conclusion was also realized with the *Scientists* group, tied with *Search & Rescue* in the number of votes received. All of these groups tend to have clearly defined goals that they wish to accomplish on the trail.

5.2.3 Assisting Versus Inhibiting

An unanticipated though interesting discussion emerged when considering the *Physical/Mental Rehab* group: the *yellow* team made a distinction between the *mental* and the *physical* elements of the hiking group, thus initiating a question regarding the efficacy of current technology, and possible technological innovations and applications to be used for purposes of mental rehab on the trail. Further, a debate was sparked on whether the technology would benefit or inhibit the experience of this group on the trail. Technology can be tied to mental stresses, suggesting that it should be avoided on trails. The exercise and the discussions revealed common use patterns that present opportunities for design, and also common themes that reveal tensions between and within groups.

5.2.4 Presence Versus Distraction

The teams were in agreement in attributing the most explicit source of tension/conflict between hikers groups to technology that distracts from the moment: Email, social media, notifications, etc. They were considered to negatively impact *Tourists*, for example, in contrast with those that undermine the trail experience of a hiker-group altogether like *Mental/Physical Rehab*. The *yellow* team was specific in differentiating between *Mental* and *Physical* aspects of rehab shown in Fig. 1) and vociferous in their opposition to technology because of the negative effects on mental well-being.

5.2.5 Experiential Versus Practical

Based on the discussion post-clustering, tension emerges between groups where the line between experiential and practical gains is blurred. *Families* is one group where the debate was whether the benefit the family gains from spending time chronicling the trail experience detracted from the experience of spending time with each other. The debate on *Guide-Book Authors* considered the redundancy of Guide-books with the popularity of online guides, against a preference for technology agnostic alternatives for some users on the trail.

5.2.6 Professional Versus Amateur

The user expertise level mattered in the discussions about whether they would benefit from technology or not. This was reflected in the votes for groups that would benefit from technology: *Search and Rescue Workers*, *Scientists*, and *Hunters*-as there was a perceived distinction on the expertise of these users and in how technology assisted in acquitting their work.

5.2.7 Limitation: Known Versus the Unknown

We acknowledge that the cause of tension between understood groups and those not well known. Our affinity diagramming sessions reflect the areas that are well known by the participants, particularly topics of interest to multiple people. This phenomenon was especially evident in the contrast between groups that got all green votes compared to those groups that did not receive any votes (e.g., *Solo Hikers*), or groups that received one vote from a knowledgeable participant that did not inspire others to vote for it (e.g., *Hunters*). We also note the explicit cases where the teams self-identify groups of hikers of which they do not fully grasp the breadth of what is involved in the technology: The *Farmers* group fell under this latter case.

6 Groups versus Communities on the Trail

After successfully identifying the technology space for design, there was a need to distinguish transient vs permanent trail users. Permanent users, unlike transient users, inhabit the trail and the area around it year-round and are affected by the choice of technology and habits of the transient users. We distinguished these users into *Groups* to describe the loose coupling of transient trail users, and *Communities* to refer to the users who live permanently on, or close to the trail. We found this differentiation to be important in helping to determine the impact of interactions and the effect of technology on the individual or a collective, either as a transient user or a permanent inhabitant of the trail.

From the users identified in the exercises we've described earlier in the chapter, and inspired by existing research that focus on these individual trail users (Schuring 2019), we considered the case of three types of users in an effort to delve deeper in understanding (1) their trail use, (2) their technology needs and/or technology used on the trail, and (3) interactions with other trail users, and the tensions and/or conflicts that emerge from these interactions.

6.1 Case 1: Thru-Hikers

Hiking as an activity can be done for recreation, wellness and fitness, competition, experiencing nature, and more. Hikers in the United States also tend to avoid urban areas and seek to embrace the wilderness (Bryson 1998). The thru-hiker has the goal of completing a chosen trail in its entirety within one hiking season (Fondren 2016; Shaffer 2004; Strayed 2012). An attempt of the 2,190 mile Appalachian Trail (AT), for example, would take several months to complete in one hiking season (Fondren 2016).

The community tends to be important to thru-hikers, given the numerous Facebook pages, blogs, planned meet-ups, and other social media and activities that are customarily used before, during, and after the hike (Kotut et al. 2020). Additionally, many hikers embrace the notion of a group with fellow hikers—often seeking to camp together, share meal planning, and splitting the weight of tents and cookware (Bryson 1998). In addition to this, thru-hikers are also known to remain connected with other groups (e.g., families, co-workers) and find ways to maintain those social bonds even while undertaking the hike.

Despite the commonality of the overarching "thru-hike" goal, conflict arises between groups on issues of preferences such as taste in (or absence of) music, communication styles, etc.

6.2 Case 2: Exercisers

Examples of trail users considered as exercisers include day hikers, bikers, joggers, and horseback riders. This classification emerged through consideration of shared goals associated with exercises and training: losing weight, muscle building, endurance training, general fitness, or simply as a means of deriving personal fulfillment and pleasure. These on common bities may be derived from the environment/place that such individuals choose to use-that is, the choice of outdoors as a means of engaging in exercise activity over indoor alternatives. This suggests that exercisers seek to fulfill specific wants, needs, and goals that may be either inter-connected or independent of the activity and exercise-related goals. Perceptions of enhanced enjoyment, fulfillment, motivation, sense of peace, solitude, and/or richer stimulus, may all be reasons why such individuals opt to use the outdoors because users have inter-related, competing, and sometimes conflicting priorities in terms or want and need fulfillment.

As such, a number of perspectives may emerge. For a given exercise, one may argue that these individuals may be viewed to be a group or a community depending on their level of involvement, interaction, and commitment. A great many devices and exercise programs leverage group behaviors, either cooperatively or competitively. From the community perspective, some shared norms, behavior, or culture related to preserving individual community member's "sense" of the outdoor medium emerge and influence the actions of the members. This may include an increased awareness of, and respect for, the outdoor exercise experience of a fellow member of the community of outdoor exercisers. A member of such a community may be more aware of the effect of intrusive stimuli; for example, noise pollution from a jogger listening to music without the aid of headphones. As such, they are likely to engage in their activity in a manner that preserves the sense of place.

6.3   Case 3: Activists

Activists as trail-users emerged from the original exercise when considering peo-ple who care about the trail, in combination with short-term goals (e.g., proper trash disposal) and long-term strategies (e.g., sustainability as evidenced by activists protesting pipeline construction impacting the trail (Appalachian Trail Conservancy 2018)). In reviewing our prior clustering activity, participants considered the trail-user placement on a social scale based on willingness to socialize, where *anti-social* and *extremely social* emerged as opposing extremes on the axis. Trail users tend-ing toward the *extremely social* end of the scale were labeled as "people to meet while hiking on the trail" (Kotut et al. 2018a), and the activists' nature of promot-ing/protesting actions on the trail and the inevitability of encounters with other trail users lend them toward this group categorization.

However, the goals of activists can differ. Does the need of those who call for the preservation of the integrity of the trail usurp those who lobby for economic benefits from a pipeline? This possibility of sharply opposing goals seems to preclude the categorization of activists as a community. Diverging goals aside, however, what we find to be common concerns across different activist groups are issues of reach—given what definition emerged during the activity and considering examples from the trail (Appalachian Trail Conservancy 2018), and that is mobilization.

7 Discussion

Before designing for the trail, we argue that we need to understand the users and the tensions they experience. From our findings resulting from the three workshop sessions we describe above, we posit that differences within fairly well-defined professions, hobbies, and activities can highlight conflicts.

Our pursuit of approaches for designing for the trail necessitates understanding the tension between trail users and how they interact with technology. Based on the discussions, we underscore the importance of distinguishing between experiencing the trail and assisting on the trail. Planning with this consideration in mind allows us to design to assist and augment the enterprise, without detracting from the experience.

Future exercises should consider explicit tensions that may follow the common themes we have discussed in this paper that would additionaly serve to inform further design opportunities. We argue that the tensions that were identified should lead to focus groups with key stakeholders, rich persona identification that highlights a depth of features, and scenarios of use that provide narrative descriptions of technology on the trail.

8 Recommendations and Conclusion

The insights gained from the three exercises and the respective discussions provide a launching point in considering future directions:

- Having an understanding of the dynamics of hikers within a group and the relationship between different groups can reveal the gaps that present the design opportunities for encouraging community and defusing intra- and inter-group conflict.
- Opportunities emerge for reaching out to specific groups or individuals within a group to aid our understanding of both the dynamics and the context of these hikers.
- When considering design opportunities in general, we have different levels of abstraction to explore: Designing for a group, for intra-group hierarchy, for group size and for different combinations of axes.
- Future work might also consider which affordances available from current technologies (e.g., GPS tracking, biometric sensing) are relevant to specific groups and which are not.
- Other work sessions could serve to showcase these insights and offer an opportunity to incorporate feedback.

In conclusion, we highlight four takeaways from the insights we gained from the three exercises: (1) The population of people who use the trail in various grouping and with differing goals provide a rich source for both design consideration and design feedback. (2) There is an immense space to consider and design technology to be used either on the trail or in the general outdoors, and while (3) technology is already being (re)used in the trail by different users in pursuit of different goals, examining its use/non-use would lead to a deeper understanding of trail needs by different users, and finally, (4) there are ample opportunities to understand and design for technology–human interaction in a manner that accounts for inter-group tensions or that mitigates group–community conflict.

References

Anderson Z, Lusk C, Jones MD (2017) Towards understanding hikers' technology preferences. In: Proceedings of the 2017 ACM international joint conference on pervasive and ubiquitous computing and proceedings of the 2017 ACM international symposium on wearable computers, UbiComp '17, New York, NY, USA. ACM, pp 1–4

Bartolome A (2018) Describing trail cultures through studying trail stakeholders and analyzing their tweets. Master's thesis, Virginia Tech, Blacksburg, Virginia, 8

Berg A (2015) "To conquer myself": the new strenuosity and the emergence of "thru-hiking" on the appalachian trail in the 1970s. J Sport Hist 42(1):1–19

Bryson B (1998) A walk in the woods: rediscovering America on the Appalachian Trail. Broadway, New York, NY, USA

Appalachian Trail Conservancy (2018) A prime example of bad energy development

Corbin JM, Strauss A (1990) Grounded theory research: procedures, canons, and evaluative criteria. Qual Sociol 13(1):3–21

Druin A, Dix A, Harmon E, Su N (2017) Technology on the trail 2017 workshop

Fields SG (2017) Technology on the trail: Using cultural probes to understand hiker. Master's thesis, Virginia Tech, Blacksburg, Virginia, 8

Fondren KM (2016) Walking on the wild side: long-distance hiking on the Appalachian Trail. Rutgers University Press, New Brunswick, NJ, USA

Goldenberg M, Hill E, Freidt B (2008) Why individuals hike the appalachian trail: a qualitative approach to benefits. J Exp Educ 30(3):277–281

Grudin J (1994) Computer-supported cooperative work: history and focus. Computer 27(5):19–26

Hardy J, Dailey D, Wyche S, Su NM (2018) Rural computing: Beyond access and infrastructure. In: Companion of the 2018 ACM conference on computer supported cooperative work and social computing. CSCW '18, New York, NY, USA. ACM, pp 463–470

Hardy J, Phelan C, Vigil-Hayes M, Su NM, Wyche S (2019) Designing from the rural. Interactions 26(4):37–41

Hoggett P (1997) Contested communities: experiences, struggles policies. Policy Press, Bristol, England

Jones MD, Anderson Z, Häkkilä J, Cheverst K, Daiber F (2018) Hci outdoors: understanding human-computer interaction in outdoor recreation. In: Extended abstracts of the 2018 CHI conference on human factors in computing systems, CHI EA '18, New York, NY, USA. ACM, pp W12:1–W12:8

Kondur N (2018) Using k-mode clustering to identify personas for technology on the trail. Master's thesis, Virginia Tech, Blacksburg, Virginia, 6

Kotut L, Horning M, Harrison S, McCrickard DS (2018) Opportunity in conflict: understanding tension among key groups on the trail. In: HCI Outdoors Workshop at ACM CHI

Kotut L, Horning M, McCrickard S (2018) Who's on the trail: identifying trail uses with affinity diagrams. In: Technology on the trail workshop at ACM GROUP

Kotut L, Horning M, Stelter TL, McCrickard DS (2020) Preparing for the unexpected: community framework for social media use and social support by trail thru-hikers. In: Proceedings of the SIGCHI conference on human factors in computing systems, CHI '20, New York, NY, USA. ACM

McCrickard DS (2017) Technology on the trail

McCrickard DS, Horning MA, Harrison S, Harmon E, Dix A, Su NM, Stelter T (2018) Technology on the trail. In: Proceedings of the 2018 ACM conference on supporting groupwork, GROUP '18, New York, NY, USA. ACM, pp 365–368

Mills AS, Butler TS (2005) Flow experience among appalachian trail thru-hikers. In: Proceedings of the 2005 northeastern recreation research symposium, US Forest Service, Newtown Square, PA, USA, pp 366–370. US Forest Service, Northeastern Research Station

Nash R (2014) Wilderness and the American Mind, 5th edn. Yale University Press, New Haven, CT, USA

Ospina D (2017) The difference between communities, groups, and networks

Schuring SA(2019) Meandering motivations: a look into the changing motivations of appalachian trail thru-hiker. Master's thesis, Ohio University, Athens, Ohio, USA

Shaffer EV (2004) Walking with Spring. Appalachian trail conference, harpers ferry, WV (1st edn)

Stelter T, McCrickard DS (207) Hiking the appalachian trail with technology. In: NatureCHI 2017 workshop at MobileHCI 2017

Strayed C (2012) Wild: from lost to found on the pacific crest trail. Vintage, New York, NY, USA

Su NM, Cheon EJ (2017) Reconsidering nature: The dialectics of fair chase in the practices of american midwest hunters. In: Proceedings of the 2017 CHI conference on human factors in computing systems, CHI '17, New York, NY, USA. ACM, pp 6089–6100

Wellman B, Milena G (1999) Virtual communities as communities. Communities in cyberspace, pp 167–194

Shared Family Experiences Over Distance in the Outdoors

Carman Neustaedter, Yasamin Heshmat, Brennan Jones, Azadeh Forghani, and Xiaoxuan Xiong

Abstract When family and friends live apart, they often want to connect over distance to stay in touch and be a part of each other's lives. Yet this can be challenging with existing technologies. Video chat systems begin to bridge this gap by providing views into remote spaces and of remote people. However, such systems are often designed to support conversations and not richer activities that a person might like to do with a family member or friend as if they were together in person. For example, this might include going for a walk together, riding bicycles, or site seeing. We have designed a number of 'shared family experiences' over distance that allow family members and friends to participate in outdoor activities together regardless of where they are located. The emphasis is on two-way video and audio links. Through two example projects—Shared Bicycling and Beam Geocaching—we describe the challenges and nuances of designing to support shared experiences over distance in the outdoors. We focus on how feelings of presence can be created, the sensations of the outdoors, and privacy challenges from the participation in 'private' activities in public spaces.

C. Neustaedter (✉) · Y. Heshmat · B. Jones · A. Forghani
School of Interactive Arts and Technology, Simon Fraser University, Surrey, Canada
e-mail: carman@sfu.ca

Y. Heshmat
e-mail: yheshmat@sfu.ca

B. Jones
e-mail: bdgjones@ucalgary.ca

A. Forghani
e-mail: azadehf@sfu.ca

B. Jones
Department of Computer Science, University of Calgary, Calgary, Canada

X. Xiong
School of Design, Hunan University, Changsha, China
e-mail: Sanzhichazi@icloud.com

© Springer Nature Switzerland AG 2020
D. S. McCrickard et al. (eds.), *HCI Outdoors: Theory, Design, Methods and Applications*, Human–Computer Interaction Series,
https://doi.org/10.1007/978-3-030-45289-6_8

155

1 Introduction

Many people live far away from their family members or close friends. This happens across the lifespan as people move to different cities for work or school, as well as a multitude of other reasons. Despite the distance separation, people often still want to stay connected with their loved ones to know what they are up to and feel like they are part of their lives (Neustaedter et al. 2006, 2013a, b). Common ways of connecting over distance include using the phone, text messaging, and video chatting (Neustaedter et al. 2006). By video chat, we refer to video-based calls using software such as Skype, Apple FaceTime, or Google Hangouts. Video chat has shown to offer promise for a multitude of relationships because of the technology's ability to show remote people and their environment (Ames et al. 2010; Judge and Neustaedter 2010; Kirk et al. 2010; Forghani and Neustaedter 2014). This includes grandparents and grandchildren, long-distance partners, and parents and their adult children. However, the challenge with the way that video chat systems are commonly designed is that they tend to focus on supporting conversations, as opposed to the sharing of activities and experiences over distance (Brubaker et al. 2012; Inkpen et al. 2013). As an example, while it might be easy for long-distance partners to talk to each other about their day over video chat and see each other's facial expressions to understand one's emotional response, it is much more difficult for the couple to actually participate in an activity together like cooking, watching a movie, or playing a game. This is important because leisure activities have been found to help people establish strong relationships and high degrees of life satisfaction (Agate et al. 2009; Zabriskie and McCormick 2003). Shared activities are also a core part of healthy couple relationships (Stafford 2005).

We also know that many of the activities people like to do with their family and friends occur in the outdoors and rightfully so. The outdoors brings the opportunity to travel to different places, experience new sites, and participate in activities that promote healthy lifestyles. Depending on the person, outdoor activities might include, for example, bicycle riding, walking or hiking, site seeing, or playing sports together. Naturally, doing such activities with a collocated family member or close friend is relatively easy. The difficult part comes when people live far apart. Most video chat systems today support calls from a mobile phone, which could easily happen outside. Yet it can be especially cumbersome to do more than just talking with someone while outdoors and mobile. This means that activities such as bicycle riding or site seeing with a distance-separate loved one are very difficult to do or quite sometimes even impossible.

Our research has explored this space by studying shared outdoor experiences over distance and designing technology probes to support family and friend connections. A *shared experience* is one where two people participate in an activity together over distance like walking or bicycle riding using video chat technology to connect them. Here, they can see each other or their environment and have conversations while they do the activity, as desired. This is in contrast to just having a conversation where two people look at each other and talk. For example, people may video call each other from home and have a conversation while at their dining table. In this case, no activity takes place besides conversing. In this chapter, we talk about two explorations of shared experiences—Shared Bicycling and Beam Geocaching—that make use of audio and video links to connect people over distance. We have selected these two projects as focal points given the diversity in the technology being used. The first, Shared Bicycling, uses a configuration of mobile phones linked to a bicycle to allow two people to experience a bicycle ride 'together' while seeing the remote location and sharing conversation. The second, Beam Geocaching, uses a telepresence robot called a *Beam* (made by Suitable Technologies) to provide a physical form or 'embodiment' for a remote family member that can aid the shared experience of walking, site seeing, and searching for 'hidden treasures' as a part of the location-based game of geocaching. We use these two examples to draw out opportunities and challenges for designing shared family experiences over distance in the outdoors.

2 Shared Bicycling

Bicycling is a common activity that many people do around the world either alone or with others. As an outdoor leisure activity, it is interesting because it can be fairly fast-paced, or it can be slow. It raises interesting safety questions since there can often be bystanders or motorized vehicles where a person is bicycling.

We were interested in understanding how two people may be able to participate in a bicycle ride together over distance in two situations. First, we wanted to learn what it might be like for two people to go bicycling at the same, but in two different locations where they would connect through video and audio links. Second, we wanted to explore the experience if one person was at home and connecting to another person who was bicycling. We felt this situation might arise if a person was, for example, facing health issues and could not leave their home. This could allow a home-bound person to still experience aspects of the outdoors despite not physically being able to do so.

One of the goals of our research is to rapidly prototype technologies so that we can try them out in realistic situations. The effort is focused on understanding the experience the technology creates rather than spending large portions of time intricately developing and implementing the technology. As a result, we often use commercial systems for study explorations or will alter existing systems, including both software and hardware, in new and interesting ways. For Shared Bicycling, we took existing commercial video chat software, in the form of Google + Hangouts, along with smartphones, and created a four-way video call system that could be attached to two bicycles. Figure 1 shows a cyclist riding with the technology setup and Fig. 2 shows a close-up view of the smartphones. One smartphone is facing towards the cyclist's face so that the camera captures and streams the person, while the second smartphone is facing towards the cyclist's environment. This provides a view of one's context and anything that they may wish to show the remote family member. A single Google + Hangouts video call shares the four video feeds, two from each bicycle. The cyclist can tap on a thumbnail of each video on the smartphone to change

Fig. 1 A cyclist riding a bicycle while streaming the experience to a remote family member

Fig. 2 The technology setup for Shared Bicycling showing the remote cyclist

which view is shown (Fig. 2). In this way, the video feeds are selectively available whenever the cyclist glances down at the display. This might be, for example, when they stop to take a short break, or when there is not a lot of traffic around. Of course, we recognize the safety issues with 'distracted driving' and return to this topic later. Family members share audio during the experience using an earbud with a built-in microphone. Additional details about the technology probe can be found in Neustaedter et al. (2017).

We studied Shared Bicycling with fourteen pairs of family members or friends within Vancouver, Canada (full details are in Neustaedter et al. 2017). In the study, half of the pairs tried out Shared Bicycling as a parallel experience. Here, both partners went for a bicycle ride at the same time but in different areas to simulate the idea that the two partners were connecting over a large distance. The other half of the participants engaged in a mixed experience where one person went bicycling and the other connected from a location of their choosing, e.g., home, coffee shop. Here, we tried to simulate the situation of a person being unable to go outdoors due to health conditions. In both study setups, participants were able to choose their own bicycle route and duration, though we asked them to try and ride anywhere between 30 and 60 min (in addition to training time). We felt this would provide enough time for them to get used to the technology and the shared experience, while not making the study overly long to participate in. Participants rode in areas containing parks and sometimes tourist attractions.

After their bicycle ride, we conducted semi-structured interviews with each participant to understand what their experience was like, where the technology probe worked well, and where it made the shared experience more challenging. We transcribed all of the interviews and then performed a thematic analysis on the transcriptions. This involved noting all of the reactions from participants to the experience, grouping them visually using an affinity diagramming process, and selecting what we felt were main themes. In the following sections, we describe the core themes that we feel are important for the design of shared outdoor experiences based on our Shared Bicycling study.

2.1 Camera Work and Video Usage

Camera work is the continual orientation and placement of a mobile video camera to provide good views for remote users (Inkpen et al. 2013; Jones et al. 2015; Rae et al. 2015). Prior research has found camera work to be difficult when sharing experiences using video chat because it can be hard for people to orient their camera to show exactly what they want when holding and using a smartphone (Inkpen et al. 2013). In turn, remote viewers often want more control over the view than they are able to see, which puts pressure on the person operating the phone and its camera (Massimi and Neustaedter 2014). With Shared Bicycling, the camera work was automated in the sense that one camera automatically captured the bicyclist's face, and the other camera automatically captured whatever the bicycle was pointing at. This would shift if the cyclist turned the bicycle's handlebars creating more control over the view, yet control was limited because the bicycle had to correspondingly be steered in a safe manner. For example, Fig. 3 shows a situation where a cyclist stops to point the camera at a water fountain to show a remote partner.

Participants in our study valued being able to see both the third-person view of their partner's face and they also valued seeing the environment through the first-person view. For both the parallel and mixed experiences, the view of one's partner

Fig. 3 A cyclist stops to show their remote partner a water fountain

was most valuable though in terms of creating a sense of connection and closeness because people loved to see the facial reactions of their partner. This is what made them feel close. Because participants could only see one view at a time, it meant they would have to switch views by touching the screen on the smartphone. This tended to happen infrequently and only in cases where partners really wanted to show each other something. For example, one participant stopped riding for a moment to show his partner the view of an airplane taking off from the airport. Otherwise, the remote partner spent nearly the entire bicycle ride with her partner's face shown on the video feed. Other participants described showing interesting sites near them and other people of interest, e.g., people staring at them, people wearing funny clothes, a wedding in the park. This worked well if the thing they were looking at took some time to see. People were less apt to stop and show something if it was easily passed by because this meant it would be quickly gone before they could show their remote partner.

Some of the most rewarding experiences we saw in our study were in the mixed setup where one person was able to watch their partner's bicycle experience. This was especially valuable when the remote partner had not been to the cyclist's location. For example, one pair of participants was long-distance siblings who had not talked in months. One was local to our study and rode the bicycle to show her remote brother what the city was like. This sibling lived in Germany and had never been to Vancouver, Canada. The stationary user-watched both camera views quite heavily during the study, while the local participant toured the remote sibling around the area. Here, she shared views of the harbor, local restaurants, and statues.

We also observed safety challenges when performing Shared Bicycling. As previously mentioned, there are potential safety issues when there are lots of people or motor vehicles around the cyclist. It can be unsafe to look at a video stream of one's partner. Participants generally felt safe in using a video feed while bicycle riding in our study, but it was not before developing careful strategies around when and how to look at the video feed. Bicycling participants used audio throughout the ride to communicate with their partner while the video was used during times that they deemed were more appropriate, i.e., when streets were not busy when there were fewer people around. When looking at the video feed, they recognized the need to glance rather than stay focused on it. In mixed setups, because one person is not actually riding a bicycle, the safety concerns may lessen, in particular for the remote participant. The caveat is that an asymmetry exists in the experiences; while the remote participant can easily watch the camera's views, the local participant riding the bicycle cannot.

2.2 Intimacy and Engagement

Participants in our study shared an audio link using headphones and a built-in microphone. This allowed them to have a conversation whenever they liked throughout the activity. Given the placement of the earpiece in each partner's ear, it gave partners a very intimate level of access to each other. Some participants described it in a way that was similar to how one might whisper in another person's ear to share intimate details about a situation where others around are not able to hear. This intimate access to one's partner created strong feelings of presence and closeness when riding together or when watching the remote partner ride. Engagement with one's partner was continuous and lasted throughout the study for nearly all pairs. Participants were not interrupted by others around them and they did not stop to talk with bystanders. Instead, they stayed engaged in the activity solely with their partner. The speed of the activity and the continuous movement of the bicycle meant that it was much more difficult to be engaged with others around oneself. Given the value of the audio link, participants said that the video link was of secondary importance to them. This was especially the case during parallel experiences because it was harder to look at the camera view while cycling.

Conversations between partners tended to be about the same things that a pair said they would normally talk about over the phone or when in person. This included their day-to-day activities, relationships, work, or school, etc. Thus, the conversation was much less about the activity of bicycling and more about life in general. That is, participants tended to stay with the familiar—what they might normally talk about over video chat—rather than create new kinds of conversations that might focus around the novelty of the activity itself, the act of bicycling, or what they were seeing around them. Participants in the mixed set-up talked more about their surroundings because the stationary participant was able to concentrate more on the video feeds and ask questions about the surroundings. This was particularly important for those who were unfamiliar with the remote location.

Many outdoor activities involve physical activity and, clearly, this is the case for bicycling. Bicycling is not always easy and, for some people, its strenuous nature can affect how connected one feels with a remote partner. Some participants were not used to bicycling and felt that having to bicycle while using the technology probe was tiring. Not all had chosen bicycling routes that were easy to do and some involved steep inclines. Other participants were not used to bicycling regularly and even flat roads were challenging. Thus, the physicality of the activity made it difficult to stay engaged with a remote partner because they had to focus more on bicycling than conversing or glancing at the partner's view. Participants said that conversations were sometimes not very deep because they were talking and concentrating on bicycling at the same time.

2.3 Privacy and Embodiment Challenges

When participating in an outdoor activity, the outdoor environment often creates environmental constraints that affect the activity. For example, the wind blows or there might be sounds from traffic. These types of things can affect the experience. Participants in our study talked about having to raise their voices when bicycling so that their partner could hear them. They also had to sometimes listen hard. Participants even noted that they would sometimes self-filter what they would say aloud because they knew they were talking more loudly than normal and that others around might be able to hear them. This caused some participants to gossip less, talk less about the people around them, or choose words carefully (e.g., no swearing).

In addition, we found that the lack of embodiment for the remote person created interesting dynamics. By embodiment, we are referring to the way a person is physically represented in a remote space. In Shared Bicycling, the remote person is embodied on the video display itself since that is where the remote person can be seen. Yet given the setup, the only person who can really see the remote person is the cyclist. In addition, the remote person is embodied by earbuds that the cyclist wears. That is, other people in the area of the cyclist can tell that the cyclist has earbuds in their ears if there is a wire coming from the phone, as found in Fig. 4. This typically suggests one of two things: either the cyclist is listening to music, or the cyclist is having a phone call with a remote person. In these ways, the remote person is physically represented in the experience, but it is ambiguous, and bystanders do not know for sure who is 'there.' It is likely the case that they would not expect that one would also have a video stream to view in addition to an audio link with the cyclist. Participants commented on this experience as some people received awkward looks or stares from bystanders because they were talking in what could be considered a loud voice. There are also likely privacy concerns from bystanders who would be susceptible to being streamed by the video link without even realizing it (Singhal et al. 2016).

Lastly, the setup of the technology probe sometimes created feelings of awkwardness in terms of where one of the cameras was placed. The camera tended to look up at participants and so it would often capture views up one's nose (Fig. 5). Depending on a person's height, cameras sometimes would look directly at one's chest. This

Fig. 4 The earbud cable acts as an embodiment for the remote person

Fig. 5 An awkward camera angle up a person's nose

was felt to be inappropriate by some of the female participants in our study. Even if the camera was not initially aimed at a participant in an awkward or socially inappropriate way, because of the nature of the activity and the shaking of the bicycle, the mounts holding the smartphones could easily adjust and change the orientation of the camera. These issues raise challenges around where cameras are placed and how they might change over time.

3 Beam Geocaching

Following our experience with Shared Bicycling, we were interested in exploring what might happen if a remote person had greater control over their camera view as well as a much richer embodiment in the remote space. That is, we were curious about what would happen if they had an actual *body*. Here, we turned to telepresence robots. Telepresence robots are remotely drivable video conferencing systems, as seen in Fig. 6. For our work, we used the *Beam* + telepresence robot. The top of this robot contains a display with an embedded camera. There is also a camera facing the ground to aid navigation. The remote user can drive the robot using a computer keyboard or a video gaming controller plugged into their computer. Their computer shows the two camera views, as shown in Fig. 7.

Fig. 6 The telepresence robot used in Beam Geocaching

Fig. 7 The telepresence robot view while driving, using the Beam's default cameras

Telepresence robots have been found to increase one's sense of presence in remote workplaces and home environments due to their mobility (Lee and Takayama 2011; Rae et al. 2013; Neustaedter et al. 2018; Rae and Neustaedter 2017). That is, because a remote user has a physical body and takes up space, they can feel more present (Yang and Neustaedter 2018). Similarly, simple acts that might seem frustrating, like bumping into objects, actually help to create a stronger sense of presence in

Fig. 8 A geocache hide under some trees (left) and a geocache container (right)

the remote space (Yang et al. 2018). While telepresence robots have been studied in many locations and contexts (e.g., work, home, schools, hospitals), there are very few studies of their usage in outdoor settings.

The shared activity we decided to study was geocaching. Geocaching is a location-based game where players use GPS coordinates shown in a mobile phone app to find 'hidden treasures,' often metal or Tupperware containers with toys and a logbook to record one's name after a find (Fig. 8). Geocaching is a highly collaborative activity where groups of family or friends go searching for geocaches together when collocated (O'Hara 2008; Neustaedter et al. 2013a, b). People travel to new locations to find geocaches as a part of explorations. They also intertwine geocaching hunting with their everyday activities, like going to the grocery store or a child's sporting event (O'Hara 2008). What makes geocaching interesting is its incorporation of a variety of outdoor activities, including hiking and site seeing. It is also a slower paced activity than bicycling, which lends itself to a different type of context.

We studied Beam Geocaching with 14 pairs of participants: one person in each pair used the telepresence robot to go with a partner who geocached in-person. For half of the geocaching activity, the remote partner operated the robot using its two normal cameras: one facing forward and one facing the ground. For the other half of the activity, they used the robot with a 360° camera attached to the top of the robot (Fig. 6, with foam around the robot to protect it from falling). They used a virtual reality (VR) headset to see the 360° camera view; Fig. 9 shows the user with a VR headset on and Fig. 10 shows the 360° view in an equirectangular format. This view meant that participants could turn their head in any direction and see what was happening in the remote space, without having to turn the robot using their gaming controller. Partners went geocaching within a local park next to our university campus.

We observed all of the participants by going along with them during their geocaching activity and observing from a short distance away. After they were finished, we conducted semi-structured interviews individually to understand their experience. We asked questions about what worked well and what did not work well with technology and activity. Interviews were fully transcribed and then we using

Fig. 9 A participant drives the telepresence robot using a gaming controller while wearing a VR headset to see a 360° view around the robot

Fig. 10 The 360° view while geocaching in a telepresence robot

coding techniques to analyze them. This included the use of open, axial, and selective coding to figure out what themes were occurring, group the themes into categories, and then select the most important themes, respectively. Full details of the study setup and its results are in Heshmat et al. (2018). In the following sections, we describe the ways in which the technology made people feel present with one another over distance, how the sensations of being in the outdoors were transmitted (or not) and the privacy concerns that arose. We directly compare these findings to those from Shared Bicycling.

3.1   A Physical Embodiment

In this study, we learned that the physicality of the robot itself aided the experience of 'being with' one's partner as a whole. Partners, who were local to the robot in the environment, even imagined that the robot's body *was* their partner. Thus, they were able to extend their mental representation of their remote family member or friend to the robot itself. In turn, the remote participants who were driving the robot especially valued the ability to move around in the outdoors. This created strong feelings of being in the remote space because they could move through it, 'feel' the bumps in the sidewalk of the park (as the robot bounced the camera view), and turn the robot to look around or turn their head if they were using the 360° camera and VR setup. Sometimes the remote person even accidentally bumped into their local partner who was with the robot. This was a reminder to both people that they were there 'together' doing the activity. Such feelings were not present in Shared Bicycling because remote partners did not have a physical presence in the space; rather, they could only see it.

As an activity, geocaching involves walking to a general location shown by the GPS coordinates. This is an activity that people typically do together, talking as they go (Neustaedter et al. 2013a, b). Once there, players search for the hidden container amongst bushes, trees, rocks, and any other objects nearby that it might be hidden under or behind. Here, people often spread out and independently work to find the container (Neustaedter et al. 2013a, b). In our study, remote participants felt empowered as they could do both activities. They could drive to a specific location and talk with their partner as they went. Once arriving, they could independently move around and look for the geocache too. This additional mobility made them feel more immersed in the remote space given the autonomy and freedom to control what they saw and when they saw it. They could look for the geocache themselves and they could also enjoy the outdoor environment by looking around.

Yet not everything was easy to do in the physical environment using the robot and cameras. The robot drove slower than a person's typical walking pace, so participants local to the robot had to walk more slowly to be 'with' their partner. Different speeds of movement could create undesirable power dynamics, e.g., the local partner can sometimes feel like they have to always wait for the remote person's robot. The cameras were not always good enough to see the specifics of the locations that the geocaches were hidden in. Because the robots didn't have arms, remote participants couldn't move objects to look behind them for the geocache container. In these ways, the experience using the telepresence robot felt more 'real' than simply using video chat software and a phone, but the robot was still not enough to mimic the experience of actually performing the activity in person.

3.2   Outdoor Effects

The outdoors come with a range of sensations not typically experienced in indoor settings. In the environment where people geocached, this included the smells of flowers in the park, freshly cut grass, the occasional wind breeze, a warm sun, and ambient noises from vehicles driving on the adjacent roads. The remote participants in our study talked about how some of these aspects were noticeably missing when geocaching. They experienced the sights and sounds of the park but missed out on the smells and environmental feelings of being in the outdoors. Participants talked about how these additional aspects of the outdoors would sometimes calm themselves. For example, the warmth of the sun sometimes puts people in better moods, or the smell of flowers may remind them to enjoy the simple things in life. In the Shared Bicycling study, these feelings were present for both participants when they were both in the outdoors, yet there could have been differences in what the two remote environments provided to each participant.

The outdoors also come with varying types of surfaces that a person moves over. In the park, this was a concrete sidewalk and grass areas. People sometimes had to step into dirt flower beds to reach in for a geocache container or to move shrubbery to see if a container was hidden. The telepresence robot was only able to move around on the sidewalks, but it was not always easy. Sometimes the robot would get stuck on cracks on the sidewalk. Some participants were apprehensive about driving the robot in certain areas for fear it might tip over. This created feelings of asymmetry; that is, the remote participant was not able to do everything that the local person could do. Participants local to the robot would sometimes feel a sense of responsibility for the robot, wanting to make sure it didn't tip over or being ready and able to catch it if it did. In these ways, the technology took away from the shared experience. This could in turn have negative effects on a relationship if one must depend on another in a way that is new or unexpected. In the Shared Bicycling work, we did not see such dependencies emerge when both participants were bicycling because they were in two separate spaces, and not the same location. The activity was also relatively passive in nature and did not involve coordination (e.g., mutually hunting for an object). Thus, there are differences when you join people together in the same 'shared place' as compared to connecting two distinctly separate spaces, especially when coordination is needed to complete an activity.

Fig. 11 A participant leans in to talk to his remote partner

3.3 Privacy and the General Public

Because the activities in Beam Geocaching are at a much slower pace (e.g., walking) than Shared Bicycling and riding a bicycle, environmental attributes like the wind did not affect the ways in which people talked with one another. That is, they did not typically need to talk louder to be heard. Moreover, the sound from the remote participant came out of the robot, as opposed to a pair of earbuds like Shared Bicycling. This meant that anybody in the general public who was in close proximity could hear conversations between partners, much like what would happen if people were geocaching together in person. As a result, some participants would move closer to each other (to the robot) to talk privately (Fig. 11). This resembled collocated geocaching.

The telepresence robot was considered a novel technology by participants and it received a large number of looks from bystanders in the park. Not all participants liked this additional attention. Remote participants felt they were 'on display' because their face was typically the only thing shown on the robot's screen and it was relatively large. This contrasts with Shared Bicycling because the remote person is really not visible to bystanders given that they are only shown on a smartphone pointed towards the cyclist. The additional attention meant that some participants felt like they were not doing an activity just with their partner. Instead, it was more of a public spectacle than an intimate shared activity with a family member or friend.

Participants recognized that the nature of the activity was somewhat slow-paced, and this meant that the robot's camera was often fixed on areas for long periods of time. This is different than Shared Bicycling because the bicycle moves quickly as does the view of what is shown over the video link. Participants were concerned that people around them in the park may not know that they weren't recording their activities and might be bothered by the camera facing them. This became the reality when some people in the park would walk by the robot with questioning looks on their faces. Some people even shouted profanities at the pairs as they geocached, questioning what they were doing and what the robot was being used for.

4 Conclusions

Overall, our explorations of Shared Bicycling and Beam Geocaching have raised design challenges and opportunities for creating shared experiences for family members over distance in the outdoors. We highlight three aspects that we think are especially important when designing such experiences.

First, the type of embodiment used to represent the remote person can have a large impact on the type of experience that family and friends have and should be carefully considered. When activities occur in the outdoors, they are naturally in the public eye with possibly many other people around. This means that people will see the embodiment if there is one. When thinking about the multitude of outdoor activities that people could do together, one could similarly imagine a whole host of ways of representing the remote person. In Shared Bicycling, the remote person was represented on small video displays attached to the bicycle and through earbuds. In Beam Geocaching, the remote person was represented by a much larger telepresence robot. Small embodiments like in Shared Bicycling mean that bystanders in the outdoor setting cannot easily know that a person is participating in an activity with a remote user. Larger embodiments like telepresence robots are highly visible and even garner additional attention. Thus, the selection of the embodiment for a shared outdoor experience will play an important role in how close the family or friends feel when doing the activity, and it can also have implications for their privacy and those around them. Again, this is because the activity is taking place in the outdoors with a broader audience composed of the general public. Similarly, the availability of audio links and where they are located can affect the intimacy of the experience. For example, audio going to an earbud and only heard by one person can feel much more intimate than audio being publicly broadcast through a telepresence robot's speaker. It is also clear from our studies that the pace of the activity (e.g., fast or slow movement) is important when it comes to designing shared outdoor experiences.

Second, there are both benefits and challenges when it comes to asymmetry and what remote partners can and cannot do in a shared outdoor experience over distance. In Shared Bicycling, remote partners could go for a bicycle ride at the same time as their partner, or they could watch from home. In Beam Geocaching, remote partners only had the opportunity to participate from the remote home through the telepresence robot. In cases where a person is not physically outside themselves, there can be an asymmetry in what they are able to do compared to a person who is actually outside. In some ways, this can be highly beneficial. It means that people who might be unable to actually go outdoors due to health concerns or chronic illness can still experience aspects of the outdoors through a shared experience with a partner. Yet connecting mixed contexts (indoor person to outdoor person) can create asymmetries in how they can actually participate and what they are able to do. For example, people using the telepresence robots in our study could not move as fast as those walking and they could not move or touch objects. With Shared Bicycling, both partners could go cycling at the same time. In both situations, there are also real-world pragmatic challenges associated with being in the outdoors that can affect the activity and how people experience it. This includes varying types of terrain, surface conditions (e.g., bumpy sidewalks), or even traffic (for bicycling). The experience can even be affected by poor Internet connections, which may cause connections to drop off or decrease in fidelity. These aspects need to be considered when thinking about the design of shared outdoor experiences.

Third, and related to aspects of asymmetry, there are design opportunities to consider the full range of sensations that the outdoors brings to people. This includes feelings beyond seeing and hearing a remote partner to things like the wind, the warmth or cold, and smells associated with the outdoors. When one partner connects to another from an indoor location, they don't get the full experience that a partner who is actually in the outdoors would get, even with an immersive 360° view. However, the challenge is that it can be much more difficult to design for broader aspects of the outdoors than the sights and sounds. Designs intended to convey things like the wind or smells can be challenging to create (Tolley et al. 2019) and may feel artificial at best. Yet these sensations are still highly important because they are what often bring people to the outdoors. That is, people go outside to get fresh air, to feel the weather (be it warm or cold), and to experience things not normally attributed to being inside. As such, we feel that the design space of shared outdoor experiences over distance is still ripe for exploration. We explored a small number of designs and activities, with a large emphasis on video and audio links. Future work should continue to explore other activities, embodiments, and the additional sensations that come with the outdoors.

Acknowledgments We thank Anezka Chua for her help conducting the study of Shared Bicycling. We thank NSERC, SSHRC, and the GRAND NCE for funding this research.

References

Agate J, Zabriskie R, Agate S, Poff R (2009) Family leisure satisfaction and satisfaction with family life. J Leisure Res 41(2):205–223

Ames M, Go J, Kaye J, Spasojevic M (2010) Making love in the network closet: the benefits and work of family videochat. In: Proceedings of the 2010 ACM conference on computer-supported cooperative work (CSCW '10). ACM, New York, NY, USA, pp 145–154. https://doi.org/10.1145/1718918.1718946

Brubaker J, Venolia G, Tang JC (2012) Focusing on shared experiences: moving beyond the camera in video communication. In: Proceedings of the designing interactive systems conference (DIS '12). ACM, New York, NY, USA, pp 96–105. https://doi.org/10.1145/2317956.2317973

Forghani A, Neustaedter C (2014) The routines and needs of grandparents and parents for grandparent-grandchild conversations over distance. In: Proceedings of the SIGCHI conference on human factors in computing systems. ACM, New York, NY, USA, pp 4177–4186

Heshmat Y, Jones B, Xiong X, Neustaedter C, Tang A, Riecke B, Yang L (2018) Geocaching with a beam: shared outdoor activities through a telepresence robot with 360° viewing. In: Proceedings of the ACM computer human interaction (CHI). ACM Press, New York, NY, USA

Inkpen K, Taylor B, Junuzovic S, Tang J, Venolia G (2013) Experiences2Go: sharing kids' activities outside the home with remote family members. In: Proceedings of the 2013 conference on Computer supported cooperative work (CSCW '13). ACM, New York, NY, USA, pp 1329–1340. https://doi.org/10.1145/2441776.2441926

Jones B, Witcraft A, Bateman S, Neustaedter C, Tang A (2015) Mechanics of camera work in mobile video collaboration. In: Proceedings of the 33rd annual ACM conference on human factors in computing systems (CHI '15). ACM, New York, NY, USA, pp 957–966. https://doi.org/10.1145/2702123.2702345

Judge TK, Neustaedter C (2010) Sharing conversation and sharing life: video conferencing in the home. In: Proceedings of the SIGCHI conference on human factors in computing systems (CHI '10). ACM, New York, NY, USA, pp 655–658. https://doi.org/10.1145/1753326.1753422

Kirk DS, Sellen A, Cao X (2010) Home video communication: mediating 'closeness'. In: Proceedings of the 2010 ACM conference on computer supported cooperative work (CSCW '10). ACM, New York, NY, USA, pp 135–144. https://doi.org/10.1145/1718918.1718945

Lee MK, Takayama L (2011) "Now, I have a body": uses and social norms for mobile remote presence in the workplace. In: Proceedings of the SIGCHI conference on human factors in computing systems (CHI '11). ACM, New York, NY, USA, pp 33–42. https://doi.org/10.1145/1978942.1978950

Massimi M, Neustaedter C (2014) Moving from talking heads to newlyweds: exploring video chat use during major life events. In: Proceedings of the 2014 conference on designing interactive systems. ACM, New York, NY, USA, pp 43–52

Neustaedter C, Elliot K, Greenberg S (2006) Interpersonal awareness in the domestic Realm, In: Proceedings of the 18th Australia conference on computer-human interaction: design: activities, artefacts and environments. ACM, New York, NY, USA, 15–22

Neustaedter C, Tang A, Judge TK (2013) Creating scalable location-based games: lessons from Geocaching. Personal Ubiquitous Comput 17(2):335–349 (Feb 2013). http://dx.doi.org/10.1007/s00779-011-0497-7

Neustaedter C, Harrison CS, Sellen A (2013). Connecting families: an introduction, in connecting families

Neustaedter C, Procyk J, Chua A, Forghani A, Pang C (2017) Mobile video conferencing for sharing outdoor leisure activities over distance. Human–Computer Interaction

Neustaedter C, Singhal S, Pan R, Heshmat Y, Forghani A, Tang J (2018) From being there to watching: shared and dedicated telepresence robot usage at academic conferences. In: Transactions on human computer interaction

O'Hara K (2008) Understanding geocaching practices and motivations. In: Proceedings of the SIGCHI conference on human factors in computing systems (CHI '08). ACM, New York, NY, USA, pp 1177–1186. https://doi.org/10.1145/1357054.1357239

Rae I, Neustaedter C (2017) Robotic telepresence at scale. In: Proceedings of the 2017 CHI conference on human factors in computing systems (CHI '17). ACM, New York, NY, USA, pp 313–324. https://doi.org/10.1145/3025453.3025855

Rae I, Takayama L, Mutlu B (2013) In-body experiences: embodiment, control, and trust in robot-mediated communication. In: Proceedings of the SIGCHI conference on human factors in computing systems (CHI '13). ACM, New York, NY, USA, pp 1921–1930. https://doi.org/10.1145/2470654.2466253

Rae I, Venolia G, Tang JC, Molnar D (2015) A framework for understanding and designing telepresence. In: Proceedings of the 18th ACM conference on computer supported cooperative work & social computing (CSCW '15). ACM, New York, NY, USA, pp 1552–1566. http://dx.doi.org/10.1145/2675133.2675141

Singhal S, Neustaedter C, Schiphorst T, Tang A, Patra A, Pan R (2016) You are being watched: bystanders' perspective on the use of camera devices in public spaces. In: Proceedings of the ACM conference on computer human interaction

Stafford L (2005) Maintaining long-distance and cross-residential relationships. Lawrence Erlbaum Associates, Inc

Tolley D, Nguyen TNT, Tang, Ranasinghe N, Kawauchi K, Yen CC (2019) WindyWall: exploring creative wind simulations. In: Proceedings of the thirteenth international conference on tangible, embedded, and embodied interaction (TEI '19). ACM, New York, NY, USA, pp 635–644. https://doi.org/10.1145/3294109.3295624

Yang L, Neustaedter C (2018) Our house: living long distance with a telepresence robot. In: Proceedings of the ACM in human-computer interaction. CSCW

Yang L, Jones B, Neustaedter C, Singhal S (2018) Shopping over distance through a telepresence robot. In: Proceedings of the ACM in Human-Computer Interaction. CSCW

Zabriskie R, McCormick B (2003) Parent and child perspectives of family leisure involvement and satisfaction with family life. J Leisure Res 35:163–189

Designing Technology for Shared Communication and Awareness in Wilderness Search and Rescue

Brennan Jones, Anthony Tang, Carman Neustaedter, Alissa N. Antle, and Elgin-Skye McLaren

Abstract Wilderness search and rescue (WSAR) is a carefully planned and organized team operation, requiring collaboration and information sharing between many volunteers who are spread out across various locations in the outdoors. Workers play a variety of roles, both on the ground and at a command post, and they need information and awareness specific to those roles. In our work, we are interested in understanding how this information is gathered and passed around, how it helps WSAR workers achieve their goals, and what challenges they face in sending and receiving information as well as in maintaining proper awareness. We conducted a study where we interviewed WSAR workers and observed a simulated search. Our findings reveal that WSAR workers face challenges in maintaining a shared mental model when radio and network connectivity are sparse. Our insights reveal opportunities for new communication modalities, such as (but not limited to) video communication, augmented reality, drones, and team-collaboration platforms to provide awareness and make communication and coordination easier remotely across various locations, but particularly between the field teams and Command workers. However, such technologies should also be designed to anticipate gaps in radio reception, and provide opportunities for workers to communicate

B. Jones (✉)
Department of Computer Science, University of Calgary, Calgary, Canada
e-mail: bdgjones@ucalgary.ca

B. Jones · C. Neustaedter · A. N. Antle · E.-S. McLaren
School of Interactive Arts and Technology, Simon Fraser University, Surrey, Canada
e-mail: carman@sfu.ca

A. N. Antle
e-mail: aantle@sfu.ca

E.-S. McLaren
e-mail: emclaren@sfu.ca

A. Tang
Faculty of Information, University of Toronto, Toronto, Canada
e-mail: tonytang@utoronto.ca

© Springer Nature Switzerland AG 2020
D. S. McCrickard et al. (eds.), *HCI Outdoors: Theory, Design, Methods and Applications*, Human–Computer Interaction Series,
https://doi.org/10.1007/978-3-030-45289-6_9

175

asynchronously and see relevant 'offline' information in a context-dependent manner. We present design ideas that pursue some of these opportunities.

1 Introduction

When a hiker gets lost in the woods or a skier does not return home from the mountain, a search crew needs to be called to find the missing person and bring them out of the wilderness safely. Wilderness search and rescue (wilderness SAR, or WSAR) is time critical, in that personnel need to find the missing person (called the *subject* of the search) as soon as possible, as surviving in the wilderness for a long period of time is incredibly difficult, especially for someone who may be injured. In many parts of the Western world, WSAR groups are volunteer based, though volunteers are professionally trained, and their training is consistent among members. As a result, they have a shared understanding of work protocols and language. However, each member also has a unique set of skills and a unique perspective to provide to the operation. For example, some are managers with a higher-level overview perspective, while others are ground workers with a lower-level and more-focused perspective.

In a typical scenario in Western Canada (which is similar to other parts of the world), a SAR agency would be called to respond to a report of a missing person (Justice Institute of British Columbia 1999, 2015), herein called the *subject* of the search. The *SAR manager* on duty for the agency would respond and send a callout to available members of the agency to meet at a staging area, which is usually set by the manager to be a convenient location near the search area. As members arrive, they form one or more *field teams* who are given assignments to search specific areas of the field using different search techniques. The manager and her management team (herein called *Command* for simplicity) set up a mobile office, which is usually a trailer or set of trailers, at the staging area in advance of the members' arrivals (Fig. 1, left). This is the base location where Command works coordinating and keeping track of teams and equipment, overseeing the operation, and making planning decisions. As field teams search their assigned areas (Fig. 1, right), they report back important

Fig. 1 WSAR involves careful communication, coordination, and information sharing between managers at a command post (left) and searchers in the field (right)

information (e.g., clues found, environmental hazards that could pose a threat to other teams, etc.) to Command. Many SAR agencies in Western countries work on a collaboration basis, where teams will call for assistance from other teams in the event that a missing person is not found within a few hours, or in the case where stakes are high; e.g., there are multiple missing people, or the weather is severe and they need to find the missing person as soon as possible (Justice Institute of British Columbia 1999, 2015).

WSAR teams look for and rescue lost people in *wilderness* areas, which are natural areas on land not built up with a lot of infrastructure. Besides a hiking trail and a few sign posts, the majority of the area is untouched nature. Often, these areas contain dense forests, rivers, lakes, mountains, valleys, and wildlife. This is in contrast to urban SAR, which takes place in urban areas and collapsed buildings, usually after a disaster; marine SAR, which takes place in the open sea and other large bodies of water such as the Great Lakes, usually for lost vessels such as ships and crashed airplanes; and, combat SAR, which is the search for and extraction of people from war and conflict zones.

For our work, we are interested in understanding what challenges WSAR workers face in remote communication and distributed collaboration, and exploring how newer collaboration technologies such as augmented reality, video communication, drones, and shared digital workspaces could help address some of those challenges. In WSAR, there is a lot of information sharing between managers at Command and workers in the field. This information is used to keep Command aware of the statuses and activities of field teams, and to aid in planning the future actions of the responding agency as a whole. We are interested in understanding how this communication and information sharing happen, what goals they support, and how we can design newer technologies to better support this information sharing so that they aid WSAR workers in maintaining the situation awareness (Endsley 1995) and team cognition (Salas 2004; Hollan et al. 2000) they need. We have been working closely with WSAR groups in Western Canada for this purpose.

Past and ongoing research has explored how to design and build collaboration technologies for other emergency-response and high-stakes situations such as firefighting (Khan. 2019; Kerne. 2007; Toups et al. 2009) and disaster response (Alharthi et al. 2018a, b; Bharosa et al. 2010; Cheung et al. 2011; Chokshi et al. 2014; Starbird and Plane 2013; Turoff et al. 2004). We can learn from some of the insights of this work and apply it to WSAR contexts. For example, WSAR shares some similarities with firefighting in that there are many workers 'on the ground' responding to an emergency, communicating and coordinating with each other, and answering to a commander (Kerne 2007). Roles are highly structured, usually in accordance to a standard protocol such as the *Incident Command System* (ICS) (Cardwell and Cooney 2000; Hannestad 2005; FHWA Office of Operations 2019), and information typically flows between personnel based on their roles, responsibilities, and positions within the pre-defined hierarchy. It also shares some similarities with disaster response (Starbird 2013; Starbird and Plane 2013; Zade et al. 2018), in that response efforts happen over longer periods of time, and commanders make use of information from multiple distributed sources 'on the ground'.

Implicit communication (sometimes called *consequential communication*) happens when a message is sent or received that is not *intended* to be communication. It is unintentional communication that happens as a result of one's use of or inter- actions with a tool or artifact (Serfaty 1999). For example, someone putting on their jacket and hiking boots communicates that that person is about to go outside and on a hike. The act of putting on the jacket and boots is not intended to be a communicative act, but it still communicates a message. This is in contrast to *explicit communica- tion*, which is when an act is solely a communicative act, intended to be interpreted as communication (Serfaty 1999). Implicit communication is usually done through non-verbal actions, whereas explicit communication can happen through both verbal words and non-verbal actions. Both implicit and explicit communication are impor- tant for team emergency-response situations such as firefighting (Gabor 2015; Kerne 2007) and avalanche rescue (Desjardins et al. 2014).

In addition to the insights that work on other emergency situations provide, we must also take into account some factors that make WSAR unique. For example, compared to urban firefighting contexts, WSAR workers operate for longer periods of time on average, and in remote wilderness environments with unpredictable terrain and weather. Teams are scattered across distances and isolated from most of their colleagues, aside from those on their field team. This reduces opportunities for face-to-face interactions with others, and particularly with managers and planners at Command. With this being the case, remote communication is heavily emphasized. Field teams need information and instructions from Command, and Command needs information from the field. A great deal of information is passed along remotely, which brings about challenges in properly transmitting, receiving, and handling this information so that it is made the best use of.

Furthermore, because WSAR takes place in natural areas with little built-up infrastructure, the search areas often contain poor cellular coverage. Additionally, geographic features such as mountains and valleys can block radio signals, resulting in radio 'dead zones' and in situations in which field teams transition between varying states of connectivity to other teams and to Command. This creates a lack of reliable realtime communications between all members of a responding agency, thus making it harder to maintain a *shared mental model*. A shared mental model is a shared awareness, understanding, and agreement, of the progress made in the operation and the status of teams, workers, and equipment; and the ability to project that knowledge to understand what will happen next and make future plans (Cannon-Bowers et al. 1993).

We focus our work on addressing the following research problems:

(1) What types of information do WSAR workers pass along to each other remotely? Who passes along this information? To whom is it sent to? And what purposes do remote communication and information sharing fulfill in WSAR?
(2) What challenges do WSAR workers face in sending and receiving information remotely? What challenges do they face in understanding and making good use of information that is passed along remotely?

(3) How can we design technologies that better support remote communication and information sharing in WSAR?

In this chapter, we discuss an investigative study we conducted to understand WSAR communication and collaboration contexts and challenges. We also discuss technology prototypes we designed that present solutions to some of the challenges raised in our study.

2   Investigative Study

Our first goal was to understand the communicative and collaborative needs of WSAR workers and teams, the challenges that they face in remote communication, distributed collaboration, and maintaining a shared mental model, as well as the design opportunities and recommendations for distributed-collaboration tools for WSAR. In order to do this, we conducted an investigative study (Jones et al. 2020) consisting of two components: (1) an *interview* component and (2) an *observation* component.

For the first component, we interviewed 13 WSAR workers (11 men and two women), including four managers and five field team leaders. Interviews were each at least one-hour long and conducted in-person, over the phone, or via Skype, depending on the participant's preference and availability. We recruited participants from volunteer SAR agencies in Western Canada, serving communities near mountains, lakes, rivers, and forests. Our participants were between the ages of 32 and 65 (M = 49, SD = 13), and had between 4 and 21 years of experience working in WSAR (M = 10, SD = 7). Though we aimed for as much diversity in our participants as possible, the gender imbalance of our participants stems from the fact that, in Canada at least, there are more men serving as WSAR volunteers than women.

For the second component, we observed a mock WSAR activity where over 100 volunteers from 14 local SAR agencies gathered to search for 15 fictional lost subjects in a forested area surrounded by mountains. This operation lasted for a full day and was organized by a local SAR agency for training purposes. The event simulated the entire experience of a normal WSAR operation from beginning to end, including setting up the command post on site, organizing search assignments and sending out field teams. Only the organizers, who were not actually involved in the mock search as participants, knew all of the details of the simulation. Thus, none of the actual participants in the simulation knew all of the details beyond what they would learn on their own through carrying out the operation. A researcher on our team observed the operation from the command post, as a fly on the wall, took detailed notes, and asked contextual questions to volunteers whenever they had a free moment. Due to safety and liability concerns of the organizers, we were unable to get a researcher to observe from the field perspective.

We used open, axial, and selective coding to analyze the interview and observation data and reveal higher-level themes. We looked at the phenomena from the perspectives of both the field and Command, to understand the similarities, differences, and tensions between the two settings. Open codes included things such as *sending information, receiving information, location awareness*, and *activity awareness*, while axial codes included categorizations of the open codes such as *information sharing* and *awareness*. Selective codes and themes included *communication goals, communication challenges*, and *workarounds*.

Next, we present an overview of our findings, followed by a set of design opportunities for WSAR remote-collaboration technologies. We then present design ideas following those opportunities and make suggestions for future work in this area.

2.1 Findings and Design Opportunities

2.1.1 Distributed Cognition and Awareness

Workers at Command have many opportunities for implicit communication and awareness, given that they are co-located. Their interactions with each other are similar to those found in settings such as emergency coordination centers (Artman 1999) and other control rooms (Heath1992; MacKay 1999; Patterson et al. 1999). In particular, workers communicate both explicitly and implicitly. We observed that managers made great use of written forms and physical artifacts, as well as their positions in the command office (Fig. 2), in maintaining a mental model of the status of the operation. They used these artifacts for record keeping, planning future actions, and maintaining awareness of the progress of the search, including the statuses of personnel and resources. In accordance with distributed cognition, they offloaded this knowledge into the artifacts spread out across the command vehicle, thus making it easier for the management team to maintain a shared mental model of the operation. This was especially useful during role changeovers, which can happen during larger searches spanning several days.

We observed that managers at Command communicate explicitly through talking directly to each other, and implicitly through keeping notes on paper and whiteboards, passing paper notes, clustering forms in various locations on the wall, displaying maps and progress information on large screens, and playing back incoming radio messages on the speaker so that everyone in the command post can hear them. The shared artifacts at Command, such as the forms, sticky notes, and digital information on screens, acted not only as artifacts for offloading knowledge (as per distributed cognition), but also as mediums for communication; i.e., *feedthrough* artifacts (see (Dix. 1994)). In other words, we observed managers at Command making use of these artifacts, pointing at forms, referencing locations on maps, and passing sticky notes, to support their communication with each other. The artifacts at Command also act as knowledge containers, conveying and keep track of people's roles, tasks, team assignments, availability of equipment, and search areas that have been covered, and so on so forth. Workers wear different-colored vests indicating their roles. These vests act both as communication artifacts (i.e., 'I am wearing a *Planner* vest, therefore I

Fig. 2 The inside of the mobile office at the command post, where the SAR management team oversee the operation, make planning decisions, and coordinate field teams

am a *Planner*') and artifacts storing knowledge (i.e., 'the *Planner* vest is located on this person, thus she is the *Planner*'). At Command, it is generally easy for someone to get the information they need simply by paying attention to their surroundings or by looking through artifacts and notes around the command vehicle. Workers can quickly figure out one's status through this implicit communication. Though when it comes down to understanding the situations of field teams, given that they are far from the command post, management is more-heavily reliant on the artifacts at Command, since they cannot directly observe the field teams.

During the mock search, when Command deployed field teams, they gave them each a set of paper maps and forms with the subject description, as well as notes on what type of search to conduct and where to search. Field teams would then take these forms out to the field with them and use the information on them for their duties. Both the field team and Command had a photocopy of the same forms. Command placed their copies of the forms on the wall in the command vehicle, to keep track of who was in the field and what they were doing. Each field team carried a GPS device and walkie talkie with them in the field, which they used to communicate with Command. When a team returned, they would debrief with Command. It was at this stage that they would share in-person any information that had not been shared yet, or discuss in-detail information that could not have been shared easily over the radio. They would make references to their GPS records and locations they 'starred' or 'pinned' using their GPS devices when discussing what they found. They would also return their copies of the forms to Command, where they would then be paired with Command's copies and moved to a special section of the wall containing the completed task assignments.

While implicit communication through *feedthrough* and *deictic referencing* (Dix 1994) between Command and a field team was easy when the team was at Command (either before or after an assignment), it was non-existent during an assignment, when a team was out in the field. Field teams could refer to annotated maps and notes from Command when out in the field, but when communicating via the radio, they could not make deictic references to their surroundings (e.g., *'Look over here!'*) or use objects as mediums for communication with Command. Instead, field teams had to be very descriptive when describing their surroundings or asking for help, as they had to be sure Command understood everything as much as possible. We noticed that sometimes teams even had to repeat their messages or reword them in order to get Command to understand them, and even then misunderstandings would still occur.

We observed that the management team logged all radio messages from the field carefully and with a lot of detail. They did this to have a time record of key events to be able to refer to later if needed, and to protect themselves for liability purposes. In accordance with distributed cognition, the knowledge contained in the radio messages was transferred to the communications log, and thus was contained in the workspace and belonged to the organization as a whole. The knowledge could then be used by others in the organization at a later time.

In contrast to the management team, who had an awareness of the bigger picture, field teams had a more-focused lower-level picture of things, in relation to their current task assignments. According to some SAR workers, this level of detail was usually enough to complete their duties.

Though field teams are expected to stay focused on their tasks, we were told that sometimes they deviate from their assignments for various reasons. The overarching reason is usually that teams have a perspective from the field that is different from that of Command. They can see and experience things first hand that Command cannot from their mobile office. Thus, they may be making decisions based more on what they are experiencing first hand and less on what Command is suggesting to them. The realities of what is in the field may be different from what Command assumed the situation to be in the field. For example, a path that Command asked the team to search along might not exist or might be unsafe to traverse.

2.1.2 Consistency and Control

WSAR workers used documentation and communications to maintain a shared mental model and consistent agreement and understanding of what was happening, what progress was made, and what everyone is supposed to be doing. Command wanted workers' knowledge to be as symmetrical as possible, and did not want there to be serious discrepancies in workers' knowledge or in what they are doing versus what Command expects them to be doing.

We observed that managers at Command maintain radio communications with field teams to build a higher-level situation awareness and shared mental model of the current status and progress of the search. They need this awareness for four main reasons: (1) to ensure that the teams in the field are safe, (2) to make sure they are on the right track in their assigned duties, (3) to understand the challenges they are facing, and (4) to prompt them for information and updates from the field (e.g., on clues they have found) in order to make informed decisions on what actions to take next. Command wanted new information to keep flowing in from the field so that their mental model would continue to update. Furthermore, Command wanted to keep in touch with field teams in order to update them with new information that was relevant to them, thus updating their mental models to the extent necessary, and keeping workers' knowledge consistent and symmetrical.

2.1.3 Network Sparseness

One challenge our participants raised though was that radio reception is usually unreliable in the wilderness. This leads to incomplete information and asymmetries in knowledge, which makes it more difficult for WSAR responders to maintain a shared mental model. Some teams experience complete radio silence, or are in a state of being 'offline' from communications, often for several hours, which results in gaps and delays in information transmission. Command may not receive new information from a field team for several hours, and this information may be out of date by the time they receive it. Similarly, a team that is in a radio gap may not hear updates about the bigger picture of the operation until they return to Command or step back into radio range. This contributes to asymmetries in workers' knowledge and their individual mental models. In some extreme cases, this could mean a team continues to search their assigned area for hours after the subject is found.

Furthermore, radio gaps sometimes resulted in a field team being in a 'partially-offline' state, in which they are able to hear the radio transmissions of some teams but not of other teams. Hearing parts of a conversation made it difficult for teams to put it into context, as there was missing information. The 'severity' of 'online/offline' state depends not only on how many others the team is able to contact, but more so on *whom* they are able to contact. For example, not being able to contact Command may be worse than not being able to contact another field team that is searching a location several kilometers away.

2.1.4 Prioritizing Communication

Different types of information need to be sent back and forth between Command and the field. Though they all need to go through, they have different levels of priority. Regardless of this, our findings reveal that the two-way radios that WSAR workers use do not always make it easy to convey the priority of messages.

For one, all radio messages were sent and received in the same way, regardless of priority. Some messages were high priority and needed to be responded to immediately (e.g., a field worker was injured and needed medical attention), while others were less urgent (e.g., a field team was giving a routine update to Command on their current location and progress in their task). However, two-way radios treat all messages the same (in a technological sense, at least), making it more difficult to distinguish between high- and low-priority messages. This introduced the potential for the recipient to not understand the true priority of the message. Workers had to resort to using verbal terms to convey the urgency of messages, such as *"pan-pan"* (i.e., the situation is urgent but not life-threatening) or *"mayday-mayday"* (i.e., the maximum urgency level; the situation is life-threatening).

In addition, all messages required the same amount of work to attend to, regardless of their priority. Field workers said that they often have to stop what they are doing and find a location where they have radio connectivity with Command in order to send a message, rather than being able to queue up less-important messages to be sent as a text later. Command has to listen to and respond to messages at the moment they come in; rather than having less important messages arrive in an inbox and being able to attend to them at a more convenient time.

In other cases, field teams wait until they return to Command before giving them some less-crucial piece of information, in order to avoid cluttering the radio with mundane messages. This is effectively asynchronous communication. As an example, we observed that when a team returns to Command, they would give an SAR manager their GPS device, containing a record of all the locations they traversed in their assignment. The manager would then upload the GPS record to a computer that would then display the path overlaid on a map. Over time, this digital map would populate with all of the paths of the teams' completed search assignments, as well as pins indicating special locations highlighted by teams as 'points of interest'. This digital map would act as a representation of the status and progress of the search, as well as of the organization's collective knowledge and shared mental model. This also gave field teams an opportunity to explain, in-person, what they found in the field. This was easier to do when the team was back at the command post, rather than while in the field in the midst of their assignment. The lack of clarity of some messages over the radio, the difficulty of using the radio while trudging through the wilderness, and radio reception gaps made it more feasible to share this larger amount of information at Command, after it had already been logged automatically by a device.

2.1.5   Awareness in the Field

Field workers have told us that they want to have some awareness of other teams' activities and the bigger picture of the operation, even when they are focused on their specific duties. They want to know, to the extent that it is relevant to them, how the bigger picture is evolving, what their impact is on the search operation, and how their remote team members are doing. Given that teams tend to spend hours in the wilderness, at the very least this awareness could boost their morale and make them feel less isolated from the rest of the organization.

While this is the case, field teams generally benefit from a narrower scope of awareness, according to SAR managers, as they are supposed to be focused on their own duties. This creates an important design tension. High focus and structure are important, though some awareness of the bigger picture and how one's actions fit within it could boost motivation and morale. This is similar to how players of online video games feel a higher sense of team commitment when they are able to hear and communicate with their team members (Dabbish et al. 2012). Field workers sometimes try to gain this awareness by eavesdropping on communications between other field teams and Command on the radio channel. There is always an inherent curiosity about what others are doing and what they have found in the field. Sometimes this awareness can be useful, in that they could overhear relevant information from nearby teams, and potentially coordinate based on that. For example, if Team A discovers an obstacle and tells Command about it on the radio, Team B nearby could overhear that message and adjust their actions based on that nearby obstacle; and potentially talk to Command or Team A directly about it. While it could have some benefit, hearing too much side communication can distract workers from focusing on their work and listening/watching for the subject.

While teams can overhear a lot of radio communications between the field and Command, they are generally prohibited (with some exceptions) from communicating directly with each other on the radio without permission from Command. There are two reasons for this: (1) Command wants to prevent the radio channel from having too much traffic, since they need to listen to and record all communications on the shared channel, and (2) Command wants to have control and awareness of communications. Usually, when Command grants permission for two teams to talk directly to each other, it is for nearby teams that need to coordinate actions or resources in the field directly, without the inefficiency of having to go through Command first. For example, two nearby teams may need to talk to each other to help each other navigate around obstacles. In these types of cases, communication is quicker and more efficient if it is more direct, and the teams need to coordinate to get something done together as quickly and efficiently as possible.

2.1.6 Use of Alternative Remote-Communication Modalities

While the radio is useful for certain communications, there are other times when workers may want to send information through other channels beyond just audio. For instance, visuals and information rich in detail may be difficult or time-consuming to describe verbally, and in some cases it may be helpful to send a photograph or video. Some SAR agencies already do this; allowing their members to send photos and videos of clues, as well as text descriptions, via SMS/MMS messaging to a manager at Command.

The main challenge with introducing multiple communication modalities though, according to SAR managers, is that it could make it more difficult for Command to build a bigger-picture understanding of what is happening, as they then have to pay attention to multiple streams of information. In addition, it also adds a cost, as workers have to then be trained in how to properly utilize new communication channels (e.g., they may need to learn how to send an effective video message). This suggests two things: (1) it may be more beneficial to aggregate existing communication channels and information streams before introducing new ones and (2) WSAR workers and agencies should carefully consider whether or not a new information stream is actually necessary before adding it, as there could be a cost overhead of adding it (it is something else that has to be paid attention to).

2.1.7 Summary, Design Opportunities, and Recommendations

The findings from this study demonstrate that while maintaining a shared mental model is important for a WSAR response, there are many aspects of WSAR that make this challenging. We highlight the following design opportunities:

[Design Opportunity #1] *Technology can be designed to support a shared mental model among WSAR workers responding to an incident.*

During a search, most communication happens on a single radio channel. This has the unintended side effect of keeping everyone in the loop, and aware at a higher level of what is happening, thus helping to foster a sense of inclusivity, teamwork, and purpose for one's work. Beyond overhearing radio communications, there are potentially other opportunities for technology design to foster this sense of belonging to a team. For example, technology that allows field workers to see the areas they have covered, the areas their colleagues have covered, and a collection of clues their colleagues have found as well as the messages they have sent (e.g., as text snippets) would allow them to see their actions and contributions in relation to their teammates, and this could foster a sense of community.

[Design Opportunity #2] *Gaps in radio and cellular reception bring about unique challenges in maintaining shared mental models across scattered locations, and so there is a necessity to support building and maintaining a shared mental model in network-sparse situations.*

While there are some technological solutions, like radio repeaters and mesh-networking technologies (e.g., goTenna Pro 2019) that could help minimize disconnectedness between teams and Command, more could still be done to provide WSAR workers with relevant information and awareness and maintain a shared mental model while disconnected. For example, it could be valuable to explore technologies that present field workers with relevant 'offline' information; or in other words, information that is *already there*, that can be presented to the user at relevant times while out of radio contact, or while 'offline'. To illustrate a simple example: technology could show a field team how much of their assigned area they have covered, or show Command a prediction (through a statistical model) of where out-of-contact teams may be located and how much progress they are likely to have made at the current time, based on information that is already known, such as their given task assignments, their last-known position, weather, etc. While the information may not be perfectly accurate (e.g., it may be out of date or 'stale'), it could still provide users with more to work with than just seeing nothing. Another example: when field workers are 'offline', technology could give them relevant information such as expected weather changes, predictions of where the other field teams are located, and predictions of when Command might want to receive an update from them.

[Design Opportunity #3] *There could be benefit to introducing increased awareness between field teams and Command.*

This already exists to some extent, as Command is able to observe the GPS locations of teams, look at forms, and listen in on radio conversations. Even with all of this though, Command still needs to put a lot of effort into communicating explicitly with the field teams to get an update of their statuses. There could be benefit to having more of this information come in automatically. It could save time for Command, allowing them to put more attention toward other activities. For example, it may be worth exploring wearable 360° cameras worn by field workers that automatically take and send geotagged photos of their surroundings to Command, where they are then displayed over maps of the search area. Photos could come in periodically (e.g., every 10 min, or every 500 m) or during key events such as when they have reached a certain location or when they are stopped for a long time.

In addition to these opportunities, we also make the following recommendations:

[Recommendation #1] *While shared mental models are important, new technologies should not burden workers with too much irrelevant information and should filter information and messages depending on one's duties, role, location, time, and cruciality of the information.*

If field teams receive too much information that is irrelevant to them and their duties, they could easily become distracted or overwhelmed, and start to miss or ignore important messages. Only the most important details, such as information relevant to the team's duties, basic bigger-picture details (such as *is everyone okay, has the subject been found*, etc.), and the teams' contributions to the bigger picture should be presented.

[Recommendation #2] *Before introducing more communication channels and information streams (such as videos, pictures, and text), designers should first focus on aggregating the existing channels together and presenting the information in a simplified way to the necessary people.*

While more information gives workers more ways of exploring the data they collect, it also increases the risk of mental overload. Thus, the information should be carefully managed, aggregated, and presented such as to not overwhelm the intended user. Based on our findings, we recommend presenting information in different ways (e.g., as a location on a map or an event on a timeline) and with different levels of detail, depending on who is viewing it and in what context they are viewing it. For example, if a manager pulls up a task assignment number, they may be interested in looking at the rough search path and the area covered. If a field worker pulls up the same assignment number, they may be interested in seeing lower-level details on the search techniques to carry out, the landmarks in the field to watch out for, and the equipment they need to bring with them. Moreover, a field worker may be interested in seeing the search path in relation to their own first-person view of the environment, whereas Command may be interested in seeing it overlaid on a map.

[Recommendation #3] *Given the mental and physical demands that workers face, WSAR communications should be as simple, minimal, quick, and distraction-free as possible.*

This is true for both field workers and Command. For Command, technology should provide minimal distractions from planning and operations duties. For field workers, technology should provide minimal distractions from immediate surroundings, allow them to communicate hands-free if possible, reduce the time needed to send and receive messages, allow them to respond to less-crucial messages when they are less busy, and allow them to focus on listening and being on the lookout for the lost person.

3 Technology Designs

While WSAR agencies are starting to use more modern technology such as text and picture messaging, this can lead to multiple information streams, and the possibility of valuable information being overlooked. While the introduction of new technologies may come at a cost for SAR agencies, we believe that modernizing communication technology could ultimately bring benefits. In the following section, we introduce two design ideas for supporting WSAR distributed collaboration. The first aggregates multiple information streams into a single tabletop system. The second involves the use of drones as tools to allow managers at Command to communicate with and assist field teams on the ground; allowing Command to (a) see a field team in context with their surrounding environment and (b) communicate 'non-verbally' with the team via the drone's movements (e.g., movement cues for navigational instructions).

3.1 Terrain Table for Manager Awareness

We designed a tangible interface for supporting managers at Command in building and maintaining awareness of an ongoing operation (Jones et al. 2018). Called the *WSAR Terrain Table* (Fig. 3), this interface brings together information from multiple sources and presents them in a single location, and thus is an early attempt at aggregating multiple information streams. The base of this tool is a physical terrain model of the search area. Placed over the terrain are physical props indicating information that remains constant or changes infrequently (e.g., the locations of the

Fig. 3 The *WSAR Terrain Table*, a tangible interface for supporting SAR managers in building and maintaining higher-level awareness of an operation. From (Jones et al. 2018)

command posts). Projected over the terrain are digital representations of information that changes frequently, such as weather information (e.g., wind direction and speed, cloud cover), the makeup of the terrain (e.g., which parts are covered by snow, which parts are water and which are ground), the current locations of the field teams, the paths the teams have taken, and the locations of clues. This tabletop interface is intended to be placed in a convenient, accessible, and easy to see location in the command post. It is meant to support workers at Command in their management and planning duties by allowing them to inspect the statuses of the search environment, the field teams, and the progress of the search through visual observations from multiple viewpoints as well as via inspections through touch and physically handling objects on the terrain.

To illustrate a simple usage scenario: Elizabeth, a WSAR manager, is called to join an ongoing search response and take over for another manager, Lucy, who had been on duty for the past 12 h. Elizabeth needs to familiarize herself with the progress of the operation and the status of the personnel and resources. Lucy briefs Elizabeth with details about the operation, and while doing so, they both approach the tabletop and interact with it. Lucy also uses the interface to help demonstrate the key points she describes Elizabeth, communicating through both feedthrough (e.g., moving flags on the terrain) and deictic referencing (e.g., pointing to spots on the terrain where digital icons indicate that teams are located). She also gestures at areas where the interface shows there is cloud buildup, suggesting that a storm could be imminent. Lucy also presses her hands on some of the steeper mountains on the terrain, indicating to Elizabeth to instruct teams that she sends to those areas to bring the equipment necessary for steep ascents. Once Lucy is confident that Elizabeth is ready to take over, she hands her the manager vest and lets her take over.

3.1.1   Drones for WSAR Distributed Collaboration

We are also exploring the use of drones for supporting distributed collaboration in WSAR. Drones could provide a unique overhead perspective, which could be useful for both field workers and Command, allowing them to inspect the space from angles that would otherwise be unachievable (Jones et al. 2016). This perspective could be especially beneficial for WSAR, as it allows workers to see things they would otherwise not be able to see from the ground; potentially even spotting the lost subject.

Drones can be used to accompany a field worker as they communicate with and receive assistance (e.g., navigational instructions) from a manager at Command. We have explored similar scenarios with general (non-WSAR) users in a previous study we ran (Jones et al. 2016). In this work, we designed a drone-video-conferencing interface in which the drone follows the local (outdoor) user (Fig. 4) and the remote (indoor) user views through the drone's camera feed (Fig. 5). With this system, we ran a study with pairs of participants, one remote at an indoor location and the other outdoors with the drone. Pairs worked on activities involving searching through and organizing objects around a park. The local (outdoor) partner had to do the physical work required for the tasks, while the remote (indoor) partner had

Fig. 4 Drones can be used to enable video-based remote collaboration between a remote user indoors and a co-located user in the field. Such a setup could allow a worker at Command to assist a team in the field. Figure from (Jones et al. 2016)

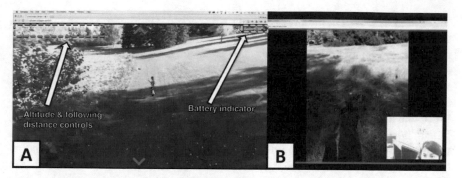

Fig. 5 The interface for a video-conferencing system that allows an indoor user to assist an outdoor user with the help of a drone's camera view. Figure from (Jones et al. 2016)

to assist using the visual information visible in the drone's camera view. We found that while this setup allows users to collaborate on such tasks more easily than with Skype-like video-chat interfaces, the introduction of the drone camera view brings about new challenges. For example, indoor users sometimes had difficulty translating navigational directions from the frame of reference of the drone to that of the local partner. For example, the indoor user might say '*move up*' or '*move down*', though *up* and *down* from the perspective of the drone might translate to *forward* and *backward* from the perspective of the person on the ground. In addition, indoor users sometimes had trouble comprehending and contextualizing all of the information visible in the drone view. Outdoor users were sometimes distracted by the drone, but also saw it as a unique embodiment that could be used to convey non-verbal (consequential) communication from the indoor user. In this way, drones can be used as, for example, navigation tools (similar to Brock et al. 2018; Knierim et al. 2018; Szafir et al. 2014, 2015) controlled by Command to help guide a field team to an area that is difficult to find from the ground but easy to see from up in the air.

4 Conclusion

Overall, our work opens up the design space for new technologies for supporting distributed collaboration in WSAR, with lessons that could also inform the design of technologies for distributed collaboration in other high-stakes activities taking place in network-sparse environments. Our investigative study outlined communication, awareness, and information-sharing activities and challenges of WSAR workers both in the field and at Command, as well as opportunities for design to address these challenges. We also presented design ideas to address these challenges. We plan to work closely with WSAR members and agencies to continue iterating on these designs and evaluate them to further understand the opportunities they bring and additional challenges that may need to be addressed.

Beyond WSAR, the findings from our work could potentially inform the design of remote-collaboration technologies for other high-stakes collaborative activities taking place in network-sparse situations. Such activities could include other types of SAR (e.g., urban, marine), military activities such as combat or peacekeeping, or large-scale disaster response in areas where communications infrastructure is down. Technologies that provide more opportunities for asynchronous communication could allow workers to share and receive information when they have a connection. When users do not have a connection, it would still be useful for technologies to attempt to provide valuable information and fill knowledge gaps. This could be done through displaying to the user (or reminding the user of) information that is already known and that is relevant in the current context or at the current location. For example, a system that knows that the user is approaching a mountain could tell the user the current conditions of that mountain, such as snow buildup or the weather forecast. Such information would already be 'saved' or 'stored' on the device after having been fetched when in 'online' or in radio contact with others, but only provided to the user when it is needed. Another way this could be done is through providing statistical predictions of information that is not known, but can be inferred with what *is* known. For example, the location of a colleague or team in a radio dead zone may not be known, but could be predicted using their last-known location, their path or direction of travel (which may be known in an activity like WSAR if they have a task assignment), their speed of travel, and the amount of time that has passed. This prediction could be presented to a user who wants it, alongside a confidence rating. Lastly, technologies for remote collaboration in network-sparse conditions should warn users of 'radio dead zones', so that they are able to anticipate and plan for when they are about to enter such zones.

Acknowledgments We thank the Natural Sciences and Engineering Research Council of Canada (NSERC), Alberta Innovates Technology Futures (AITF), and the University of Calgary for funding and supporting this research. We also thank the British Columbia (BC) Search and Rescue Association (BCSARA), SAR Alberta, and the SAR agencies and volunteers from BC and Alberta, Canada whom we have been in contact with for their ideas and their support of this work.

References

Alharthi SA, LaLone N, Khalaf AS, Torres RC, Nacke LE, Dolgov I, Toups ZO (2018a) Practical insights into the design of future disaster response training simulations. In: Proceedings of the 15th international conference on information systems for crisis response and management

Alharthi SA, Sharma HN, Sunka S, Dolgov I, Toups ZO (2018b) Designing future disaster response team wearables from a grounding in practice. In: Proceedings of technology, mind, and society, TechMindSociety, vol 18

Artman H, Wærn Y (1999) Distributed cognition in an emergency co-ordination center. Cogn Technol Work 1(4):237–246 (Dec 1999). https://doi.org/10.1007/s101110050020

Bharosa N, Lee JK, Janssen M (2010) Challenges and obstacles in sharing and coordinating information during multi-agency disaster response: Propositions from field exercises. Inf Syst Front 12(1):49–65 (Mar 2010). https://doi.org/10.1007/s10796-009-9174-z

Brock AM, Chatain J, Park M, Fang T, Hachet M, Landay JA, Cauchard JR (2018) FlyMap: interacting with maps projected from a drone. In: Proceedings of the 7th ACM international symposium on pervasive displays (PerDis '18), pp 13:1–13:9. https://doi.org/10.1145/3205873. 3205877

Cannon-Bowers JA, Salas E, Converse S (1993) Shared mental models in expert team decision making. Individual and group decision making: Current issues. Lawrence Erlbaum Associates Inc, Hillsdale, NJ, US, pp 221–246

Cardwell MD, Cooney PT (2000) Nationwide application of the incident command system: standardization is the key. FBI L. Enforc Bull 69(2000):10

Cheung V, Cheaib N, Scott SD (2011) Interactive surface technology for a mobile command centre. In: CHI '11 extended abstracts on human factors in computing systems (CHI EA '11), pp 1771–1776.https://doi.org/10.1145/1979742.1979843

Chokshi A, Seyed T, Rodrigues FM, Maurer F (2014) ePlan multi-surface: a multi-surface environment for emergency response planning exercises. In: Proceedings of the ninth ACM international conference on interactive tabletops and surfaces (ITS '14), pp 219–228. https://doi.org/10.1145/2669485.2669520

Dabbish L, Kraut R, Patton J (2012) Communication and commitment in an online game team. In: Proceedings of the SIGCHI conference on human factors in computing systems (CHI '12), pp 879–888. https://doi.org/10.1145/2207676.2208529

Desjardins A, Neustaedter C, Greenberg S, Wakkary R (2014) Collaboration surrounding beacon use during companion avalanche rescue. In: Proceedings of the 17th ACM conference on computer supported cooperative work & social computing (CSCW '14), pp 877–887. https://doi.org/10.1145/2531602.2531684

Dix A (1994) Computer supported cooperative work: a framework. In: Rosenberg D, Hutchison C (eds) Design issues in CSCW. Springer, London, pp 9–26. https://doi.org/10.1007/978-1-4471-2029-2_2

Endsley MR (1995) Toward a theory of situation awareness in dynamic systems. Hum Factors 37(1):32–64 (Mar 1995). https://doi.org/10.1518/001872095779049543

Entin EE, Serfaty D (1999) Adaptive team coordination. Hum Factors 41(2):312–325 (June 1999). https://doi.org/10.1518/001872099779591196

FHWA (2019) Office of operations—glossary: simplified guide to the incident command system for transportation professionals. https://ops.fhwa.dot.gov/publications/ics_guide/glossary.htm. Accessed 2 Apr 2019

Fiore SM, Salas E (2004) Why we need team cognition. In: Team cognition: understanding the factors that drive process and performance. American Psychological Association, Washington, DC, US, pp 235–248. https://doi.org/10.1037/10690-011

Gabor E (2015) Words matter: radio misunderstandings in wildland firefighting. Int. J. Wildland Fire 24(4):580–588 (June 2015). https://doi.org/10.1071/WF13120

goTenna Pro—Lightweight (2019) Low-cost tactical mesh-networking comms. goTenna Pro. https://gotennapro.com/. Accessed 20 June 2019

Hannestad SE (2005) Incident command system: a developing national standard of incident management in the US. In: Proceedings of the ISCRAM conference

Heath C, Luff P (1992) Collaboration and control: crisis management and multimedia technology in London underground line control rooms. Comput Supported Coop Work 1(1–2):69–94 (March 1992). https://doi.org/10.1007/BF00752451

Hollan J, Hutchins E, Kirsh D (2000) Distributed cognition: toward a new foundation for human-computer interaction research. ACM Trans Comput-Hum Interact 7(2):174–196 (June 2000). https://doi.org/10.1145/353485.353487

Jones B, Dillman K, Tang R, Tang A, Sharlin E, Oehlberg L, Neustaedter C, Bateman S (2016) Elevating communication, collaboration, and shared experiences in mobile video through drones. In: Proceedings of the 2016 ACM conference on designing interactive systems (DIS '16), pp 1123–1135. https://doi.org/10.1145/2901790.2901847

Jones B, Tang A, Neustaedter C (2020) Remote communication in wilderness search and rescue: implications for the design of emergency distributed-collaboration tools for network-sparse environments. In: Proceedings of the ACM on human-computer interaction 4, GROUP. https://doi.org/10.1145/3375190

Jones B, Tang A, Neustaedter C, Antle AN, McLaren E-S (2018) Designing a tangible interface for manager awareness in wilderness search and rescue, pp 161–164. https://doi.org/10.1145/327 2973.3274045

Justice Institute of British Columbia (1999) Ground search and rescue (GSAR) manual (2nd ed). Justice Institute of British Columbia. http://www.jibc.ca/sites/default/files/emd/pdf/SAR100% 20GSAR%20Participant%20Manual.pdf

Justice Institute of British Columbia (2015) Search and rescue management level 1 participant manual (Selected Pre-Read Material). http://www.jibc.ca/sites/default/files/emd/pdf/EMRG_1 783_PreRead_Chapters_for_Web_20150624.pdf

Khan N (2019) An exploratory study of the use of drones for assisting firefighters during emergency situations. In: CHI 2019: proceedings of the 2019 sigchi conference on human factors in computing systems. https://doi.org/10.1145/3290605.3300502

Knierim P, Maurer S, Wolf K, Funk M (2018) Quadcopter-Projected in-situ navigation cues for improved location awareness. In: Proceedings of the 2018 CHI conference on human factors in computing systems (CHI '18), pp 433:1–433:6. https://doi.org/10.1145/3173574.3174007

MacKay WE (1999) Is paper safer? The role of paper flight strips in air traffic control. ACM Trans Comput-Hum Interact 6(4):311–340 (Dec 1999). https://doi.org/10.1145/331490.331491

Patterson ES, Watts-Perotti* J, Woods DD (1999) Voice loops as coordination aids in space shuttle mission control. Comput Support Cooperative Work (CSCW) 8(4):353–371 (Dec 1999). https://doi.org/10.1023/A:1008722214282

Starbird K (2013) Delivering patients to Sacré Coeur: collective intelligence in digital volunteer communities. In: Proceedings of the SIGCHI conference on human factors in computing systems (CHI '13), pp 801–810. https://doi.org/10.1145/2470654.2470769

Starbird K, Palen L (2013) Working and sustaining the virtual "disaster desk." In: Proceedings of the 2013 conference on computer supported cooperative work (CSCW '13), pp 491–502. https://doi.org/10.1145/2441776.2441832

Szafir D, Mutlu B, Fong T (2014) Communication of intent in assistive free flyers. In: Proceedings of the 2014 ACM/IEEE international conference on human-robot interaction (HRI '14), pp 358–365. https://doi.org/10.1145/2559636.2559672

Szafir D, Mutlu B, Fong T (2015) Communicating directionality in flying robots. In: Proceedings of the tenth annual ACM/IEEE international conference on human-robot interaction (HRI '15), pp 19–26. https://doi.org/10.1145/2696454.2696475

Toups ZO. Kerne A (2007) Implicit coordination in firefighting practice: design implications for teaching fire emergency responders. In: Proceedings of the SIGCHI conference on human factors in computing systems (CHI '07), pp 707–716. https://doi.org/10.1145/1240624.1240734

Toups ZO, Kerne A, Hamilton W, Blevins A (2009) Emergent team coordination: from fire emergency response practice to a non-mimetic simulation game. In Proceedings of the ACM 2009 international conference on supporting group work (GROUP '09), pp 341–350. https://doi.org/10.1145/1531674.1531725

Turoff M, Chumer M, Van de Walle B, Yao X (2004) The design of a dynamic emergency response management information system (DERMIS). J Inf Technol Theory Appl (JITTA) 5(4):3

Zade H, Shah K, Rangarajan V, Kshirsagar P, Imran M, Starbird K (2018) From situational awareness to actionability: towards improving the utility of social media data for crisis response. In: Proceedings of the ACM on human-computer interaction 2. CSCW, pp 195:1–195:18 (Nov 2018). https://doi.org/10.1145/3274464

Design for Outdoors

Technology and Mastery: Exploring Design Sensitivities for Technology in Mountaineering

Keith Cheverst, Mads Bødker, and Florian Daiber

Abstract The idea of man's 'mastery over nature' is ubiquitous in western philosophy and in western thinking. Technology has been widely used in support of this end. Given the growing interaction design opportunities for personal digital technologies in supporting outdoor and recreational nature activities such as mountaineering, it is timely to unpack the role that technology can play in such activities. In doing so, it is important to consider the intrinsic and extrinsic motivations at play for the individual and the accepted social norms or 'rules' that are associated with the activity through its community and passed on through its community of practice. Technologies that may be considered as a form of 'cheating' when first introduced (such as handheld GPS) can later become accepted through common practice, although the rules are often nuanced. For example, it is widely regarded that GPS should not replace the skill of map reading and navigation. In this chapter, we consider different forms of mastery over nature that technology can support and reflect on the design sensitivities that these provide.

1 Introduction

The idea of man's 'mastery over nature' is ubiquitous in western philosophy and in western thinking. As a particular term, it can be attributed to Frances Bacon's Novum Organum, but it can be traced back to key passages in the old testament. Here, man (!) is told to

K. Cheverst (✉)
School of Computing and Communications, Lancaster University, InfoLab21, England, UK
e-mail: k.cheverst@lancaster.ac.uk

M. Bødker
Department of Digitalization, Copenhagen Business School, Frederiksberg, Denmark
e-mail: mb.digi@cbs.dk

F. Daiber
German Research Center for Artificial Intelligence (DFKI), Saarland Informatics Campus, Saarbrücken, Germany
e-mail: florian.daiber@dfki.de

© Springer Nature Switzerland AG 2020
D. S. McCrickard et al. (eds.), *HCI Outdoors: Theory, Design, Methods and Applications*, Human–Computer Interaction Series,
https://doi.org/10.1007/978-3-030-45289-6_10

fill the earth and subdue it; and have dominion over the fish of the sea and over the birds of the air and over every living thing that moves upon the earth. (Genesis, 1:28).

In considering the relationship between human, technology and nature/world, Don Ihde inquires upon:

"The isolation of a difference between technologically mediated and non-technological experiences of the world..." with the observation that "...such a difference almost always gets crossed with either a romantic or an anti-romantic interpretation in most examinations of technology via- à-vis human life." (Ihde 1990)

Ihde's suggestion is that 'being human' is a condition of thorough entanglement with technology, and hence inquiries into human life need to consider how particular forms of technology and their affordances give shape to forms of life, experience or knowledge. The 'form' of technology: the agendas, economic, political, ethical or historical commitments embodied by technologies constitutes a *leitmotif*—a guiding 'idea' that directs efforts of design and development. This chapter aims to suggest how 'mastery over nature' is one such dominant leitmotif (Hallnäs and Redström 2002) that can be seen to shape the development of digital technologies for use in 'nature'. In considering issues around technology use in nature it is helpful to consider the reflections articulated by Bødker (2006) on the second and third wave of HCI:

The second and the third wave seem to be stuck on either side of the divide between work on the one hand and leisure, arts, and home on the other; between rationality on the one hand and emotion on the other. While development on either side may lead toward a true third wave, I don't believe that we will get there until we embrace people's whole lives and transcend the dichotomies between work, rationality, etc. and their negations.

While everyday uses of digital technology certainly involve the consumption of natural resources (power) we use examples of 'technology in nature' to emphasize how the image of "man over nature" plays out when considering the particular recreational nature activity of mountaineering/climbing. This activity is chosen because of its rich set of values and associated motivations and for the fact that popular discussions of the activity often includes appeals to a particular discourse that include metaphors such as 'conquering' or 'bagging' a rock face or a mountain (Michael 2002)—clearly resonating with the image of man's 'conquest of nature' originates in the works of enlightenment philosophers such as Frances Bacon (Merrill 2008).

As part of this study, we consider how such understanding can play a generative role in design by deriving a set of design sensitivities. As noted by (Ciolfi 2004):

Design sensitivities do not impose predetermined solutions, but rather define spaces for discussion on how the design of interaction could deal with the issues that they express.

In (Jensen et al. 2014), the authors describe their design work involving interactive sport-training games and argue that design sensitivities can:

emphasize issues, challenges and opportunities, important for the design, development and analysis.

We use a variety of observations and engagement in the activity of rock climbing to support the idea that designing for these forms of nature experience is typically predicated upon an overarching ideology of mastery of nature. Sketching out four selected design sensitivities, we suggest how these are imbued with tropes of mastery. We then consider how this ideology of mastery might be limiting the design space and opportunities for a designerly engagement with the development of digital technologies for climbing. Following Coyne's paraphrase of Derrida, we suggest that "every appeal we make to the existence of nature in the raw is already imbued with artifice—in other words, technologies" (Coyne 2014) as a view that opposes the strict separation of the human and the technology.

From this view, we suggest how attributes of more artistic/speculative design traditions can be leveraged to suggest other hybrid futures of activities such as climbing as counterpoints to the dominant trope of mastery. Speculative design (Dunne and Raby 2014) and related work under the tenet of Critical Design (Dunne 1999; Dunne and Raby 2001) have been addressed in HCI design, and tends to favour the articulation or construction of (sometimes far-fetched or playful) *what-if* scenarios with digital technologies that go against the grain of 'good design' including the traditional HCI focus on functionality and efficiency (Wong and Khovanskay 2018; Gaver and Martin 2000; Blyth et al. 2015). Such work can also reverse the functional aim to facilitate transparency, working instead to create instances of wonder or reflection (Sengers et al. 2005) and challenge design's traditional allegiance to consumer capitalism (Bardzell and Bardzell 2013).

In our reflections below, we suggest how speculative design approaches might be useful for articulating some more nuanced and diverse understandings of digital technologies in nature. In this way, the chapter contributes with a design-oriented discussion and reflection on the relationships and tensions between the "mastery" trope and the design of digital technologies.

In the following sections, we describe our study focus, climbing and mountaineering, before proceeding to derive and present four design sensitivities.

2 Study Focus: Climbing and Mountaineering

In this section, we consider the outdoor/nature activity of rock climbing and mountaineering to unpack and consider more concretely the relationship (and associated issues) between new technology and 'mastery over nature'.

2.1 Digital Technologies and Services to Support Climbing and Mountaineering

Early research considering the community aspects of climbing in relation to interaction design is presented in Rouncefield et al. (2005). In this research, the authors describe their study of a university climbing club as a climbing community and

consider how digital technology might be used to support the production and maintenance of this community with particular reference to the three aspects of Boundaries,
Relationships and Change.

The research literature includes examples of potential advanced technologies
that can support the activity of climbing. For example, early work by Schöning
et al. (2007) presents design ideas based around Location Based Services to support
climbing activities. Based on this concept (Daiber et al. 2016a, b) envisioned an
approach that consists of a wearable device and a personal drone to guide climbers
and allow lifelogging of their climbing experience. Mayer et al. (2017) also consider
the potential of personal drones in the support of backcountry activities. One example
scenario presented in this research is the use of a drone in facilitating an emergency
rescue.

The ClimbAX system by (Ladha et al. 2013) is a wristband for automatic skills
assessment that is able to detect power, control, stability and speed in climbing
sessions and consequently focuses on (ambitioned) training for climbing. Similarly,
the ClimbSense system presented in (Kosmalla et al. 2015) is also a wrist-worn
device that is capable of automatically recognizing the routes climbed in a gym and
thus allowing the logging of training sessions and comparison between climbers. In a
survey on technology acceptance in climbers, (Daiber et al. 2016a, b) identified two
distinct groups of climbers: "outdoor nature lovers" and "indoor training enthusiasts".
Their findings imply that this latter group of typically performance oriented climbers
are more likely to accept and adapt novel technologies than more traditional climbers
that tend to value the outdoor experience higher than the difficulty of an accent.

In Mencarini et al. (2018), the authors describe findings from a field study carried
out in a climbing gym that revealed the learning difficulties of beginner climbers and
the negative emotions (such as fear) which they experienced. The authors use the
findings of the field study to inform their considerations on design opportunities for
wearable devices as a means for augmented communication between the climber,
the belayer, and the instructor.

2.2 Understanding the Potential Role of Technologies for Climbing and Mountaineering

In understanding the potential role and adoption of technologies for climbing, it
is important to consider the different personal motivations at play. In (Csikszentmihalyi and Rathunde 1993), the authors unpack motivation into two broad types,
namely: intrinsic and extrinsic and both types are present in climbing and mountaineering (Loukova and Vomacko 2008). In more detail, one example of an intrinsic
motivation could be the sense of personal satisfaction from skill mastery leading to
the accomplishment of a personally challenging ascent. Conversely, one example
of extrinsic motivation could be the peer recognition that a climber may seek from
achieving a notable first ascent or speed record for a particular climb.

In considering the role that technology (in a broad sense) can play in these motivations and the dynamic nature of technology acceptance in mountaineering/climbing it is helpful to consider the so-called 'rules' associated with the activity (and sub-activities). In his seminal article entitled "Games Climbers Play" (Tejada-Flores 1968) Lito notes how:

> ...the rules of various climbing-games are determined by the climbing community at large, but less so by climbers approaching the two extremes of ability. One of these elements is composed of those fainthearted types who desire to overcome every new difficulty with some kind of technological means rather than at the expense of personal effort under pressure, The other group is the small nucleus of elite climbers whose basic concern is not with merely ethical climbing but with minimising the role of technology and increasing that of individual effort in order to do climbs with better style.

Lito also points to the interplay of adhering to rules and value, i.e. What might be considered 'good' practice.

> It is important to realise at the outset that these rules are negatively expressed although their aim is positive. They are nothing more than a series of 'dont's': don't use fixed ropes, belays, pitons, a series of camps, etc. The purpose of these rules is essentially protective or conservative. That is, they are designed to conserve the climber's feeling of personal (moral) accomplishment against the meaninglessness of a success which represents merely technological victory

The rules are, however, dynamic in nature and so a technology that is deemed 'cheating' when first introduced may later be considered acceptable and compatible with a 'good' style of ascent. For example, in the early 1980s so-called 'Sticky rubber' soles were introduced to climbing shoes that provided superior adhesion on the rock. The extra adhesion afforded by this sticky rubber meant that, all other things being equal, a given climber would be able to use (i.e. stand on without slipping) a poor, low friction, foothold which would not have been possible with the traditional non-sticky rubber. At the time of its introduction, some members of the climbing community considered its use to be 'bad form' because it could be considered as reducing the physical strength required to ascend a given climb (because climbers would be able to reduce the force on their arms by putting more force through their feet) and therefore effectively reducing the natural challenge posed by the climb.

In order to further illustrate the complicated nature of climbing ethics consider the potentially controversial climbing situation shown in Fig. 1. Visible in this image are a pile of stones positioned at the base of the climb. A climber may choose to stand on these stones in order to help reach the first handholds on the climb but this could be considered a somewhat dubious tactic especially if this 'point of aid' was not used by the first ascensionist.

Fig. 1 Image showing residual climbing chalk on a rock face and a 'cheat' boulder at the base of the climb (left of the climbing rope)

3 Design Sensitivities

In this section, we consider four design sensitivities (peer recognition, physical strength, technical skill, and the aesthetics of climbing) by which to consider potential adoption issues relating to digital technology support for climbing and mountaineering. The sensitivities point away from the dominant ambitions of 'mastery' by highlighting a number of issues beyond the explicit aim of simply 'bagging' a mountain or conquering nature. Discarding mastery as the primary *leifmotif* for design allows designers to focus on less well known and less recognizable aspects of increasingly digitally mediated natural encounters.

3.1 Design Sensitivity 1: Peer Recognition

One notable extrinsic motivation associated with climbing and mountaineering is that of peer recognition. Such recognition is particularly important for the professional climber or mountaineer where the extrinsic reward can be new or continued financial sponsorship deals from established equipment manufacturers.

Unfortunately, situations have arisen where claimed ascents have been questioned by the climbing community and several recent news articles have pointed to the use of GPS traces in order to 'prove' summit claims (for example: https://af.reuters.com/art icle/worldNews/idAFKBN16R177) or video footage to 'prove' the successful accent of iconic sport climbing route such as 'Action Directe' (https://www.rokblok.de/post/ fame-is-a-bitch).

In the lifelogging scenario proposed by (Daiber et al. 2016a, b) a drone is deployed in order to capture video footage of a climb. Such an approach could be also used to record the style of an ascent and this video could then be shared with the climbing community in order to facilitate peer recognition and associated extrinsic rewards. Note that this acknowledgement of peer recognition resonates strongly with the extended Technology Acceptance model (Venkatesh and Davis, 2000) which includes social influence as a key factor influencing technology adoption.

Design sensitivity 1: *technologies that may capture proof on an ascent and the style of an ascent may be adopted in order to facilitate peer recognition and defend a climber against peer scepticism relating to a claimed ascent.*

3.2 Design Sensitivity 2: Strength to Weight Ratio

The given physical strength (or more accurately, *strength to weight* ratio) of a climber is (along with technical skill) a key factor that helps determine whether the climber is capable of ascending a given route. As discussed in Sect. 2.2, when describing the controversial introduction of 'Sticky rubber' soles, the use of non-traditional aids/technologies that can be perceived as reducing the physical strength required by a climber may receive criticism.

Another example of a controversial technology that was introduced into climbing was climbing chalk. The chalk (magnesium carbonate) would be applied by climbers to their hands in order to improve their grip on the rock, especially in situations where they might sweat through their fingertips. The use of chalk often results in some of the chalk remaining on the rock. An illustration of the resulting white markings left visible on the rock can be seen in the top left of Fig. 1.

The use of climbing chalk was deemed by many in the climbing community (and especially those belonging to the so-called 'Clean Hand Gang') as cheating when it was first introduced because it effectively increased the friction co-efficient of a climbers fingers with the rock (Amca et al. 2012) and therefore (and in common with 'Sticky rubber') could be viewed as reducing the strength and technical skill required for a given ascent.

One could imagine a scenario in which a personal drone could be flown close to a rock face (see Fig. 2) and augmented in such a way as to provide the climber with an upward force by attaching to the climber via a suitable cord or rope. Effectively, the lift provided by the drone would reduce the weight of the climber and therefore reduce the physical strength needed to execute moves up the climb. Such direct assistance provided to the climber would likely not be accepted by the climbing community. Similarly, the use of a personal drone for lifting gear to a climber (and thus reducing the weight of the climber by enabling them to carry less gear) during a climb would not be accepted. However, if the climber's partner were able to throw climbing gear to the climber then this would not be considered cheating as this would be considered within the scope of a team effort.

Design sensitivity 2*: caution should be used when designing and introducing technologies that may be perceived as reducing the physical strength required to achieve a particular climbing ascent as such ascents are likely (at least initially) to receive peer criticism.*

Fig. 2 Experiencing the usage of a drone while climbing during the UbiMount Workshop at UbiComp 2016

3.3 Design Sensitivity 3: Technical Skill

The notion of technical skill appears a key factor in the values associated with a 'good' style of ascent and consequently it is technologies that can be perceived as reducing the level of technical skill required that are likely to receive criticism.

In terms of digital technologies, the introduction of handheld GPS units was initially regarded with scepticism but rather than 'cheating' as such the main concern was that the positioning service would lead to a reduction in the technical skills associated with map reading and navigation and in-turn lead to an over-reliance on the technology and the potential for accidents related to getting lost in the mountains.

Recognizing the strong value placed on technical skills within moun-taineering/climbing can be used to help generate design ideas that are more likely to receive acceptance and to recognize design ideas that are likely to cause adoption issues if introduced.

Consider a scenario involving a drone to support the collection and appropriate disposal of detritus after a mountain ascent, e.g. collecting water/oxygen bottles, climbing gear left behind, etc. In such a scenario, the use of the drone would not reduce the technical skill of the climb as such and would be unlikely to prove controversial to the climbing community (apart perhaps for the noise generated by the drone).

Design sensitivity 3: caution should be used when designing and introducing tech-nologies that may be perceived as reducing the technical skill required to achieve a particular climbing ascent as such ascents are likely (at least initially) to receive peer criticism.

3.4 Design Sensitivity 4: The Aesthetics of Climbing

Both the drone example and the chalk mark example seem to invoke questions of how technologies influence the experience of 'raw' nature or the beauty of nature. Experiences in nature are often couched in a language of the sublime (Day 1996; McNaughten and Urry 1998), where contact with nature facilitates awe, astonishment and perhaps a spiritual sense of 'transcendence'—feeling small or insignificant in the face of a spectacular and unruly nature.

The chalk marks discussed in Sect. 3.2 are, to some, not only signs of cheating or the distribution of a raw human effort/capacity to a kind of technological inter-vention. The chalk marks might also be considered offensive due to leaving marks on an otherwise untainted rock (see e.g. https://www.ukclimbing.com/articles/ski lls/series/respecttherock/chalk_use-9892). Drones are not necessarily cheating or a means of offloading the human effort to a machine. They may incur radically upon a climber's sense of aesthetics and the raw beauty of nature; chalk leaves lines or marks on a rock wall, drones can be noisy, mechanical beasts that potentially disrupt the sense of solitude or having escaped civilization. Similarly, the use of the near-ubiquitous smartphone in nature can be perceived as 'out-of-place' since its use seems to connote 'connectivity', scattered attention, work, addiction and similar civiliza-tional ailments. The aesthetics of rock climbing and what could be characterized as a sublime or spectacular experience is challenged by technology that is 'out-of-place' and frames the "raw" experience as somehow dependent on or entangled with technology.

Design sensitivity 4: have regard for the figure of 'nature' as pure or 'wild', and how technologies play a role in the construction of this figure. This, we suggest, is a question of aesthetics, a judgment of the immediate sensory as well as conceptual 'totality' of an activity. Designers need to be sensitive to how technologies frame the activity, and whether technologies bring about unwanted interference to the appreci-ation of being in nature. This is not merely a question of maintaining a pleasing visual scene (e.g. no chalk marks) or a situation free from unwanted 'artificial' sounds (e.g. a noisy drone). We suggest that an aesthetic concern must also cover more proces-sual aspects such as a meaningful simplicity or the elegance of interaction with technologies.

4 Discussion and Reflections

In the following section, we discuss the relations between the suggested leitmotif of "mastery" as a form of relation to nature and our design sensibilities. In the reflec-tions below, we also extend the dominant view by suggesting how speculating on alternative technological futures and figures of the relationships between humans and nature can aid in articulating design agendas that go beyond the prevalent discourse of human mastery.

First, in our design sensitivities, seemingly "natural" and *embodied skills* are valued, and hence digital technologies should be built in ways that retain a sense of "mastery of nature", without explicitly interfering with the (embodied) capacities of the individual climber. Designing digital and high-tech devices or services for climbing needs to be done with a view to balance between technologies that directly reduce the need for acquiring skill or strength to those that subtly augment a skill or aids a climber in an aesthetically pleasing way. The design sensitivities developed in the previous sections rely on the trope of mastery in the sense that they priori-tize a certain 'backgrounding' of technologies to emphasize or frame human agency (muscle and mental strength, agility, courage, technique, etc.) as unmediated by tech-nology. Acceptable technologies tend to become 'backgrounded' in their relations to the practices they afford, in the sense that they are not 'experienced' as technology, but tacitly provide a context or environment for other experiences (Ihde 1990).

As we have discussed, e.g. using chalk and the 'Clean Hand Gang' opposition to this, perceptions of the acceptability of certain technologies change over time. As an example, current digital technologies are being designed and broadly adopted for 'nature' activities. While some safety-oriented and more passive technologies such as GPS tracking beacons for wilderness solo hiking are broadly accepted (and recommended in some areas), there is considerable resistance to using GPS devices to replace physical map reading and compass orientation. Experienced hikers and search and rescue organizations seem to consistently warn against the over-reliance on GPS for navigation and the false sense of safety provided by carrying a cell phone to call for help. Particularly with the growing interest in climbing and other wilderness pursuits, such warnings are probably warranted. However, as network connectivity, reliability of services and hardware components such as batteries as well as the general computing capacity of devices increases, digital technologies will arguably come to play new roles and be more broadly accepted in outdoor activities such as climbing.

If mastery is a dominant theme, we suggest that it might occlude other possible, useful or potentially unsettling motifs that could allow us to find other ways of thinking about human–technology relations in the kinds of activities we have described in our case. How might future design speculation engage critically with the idea of 'mastery' in order to widen the conceptual landscape of design?

4.1 Beyond Mastery

Climbing, at the same time as it relies profoundly on particular human embodied skills and trained endurance, is an activity that is already thoroughly entangled with a number of technological aids. Rope, carabiners, harnesses, light-weight food and energy bars, chalk, protective gear, carrying gear, clothing, shoes, and sometimes camping and sleeping equipment all play crucial parts of the activity. Climbing as recreation also relies crucially on a range of "mundane" technologies such as mobility, transportation and infrastructure; awareness of and easy access to climbing spots as well as maintenance and regulation of climbing spots are key to facilitating climbing. In this way, "mundane technology mediates […] a particular, valued relation to the 'natural environment'" (Michael 2002: 48).

Thinking beyond the 'human mastery' trope, any "natural" relation to the world is a fundamentally entangled affair. While climbing and mountaineering are often couched in a language of conquest, domination, signifying an expression of man's (sic!) natural disposition (e.g. Mallory's famous answer to a journalist who, in the late 1920s, inquired why he'd want to scale Mt. Everest; "Because it's there"), on an opposing view, climbing is a hybrid/cyborg pursuit with equipment entangled with or mediating relations to nature and giving shape and meaning to the practice.

Put otherwise, a key difference here is fundamentally between a dualist (i.e. dual nature, man vs. nature) and a monist (single nature, everything-is-one) conception of nature. 'Man's mastery of nature' is aligned with a dualistic concept of the relationships between humans and their world, since 'mastery' requires a fundamental difference and hierarchy to be a meaningful concept. The trope of mastery relates to a masculinist and rationalistic conception of knowing, a position critiqued in, for example, feminist science studies and philosophies:

Reason in the western tradition has been constructed as the privileged domain of the master, who has conceived nature as a wife or subordinate other encompassing and representing the sphere of materiality, subsistence and the feminine which the master has split off and constructed as beneath him. (Plumwood 1993: 3).

Design often relies uncritically (and unconsciously) on such dominant, inherited philosophical grounds. Speculative design has been used as a means for examining those philosophical 'truths' that guide or obscure other more challenging views of the relations between humans and designed objects or environments. Speculation allows designers to not merely extrapolate from existing situations or observations in what seems to be a linear, rational or logical fashion, but to widen the future potentials of technologies in ways that challenge the metaphors, ideologies or discourse that currently guides design practices.

We have suggested how the inherited idea of "man's mastery of nature" plays out in the practical engagement and judgment of equipment and technology in the space of climbing and natural experiences. Some implications of a speculative engagement with climbing and other 'nature' experiences could be

1. Rather than emphasizing mastery as the conceptual foundation for a successful design, we imagine that there is room for extending the practices of climbing into more 'hybrid' territories. What if designing for climbers is approached as the creation of 'cyborgs' in a way that de-emphasizes the focus on maintaining the (illusion of a) spectacular and raw experience of nature to instead emphasize the pleasure of technological entanglement (Haraway 1985)?
2. Extending beyond the idea of 'good design' based on tracing and representing current situations, freeing the imagination from the shackles of the present can point to new directions. Digital technologies, services and infrastructures are in constant flux, and their systemic future affordances are unpredictable. By venturing into possible speculative and science fictional territories, for example by considering far-fetched ideas that are on the limits of technical feasibility or social desirability, it becomes possible to imagine different relations to nature that are less imbued with the idea of mastery. Such speculative approaches resonate with environmental concerns as they challenge the dominant 'backgrounding' of technology in nature and instead begin to make an account for the all-pervasive networks of technology (politics, cultures, discourses) that 'enable' nature. In other words, speculative design in the broader space of designing for natural encounters needs to reflect on how 'nature' is mediated by technology (Ihde 1990) and how this mediation creates certain experiences, expectations, ways of accounting and so forth. This, we suggest, presents designers with ways to ponder more complex entanglements of technology/nature, and might also be harnessed to facilitate more reflective and responsible relations to nature.

These suggestions not only have consequences for activities such as mountaineering and climbing, but could also be relevant for a design-oriented engagement with new digital technologies and the ways in which they mediate other encounters with nature. The popularity of GPS equipped trail apps for hikers indicates a need for easy-to-use navigational aids, but also entail the danger of congested routes or crowded natural sites as they are becoming increasingly accessible. Creating navigational tools that introduce elements of chance and serendipity or interesting detours on popular route, thus de-emphasizing the mastery trope, might create new dynamics in the use of natural places and new forms of playful, enjoyable and not least sustainable activities in nature might occur.

5 Summary and Concluding Remarks

In this chapter, we have reflected upon the image of 'man mastering nature' as a perspective for considering the design of technology in nature. Focusing on the activity of climbing and mountaineering, we derived four design sensitivities that may function as an inspiration for the design of new digital technologies.

The design sensitivities considered related to peer recognition, a given climber's strength to weight ratio and a given climber's technical skill. When considering these design sensitivities, we used imaged scenarios based on drone technology to consider the likely acceptance or otherwise of the use of technology by the climbing community. For example, the use of a drone to effectively reduce the weight of a climber would not be acceptable but the use of a drone to record the video footage of a notable climb would be acceptable. Either way, the acceptance of the same technological artefact in the same context might differ between people, groups and communities. The use of a drone for material transport to a climber might foster similar discussions as support in high-altitude mountaineering (Sherpas, oxygen use, etc.), or might be at least be valued differently such as supported, self-supported and unsupported fastest known time (FKT) records in thru-hiking (https://thetrek.co/app alachian-trail/fkts-explained/).

A variety of examples of "man's mastery of nature" exist that go beyond climbing and indeed a lot of controversies frequently emerge in other outdoor disciplines (e.g. the current popularity of electric mountain bikes). In future work, the proposed approach of design sensitivities can be easily adapted to the design of digital technologies for other outdoor activities.

Developing the design sensitivities from our observations, we have suggested how some tenets from speculative design allow us to extend or deconstruct the "mastery" trope.

References

Amca AM, Vigouroux L, Aritan S, Berton E (2012) The effect of chalk on the finger–hold friction coefficient in rock climbing. Sports Biomech 11(4):473–479 (Nov 2012). https://doi.org/10.1080/14763141.2012.724700

Bardzell J, Bardzell S (2013) What is "Critical" about critical design? CHI '13. In: Proceedings of the SIGCHI conference on human factors in computing systems, pp 3297–3306

Blyth P, Mladenović M, Nardi B, Su N, Ekbia H (2015) Driving the self-driving vehicle: expanding the technological design horizon. In: Proceedings of the international symposium on technology and society technical expertise and public decisions

Bødker S (2006) When second wave HCI meets third wave challenges. In: Mørch A, Morgan K, Bratteteig T, Ghosh G, Svanaes D (eds) Proceedings of the 4th nordic conference on human-computer interaction: changing roles (NordiCHI '06). ACM, New York, NY, USA, 1–8

Ciolfi L (2004) Situating 'Place' in interaction design: enhancing the user experience in interactive environments. Department of computer science and information systems. University of Limerick, Ireland

NatureCR (2014) vs smartphones. Interactions 21(5):24–31. http://dx.doi.org/10.1145/2656933

Csikszentmihalyi M, Rathunde K (1993) The measurement of flow in everyday life: toward a theory of emergent motivation. In: Jacobs JE (ed) Developmental perspectives on motivation. University of Nebraska Press, Lincoln, pp 57–97

Daiber F, Kosmalla F, Wiehr F, Krüger A (2016a) Outdoor nature lovers versus indoor training enthusiasts: a survey of technology acceptance of climbers. In: Proceedings of the ACM CHI workshop on unobtrusive user experiences with technology in nature (NatureCHI). CHI workshop on unobtrusive user experiences with technology in nature (NatureCHI-16), located at CHI 2016, May 8, San Jose, CA, USA. NatureCHI

Daiber F, Kosmalla F, Wiehr F, Krüger A (2016b) Towards guidance in and life-logging of multi-pitch climbing using wearables and drones. In Proceedings of the ACM UbiComp workshop on ubi- quitous computing in the mountains (UbiMount). International joint conference on pervasive and ubiquitous computing (UbiComp-16), Heidelberg. UbiMount

Day A (1996) Romanticism. Routledge, London

Dunne A (1999) Hertzian tales: electronic products, aesthetic experience and critical design. Royal College of Art, London

Dunne A, Raby Fiona (2001) Design Noir: the secret life of electronic objects. Birkhäuser, Basel

Dunne A, Raby F (2014) Speculative everything—design, fiction, and social dreaming. MIT Press, Cambridge, MA

Gaver B, Martin H (2000) Alternatives: exploring information appliances through conceptual design proposals. In: Proceedings of the SIGCHI conference on human factors in computing systems, 01–06 Apr 2000. The Hague, The Netherlands, pp 209–216

Hallnäs L, Redström J (2002) From use to presence: on the expressions and aesthetics of everyday computational things. In: ACM transactions on computer-human interaction (TOCHI) TOCHI homepage archive, vol 9, issue 2, pp 106–124, June 2002

Haraway D (1985) A manifesto for cyborgs

Ihde D (1990) Technology and the life world. From garden to earth. Indiana University Press, Bloomington

Jensen MM, Rasmussen MK, Grønbæk K (2014) Design sensitivities for interactive sport-training games. In: Proceedings of the 2014 conference on designing interactive systems (DIS '14). ACM, New York, NY, USA, pp 685–694

Kosmalla F, Daiber F, Krüger A (2015) ClimbSense: automatic climbing route recognition using wrist-worn inertia measurement Units. In: Proceedings of the 33rd annual ACM conference on human factors in computing systems (CHI '15). ACM, New York, NY, USA, pp 2033–2042

Ladha C, Hammerla N, Olivier P, Plötz T (2013) ClimbAX: skill assessment for climbing enthusiasts. In *Proceedings of the 2013 ACM international joint conference on Pervasive and ubiquitous computing* (UbiComp '13). ACM, New York, NY, USA, 235–244

Loukova T, Vomacko L (2008) Motivation for climbing and mountaineering. In: 4th international mountain and outdoor sports conference. Outdoor Activities in Educational and Recreational Programmes, pp 135–139

MacNaghten P, Urry J (1998) Contested Nature. Sage Publications, London

Mayer S, Knierim P, Wozniak P, Funk M (2017) How drones can support backcountry activities. Retrieved from the NatureCHI workshop: http://www.naturechi.net/papers/NatureHCI2017-Mayer.pdf

Mencarini E, Chiara L, Cappellettia A, Giovanellia D, De Angeli A, Zancanaro M (2018) Co-Designing wearable devices for sports: the case study of sport climbing. Int J Hum-Comput Stud 124. https://doi.org/10.1016/j.ijhcs.2018.10.005

Merrill TW (2008) Masters and possessors of nature, The New Atlantis, Number 19, Winter 2008, pp 91–107

Michael M (2002) Reconnecting culture, technology and nature: from society to heterogeneity. Routledge, London/New York

Plumwood V (1993) Feminism and the mastery of nature. Routledge, London

Rouncefield M, Cheverst K et al (2005) Understanding space, place and 'community'. In: Proceedigns of interact 2005 workshop on 'space, place and experience in HCI'. Rome, Italy. Sept 2017

Schöning J, Panov I, Kessler C, 2007. No vertical limit—conceptual LBS design for climbers. In: Extended abstracts on human factors in computing systems—CHI EA'07, pp 1–5

Sengers P, Boehner K, David S, Kaye J (2005). Reflective design. In: Bertelsen OW, Bouvin NO, Krogh PG, Kyng M (eds) Proceedings of the 4th decennial conference on critical computing: between sense and sensibility (CC '05). ACM, New York, NY, USA, pp 49–58

Tejada-Flores L (1968) Games climbers play. Alpine J 46–52

Venkatesh V, Davis F (2000) A theoretical extension of the technology acceptance model: four longitudinal field studies. Manage Sci 46(2):186–204

Wong RY, Khovanskaya V (2018) Speculative design in HCI: from corporate imaginations to critical orientations. In: Filimowicz M, Tzankova V (eds) New directions in third wave human-computer interaction: volume 2—methodologies. Human-Computer Interaction Series, Springer, Cham

The Design of Outdoor Technologies for Children

Jerry Alan Fails and Michael Jones

Abstract Children have different needs, motivations, interaction styles, and perspectives than adults as they utilize technology and explore the world around them. We present an overview of technologies for children outdoors and lessons learned from developing some of those technologies as well as a survey of adults' experience with technology while hiking. The literature and our experience inform our recommended design considerations for technology for children outdoors, namely that it should: support social interactions; accommodate groups that are generally led by an adult; motivate via a narrative that piques children's interest; promote exploration in open, generative and creative ways; and keep children safe and allow communication with parents.

1 Introduction

Interactive computing is a routine part of life for many children. Many children under the age of 16 in 2019 have no memory of life pre-Internet and have used technologies including tablets and smartphones from an early age (Rideout 2017). At the same time, children tend to stay inside more than they used to (Outdoor Participation Report 2018). This is documented in the best-selling book "Last Child in the Woods" (Louv 2008), and in a more recent study investigating people's participation in outdoor activities (Outdoor Participation Report 2018). Technology is often maligned for incurring these negative consequences on children—keeping them indoors (Kellert et al. 2017) and isolating them (Turkle 2011). The apparent correlation between increased use of technology and decreased experience of nature has motivated some organizations to call for dramatic restrictions of technology use by

J. A. Fails (✉)
Boise State University, Boise, ID 83646, USA
e-mail: jerryfails@boisestate.edu

M. Jones
Brigham Young University, Provo, UT 84602, USA
e-mail: jones@cs.byu.edu

© Springer Nature Switzerland AG 2020
D. S. McCrickard et al. (eds.), *HCI Outdoors: Theory, Design, Methods and Applications*, Human–Computer Interaction Series,
https://doi.org/10.1007/978-3-030-45289-6_11

children, some going so far as to position nature and technology as being diametrically opposed to one another (Cordes and Miller 2000). We believe that this approach is not only unrealistic, but ignores the great potential that technology has, to bring people together and encourage outdoor exploration. Technology can be empowering, promote exploration, and be uniting.

In this chapter, we review systems designed for children outdoors and then synthesize two research perspectives—adult and child—that lead to design considerations for outdoor technologies for children. One perspective involves children in a series of participatory design exercises aimed at creating informal education systems for use outdoors. The other explores adults' use of mobile computing in hiking. While the study involving adults did not focus on children, children appeared in several responses to open-ended survey questions, interview question responses, and our on-trail observations.

Results from participatory design sessions suggest that children feel a sense of curiosity about the outdoors, which increases as they are motivated by creating or following a story related to their outdoor environment. They also like to socialize with their peers while outside. Generative and constructive systems fostered exploration, sharing, and socializing. In addition, children often spend time outdoors as part of a group supervised by adults and seek approval from those adults.

The study of children from adults' perspective on technology and hiking found that adults used technology or the outdoors to shape children's behavior outdoors. Adults also used technology to facilitate communication with children. We also observed adults leading groups of children outdoors.

Synthesizing the results from these two perspectives leads to the following design considerations within the context of HCI and children outdoors:

- **Support social interactions**. Children see time outdoors as a chance to socialize with their peers. Computing systems for children outdoors can support that social interaction.
- **Include narrative and generative elements**. These elements often motivate children to participate and keep them engaged.
- **Consider safety and ethical issues**. Interactive systems for children should be safe for children to use.

2 Outdoor Technologies for Children

There are many technologies that have been developed for children. In this section, we briefly present some that have been used in outdoor settings. This brief overview of technologies includes outdoor games, fitness applications, and educational/field-trip technologies. The experiences of children with these systems begin to frame the problem of understanding how children view interactive computing in the outdoors.

2.1 Gaming Apps in the Outdoors

With the decrease in children's outdoor play (Outdoor Partcipation Report 2018; Kellert et al. 2017; Loucv 2008), technologists have grappled with how to engage children and get them actively engaged outside. Soute et al. started addressing this by first creating a small set of "heads up games" (HUGs) which then evolved into build a rapid prototyping platform (RaPIDO) to build children's outdoor games that engage them in physical interaction outdoors (Soute et al. 2013, 2017). The focus of HUGs is to empower users to perform embodied interactions in an outdoor, physical space without being hampered by technology that demands their attention. These games were intended to be with or against others and therefore are highly social in nature. They further developed GameBaker which allowed children to customize games using a software interface and the RaPIDO rapid prototyping hardware (Avontuur et al. 2014).

A discussion about outdoor games would be remiss without including the widely popular game: Pokémon Go. Gaming studies seeking to understand its popularity, usage, and user motivations are widespread. Some of the factors leading to its mainstream usage have been identified as the game being: fun, social, and that it relates to a globally well-known brand (Paavilainen et al. 2017). With particular regards to children (and families), one study identified the impact on families through the lens of joint media engagement and how parents and children interacted with the game and its content as well with one another (Sobel et al. 2017). Families noted how the dynamic outdoor context led to various forms of joint learning not only about the content of the game (Pokémon), but also about the environment (e.g., the park they were walking in). This is evidence of the impact that social engagement has with regards to having a positive experience with this outdoor technology. Additionally, other research identified a relationship between Pokémon Go and the concept of affinity spaces (from the online learning paradigm) that allowed users to share and collaborate (Pauw et al. 2017). Pauw et al. also noted how Pokémon Go did not need an elaborate technological social feature, but the flow of the game and social interactions naturally supported the strengthening of relationships of those playing together and also piqued their interest in the physical spaces they explored while playing the game (Pauw et al. 2017). Other mainstream apps exist that encourage children to play outside.[1] The primary characteristics of the apps include a focus on social, embodied, and generative activities.

2.2 Fitness Applications

In addition to getting people outdoors and in their environment, other applications focus on encouraging children to be physically active—in part to combat the global obesity epidemic (What is Childhood Obesity 2019). Apps like UbiFit Garden

---

[1] https://www.commonsensemedia.org/lists/apps-that-inspire-kids-to-play-outside.

(Consolvo et al. 2008) and FitPet (Tong et al. 2020) encourage children to be active by measuring their activity and providing a persuasive display that either illustrates a garden growing or a pet being fed (or receiving care and nourishment) as a result of a child's physical activity. A recent review of several papers of design interventions for promoting adolescents' physical activity, identified that the key factors that were addressed (in decreasing order of prevalence) were physical activity, promoting social experiences, gameplay experiences, and learning (Ma et al. 2019).

In our own research on fitness trackers and applications for children, a survey of ($n = 98$) parents of children ($n = 113$) ages 6–11 regarding their usage or fitness trackers revealed the importance of social and familial influence on acquiring and using a fitness tracker (Samariya 2019). A subsequent user study revealed that children enjoyed the social interaction provided by fitness games, with short, synchronous game play. They noted that physical activity was hampered when it was cold outside (e.g., winter) (Samariya 2019). In addition, we conducted several participatory design sessions where children and adults worked together as design partners to identify the aspects that were deemed desirable and fun—particularly by the children in the group—with regards to various fitness applications available for children (Samariya and Fails 2018; Samariya et al. 2018). Our initial study looked at Zombies Run, Virtual Walk, and NFL Play 60 and identified the characteristics that children deemed most influential to enjoying their engagement with these apps as the enabling of social interaction, the existence of a narrative, and the ability of flexibility so they could add their own creative elements to the engagement (Samariya and Fails 2018).

2.3 Educational/Field-Trip Technologies

The location services and technologies (e.g., GPS) on mobile devices enable applications to provide location- and context-based content. One of the primary ways this is exposed to children is via outdoor field-trip technologies. Ambient Woods was one of the earlier technology-enabled mobile device systems designed to enable children to explore the outdoors, capture data and information, and promote some experimentation (Rogers et al. 2004). This system supported and encouraged children via scaffolding provided in structured lessons to work in teams to find information, analyze it, and discuss and share it.

Field-trip technologies and other inquiry-based learning tools have been developed to help bridge the gap between the natural/physical and digital worlds. These have been utilized to enhance cultural heritage and archaeological parks with contextual sounds by mobile phones that supported children (ages 11–13) as they explored orientation and engagement (Ardito et al. 2012). Quick Response (QR) codes have also been utilized to bridge the digital and physical worlds to support students as they explore and learn various tree species (Eliasson et al. 2013).

One of the authors of this chapter has helped develop several collaborative, field-trip technologies that utilized context- and location-based technologies including Tangible Flags (Chipman et al. 2006, 2011; Fails et al. 2014, 2015), Mobile Stories

(Fails 2007; Fails et al. 2010), and Geotagger (Fails et al. 2014, 2015). Tangible Flags allowed children to use a physical flag (equipped with an RFID tag) to place a marker in the environment (Chipman et al. 2006, 2011; Fails et al. 2014, 2015). They could then make a digital annotation which could be a comment or a question. Other visitors in the space could see the flag and scan it to see the digital annotations upon which they could further comment. The flag acted as a bridge from the physical to digital world and allowed them to contextualize the annotations within the natural world. After a flag had been scanned once in the physical world, the child was then allowed to revisit that flag in the digital world as they had already formed the real-world contextualization of that flag.

Mobile Stories built on the findings of Tangible Flags and further enhanced the social aspect by allowing children to create a shared narrative regarding an experience, such as co-creating a narrative or shared understanding of a class visit to Fort McHenry National Park (Fails 2007; Fails et al. 2010). Children using Mobile Stories could see the various pages within a shared story and see the updated story parts of their fellow child collaborators. Even though children could see one another's work, it was observed that children would still frequently call out to one another and run to share what they had learned and added to the shared narrative. This led to further explorations as to how to utilize both devices in a collocated shared experience as it was observed that often when this occurred one of the devices was left unutilized while children shared their moment together discussing the additions or edits they had made to the shared narrative.

Geotagger is a collaborative environmental inquiry platform designed for children to enable them to observe the world around them, document that observation, share it, and engage in informal discussions about their observations (Fails et al. 2014, 2015). Geotagger leverages the rampant use of, and affinity for, technology to encourage people to observe the natural world around them and to share and discuss that information with others. In this system, children could follow along a predefined set of geo-located observations, read what others had noted about the locations, add to the discussion about the location, and/or add new locations/observations. Geotagger supports creating, collaborating, and sharing. Geotagger encouraged collaborative discussions about the environment and enabled generation of content, social interaction, and exploration and learning about one's environment.

Critical to the development of Tangible Flags, Mobile Stories, and Geotagger was a participatory design process where children and adults work together as design partners (Fails et al. 2013; Guha et al. 2013; Druin et al. 1999). Tangible Flags began as an investigation as to how to enable children to connect with their physical environment. Through the participatory design process, it was identified that in order to enable the connection between the digital and the physical, we also need to enable generative processes and therefore support the creation of content, as well as provide mechanisms for collaborative social aspects that allowed children to see one another's work and collaboratively work together. Core to these systems was the ability for children to not just be consumers of information, but allow them to be creators and participate in generative and creative processes. In addition to this social engagement, narrative elements were deemed critical by the participatory design team.

The overview of technology in this section illustrates how varied technologies used by children outdoors and points to salient and necessary characteristics, namely, that in seeking ways to connect to the environment, child systems need to support social interaction (Kellert et al. 2017), incorporate an element of narrative element (e.g., Pokemon Go and Samariya and Fails 2018), and promote exploration via generative activities.

3   Child Motivations for Using Technology Outdoors

Basic user-centered design approaches teach us that adults and children will likely have different technology needs and motivations. While children utilize technologies designed for adults all of the time, there is a large body of research that seeks to involve children in the design of technologies intended to be used by them (Fails et al. 2013). Children, however, have a very different mindset than adults as they have different experiences with technology. A case reinforcing this point is that children these days do not remember when smartphones were not ubiquitous.

The characteristics described in the previous section that are common among technologies for children outdoors, align with research by Cumbo et al., who utilized participatory design to help identify what motivates children to interact with nature and how technology may enhance their engagement with nature (Cumbo et al. 2014a, b). By interacting with children in participatory design sessions, they identified several key motivators including opportunities to learn, special attention from parents and other social opportunities, feeling peaceful, and experiencing new things. A follow-up focus group with parents further identified the importance of having fun, being social, creating, having rewards, competing, spending time with family, learning, and including storytelling and narratives.

We share some additional motivations for children using outdoor technologies based on our experience interacting with children in developing technologies and conducting collaborative design studies (Chipman et al. 2006, 2011; Fails 2007; Fails et al. 2013, 2014, 2015). As part of this, we consider how children may interact with computing devices as they hike or explore an environment. Of note, from our observations, the differentiator is not so much about minding the gap between the natural and civilized worlds, but more about leveraging technology to draw them to the natural world to encourage them to playfully or thoughtfully interact with it and one another in safe and productive ways. We have observed that technology that encourages generative constructive activities not only can encourage informal scientific inquiry of the environment, but are also engaging and fun (Chipman et al. 2006, 2011; Kamarainen et al. 2013).

It is of note that children generally do not go outside without parental permission or encouragement. Adults make an active decision to engage with the outdoor environment, whereas children sometimes are passive, in that the decision is made for them. As such, a bridge or enticement can encourage more engagement with the environment. Contrary to adults who often explore the nature in search of enjoyment and relaxation (Posti et al. 2014), children are fascinated by the various forms of life and colors nature offers. Be it in a zoo or a jungle safari, kids are excited to see things that differ from the civilized world and enjoy capturing that information with technology to review or share it with others. This reinforces the need for children's outdoor technologies to empower children by allowing them to generate, create, and share content that they explore while they are outside. It also reflects the necessity for outdoor technologies for children to support social engagement.

With regards to social engagement, children may visit the outdoors with their family, an outdoor club (e.g., boy/girl scouts), to play outdoor games, or perhaps on a field trip associated with school. Often this social aspect is partially due to logistics (to minimize the oversight needed) or safety concerns (an important aspect even to adults Anderson et al. 2017). Beyond just ensuring the safety of children, additional people being present allows children to socialize with their family, friends, and/or peers. In order to be able to capture children's focus on the environment and the social interaction, some groups (e.g., schools, scouts) ask children to not use or bring technology as it can be a distraction. Some parents, however, utilize technology that children take with them to track or monitor their locations. In summary, technology has the ability to enhance social activity and increase safety both of which are viewed positively.

Another class of technologies utilized for children is fitness trackers for children. These allow children and parents to track their physical activity and stay safe. On the one hand, the intent is to motivate children to be more active and healthy, however, often the impetus to acquire a fitness tracker is initiated by the parent: either because they hope to influence their child's activity levels directly or because their children see their parents have and use them and their children want to emulate them (Samariya et al. 2018). These trackers come with a variety of features including contacting family in case of emergency, GPS tracking where parents can track the location of their children and draw a virtual fence, which if the child exits the parent gets an alert. So in addition to the physical activity, they aspire to inspire, they reflect an additional motivation of parents (in particular) to monitor the safety of their children.

4 Adult Views on Technology and Children Outdoors

In 2018–2019 we conducted a three-part study to understand how adults use interactive computing in the outdoors in the context of recreational hiking. In this section, we present and discuss adult responses that refer to children's use of technology outdoors. In most cases, the adults are the parents of the children. These responses can help us frame issues around interactive technology for children and highlights the need to involve children in the design process from the beginning.

We gathered data through survey, interviews, and observations. We collected 256 survey responses from adults in the United States using Amazon Mechanical Turk. After asking respondents to list the devices they take with them when they go hiking, the survey asked open-ended questions of the form "why do you bring *techology-X* when you hike?" or "why don't you bring *technology-X* when you hike?" In order to be compensated, participants had to give 3 sentences in response to each question. We also conducted 17 semi-structured interviews with adults. These lasted from 5 to 20 min and focused on issues around technology use while hiking. Finally, we spent 40 h on hiking trails observing people hiking and interacting with technology.

None of the data included specific questions about children and technology. However, the topic came up in some of the responses to open-ended survey responses and in some responses to interview questions. We did not set out to observe children in our observations, but we did observe children on two occasions.

4.1   Surveys

Most mentions of children in the open-ended questions of the survey responses referred to making sure that one's children can "get in touch with me" while the parent is out hiking. These issues appear in 5 of 256 responses. A variation on this theme is making sure that all members of a hiking party, including children, can reach each other during the hike. One adult wrote "the phones help ensure either ourselves or our children don't get lost 'in the woods'" (P166).

When asked why they bring headphones when hiking, two respondents mentioned the role of headphones in mediating communication between themselves and children. This happened both in the sense of limiting communication: "I also were sic them to drown out my kids sometimes" (P28) and in the sense of allowing communication "since I do 99% of my hiking with my wife and kids, it wouldn't be cool for me to just put headphones on and tune everyone out" (P36).

4.2   Interviews

Children, technology, and hiking came up in 3 of 17 interviews. Two participants are married with children and discussed their children, hiking, and technology; the other participant volunteers with a local youth group.

The married participants, IP9 and IP11 are both avid hikers and described how they modified their hiking goals and plans to create a better experience for their children. Both IP9 and IP11 discussed technology and hiking with children. Both participants spoke of technology in the context of shaping childrens' behavior. IP9 appreciated that hiking took children out of screen-based behaviors:

> The kids want to be on video games. They want to be doing all that. So to me it's nice that they can leave that stuff behind and then we can just get out and be together, you know as a family, enjoying nature and just kind of, you know, making that time to create memories.

In contrast, IP11 used technology on the trail to encourage more hiking:

I use that All Trails App so I can track. Because they're nothing worse than your kid going, "How far have we gone? How much longer?" They always ask, when you're like, "Look, we're like a quarter of a mile away. We've already walked two miles." Like, "Yeah, I can make it."

The other participant who mentioned children, hiking, and technology (IP6) is a volunteer leader of youth who regularly takes teenagers with different experience levels hiking. This person discussed efforts to teach teenagers how to function on the trail and lamented the fact that "young people don't know how to travel without electronics" meaning that younger people lacked the ability to use a compass and a paper map. Instead, they rely on GPS and phone screens.

4.3   Observations

In our observations, we noted two incidents involving children, hiking, and technology. One happened on a local hiking trail in the early morning. The trail is a strenuous 1.8 km climb of 327 m in the mountains on the urban forest interface. In the trailhead parking lot, a man gathered a group of 6 children around him at the trailhead map kiosk. After gathering the children around the map display, he took a picture of them together. They then started up the trail.

The other incident happened near an alpine lake at nearly 4000 m altitude. This lake is near a large city and is popular with families and casual hikers. The incident occurred about 3 km from the large trailhead parking lot. The incident involved a man and two teenage children (one male and one female). The group was likely a father with 2 children. As the group got near the lake, the girl held a phone in two hands and focused intently on the screen while walking through a section of the trail littered with rocks around 0.33 m diameter. She tripped and fell (but was not injured). Once they crested the hill below the lake, the boy said argumentatively to the man "I saw the lake first, you said if I saw the lake first I could use the phone!"

4.4   Discussion

This study of technology and hiking did not focus on children, but the adult perspectives and observations that occasionally included children. In those responses and observations, we identified three themes: facilitating communication, shaping behavior, and hiking together.

Facilitating communication means using technology while hiking to facilitate communication between parents and children either when the parent is on a hike alone or when the parents hike with the children. This theme appears in the survey data only. However, we observed communication using a smartphone in interview responses and on the trail—but not explicitly involving children. As it relates to children, communication using technology while hiking is likely to focus on communication between parents and children.

Shaping behavior refers to adult's manipulation of technology and hiking to shape the behavior of children participating in the hike. Our study found two forms of shaping behavior. One form was hiking as a means to remove children from screen time. The other form was using technology to encourage more hiking.

Hiking together involves children hiking with adults and specifically with family or groups. This is not unexpected given that we talked to *adults* about hiking and their answers involved themselves.

A limitation of our study is that it includes only the adult perspective on hiking, children, and technology. The child's perspective will be needed to better understand these issues. Another limitation is a small sample size that likely includes people who are avid hikers. Interviews and observations of different people may give different results.

5 Design Considerations for Outdoor Technology for Children

Based on the above literature and our experience, we propose the following design considerations for those designing technologies for children to use outdoors.

5.1 Support Social Interaction

The research presented herein, and our experience designing technologies for children illustrate the need and desire for the support of social interactions. This interaction includes interacting with adults (e.g., a group leader and/or parents), as well as peers—primarily those that are co-located or have experienced that same location. This can be through supporting co-located experiences or capturing and sharing experiential information for others to see and interact with at another time and place.

Social interaction can be between children and others they already know. This kind of social interaction builds upon existing relationships. Social interaction within existing relationships can also lead to better engagement with an application and with others (Samariya 2019).

When facilitating social interaction, especially among children who know each other, it is important for responsible adults or moderators (e.g., a group leader, a parent, a teacher) to be involved in the group formation stages. Initial stages of group formation can be a critical time for children. Curation of groups allows a teacher or adult leader to shape the group composition and dynamics. This kind of social interaction is different than the free-form interaction one might find on a social networking platform.

Finally, when designing social interaction in a computer-based platform, it is important to preclude unsafe interactions with strangers. This is not difficult when computer-mediated interaction happens between people in the same physical location. But if social interaction includes remotely located people, the system should prevent adults from masquerading as children and participating as children.

5.2 Narrative Elements

Stories are often used to engage attention, and this has been shown to be effective in outdoor technologies for children as well. Designers of outdoor technologies for children should consider what narrative elements are used to engage the users and support the social interactions of the outdoor technology. Plot or story-line, setting, characters, point of view, style, theme, symbolism, conflicts, resolution or reward are all narrative elements that can be utilized within the technology to engage children with the environment and with one another.

5.3 Generative Elements

Children are inherently curious and creative—they love to create and explore. Allowing them to generate, create, construct meaning, and share information outdoors helps engage them further and can encourage them to explore the outdoors further. Outdoor technology can be designed to engage children's curiosity by allowing them to make decisions, discover things previously unknown to them, and create—and even co-create artifacts—to share their discoveries with those whom they are concurrently experiencing the outdoors with or with others at a different place and time. Enabling children's generative processes increases engagement and promotes active learning, which is contrary to scripted experiences (e.g., an app directed audio-visual tour) that place children more in a role of being a consumer of information. We recommend generative elements be leveraged in designing outdoor technologies for children as it will engage their creativity, and urge them to explore and engage more with the outdoors and with others.

5.4 Other Ethical and Safety Considerations

Since children are a vulnerable population, it is ethically imperative that their safety be considered when developing outdoor technologies. From an ethical perspective, designers should consider the values and behaviors a technology reinforces (or inhibits) and how that impact children now and in the future (Frauenberger et al. 2018; Hourcade et al. 2017). Parents note safety as a primary concern for themselves and for children in general, but also specifically with regards to outdoor technology. In addition to physical safety, there are other considerations including who and how they interact with others especially in cases where the technology supports social interactions.

6   Conclusion

Perceptions and motivations for being outdoors are different for adults and children. Whereas adults may look at being in nature as a reprieve or for health, children may perceive it as an opportunity to explore, be curious, or perhaps even a place their parents are "dragging" them to. In all of these situations, technology can be a facilitator or activator to engage with the environment. Engaging with the environment with technology provides opportunities for children to be curious, active, social, and to learn. As with adults, technology could be used to block or distract from the environment, but care can be taken through proper facilitation and appropriate apps to promote engagement with the environment. We have provided some considerations that designers can heed to more actively engage children in the outdoors via technology. While some of the motivations for adults and children are similar, the challenge remaining for designers of technology for children in the outdoors is to enable and encourage exploration via technology while not distracting users from the great outdoors.

References

2018 Outdoor Participation Report. en-US. Technical report, Washington, DC, United States of America: Outdoor Foundation, July 2018. https://outdoorindustry.org/resource/2018-outdoor-participationreport/. Accessed 29 August 2019

Anderson Z, Lusk C, Jones MD (2017) Towards understanding hikers' technology preferences. In: Proceedings of the 2017 ACM international joint conference on pervasive and ubiquitous computing and proceedings of the 2017 ACM international symposium on wearable computers, UbiComp '17, Maui, Hawaii. ACM, New York, NY, USA, pp 1–4. ISBN 978-1-4503-5190-4. https://doi.org/10.1145/3123024.3123089, https://doi.org/10.1145/3123024.3123089. Accessed 17 Sept 2019

Ardito C et al (2012) Enriching archaeological parks with contextual sounds and mobile technology. ACM Trans Comput-Hum Interact 19(4):29:1–29:30. ISSN 1073-0516. https://doi.org/10.1145/2395131.2395136., http://doi.acm.org/10.1145/2395131.2395136. Accessed 11 Sept 2019

Avontuur T et al (2014) Play it our way: customization of game rules in children's interactive outdoor games. In: Proceedings of the 2014 conference on interaction design and children. ACM, New York, NY, USA, pp 95–104. ISBN 978-1-4503-2272-0. https://doi.org/10.1145/2593968.2593973, http://doi.acm.org/10.1145/2593968.2593973/ Accessed 18 Apr 2018

Chipman G et al (2006) A Case study of tangible flags: a collaborative technology to enhance field trips. In: Proceedings of the 2006 conference on interaction design and children. ACM, New York, NY, USA, pp 1–8. https://doi.org/10.1145/1139073.1139081, http://doi.acm.org/10.1145/1139073.1139081. Accessed 14 Nov 2017

Chipman G et al (2011) Paper vs. tablet computers: a comparative study using tangible flags. In: Proceedings of the 10th international conference on interaction design and children, IDC '11. ACM, New York, NY, USA, pp 29–36. ISBN 978-1-4503-0751-2. https://doi.org/10.1145/1999030.1999034, http://doi.acm.org/10.1145/1999030.1999034. Accessed 10 Nov 2018

Consolvo S et al (2008) Activity sensing in the wild: a field trial of ubifit garden. In: Proceeding of the twenty-sixth annual CHI conference on human factors in computing systems, CHI '08. ACM Press, Florence, Italy, p 1797. ISBN 978-1-60558-011-1. https://doi.org/10.1145/1357054.1357335, http://portal.acm.org/citation.cfm?doid=1357054.1357335. Accessed 3 Jan 2019

Cordes C, Miller E (2000) Fool's gold: a critical look at computers in childhood. Alliance for Childhood. https://eric.ed.gov/?id=ED445803. Accessed 5 Sept 2019

Cumbo BJ et al (2014a) Connecting children to nature with technology: sowing the seeds for proenvironmental behaviour. In: Proceedings of the 2014 conference on interaction design and children, IDC '14, Aarhus, Denmark. ACM, New York, NY, USA, pp 189–192. ISBN 978-1-4503-2272-0. https://doi.org/10.1145/2593968.2610449, http://doi.acm.org/10.1145/2593968.2610449. Accessed 11 Sept 2019

Cumbo BJ et al (2014b) What motivates children to play outdoors?: potential applications for interactive digital tools. In: Proceedings of the 26th Australian computer–human interaction conference on designing futures: the future of design. ACM, New York, NY, USA, pp 168–171. ISBN 978-1-4503-0653-9. https://doi.org/10.1145/2686612.2686637, http://doi.acm.org/10.1145/2686612.2686637. Accessed 30 Jan 2018

Druin A (1999) Cooperative inquiry: new technologies for children. In: Proceedings of the ACM SIGCHI Conference on human factors in computing systems, CHI 1999, ACM Press, p 8. https://doi.org/10.1145/302979.303166

Eliasson J et al (2013) Using smartphones and QR codes for supporting students in exploring tree species. In: Proceedings of the 8th European conference on scaling up learning for sustained impact, vol 8095. Springer, Berlin, Heidelberg, pp 436–441. ISBN 978-3-642-40813-7. https://doi.org/10.1007/978-3-642-40814-4_35, https://doi.org/10.1007/978-3-642-40814-4_35. Accessed 11 Sept 2019

Fails JA (2007) Mobile collaboration for young children. In: Proceedings of the 6th international conference on interaction design and children. ACM, New York, NY, USA, pp 181–184. ISBN 978-1-59593-747-6. https://doi.org/10.1145/1297277.1297324, http://doi.acm.org/10.1145/1297277.1297324. Accessed 14 Nov 2017

Fails JA, Druin A, Guha ML (2010) Mobile collaboration: collaboratively reading and creating children's stories on mobile devices. In: Proceedings of the 9th international conference on interaction design and children, IDC '10. ACM, New York, NY, USA, pp 20–29. ISBN 978-1-60558-951-0. https://doi.org/10.1145/1810543.1810547, http://doi.acm.org/10.1145/1810543.1810547. Accessed 15 Nov 2017

Fails JA, Guha ML, Druin A (2013) Methods and techniques for involving children in the design of new technology for children. Now Publishers Inc., Hanover, MA, USA. ISBN 978-1-60198-720-4

Fails JA et al (2014) GeoTagger: a collaborative and participatory environmental inquiry system. In: Proceedings of the companion publication of the 17th ACM conference on computer supported cooperative work & social computing, CSCW Companion '14. ACM, New York, NY, USA, pp 157-160. ISBN 978-1-4503-2541-7. https://doi.org/10.1145/2556420.2556481, http://doi.acm.org/10.1145/2556420.2556481. Accessed 13 Feb 2017

Fails J et al (2015) Geotagger: a collaborative environmental inquiry platform. In: 2015 international conference on collaboration technologies and systems (CTS), June 2015, pp 383–390. https://doi.org/10.1109/CTS.2015.7210453

Frauenberger C et al (2018) Ethics in interaction design and children: a panel and community dialogue. In: Proceedings of the 17th ACM conference on interaction design and children, IDC '18, June 2018. Association for Computing Machinery, Trondheim, Norway, pp 748–752. ISBN 978-1-4503-5152-2. https://doi.org/10.1145/3202185.3210802, https://doi.org/10.1145/3202185.3210802. Accessed 22 Jan 2020

Guha ML, Druin A, Fails JA (2013) Cooperative inquiry revisited: reflections of the past and guidelines for the future of intergenerational co-design. Int J Child-Comput Interact 1(1):14–23. ISSN 2212-8689. https://doi.org/10.1016/j.ijcci.2012.08.003, http://www.sciencedirect.com/science/article/pii/S2212868912000049. Accessed 14 Nov 2017

Hourcade JP et al (2017) Child-computer interaction SIG: ethics and values. In: Proceedings of the 2017 CHI conference extended abstracts on human factors in computing systems, CHI EA '17, May 2017. Association for Computing Machinery, Denver, Colorado, USA, pp 1334–1337. ISBN 978-1-4503-4656-6. https://doi.org/10.1145/3027063.3049286, https://doi.org/10.1145/3027063.3049286. Accessed 22 Jan 2020

Kamarainen AM et al (2013) EcoMOBILE: integrating augmented reality and probeware with environmental education field trips. Comput Educ 68:545–556. ISSN 0360-1315. https://doi.org/10.1016/j.compedu.2013.02.018, http://dx.doi.org/10.1016/j.compedu.2013.02.018. Accessed 6 June 2018

Kellert SR et al (2017) The nature of Americans: disconnection and recommendations for reconnection: conservation tools. Technical report, April 2017, p 363. https://conservationtools.org/library_items/1574-The-Nature-of-Americans-Disconnection-and-Recommendationsfor-Reconnection. Accessed 5 Sept 2019

Ma Y et al (2019) A review of design interventions for promoting adolescents' physical activity. In: Proceedings of the 18th ACM international conference on interaction design and children, IDC '19, Boise, ID, USA. ACM, New York, NY, USA, pp 161–172. ISBN 978-1-4503-6690-8. https://doi.org/10.1145/3311927.3323130, http://doi.acm.org/10.1145/3311927.3323130. Accessed 14 Aug 2019

Paavilainen J et al (2017) The PokéMon GO experience: a location-based augmented reality mobile game goes mainstream. In: Proceedings of the 2017 CHI conference on human factors in computing systems, CHI '17, Denver, Colorado, USA. ACM, New York, NY, USA, pp 2493–2498. ISBN 978-1-4503-4655-9. https://doi.org/10.1145/3025453.3025871, http://doi.acm.org/10.1145/3025453.3025871. Accessed 10 Sept 2019

Pauw D et al (2017) Connecting affinity spaces to places and back: a look at Pokemon go. In: Companion of the 2017 ACM conference on computer supported cooperative work and social computing, CSCW '17 Companion, Portland, Oregon, USA. ACM, New York, NY, USA, pp 275–278. ISBN 978-1-4503-4688-7. https://doi.org/10.1145/3022198.3026345, http://doi.acm.org/10.1145/3022198.3026345. Accessed 10 Sept 2019

Posti M, Schöning J, Häkkilä J (2014) Unexpected journeys with the HOBBIT: the design and evaluation of an asocial hiking app. In: Proceedings of the 2014 conference on designing interactive systems, DIS '14. ACM, New York, NY, USA, pp 637–646. ISBN 978-1-4503-2902-6. https://doi.org/10.1145/2598510.2598592, http://doi.acm.org/10.1145/2598510.2598592. Accessed 2 Feb 2018

Richard L (2008) Last child in the woods: saving our children from nature-deficit disorder. Algonquin Books, English. Updated and Expanded edition

Rideout V (2017) The common sense census: media use by kids age zero to eight 2017|Common sense media. English. Technical report. Common Sense Media, San Francisco, CA, USA, p 64. https://www.commonsensemedia.org/research/the-common-sense-census-mediause-by-kids-age-zero-to-eight-2017. Acessed 1 Oct 2019

Rogers Y et al (2004) Ambient wood: designing new forms of digital augmentation for learning outdoors. In: Proceedings of the 2004 conference on interaction design and children: building a community, IDC'04, Maryland. ACM, New York, NY, USA, pp 3–10. ISBN 978-1-58113-791-0. https://doi.org/10.1145/1017833.1017834, http://doi.acm.org/10.1145/1017833.1017834. Accessed 5 Sept 2019

Samariya A (2019) Investigating the effects of social and temporal dynamics in fitness games on children's physical activity. Ph.D thesis. August 2019. https://scholarworks.boisestate.edu/td/1570

Samariya A, Fails JA (2018) Making physical activity fun & playful: investigating fitness games with children. In: 20th international conference on human-computer interaction with mobile devices and services. ACM, Barcelona, Spain. https://drive.google.com/file/d/1to1Nr12CqRimmmnqw-Xs2w93w9-x2jm9/view?usp=sharing

Samariya A et al (2018) Technology as a bridge for children to explore the world around them. In: HCI outdoors: a CHI (2018) workshop on understanding human–computer interaction in the outdoors (CHI), Montreal, Canada, April, p 2018

Sobel K et al (2017) It wasn't really about the PokéMon: parents' perspectives on a location-based mobile game. In: Proceedings of the 2017 chi conference on human factors in computing systems, CHI '17, Denver, Colorado, USA. ACM, New York, NY, USA, pp 1483–1496. ISBN 978-1-4503-4655-9. https://doi.org/10.1145/025453.3025761, http://doi.acm.org/10.1145/3025453.3025761. Accessed 10 Sept 2019

Soute I, Lagerström S, Markopoulos P (2013) Rapid prototyping of outdoor games for children in an iterative design process. In: Proceedings of the 12th international conference on interaction design and children, IDC '13, New York, New York, USA. ACM, New York, NY, USA, pp 74–83. ISBN 978-1-4503-1918-8. https://doi.org/10.1145/2485760.2485779, http://doi.acm.org/10.1145/2485760.2485779. Aceessed 11 Sept 2019

Soute I et al (2017) Design and evaluation of RaPIDO, a platform for rapid prototyping of interactive outdoor games. ACM Trans Comput-Hum Interact 24(4):28:1–28:30. ISSN 1073-0516. https://doi.org/10.1145/3105704, http://doi.acm.org/10.1145/3105704. Accessed 11 Sept 2019

Tong X et al (2020) Examining the efficiency of gamification incentives for encouraging physical activity-social collaborations or interactive mobile games? In: Proceedings of the 10th EAI International Conference on Pervasive Computing Technologies for Healthcare, https://www.researchgate.net/publication/266025077_Deconstructing_gamification_Evaluating_the_effectiveness_of_continuous_measurement_virtual_rewards_and_social_comparison_for_promoting_physical_activity

Turkle S (2011) Alone together: why we expect more from technology and less from each other. Basic Books, Inc., New York, NY, USA. ISBN 978-0-465-01021-9

What is Childhood Obesity? Published: Retrieved Sept 12, 2018 from https://www.obesityaction.org/geteducated/understanding-childhood-obesity/what-is-childhood-obesity/, https://www.obesityaction.org/get-educated/understandingchildhood-obesity/what-is-childhood-obesity/. Accessed 5 Mar 2019

CommunIT Building

An Interactive Environment Exemplar Advancing Social Interaction in Underused Public Spaces

Carlos Henrique Araujo de Aguiar and Keith Evan Green

Abstract Despite the promise of social media to bring the world closer together, large segments of local communities, globally, remain misunderstood by or invisible to mainstream society. This problem is attributed, in large part, to digital media's ascendancy over physical, public space as the locus for civic discourse—the loss of informal and structured encounters between members of communities there. This chapter presents our development and early evaluation of a novel cyber-physical platform, *communIT*, for community building across diverse local community groups. Deployed in underused public spaces, *communIT* is an origami-like, folding, robotic surface of billboard scale, with embedded peripherals, that changes form in response to group needs for group co-creation and sharing of media. By collaboratively making and sharing media with *communIT*, local groups can tell stories, share experiences and aspirations, and advocate within the larger community. Such civic discourse promises the potential to transform personal identity and self-representation, community awareness and responsibility, and wider social relationships with policy-makers.

1 Introduction

The waning significance of public, outdoor, urban space—the "commons"—is an important contemporary issue within our technologically changing world that warrants careful examination and further comprehension by HCI researchers. Historically, in many cultures and societies, public, outdoor space—the Agora of ancient Greece (Fig. 1), is an archetype—has served as the capacious physical setting for people's interactions. Recently, however, the significance of the public, outdoor

C. H. A. de Aguiar (✉) · K. E. Green
Architectural Robotic Lab, Cornell University, Design and Environmental Analysis (DEA), Ithaca, USA
e-mail: ca449@cornell.edu

K. E. Green
e-mail: keg95@cornell.edu

© Springer Nature Switzerland AG 2020
D. S. McCrickard et al. (eds.), *HCI Outdoors: Theory, Design, Methods and Applications*, Human–Computer Interaction Series,
https://doi.org/10.1007/978-3-030-45289-6_12

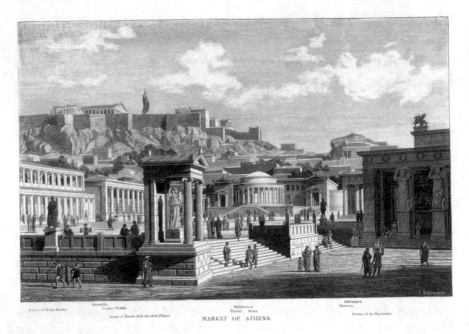

Fig. 1 Agora, in ancient Greek city Permission obtained from Alamy for use

spaces has been waning as information technology continues its global expansion and ubiquity. Information technology, readily accessible by many via smartphone, and embedded in the built environment in the form of innumerous small and large displays and sensor networks, has significantly transformed the relationship across individuals, private and public bodies, and the built environment (Oungrinis 2006; Sassen 2011; Easterling 2011; McLuhan 1994, Anderson 1992; Dublon and Portocarrero 2014). Weiser (Anderson 1992/Pinch 2010), for one, argues that ubiquitous computing produces uncertain consequences for the material world. He asks:

> At the time that digital technology seems to be dematerializing more and more of the world around us (think of books, CDs, photographs), what impact can they possibly have on the inevitable materiality of buildings and cities?

The "shift of importance from material to information" Sassen (2011), and the phenomena of "globalization and digitalization" Oungrinis (2006), have foregrounded virtual interaction among people. Undeniably, technological advances in information sciences produce many beneficial effects to society, such as efficiency and connectivity. Nevertheless, these benefits do not come without side effects. Equipped with smartphones with apps, people do not need to be in a physical space to interact with one another. As characterized by McLuhan (1994)/De Waal (2011), the flow of information has become, unlike physical space, "borderless and nonspatial": "cyberspace." The outdoor material space, once a key locus for social interaction, has lost much of its grounding in public life.

Information technology is not the first technology that has diminished the significance of the commons. Mitchel (1999) offers the historical example of the advent of plumbing infrastructure that supplanted the watering well as a catalyst for community building; with water being delivered to houses, there was no longer the need for members of the community to retrieve water from a centrally located water source where, oftentimes, citizens would have the occasion for informal exchange. This historical case illustrates how technological advances are inextricably connected with the built environment. In Mitchel's example, technology affected the material space which, in turn, affected social relations in urban outdoor spaces. Sassen (2011) and Oungrinis (2006) argue that technological advances have diminished the significance of the commons. We believe that ubiquitous computing and virtual interaction pose especially urgent challenges to human-environment interaction and the sociocultural significance. These challenges point to a new frontier to HCI researchers.

2 Rethinking the Technology-Human-Environment Relationship

The complex interrelation of people characterizes public, outdoor spaces. Historically, these spaces are cherished, multicultural, and diverse places. They work as a setting for friendly companionship and mutual interchange of ideas and political debate, crucial for democracy Oldenburg (1999). Today, there is, however, a need to rethink the relationship between people, space, and technology. De Waal, for instance, argues that technology can provide ways to enable "new forms of publicness and exchange" De Waal (2011). We believe HCI researchers should explore ways to integrate the new means of human-computer interaction with the old human-environment ("material space") interaction. More specifically, we believe there is a need to redesign public, outdoor spaces with embedded technological means to promote and enhance social interaction.

To better understand this technology-material space integration, we need to first reflect on the interaction between humans and the outdoor built environment. Pinch (2010), for instance, points out that the physical arrangement of material objects evokes particular human behavior. Reflecting on how a carrousel affects social interaction in place, Pinch says:

> There are two potential audiences (or recipients) for the role-distancing performance: fellow riders, and the watching parents and/or friends standing at the side of the merry-go-round. If the merry-go-round did not permit children to sit in close proximity to each other (so that they can monitor each others' behavior), then role distance for other riders could not be performed. In other words, the physical layout of the horses is crucial for this form of social interaction.

Pinch's idea highlights a synergetic and symbiotic relationship between people and the material arrangement of the space. In this relationship, people and the built environment have agency, each influencing the other. Pinch's idea seems to be in concordance with Pask (1969), a pioneering figure in cybernetics who also taught in the famed London architecture school, the Architectural Association. Pask's concept of "mutualism" involves the interplay between inhabitants and the built environment—the mutual relation between *"structures (any built environment entity) and men or society"* Pask (1969).

It is essential to highlight, however, that the built environment tends to be physically inelastic, despite having agency to affect people's behavior. On this topic, Pask speculates that "the dialogue (between people and the built environment) can be redefined and extended with the aid of modern techniques" Pask (1969). Pask's supposition about the adaptive environments seems to be an extension of his concept of mutualism. It also seems to involve embedding technology into the built environment. Adaptable, urban-architectural artifacts can sense, process, and respond to people's input, augmenting agency in space and providing multiple ways in which inhabitants and the built environment interact.

Our main goal is to rethink the relationship between people, space, and technology, and ultimately, to redesign urban, outdoor spaces as a vehicle for human interaction embedded with today's digital technologies. The key is not to negate technology but to reintegrate it into the built environment in order to, in Mitchell's words, "create fresh urban relationships, processes, and patterns that have the social and cultural qualities we seek for the twenty-first century" Mitchel (1999).

3   Our Response: *communIT*

Our team has been developing what we call *communIT* (Fig. 2), a cyber-physical environment responsive to the crisis of public outdoor spaces being supplanted by the ubiquity of personal, mobile computing. Practically, communIT is a foldable, large-scale origami, roughly 9ft long and 4.5 feet high, with embedded lighting, audio, and displays that changes its physical form responsively to the needs of individuals and groups. communIT is envisioned as consisting of sensible and responsive cyber-physical components that change the urban space via physically reconfigurable panels with embedded lighting, audio, and displays, among other integrated components and features.

Fig. 2   communIT in three different configurations

We envision communIT as an interactive urban environment that creates multiple "rooms" in underused public outdoor spaces. We envision these "many rooms" augmenting the services and programming of, for instance, schools, libraries, and community centers. CommunIT will allow users to interact with, and generate information in formats that are appropriate and personalized to them, including self-publishing, web design, graphic design, video production, game design, sound recording/mixing, and the creation of artifacts of a kind not yet imagined. While many of these activities can be accomplished with mobile technologies, we believe that a cyber-physical environment will more adequately serve a community's need to "find its place," literally and figuratively, in an increasingly digital society.

4 *communIT*, a Cyber-Physical Environment Increasing Social Interaction and Place Attachment in Public, Outdoors Space

The main objective of communIT is to activate underused public, urban spaces by increasing social interaction and place attachment. In this section, we present and discuss these two constructs, social interaction and place attachment, to consider how communIT affects the human-environment interplay in public, outdoor spaces. The first construct, social interaction, involves how people behave with each other. We hypothesize that communIT might shape social interaction by providing people tools to engage with activities within the public, outdoor spaces. We believe such activity engagement will provide a means for social encounters and interplay among users to increase social interaction.

The second construct, place attachment, is the cognitive and emotional bond that individuals develop toward a place (Cuba and Hummon 1993; Riley 1992). Place attachment helps to explain and predict other outcomes, such as behaviors, perceptions, and emotions (Giuliani 2003; Mesh and Manor 1998). Place attachment is organized in a three-dimensional framework: person, process, and place Scannell and Gifford (2010). The first dimension, "person," focuses on who is attached, and it involves the personal or collective meaning of attachment. The second dimension. "process," refers to how a person or a group is attached, and how individuals and groups express their attachment through affection, cognition, and behavior. The last dimension, "place," refers to what it is about the place that people are attached to—the physical quality of the place.

Place attachment has two main sub-constructs: place identity and place dependence. Place identity involves an individual's integration of place into the conception self-identity (Proshansky et al. 1978, 1983). This sub-construct indicates that self-identity depends, partially, on the place: who we depend on where we are, and consequently distinguishes us from others who are somewhere else Twigger-Ross et al. (1996). Place dependence involves the ability of the place to satisfy its inhabitants' various needs and wants. People tend to become more attached to a place when it offers significant resources supporting their activities.

We expect that communIT will impact place attachment by positively affecting its two sub-variables. For place dependence, communIT will provide new tools and attributes to help people satisfy their needs and wants. Physicality is an essential aspect of a place; we believe that communIT, as a material artifact, will help "ground" the people's dependence in a real, physical place. For place identity, we envision that communIT will provide people the opportunity to socially interact when engaging in activities in situ. We hypothesize that communIT will help users incorporate the space within their social identity by providing the means for social interaction. In the next section of this chapter, we will describe the iterative development of communIT, with particular focus on user studies, as a way of elaborating our exemplar of an HCI Outdoors artifact for advancing social interaction in underused public spaces.

5 Study 1: CoDAS, Co-design at Scale

Our research team has developed what it calls the "CoDAS method" (Co-Design at Scale) to initiate the design of communIT. CoDAS combines elements of established HCI methods—co-design Sanders and Stappers (2008) and user enactment Odom et al. (2012)—to develop larger-scale social computing artifacts. While other researchers (Sanders and Stappers 2008; Odom et al. 2012; Mokhtar et al. 2010; de Aguiar et al. 2016), have used these methods to design various types of physical artifacts, few have used this approach to design interactive, large-scale artifacts for urban, outdoor spaces. These artifacts have one particular characteristic: they have architectural (space-making) qualities, and their design involves not only the artifact per se but also the immediate surrounding environment. For instance, in order to design an architectural artifact installed in an urban environment (e.g., a kiosk in a public square), a designer will not only think about the physical shape of the kiosk but also the space around the artifact, how people occupy and behave in such space—the context.

The CoDAS method was developed to permit the design of artifacts with architectural qualities. The virtue of CoDAS is that it affords the exploration of the physical design of larger-scale interactive systems enabled by the use of a (physically small) scale model of the actual physical artifact and its surrounding physical environment. CoDAS has two main principles, based upon Brandt et al.'s "design challenge" Brandt (2012): participants and researchers co-designing, using "generative tools for co-design," a small-scale model of the artifact; and participants using "props, mock-up, and prototypes" to enact within the small-scale model, following from the co-design environment.

CoDAS is also based upon Lofland's (2006), social-setting framework, where every social setting involves actors engaging in activities with others in a particular space. Recognize that these actors may or may not be human—that "actors" can be the physical and digital artifacts that are integral to interactive behaviors. To further support CoDAS' foundation, we also used Zeizel's (1984), grand environmental behavior question: "who does what, with whom, using what, and in which setting?" From Zeizel and Lofland et al., we gained the fundamental framework for co-designing communIT and a way in which to conduct the socio-material analysis involving human and nonhuman actors, activities and behaviors, and place. More specifically, in CoDAS, these fundamental elements are the "generative tools for co-design"—the "props, mock-up, and prototypes." Co-designers and users use generative tools for co-design to imagine humans engaging in activities or behaviors within a place, and possibly use a nonhuman to accomplish those activities. These fundamental elements are the props, mock-up, and prototypes that enact this projected world.

CoDAS allows designers and participants to design attributes of an artifact socially, and to observe the environmental behavior and socio-dynamics around the designed system. The pre-definition of the elements mentioned above for designing communIT involves: (1) human actors under three conditions, (2) six nonhuman actors, (3) activities, and (4) the place, elaborated as follows:

(1) Three conditions: alone, with known people, with unknown people;
(2) Six nonhuman actors: canopy, floor, screen, bench, table, and light;
(3) A list of fourteen activities, such as working, studying, and playing: through a survey, participants were asked to select the activities they would prefer doing in an outdoor space under the three different human actor-conditions;
(4) The physical site: an outdoor urban public space that will receive communIT intervention.

Following from this pre-definition, the designer team physically fabricated the generative tools for co-design (props, mock-up, and prototypes) using manual tools and digital fabrication (Fig. 3). Design took place in the researchers' lab, where seven participants were invited to engage in the co-design of communIT. The research

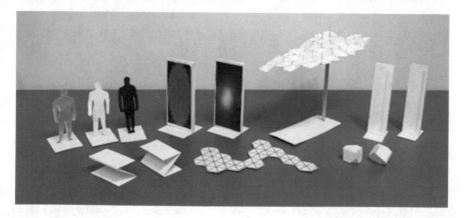

Fig. 3 The generative tools for co-design: basic design components that might make up commnIT

team first explained the essential attributes of each element included in the study and followed with the two primary co-design activities.

5.1 Study 1: Procedure

We invited seven participants, a convenience sample of university students, ages 18–30, 5 males, 2 females, to our lab to engage individually with the research team in our study. We described each of the six design components, presenting on a large computer display a photo of each modeled component, as well as a video, of its potential interactive features. For instance, a photo of the modeled canopy was displayed along with a short video that communicated the kinds of interactive features.

Using the generative tools for co-design described above, a participant and a member of the research team co-designed three different environments and drafted scenarios of actor-interactions for each of these environments (Fig. 4). For each co-design, the co-designers started the design process by picking one activity corresponding to the actor conditions; the co-designers then positioned, in the physical site model, the scale-modeled actors and design components to yield a design and an interaction scenario defined by this action.

Following the construction of the design and scenario, we asked each participant to engage in enacting the scenarios within the spaces they defined using the human figures. We asked participants to think out loud while enacting the scenarios. During the user enactment activity, the co-designer from our research team would sometimes prompt the participant co-designer with questions such as, *What are the actors doing at this instance in the scenario?*, to help focus the participant co-designer on the impacts the designs and scenarios have on their actors' behaviors, experiences, and emotions, and how these actors are negotiating this place and any other actors. The research team used the qualitative software program to organize, analyze, and

Fig. 4 Two co-designers—a participant and a research team member–collaboratively designing an environment using our "generative tools for co-design"

generate insights out of the data gathered. The analysis of the data was then used to generate insights toward advancing the development of communIT.

5.2   Study 1: Data Analysis

From the co-design task, researchers found that most of the co-designed environments were composed of a series of multipurpose micro-spaces (i.e., smaller, subdivided spaces), each with particular attributes, function, ambiance, levels of permeability, and privacy. While these micro-spaces had their characteristics, they were still connected among each other through what we call "in-between spaces" (i.e., transitory spaces, where people move from one place to another). Additionally, the researchers also noted that the overall co-designed environment, constituted by micro-spaces and in-between spaces, was generally organized in two different ways: a tight organization or a looser organization. Figures 5 and 6 show two spaces created by co-designers that correspond, respectively, to a tight and a loose overall co-designed environment. These two figures will help show this contrast better.

In Fig. 5, the overall co-designed environment is placed in the middle of the urban, scaled model, leaving the corridors at the periphery as passage, as indicated by the two gray arrows. The various nonhuman actors used in this design are grouped in a way that creates many micro-spaces closely connected. The in-between spaces (i.e., dark bubbles) in this instance are very minimal, sometimes even inexistent. The micro-space borders sometimes merge into each other in a way that their ambient influence becomes somewhat their combination. The transition between the micro-spaces, which occurs through the in-between spaces, therefore, is very immediate, as if the sum of the micro-spaces resulted in a continuum, unified (yet heterogeneous) space. Most of the peripheral micro-spaces are designed using one or two nonhuman actors, while the central one is created using many and different nonhuman actors.

Fig. 5 Looking down on the to-scale model: a compact organization of elements characterized as tight

Fig. 6 Looking down on the
to-scale model: an
organization of the elements
along two separate lines,
characterized as loose

This suggests a progressive increase of signals, stimulus, and information emitted by the nonhuman actors as the human actor moves from the peripheral micro-spaces toward the central one.

Figure 6 depicts an overall co-designed environment that is the antithesis of the previous one. While the previous environment was a tight arrangement of nonhuman actors, this other environment is a loose agglomeration of nonhuman actors. The environment is divided into two major peripheral areas leaving a passage in the middle. Despite being connected, the various micro-spaces seem to be more dispersed throughout the space compared to the previous design. One participant said he "imagine(s) the structure being semi-fixed [creating a] a semi-secluded space with permeable limits, not very constrained, allowing people to move between components" (i.e., nonhuman actors). The words of the participant suggest a looser and more flexible organization of the space.

From the enactment task, researchers found that some participants' initial response to the artifact arose from the mystery of the space they created and the curiosity the space generated. This suggests that the components' novelty and unknown nature of the setting were two aspects that initiated actors' attraction. As one participant articulated:

> I would first approach this space [i.e. a micro-space] and look at the screen or floor. And if I find something interesting, I would stay; if not, then I would move to this other space [i.e. another micro-space]…, and while moving from one micro-space toward another, passing through an in-between spaces, … I would observe these people as I move, but not get close [to the micro-space they're occupying].

Another participant offered that…

> the space allows you to do things that you don't know yet. You continuously move to the center… the periphery creates a path…. It's like climbing a mountain: the fun moment is not directly given, … but for you to explore by yourself.

These passages suggest that the initial attraction may sometimes be followed by an exploratory behavior aimed at understanding (a) nonhumans' attributes, (b) the many micro-spaces ambiance and function, and (c) the behavior of others human actors that were already in space. These passages also highlight how the space can differently constrain the human actor's behavior. Human actors seem to engage in observing the overall surroundings when transiting from one micro-space towards another (i.e., when circulating in-between space). On the other hand, a closer exploration seems to occur when the actors are inside a micro-space; such closer exploration involved the investigation of nonhumans' attributes and functions within the micro-space.

5.3   Study 1—Consecutive Design Iteration

Following from the above analysis, the design team designed (without users) a new design iteration (see Fig. 2), that was informed by findings reported above. Vyzoviti's idea of "Folding Architecture" Vyzoviti (2003), inspired our design concept. Folding Architecture involves the manipulation of space through the manipulation of surface. As Simitch and Warkere point out, a design concept is a pure design abstraction that "*poses a way of thinking about a design problem….*" Simitch and Warkere (2014). As in every design problem, we could have chosen another concept from a vast library of possibilities; but with much pondering of the problem and opportunity, our extensive knowledge of design precedent, our cumulative experience as practitioners and design researchers, and ample discussion and critical debate, we agreed on Folding Architecture as a fruitful concept for our team to build from.

Using simple pieces of paper, we started to explore potential ways to replicate lessons learned in the co-design activity. More precisely, our team of design researchers began to cut, fold, and rotate numerous pieces of paper to find forms that subdivided the space, creating various smaller spaces—micro-spaces. Figure 7 depicts four early models produced in our exploration. This design iteration aimed to replicate the general patterns, behaviors, and interactions found in Study 1.

Each micro-space, as informed from the CoDAS study, would have its own characteristics and would provide users multiple purposes, stimulus, etc. These smaller spaces would also be diverse in its organization (i.e., from tightly to loosely

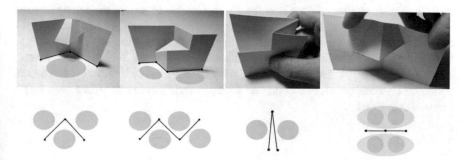

Fig. 7 Early models of communIT and how they divided the space in micro-spaces

connected) to allow different user experience within the space. The designers' overall intention was to create an environment composed of heterogeneous micro-spaces which allowed various levels of human actors' interaction and engagement. This design iteration, of course, is one possible interpretation among many designs co-designers socially constructed. As this is an early design phase, communIT's design will most likely be changed as the research design progresses.

6 Current and Future Work in CommunIT Research

In this chapter, we have presented the motivations for and iterative development of communIT. We used the CoDAS method in Study 1 to co-design communIT. Then, we used the many design cases produced by the co-designers to construct design guidelines. After having explored alternative potential designs for communIT, we produced a design that we believe encompasses essential design patterns we sought. These design patterns involved the overall organization of the space and the user's behavior.

Our research exploration of communIT has so far been conducted in a controlled lab environment, and we recognize the limitations of such research. Research in-the-wild Rogers and Marshall (2017), has the potential to further assist researchers in developing cyber-physical technologies of the kind like communIT for the outdoor spaces that aim to have a social impact. Research in-the-wild advocates the in situ understanding of technological interventions in the everyday lives of people, as well as the kind of interaction humans, have with these technologies. For communIT, more specifically, research in-the-wild could be used together with co-design activities to engage potential users in the designing, testing, and iteration of communIT's physical attributes and configurations needed and/or desired to accomplish specific activities.

Because research in-the-wild happens in situ, we intend, as a next activity, to conduct a quasi-experiment where we measure the effect of communIT on social interaction and place attachment. Specifically, we will conduct a quasi-experiment with our next, full-scale, iteration of communIT to measure its impact on both social interaction and place attachment in the wild. To measure social interaction, we will look at: (a) the number of people in the space, (b) the amount of time people spend in the space, and (c) the frequency they visit the space. We expect that communIT will attract more people to the space, instigate them to stay longer, and encourage them to return more often. For place attachment, we will use Williams and Vaske's validated scale Williams and Vaske (2003). We will do five observations—two before communIT's installation, two after, and finally, an additional one after communIT's removal (see Fig. 8).

$$O_1 O_2 X O_3 O_4 \underline{X} O_5$$

Fig. 8 Quasi-experiment, remove treatment with pre- and post-test. The letters 'O' means observation. The letter 'X' means add intervention, in this case communIT. The letter '$\underline{X}$' means "remove intervention"

7 The Importance of Interactive Physical Artifacts for HCI Outdoors

The emergence of social media has diminished the importance of physical space as a locus for collaborative activity. And despite the ubiquity of social media, which promises "to bring the world closer together" (Facebook), many segments of the population remain misunderstood by or invisible to the mainstream of society. *How might a cyber-physical system re-activate underused public spaces by offering means social interaction?* To answer this question, we have been developing communIT, a cyber-physical artifact for community building. In brief, communIT "situates" community engagement in the physical (outdoor) world as much as the digital world, serving (in the words of Malcom McCullough) "our basic human need for getting into place" McCullough (2004). CommunIT will probe unexplored opportunities in public, outdoor places for HCI artifacts at large physical scale, and will provide a deeper understanding of how people perceive and interact with each other in such new places. While other researchers have created larger-scale interactive installations (Fortin et al. 2014; Fisher et al. 2014; Peltonen et al. 2008; Grønbæk et al. 2012; Grönvall et al. 2014), communIT is distinct from these in its objective to foster place attachment and offer information services beyond the virtual world. Cyber-physical interventions at large-scale in public spaces are an inevitable future, and the communIT project aims to establish the fundamental terms of this frontier.

References

Anderson R (1992) Social impacts of computing: codes of professional ethics. Soc Sci Comput Rev 10(2):453–469

Brandt E et al (2012) Tools and techniques. In: Simonsen, Roberts (eds) Routledge international handbook of participatory design

Cuba L, Hummon DM (1993) A place to call home: identification with dwelling, community, and region. Sociol Quart 34:111–131

de Aguiar et al (2016) The networked, robotic home + furniture suite: a distributed, assistive technology facilitating aging in place. In: 2016 IEEE international conference on automation science and engineering (CASE). https://doi.org/10.1109/coase.2016.7743522

De Waal M (2011) The urban culture of sentient cities: from an internet of things to a public sphere of things. In: Shepard M (ed.) Sentient City: ubiquitous computing, architecture, and the future of urban space. The Architect League of New York, The MIT Press, pp 190–195

Dublon G, Portocarrero E (2014) Listentree: audio-haptic display in the natural environment. In: Proceedings 20th international conference on auditory display (ICAD–2014)

Easterling K (2011) The action is the form. In: Sentient City: ubiquitous computing, architecture, and the future of urban space. In: Shepard M (ed) The Architect League of New York. The MIT Press

Fisher P, Gerlach F, Acuna J, Pollack D, Schäfer I, Trautmann J, Hornecker E (2014) Movable, Kick-/Flickable light fragments eliciting ad-hoc interaction in public space. In: Proceedings of the international symposium on pervasive displays, pp 50–55 (June 2014)

Fortin C, Hennessy K, Sweeney H (2014) Roles of an interactive media façade in a digital agora. In: Proceedings of the international symposium on pervasive displays, pp 7–12 (June 2014)

Giuliani MV (2003) Theory of attachment and place attachment. In: Bonnes M, Lee T, Bonaiuto M (eds) Psychological theories for environmental issues. Ashgate, Aldershot, pp 137–170

Grønbæk K, Kortbek K, Møller C, Nielsen J, Stenfeldt L (2012) Designing playful interactive installations for urban environments—the swingscape experience. In: Nijholt A, Romão T, Reidsma D (eds) Advances in computer entertainment SE—16. Springer, Berlin, Heidelberg, pp 230–245. http://doi.org/10.1007/978–3-642-34292-9_16

Grönvall E, Kinch S, Petersen MG, Rasmussen MK (2014) Causing commotion with a shape-changing bench: experiencing shape-changing interfaces in use. In: Proceedings of SIGCHI Conference on Human Factors in Computing Systems, pp 2559–2568 (May 2014)

Lofland J et al (2006) Analyzing social settings a guide to qualitative observation and analysis. Wadsworth/Thomson Learning, Belmont, CA

McCullough M (2004) Digital ground—architecture, pervasive computing and environmental knowing. MIT Press, p 118

McLuhan M (1994) Understanding media. MIT Press, Cambridge, MA

Mesh GS, Manor O (1998) Social ties, environmental perception, and local attachment. Environ Behav 30:227–245

Mitchel M (1999) E-topia: Urban life, Jim—but not as we know it. Chapter 1, MIT Press, Cambridge, MA

Mokhtar TH, Green KE, Walker ID, Threatt T, Murali VN, Apte A, Mohan SK (2010) Embedding robotics in civic monuments for an information world. In: CHI '10 extended abstracts on human factors in computing systems (CHI EA '10). ACM, New York, NY, USA, pp 3859–3864. https://doi.org/10.1145/1753846.1754069

Odom W, Zimmerman J, Davidoff S, Forlizzi J, Dey AK, Lee MK (2012) A fieldwork of the future with user enactments. In Proceedings of the designing interactive systems conference (DIS '12). ACM, New York, NY, USA, pp 338–347. https://doi.org/10.1145/2317956.2318008

Oldenburg R (1999) The Great Good Place: cafes, caffee shops, bookstores, bars, hair salons, and other hangouts at the heart of a community. Marlowe & Company

Oungrinis K (2006) CommunITations: paradigms for designing CommunITable spaces. Harvard Design School, Cambridge, MA

Pask G (1969) The architectural relevance of cybernetics. Arch Des 39.9: 494–496. Trivedi D et al (2008) "Soft robotics: Biological inspiration, state of the art, and future research. Appl Bionics Biomech 5.3:99–117

Peltonen P, Kurvinen E, Salovaara A et al (2008) It's Mine, Don'T Touch!: interactions at a large multi-touch display in a city centre. In: Proceedings of the SIGCHI conference on human factors in computing systems. ACM, pp 1285–1294. http://doi.org/10.1145/1357054.1357255

Pinch T (2010) The invisible technologies of goffman's sociology from the merry-go-round to the internet. Technology and culture, vol 51, Number 2, Apr 2010, pp 409–424

Proshansky H et al (1978) The city and the self-identity. Environ Behav 10:147–169

Proshansky H et al (1983) Place-identity: physical world socialization of the self. J Environ Psychol 3:5783

Riley RB (1992) Attachment to ordinary landscape. In: Altman I, Low SM (eds) Place attachment. Plenum, New Yorl, pp 13–35

Rogers Y, Marshall P (2017) Research in the wild. [San Rafael, California]: Morgan & Claypool. https://doi.org/10.2200/S00764ED1V01Y201703HCI037

Sanders EB-N, Stappers PJ (2008) Co-creation and the new landscapes of design. CoDesign, 4(1):5–18 (Mar 2008)

Sassen S (2011) Unsettling topographic representation. In: Shepard M (ed) Sentient city: ubiquitous computing, architecture, and the future of urban space. The Architect League of New York, The MIT Press, pp 192–198

Scannell LD, Gifford R (2010) Defining place attachment: a tripartite organization framework. J Environ Psychol 30:1–10

Simitch A, Warkere V (2014) The language of architecture—26 principles every architect should know. Rockport, USA

Twigger-Ross et al (1996) Place and identity processes. J Environ Psychol 16, 205

Vyzoviti S (2003) Folding architecture. BIS, Amsterdam

Williams DR, Vaske JJ (2003) The measurement of place attachment: validity and generalizability of a psychometric approach. Forest Sci 49(6):830–840

Zeisel J (1984) Inquiry by design tools for environment-behavior research. Cambridge University Press, Cambridge, UK

Outdoor Auditory Wearable Interfaces: Bone Conduction Communication

Rafael N. C. Patrick, Tomasz R. Letowski, and Maranda E. McBride

Abstract Our senses not only connect us to the world around us but also protect us from harm. On any given day, we are involved in numerous activities and communication tasks but we are also exposed to a wide range of potential dangers. Whether it be hazardous toxins, slippery roads, or reckless acts that place us in such situations, our senses allow us to perceive threats in advance and provide us the opportunity to defend ourselves. However, technological advances created to make our lives better have frequently become double-edged swords limiting the effectiveness of our sensory shield by absorbing our attention and distracting us from receiving environmental warnings. Such situations recently became more prevalent and dangerous due to the wide-spread use of computers and digital technology in all aspects of our lives. For example, the use of smartphones with cellular, texting and media player capabilities, and portable computers with related visual and audio contents frequently detract us from hearing surrounding activities, which becomes especially dangerous in outdoor and hostile environments. However, in such situations, the utilization of active or open-ear wearable interfaces, such as bone conduction systems, can enable users to attend to streams of technology-based communication and/or entertainment (e.g., directions, phone conversations, music) without compromising their ability to sense the natural world and all of its salient beauty and danger. This chapter provides an introduction to auditory wearable devices, with a specific focus on bone conduction hearing and bone conduction head-mounted devices, while discussing auditory wearable device applications in outdoor environments in the context of human-computer interactions.

R. N. C. Patrick (✉) · T. R. Letowski
Grado Department of Industrial and Systems Engineering, Virginia Polytechnic Institute and State University, Blacksburg, VA, USA
e-mail: RNCP@vt.edu

T. R. Letowski
e-mail: Tolima2@verizon.net

M. E. McBride
Department of Management, College of Business and Economics, North Carolina A&T State University, Greensboro, NC, USA
e-mail: Mcbride@ncat.edu

© Springer Nature Switzerland AG 2020
D. S. McCrickard et al. (eds.), *HCI Outdoors: Theory, Design, Methods and Applications*, Human–Computer Interaction Series,
https://doi.org/10.1007/978-3-030-45289-6_13

1   Introduction

Human-Computer Interactions (HCIs) have become an important and still growing part of modern-day life. Such interactions include common activities like initiating a phone call or activating audio content on a portable listening device (PLD) carried out at work, at home, within hospital settings, during travel, and, ultimately, within all aspects of daily activity. Almost overnight, computers became critical elements of security systems, military operations, financial systems, all forms of media, and simple everyday tasks. Essentially, they became the parts of ourselves that we did not know we were missing. They are involved in both our stationary and mobile activities. Due to the vast interconnectivity of today's society, computers (and smart computer-based devices) have become ubiquitous. It is hard to imagine a modern person without some form of daily interaction with a computer or computer-controlled system. With this in mind, it is important that we take the time to examine how such interactions affect our everyday lives and, more importantly, how they may interfere with the natural behaviors we have historically relied upon to keep ourselves safe.

As smart devices and digital media become more prevalent in societies, people have begun engaging in communication- or entertainment-based activities (i.e., cell-phone conversations, texting, and/or listening to music) on a much larger scale than previously with battery-operated portable audio devices. More importantly, these activities are frequently conducted while a person performs other cognitively demanding tasks (e.g., while driving a vehicle or crossing a busy intersection). In 2010 a study reported that the estimated number of pedestrian injuries involving mobile devices was about 1,506 (Nasar and Troyer 2013). In the mid-1980s, mobile phone usage represented about 1% of the U.S. population but rapidly grew to about 14.5% or 38 million users by 1996 (Katz and Aspden 1998). In terms of the amount of usage (represented by wireless data traffic), Cellular Telecommunications Industry Association (CTIA) reported an annual wireless data traffic growth of 40x from 2010 to 2017, which equates to about 250 million people simultaneously using a mobile device to stream some form of content (Cellular Telecommunications & Internet Association (CTIA) 2018).

Due to the oversaturation of our daily activities by digital content paired with a fear-of-missing-out (FOMO), the term "Internet Addiction" has been associated with today's young population who continuously monitors their public and private digital content (Young 1999), and subject themselves to extremely dangerous situations while indulging in such activities. Although the term FOMO is generally directed toward younger users of HCI interfaces, it should be considered a widespread phenomenon among inhabitants of technologically advanced societies and its effects should be adequately assessed. Users of HCI interfaces should be aware that to effectively engage in such activities, critical periods of time elapse that may temporarily distract them from their environment, which, in turn, causes them to sacrifice precious seconds of mental concentration often required to safely complete the task at hand.

While the vast majority of HCIs take place indoors or within sheltered environments (e.g., driver-based HCI within a commuter vehicle), in recent years they have become commonplace in outdoor settings and hostile environments (e.g., dynamic military operations and outdoor leisure and recreational activities). In many ways, such interactions are coupled with multitasking activities that require a person to interact with computer components, operate mechanical equipment, engage with human counterparts outside of the HCI network, and monitor unrelated activities while concurrently maintaining a high level of vigilance. Therefore, HCI interfaces that are used outdoors during dynamic or information critical multitasking activities and/or for entertainment while performing other activities must facilitate efficient and safe human operation without being a detriment to one's ability to sense the surrounding environment and respond accordingly. In other words, the use of computer-based platforms during various communication tasks, work, or leisure activities should neither hinder our ability to perceive the immediate environment nor limit our natural ability to sense hazards and protect ourselves.

Concerning the sense of hearing, such requirements can be fulfilled by the utilization of active or open-ear wearable communication systems. Unlike the primary sense of sight, the auditory sense is omnidirectional, affording one the ability to be acoustically aware of the immediate environment regardless of which way the head is facing. The importance of hearing the surrounding environment results from the fact that we may often hear some events of concern before we are able to see it. Therefore, the ability to be aware of one's environment is critical during task performance and the accessibility of audio content (e.g., radio communication, entertainment, navigation, etc.) should not interfere or reduce one's ability to be situationally aware.

The purpose of this chapter is to: (1) provide a surface-level review of the human auditory system and auditory communication; (2) discuss advantages and limitations of auditory wearable devices with the focus on their effects on a user's auditory situation awareness (ASA); and (3) review examples of auditory wearable bone conduction HCI systems capable of allowing users the ability to maintain intelligible communication, while still sensing the immediate acoustic environment via open-ear pathways.

Throughout this chapter, the term communication will be used often. Generally, the term refers to a two-way contact and/or interaction between a "sender" and "receiver". However, the word may also be applied to the reception-only activity such as during radio reception, television watching, computer games (both interactive and non-interactive), and most forms of social media and music entertainment usages. Therefore, moving forward, the term communication will be used in this chapter not only to denote the process of information exchange but also the process of passively acquiring information from computer or various forms of media.

2   Human Auditory Perception

Sight is the sense that enables us to visually acquire and distinguish various objects
we interact with on a daily basis. We are able to recognize pleasant or toxic odors
through our olfactory sense of smell. The gustatory sense (i.e., taste) protects us from
consuming spoiled or rotten food. We distinguish between hot and cold, soft and hard,
and still or pulsating objects to protect ourselves from severe bodily harm through
the tactile sense, which allows us to feel the touch of an object. Last but not least, the
auditory sense (i.e., our ability to hear) is the sense by which we perceive the acoustic
environment. The importance of hearing in our life cannot be overemphasized. In
1982, Evans noted that "… a blind man is cut off from the world of things, whereas
one who is deaf is cut off from the world of people" (Evans 1982).

In everyday life, we receive a large variety of auditory signals resulting from
acoustic waves impinging on our head. Since some acoustic waves may be heard and
others not, those that can be heard are called sound waves[1] to differentiate them from
the others. The audibility of various sound waves depends on our hearing health (i.e.,
hearing sensitivity) and the listening condition. The main auditory sensory elements
are two organs of hearing—organs of Corti—located within the structure of the head
in fluidic capsules called the left and right inner ears. Acoustic waves transmitted
through an elastic medium (i.e., air) and impinging on the head can stimulate organs
of hearing (and be perceived as sound) through two different pathways—the air
conducting pathway and the bone conducting pathway. Both pathways are transmission chains through which acoustic signals are converted into mechanical vibrations
exciting the organs of hearing and triggering neural responses interpreted by the
brain as sound. The primary difference between the two modes of perception is that
sound can be channeled from the air into a listener's ear(s) (via AC) or by directly
affecting the mechanical structures within the human head (via BC).

In the air conduction transmission mode (pathway), acoustic waves are transmitted
to the left and right organ of hearing through two corresponding sets (left and right)
of three conducting segments called the outer ear, middle ear, and inner ear. The
outer ear consists of an external flap, the auricular—commonly called "the ear"—
channeling sound waves to the canal (auditory meatus) leading to the membrane
(tympanic membrane) separating the outer ear from the cavity of the middle ear. The
mechanical vibration of the tympanic membrane caused by impinging sound waves
is transmitted through a system of three small bones (ossicles chain), connecting the
tympanic membrane to another—much smaller—membrane separating the middle
ear from the fluidic capsule of the inner ear and to the fluids of the inner ear. In
this process, the middle ear operates as a force transformer compensating for the
differences in size and modes of vibration of both membranes. The movement of
fluid in the inner ear triggers specific neural reactions in the organ of hearing that are
transmitted through a neural network to the brain.

---

[1]the term "sound" describes a physical stimulus. However, the same term "sound" is also used
to describe the perceptual effect of auditory stimulation. Although sometimes confusing, both
meanings need to be understood and differentiated.

In the bone conduction transmission mode (pathway), acoustic waves act directly on the skull of the head, causing it to vibrate. The vibration of the bony structures of the head is directly transmitted to the fluids of the inner ear. Movement of the fluids stimulates the organ of hearing in an analogous manner as in the case of the transmission mode. In a typical listening situation, both transmission modes act simultaneously with the main difference between the modes being their sensitivity. Since the head, as a mechanical system, is not very sensitive to stimulation by minute vibrations of the air due to impedance mismatch, the transmission of acoustic energy to the fluids of the inner ear is very inefficient. As a result, sound waves impinging on the human head, with the exception of extremely strong stimuli, will not be heard through the pathway. In contrast, hearing transmission through the pathway provides both impedance matching and sound amplification and delivers auditory stimuli to the inner ear in a very effective manner. As a result, stimulation of the organ of hearing through the pathway is about 40–60 dB stronger at mid and high frequencies than through the pathway for the same sound wave acting on the head (v Békésy 1948; Zwislocki 1953; Sklare and Denenberg 1987). Therefore, in a typical everyday situation, when we receive acoustic energy through the medium of air, we hear it as sound through our air conduction pathways (the "ears") while we are not aware that it is also heard through the skull bones at the same time. However, the reception of sound can be easily improved if the sound is directly delivered to the head by solid-state coupling. Such a delivery method is the essence of the auditory wearable devices to be discussed in this chapter.

Concerning global human perception, one must be aware of the role the sense of hearing plays on human activities and overall safety. Within a given environment, hearing provides us with an involuntary (i.e., natural) advantage when caring for ourselves. It allows for distant perception and operates in a 360° spherical range. The ability to perceive distant events that we are unable to detect or identify visually serves as an important early warning mechanism for humans and animals alike. In the case of animals, signal detection of footsteps or broken twigs in the distance serves as an advanced warning of danger of an approaching predator or information about potential pray nearby. Humans utilize their auditory senses in very similar ways in both stationary and dynamic situations. Some examples of dynamic situations are outdoor activities such as urban running and walking, trail hiking, and biking. Possessing the ability to sense approaching hazards such as an oncoming vehicle in urban environments or hostile wildlife in the wilderness can be the difference between a "close-call" and severe bodily harm or even death. Unfortunately, the outdoor operation of communication systems, which are currently dominated by computer-based systems like smartphones, in hostile or hazardous environments (e.g., cave exploration, off-road driving, rescue missions, etc.) limits our ability to utilize environmental cues and can result in severe bodily harm or death if awareness of the environment is compromised. Furthermore, the use of such systems without the knowledge of how they are compromising environmental awareness can greatly increase the likelihood of harm.

In order for a person to fully utilize auditory information, the incoming sounds must be heard (detected) and their sources recognized and localized. Although adolescent humans have the ability to perceive (hear) acoustic waves with frequencies between 20 Hertz (Hz) and 20,000 Hz (range of human hearing), they need to be at certain intensities to be heard while the threshold of audibility varies across the frequencies and is affected by our health and age. The frequencies between 2,000 and 4,000 Hz are the easiest to hear while the ability to hear frequencies outside of this band decreases gradually toward low and high frequencies.

Detection of sound is the first step in auditory perception. With increasing levels of sound, auditory stimuli can be recognized (e.g., it is music) and its source identified (e.g., played by a flute). If we want to hear it, it becomes a signal to us. If we do not, it becomes a noise masking other useful signals preventing reception. In order to hear a signal, it must arrive at our ears at certain minimal (audibility threshold) or higher intensity (super threshold) and needs to be distinguishable from surrounding sounds. This typically requires a favorable signal-to-noise intensity ratio (SNR) and favorable direction of the incoming signal in comparison to the direction of the incoming or surrounding noise. In general, the higher the signal intensity (SI) the greater the likelihood that a signal can be heard. However, an increase of sound intensity above a certain level may cause discomfort for the listener and, in extreme cases, even pain. In addition, prolonged exposure to intense sounds results in some form of inner ear damage and temporary or permanent hearing loss. Therefore, people working in high intensity noise environments (e.g., around machinery noise, airplane jet noise, etc.) or exposed to high intensity sonic impulses (e.g., explosions, gunshots, etc.) are mandated by the Occupational Safety and Health Administration (OSHA) requirements (Leonard 2009), to wear hearing protection devices (HPDs) capable of protecting their hearing against damage.

HPDs have been found to decrease the level of audible noise but also prevents wearers from hearing warning or auxiliary (e.g., tactical) signals. This difficulty may be mitigated by delivering such signals through various pass/through and BC wearable devices. However, over the past decade, a series of in-field and in-lab experiments at Virginia Tech's Auditory Systems Laboratory have demonstrated that certain advanced HPDs and military Tactical-Communications-and-Protective-Systems (TCAPS), all designed to pass-through signals/communications, in fact, do not provide truly natural hearing or "transparency," and have deleterious effects on auditory situation awareness (ASA) (Lee and Casali 2016). Measures of ASA performance have included: hearing threshold (dB) at detection, accuracy, and response time in recognizing/identifying signatures and for localization, and intelligibility of communications (Casali and Lee 2016). Based on these experiments, an objective, repeatable test battery was developed for evaluating HPD and TCAPS effects on the ASA tasks of: Detection, Recognition/Identification, Localization (azimuth and frontal elevation), and COMmunication, known as "DRILCOM" (Lee and Casali 2017).

By way of the BC pathway, an individual can maintain a steady stream of intelligible communication via computer-based and audio systems while remaining acoustically cognizant of ambient sound and acoustical changes in the environment which, in turn, should increase a user's overall achievable situation awareness. Although previous research aimed at determining achievable levels of ASA while using a BC device were conducted and were found favorable (Nuamah et al. 2014), a direct device comparison (AC vs. BC) using the DRILCOM methodology would provide a much-needed body of evidence. The following section aims to discuss the concept of situation awareness in detail, more specifically, ASA and why possessing a high-level of ASA is critical during outdoor use of HCI interfaces.

3 Situation Awareness and Auditory Situation Awareness

Due to the rapid development of smartphones and the almost overnight saturation, overutilization, and addiction of social networks, individuals are now able to communicate and share their experiences with family, friends, and whoever is willing to pay attention over great distances instantly either synchronously or asynchronously. However, a negative unintended consequence of such "connectivity" throughout the society has resulted in individuals engaging in conversation or social media interactions while performing other cognitively demanding tasks. To do so, such individuals subject themselves to hazardous predicaments while indulging in such activities. Performing a simple gesture such as answering a phone call while riding a bike along a busy road or attempting to cross the street while engaging in a telephone conversation can put that individual and/or other parties in the vicinity in a very hazardous situation. Since effective communication requires an individual to first perceive what is being communicated to them, interpret the content, formulate a response, and finally articulate that response, precious time and mental energy is consumed. This, in turn, may temporarily distract them from their current environment and sacrifice critical seconds of mental concentration required to safely complete the potentially risky primary task before them.

The traditional mode of hearing or communicating via audio signals delivered by loudspeakers or headset devices requires AC sound delivery, which, in turn, decreases a person's ability to perceive auditory signals in the surrounding area. Limiting an individual's ability to perceive his/her surroundings directly limits the level of situation awareness one can achieve and; therefore, limits the ability to receive environmental cues that are essential for safety. The concept of situation awareness (SA), a person's mental model of the world around them, was first introduced in the context of the dynamic and safety-critical aviation environment by Mica Endlsey in 1987 (Endsley 1987). Defined as "the perception of the elements in the environment within a volume of time and space, the comprehension of their meaning, and the projection of their status in the near future" (Endsley 1988), SA is central to effective decision-making. Since SA involves perceiving critical factors in the environment (Level 1), understanding what those factors mean, particularly when integrated together in relation to a person's goal (Level 2), and at the highest level, an understanding of what will happen in the near future (Level 3), it is paramount for overall safety that a person is able to receive environmental cues allowing for a decision, in regards to action, to occur in a timely and effective manner.

When the concept of SA is specifically applied to acoustic environments, it can be described as auditory situation awareness (ASA). With cues from the environment, an individual can easily determine where a sound source is located due to interaural intensity differences (IID) and interaural time differences (ITD). ITD is defined as the time difference between signals arriving at one ear versus the other in relation to the signal while IID is defined as the difference in sound intensity at the ears of the listener (Wolfe et al. 2007). In the case of communication using a binaural (both ears) headset or monaural (one ear) in-ear communication device, such binaural differences are compromised and frequently misleading[2]. Although humans have bilateral auditory symmetry, once a headset or earplug obstructs the auditory canal(s), perception becomes noticeably unbalanced or nonexistent. The use of binaural headsets does not necessarily introduce auditory imbalance, but to a greater degree, isolates a person from their environment.

In an environment-deafening situation created by most over-the-head or in-ear headsets, the ear canal is blocked from receiving environmental signals. For example, a person wearing a headset while on a leisure walk through the local trails would be cut off from the acoustic environment, which, in turn, reduces that individual's overall ASA and, to a large extent, limits their ability to hear hazards and respond appropriately. Similarly, an individual wearing the same type of headset while in a seemingly controlled environment such as on a park bench or on the bleachers of a stadium while watching an audio-video rendering of a sporting event on their smartphone device would also greatly deprive themselves of hearing environmental warnings (e.g., a stranger's arrival or a warning of a fast approaching object). Regardless of the environment (i.e., wilderness or safe-space), it is essential for overall safety that the human ear remains unoccluded despite the desire to communicate or be entertained. In such cases and many others, a person utilizing any form of auditory device subjects themselves to distraction from environmental awareness whether it is purposeful or unintentional. Therefore, for the sake of safety, such distraction from the environment must be minimized unless that is the desired result (i.e., intentional noise abatement).

In 2002, research investigating soldier ASA and its detriment due to the use of hearing protection devices, communication headsets, and other types of headgear was published in Designing Soldier Systems: Issues in Human Factors (Melzer et al. 2018). This report provided further evidence that ground soldiers use all five senses to gather information, especially in an urban environment. Furthermore, interfaces that degrade a soldier's ability to sense his/her environment could compromise his/her safety. In an attempt to counteract the effects of traditional auditory communication devices on ASA, BC systems have been recommended to provide users with the

---

[2]Through conditioning, whether someone has symmetrical or unsymmetrical hearing, the brain becomes accustomed to the way the ears receive cues from the surrounding environment. Any occlusion of the ears distorts this learned behavior, which may lead to grave mistakes in interpreting one's surroundings.

ability to be aware of the acoustic environment when using audio signals in HCIs; so that sounds in the surrounding environment can be localized and understood, resulting in increased levels of safety.

As alluded to earlier, in many ways, sound can be the initial warning of events occurring within our immediate vicinity. The IID and ITD localization techniques mentioned previously enable the extraction of useful information about sounds sensed in the environment. Essentially, such information allows a listener to localize a sound source and form an auditory spatial orientation. These cues allow a listener to assess the location of the sound source in the horizontal plane (azimuth), the location of the sound source in the vertical plane (elevation), the distance to the sound source, and the volume of the acoustic space (Scharine et al. 2009). Although it has been found that humans are somewhat inaccurate at determining the absolute location of a moving sound at a particular time (Perrott and Musicant 1977), simply sensing a sound in the distance can be invaluable in regards to deciding if immediate action is necessary. However, if the ears are blocked, resulting in little or no perception of the environment, such an individual is subject to the mercy of the oncoming threat. In outdoor settings (i.e., battlefield or wilderness), this can be a very hazardous predicament to find yourself in without forewarning.

As reported by Scharine et al., in their study on ASA in urban operations, "the urban environment adds acoustical and situational features that are detrimental to a soldier's ability to detect, recognize, identify, and localize relevant sound information. For the most part, both friendly and opposing forces are faced with similar limitations. However, indigenous opposing forces have a significant advantage due to familiarity with the terrain, and experience with the local sounds and the characteristics of the environment that help them better identify and locate sounds (Scharine et al. 2009)".

If paralleled to the outdoor environment and the "friendly" soldier substituted with a casual user of an ASA deafening interface, an "indigenous opposing force" such as dangerous wildlife would have the same or more of an advantage over its prey (i.e., the oblivious hiker). Therefore, in order to have any chance to protect oneself, the hiker in this case would have to have prior warning of the oncoming hazard, formulate the appropriate response, and react immediately. Such would not be possible if that forewarning was inhibited due to obstruction of the open-ear AC pathway. As to be discussed in the following section, advancements in technology have allowed for the development of advanced auditory communication systems such as bone conduction interfaces. With such an interface, the hiker would be able to enjoy their preferred form of communication via a computer-based platform while still being able to perceive the threat.

The need for an open-ear system that allows its user to maintain high-levels of ASA so that they may interact with the outdoor experience is upon us. Experiences such as the Sonic City allows users to interactively create music by walking through a city are meant to enhance the outdoor exploration experience (Gaye et al. 2003). While other outdoor experiences have been created to support esthetic engagement with everyday surroundings through soundscape augmentation (Monastero et al. 2016) and deliberately composed musical experiences meant to be heard in the background of landscapes (Hazzard et al. 2015), all require the user to be acoustically aware of the environment to be able to effectively submerge oneself in the experience. If not for these reasons alone, additional research must be done to improve the overall quality and, ultimately, the experiences associated with the use of bone conduction communication systems since such systems are ideal compliments to such information rich environments.

4 Auditory Wearable Communication Systems: Current and Future

The concept of wearable technology is not new, in fact, the earliest adoption of a wearable device can be traced back to the development of the watch in 1500, by German inventor Peter Henlein. Worn around the neck, the first iteration of the watch was a semi-electronic device capable of providing users with a somewhat accurate account of time. Although at this point, the watch was not considered a computer-based interface, it can be considered the first stage in wearable HCI due to the fact that it warranted moderate levels of human interaction (e.g., calibration of the time). As the watch developed—into the pocket watch than the wearable form of the wristwatch—it began to evolve into the ubiquitous computing device we have come accustomed to wearing today. Originally introduced in the mid-1970 s, the Pulsar calculator watch was the penultimate step towards today's modern wrist worn gadgets like the popular Apple Watch and Fitbit.

As it relates to auditory interfaces, another early wearable technology which is often overlooked due to its relatively small targeted consumer market is the hearing aid. Typically, used by individuals with moderate levels of hearing loss, the hearing aid is a device designed to provide passive amplification by gathering sound energy and directing it into the ear canal (Bentler and Duve 2000). Worn as an in-the-canal device or external device connected to the ear canal by an ear mold, hearing aids are classified in most countries as medical devices and are regulated in their use and distribution. As technology advanced, modern devices became computerized electroacoustic systems that transform environmental sound unperceivable or poorly perceived by an individual having some form of mechanical damage to the hearing system (conductive hearing loss). Additionally, more sophisticated devices provide some levels of digital signal processing in an attempt to improve speech intelligibility and comfort by managing feedback, directionality, frequency lowering, wide dynamic range compression, and in some cases, noise reduction (i.e., similar to TCAPS). It should be noted that an important factor contributing to the overall effectiveness of such devices is the "fitting" which is the configuration of the device to match the characteristics of the intended users (i.e., type and severity of the hearing loss, physical features of the pinna and ear canal, and lifestyle).

Another form of a modern hearing aid is a surgically implanted (transcutaneous) bone-anchored hearing aid (BAHA) (Janssen et al. 2012), which is a device that utilizes the bone conduction auditory pathways previously described. Although

BAHA systems are best suited for listeners with severe conductive hearing loss, individuals with less severe (moderate, mild) conductive hearing loss have been successfully using the device for decades as percutaneous (unanchored) BC systems. Similarly, to the BAHA systems, the percutaneous systems leave the ear canal(s) open, but they do not require any surgical intervention. Historically, BC as a process of hearing enhancement is frequently credited to Ludwig van Beethoven, at the early age of thirteen, when he developed a severe case of hearing loss and was unable to hear music due to his condition. Even though it is somewhat unclear how he implemented BC stimulation, Beethoven was able to produce some of mankind's finest and most treasured musical pieces while clinically deaf and receiving sound only through vibrotactile vibrations (i.e., BC). In all likelihood, perception via BC has been known since ancient times but was not paid much attention as a means of natural communication until the end of the twentieth century when the first commercial BC interfaces were developed for military operations. As a standalone system, BC communication interfaces have successfully found their way into noteworthy aspects of general leisure-based consumer markets, dynamic-based military environments, and clinical settings.

In American clinical settings, *Radioear* BC transducers are the most commonly used device. The B81, B71, and B71W are all similar in terms of contact surface area (1.75 cm^2) yet differ in regards to the physical design, performance characteristics, and intended use. The B71W and B71 are identical in all aspects with regards to performance and materials except that the B71W does not contain lead. The B81, on the other hand, is the newest device and achieves higher output levels at low frequencies with superior distortion performance. The B81's design was based on the Balanced Electro-magnetic Separation Transducer (BEST) principle devel oped by Håkansson (2003). Another reason for developing the B81 was due to the fact that the B71 produced high harmonic distortion at low frequencies (Dirks and Kamm 1975; Dolan and Morris 1990; Parving and Elberling 1982); that altered hearing sensitivity readings which could lead to misdiagnosed hearing loss. In military settings, both BC transducers and microphones have been used or tested for potential use to varying degrees. One such device, which is still active and was developed with a U.S. Naval Special Warfare team is the *Dominator II*. This is a custom-made system developed to address issues encountered with other communication systems on the market. Lastly, consumer-based devices such as the *Trekz Air*, *Titanium*, and *Bluez 2S* developed by AfterShokz, the *Juhall*, the *Borofone*, and *Oannao*, just to name a few, have been quite popular with users of auditory wearable devices who see the value of maintaining unoccluded hearing while engaging in various outdoor activities. Currently, several BC headsets, individual transducers, as well as microphones (e.g., for divers), are available commercially, while further development of such devices is fueled by ongoing research into perception via bone and application-based exploration of BC interfaces. An exhaustive list was compiled by McBride et al. (2017), and was published in the US Army Research Laboratory's Bone Conduction Communication: Research Progress and Directions (McBride et al. 2017).

Despite a fragmented understanding, related studies have provided evidence that the use of BC pathways can be beneficial within dynamic environments where acoustic situation awareness and intelligible communication is equally valued (Nuamah et al. 2014; Walker et al. 2005; Kyte et al. 2011; McBride et al. 2011). More specifically for outdoor use, BC systems have been used for navigation to aid temporarily or permanently visually impaired persons (Wilson et al. (October 2007), and for older pedestrians (Montuwy et al. 2019). In both instances, navigational information in the form of audio content presented via bone conduction pathways were found to be accepted by its users due to its effectiveness and inconspicuous appearance. Last but not least, a study investigating the effectiveness of an advanced BC system for people who enjoy outdoor activities provides evidence that users were entertained even better with the BC interface compared to the conventional AC device (i.e., earphones) because their feeling of uneasiness was much less during walking tasks while other people were around them (Chang-Geun et al. 2011).

As a result, it is important to keep in mind the technology's potential moving forward due to its ability to allow for safe transmission of intelligible audio signals while affording its users the ability to perceive the natural world and maintain a necessary level of ASA. Although, in order for BC communication systems to become more accepted by users of auditory wearables, more research in the form of achievable situation awareness, general usability, and technology acceptance should be conducted to inform the design of future systems.

5 Conclusions

To interact in the world of today, we must communicate with each other in some way. When communicating in today's society, we are no longer limited to face-to-face verbal interactions. The concept of communication and the sharing of ideas has evolved from traditional gatherings in person to cell phone conversations, text-based messaging, and digitally formatted media. Although technological advancements constantly change the means of communication, an awareness of the surrounding environment and its changes remain essential for users' safety and task completion. As reviewed throughout this chapter, humans are able to receive auditory signals in two ways: via air conduction (AC) or bone conduction (BC). Both are modes of converting acoustic signals either in the form of acoustic waves propagating through the environment or transmitted directly to the listener through mechanical vibrations into comprehensible sounds referred to as speech, music, noise, etc. AC is considered the primary form of hearing since it is about 40 dB more sensitive than BC due to the internal amplification of sound that takes place within the middle ear. Furthermore, this form of sound perception is the way most sound producing devices (e.g., loudspeakers, headphones, and earbuds) transmit auditory stimuli to users.

One major advantage of BC perception, when it is invoked by mechanical vibrations directly applied to the skull of a listener, is that it does not rely on the existence of the external and middle ear mechanics. Utilization of the BC sound delivery mechanism for one signal source leaves the ear canals open for clear passage of signals from other sources via AC pathways. Through the utilization of the BC pathway, an individual can maintain a steady stream of intelligible communication via computer-based and audio systems, while remaining acoustically cognizant of ambient sound and acoustical changes in the environment, which, in turn, increase an individual's overall achievable situation awareness. Due to the advancement of bone conduction technology, users of such systems are now able to communicate via two-way radio, cellular device and/or other communication systems without surrendering their ability to perceive surrounding events by utilizing small, lightweight, inconspicuous bone conduction systems (interfaces). By using BC interfaces, intelligible auditory signals may be presented to a listener without obstructing the ear canal, allowing the listener to perceive the environment while maintaining a steady stream of communication and efficient HCI. Due to this reason and those outlined throughout this chapter, bone conduction communication systems can be a valuable tool for HCI users engaging in outdoor leisure and recreation activities.

References

Bentler RA, Duve MR (2000) Comparison of hearing aids over the 20th century. Ear Hear 21(6):625–639

Casali JG, Lee K (2016) An objective, efficient auditory situation awareness test battery for advanced hearing protectors and tactical communications and protective systems (TCAPS): DRILCOM (detection-recognition/identification-localization-communication). J Acoust Soc Am 140(4):3200

Cellular Telecommunications & Internet Association (CTIA) (2018) The State of Wireless 2018. https://www.ctia.org/news/the-state-of-wireless-2018. Accessed 23 Oct 2019

Chang-Geun O, Lee K, Spencer P (2011) Effectiveness of advanced bone conduction earphones for people who enjoy outdoor activities. In: Proceedings of the human factors and ergonomics society annual meeting, vol 55(1). SAGE Publications, Sage CA: Los Angeles, CA, pp 1788–1792

Dirks DD, Kamm C (1975) Bone-vibrator measurements: physical characteristics and behavioral thresholds. J Speech Lang Hear Res 18(2):242–260

Dolan T, Morris S (1990) Administering audiometric speech tests via bone conduction: a comparison of transducers. Ear and Hear 11(6):446–449

Endsley MR (1987) SAGAT: a methodology for the measurement of situation awareness (NOR DOC 87-83). Northrop Corporation, Hawthorne, CA

Endsley MR (1988) Design and evaluation for situation awareness enhancement. In: Proceedings of the human factors society 32nd annual meeting. Human Factors Society, Santa Monica, CA, pp 97–101

Evans EF (1982) Basic physics and psychophysics of sound, vol The senses (Barlow HB, Mollon JD (eds)). Cambridge University Press, Cambridge

Gaye L, Mazé R, Holmquist LE (May 2003) Sonic City: the urban environment as a musical interface. In: NIME, vol 3, pp 109–115

Håkansson B (2003) The balanced electromagnetic separation transducer: a new bone conduction transducer. J Acoust Soc Am 113:818–825

Hazzard A, Benford S, Burnett G (April 2015) Sculpting a mobile musical soundtrack. In: Proceedings of the 33rd annual ACM conference on human factors in computing systems, pp 387–396

Janssen RM, Hong P, Chadha NK (2012) Bilateral bone-anchored hearing aids for bilateral permanent conductive hearing loss: a systematic review. Otolaryngol Head Neck Surg 147(3):412–422

Katz JE, Aspden P (1998) Theories, data, and potential impacts of mobile communications: a longitudinal analysis of US national surveys. Technol Forecast Soc Chang 57(1–2):133–156

Kyte K, Goring B, Patrick R (2011) Performance implications of replacing AC with BC communication devices. Southeastern Psychological Association Annual Meeting. New Orleans, LA

Lee K, Casali JG (2016) Effects of low speed wind on the recognition/identification and pass-through communication tasks of auditory situation awareness afforded by military hearing protection/enhancement devices and tactical communication and protective systems. Int J Audiol 55(sup1):S21–S29

Lee K, Casali JG (2017) Development of an auditory situation awareness test battery for advanced hearing protectors and TCAPS: detection subtest of DRILCOM (detection-recognition/identification-localization-communication). Int J Audiol 56(sup1):22–33

Leonard B (ed) (2009) Hearing conservation (rev DIANE Publishing)

McBride M, Tran P, Letowski T, Patrick R (2011) The effect of bone conduction microphone locations on speech intelligibility and sound quality. Appl Ergon 42(3):495–502

McBride M, Tran P, Letowski T (2017) Bone conduction communication: research progress and directions (No ARL-TR-8096). US Army Research Laboratory Aberdeen Proving Ground United States

Melzer JE, Scharine AA, Amrein BE (2018) Soldier auditory situation awareness: the effects of hearing protection, communications headsets, and headgear. In: Designing soldier systems. CRC Press, pp 173–195

Monastero B, McGookin D, Torre G (December 2016) Wandertroper: supporting aesthetic engagement with everyday surroundings through soundscape augmentation. In: Proceedings of the 15th international conference on mobile and ubiquitous multimedia, pp 129–140

Montuwy A, Cahour B, Dommes A (2019) Using Sensory wearable devices to navigate the city: effectiveness and user experience in older pedestrians. Multimodal Technol Interact 3(1):17

Nasar JL, Troyer D (2013) Pedestrian injuries due to mobile phone use in public places. Accid Anal Prev 57:91–95

Nuamah J, Patrick R, Oh S, Jiang Z, McBride M (2014) Effects of the auditory conduction mode on achievable situation awareness. In IIE annual conference. Proceedings. Institute of Industrial and Systems Engineers (IISE), p 3602

Parving A, Elberling C (1982) High-pass masking in the classification of low-frequency hearing loss. Scand Audiol 11(3):173–178

Perrott DR, Musicant AD (1977) Minimum auditory movement angle-binaural localization of moving sound sources. J Acoust Soc Am 62:1463–1466

Scharine A, Letowski T, Sampson JB (2009) Auditory situation awareness in urban operations. J Mil Strateg Stud 11(4)

Sklare DA, Denenberg LJ (1987) Interaural attenuation for tubephone insert earphones. Ear Hear 8(5):298–300

v Békésy G (1948) Vibration of the head in a sound field and its role in hearing by bone conduction. J Acoust Soc Am 20(6):749–760

Walker BN, Stanley RM, Iyer N, Simpson BD, Brungart DS (2005) Evaluation of bone-conduction headsets for use in multitalker communication environments. In: Proceedings of the human factors and ergonomics society annual meeting, vol 49(17). SAGE Publications, Sage CA: Los Angeles, CA, pp 1615–1619

Wilson J, Walker BN, Lindsay J, Cambias C, Dellaert F (October 2007) Swan: system for wearable audio navigation. In: 2007 11th IEEE international symposium on wearable computers. IEEE, pp 91–98

Wolfe J, Kluender K, Levi DM (2007) Sensation & perception. Academic Internet Publishers, Sunderland

Young KS (1999) Internet addiction: symptoms, evaluation and treatment. Innov Clin Pract Sour Book 17(17):351–352

Zwislocki J (1953) Acoustic attenuation between the ears. J Acoust Soc Am 25(4):752–759

Outdoor Recreation

Designing for Interaction in Outdoor Winter Sports

Jonna Häkkilä and Ashley Colley

Abstract Winter sports define a wide variety of different activities, which are adopted especially in northern countries. The winter context sets special requirements for designing interactive systems, as the activities are typically conducted in cold temperatures, with heavier clothing and equipment than summer sports. This chapter describes the authors' experiences when designing, prototyping, and evaluating computational enhancements for use in outdoor winter sports. The chapter presents four case studies addressing different winter sports, namely cross-country skiing, downhill skiing, snowboarding, and ice skating. As a conclusion, we discuss the common themes, challenges, and lessons learnt from the case studies as a whole.

1 Introduction

Human-computer interaction (HCI) concepts are increasingly being adopted in the area of wellness, and different wellness applications and tracking technologies are today commonplace. These have been taken into use by enthusiasts, e.g., the so-called quantified-selfers (Choe et al. 2014), as well as by large user groups, illustrated, e.g., through the availability of thousands of different smartphone apps for health and wellness (Häkkilä et al. 2015). Counting steps, measuring daily activity levels, and keeping performance diaries have become popular through mobile apps (Edwards et al. 2016; Häkkilä et al. 2015), wristbands and other wearables (Berglund et al. 2016), plus other commercial solutions. Research is also actively investigating new solutions and application areas for integrating interactive technologies in the wellness domain.

Sports-related interactive systems are a specific area among wellness technologies. The sports context often sets stricter requirements for the design, as the use case is

J. Häkkilä · A. Colley (✉)
University of Lapland, Rovaniemi, Finland
e-mail: ashley.colley@ulapland.fi

J. Häkkilä
e-mail: jonna.hakkila@ulapland.fi

© Springer Nature Switzerland AG 2020
D. S. McCrickard et al. (eds.), *HCI Outdoors: Theory, Design, Methods and Applications*, Human–Computer Interaction Series,
https://doi.org/10.1007/978-3-030-45289-6_14

performance-oriented, and the users are experts in their domain. Moreover, in outdoor sports, the usage conditions can be extreme in terms of weather or the required robustness to impacts. For the sportsperson, both the experience and the performance are important elements of doing the sport (Tholander et al. 2015). HCI research has addressed a wide variety of different sports, such as running (Daiber et al. 2017b), climbing (Kajastila et al. 2016), table tennis (Mueller and Gibbs 2006), or sport as part of exertion interfaces (Mueller et al. 2011). Winter sports, however, has been a less investigated area, this being partly explained by the special and challenging conditions in which the research must be conducted. With the increasing level of interest in sports in HCI research (Nylander et al. 2015), it is relevant to look also into the possibilities of designing for the winter sports domain, as well as focusing on the design opportunities for HCI in individual winter sports, it is interesting to identify general themes and challenges across winter sports in general.

The domain of outdoor sports has particular nuances, as exercising outdoors is conducted not only as a physical activity, but also has a recreational aspect. The benefits of being outdoors in nature are both physical and mental. For instance, research on hiking reports that the mental benefits are often more important than the physical ones (Nordbø and Prebensen 2015), and escape from urban life, contact with nature, and experiencing silence have been reported as important motivations (Muhar et al. 2007; Taczanowska et al. 2014). Also, among the HCI research community, the use of technology in nature and outdoor contexts has become increasingly topical (Daiber et al. 2017a; Häkkilä et al. 2018; Jones et al. 2018).

In this chapter, we address designing interactive systems for different winter sports, especially focusing on the outdoor aspects of the activities. We present several case studies, which we have conducted on different winter sports activities, and discuss the common themes and challenges that arose. This chapter contributes by providing an inspiring overview across different winter sports domains, and is of interest for researchers and practitioners working at the cross-section of technology and winter sports or winter outdoor contexts.

2 Background

HCI research has addressed different sports (e.g., Daiber et al. 2017b; Kajastila et al. 2016; Mueller and Gibbs 2006), typically by integrating technologies such as sensors or displays into sports equipments (Mauriello et al. 2014; Schneegass et al. 2016). Mueller and Young have presented ten lenses for HCI design in a sport which represent the virtues aligned with the sports, namely, reverie, pleasure, humility, sublime, oneness, sacrifice, beauty, pain, consistency, and perseverance (Mueller 2018). These virtues supporting both physical health and personal growth. Physical activity outdoors is also promoted for both physical and mental wellbeing, e.g., for recreation (Taczanowska et al. 2014), as well as enhancing work performance (Ahtinen et al. 2016). When exercising outdoors and in nature, people often seek not only exercise, but also solitude and peace. They may desire to avoid contact with other people (Posti et al. 2014), and not to be distracted by notifications from smartphones and other technology devices.

Prior research in ubiquitous computing related to the outdoor context in winter is scarce, but some examples exist. In the winter sports domain, Fedosov et al., have investigated social behavior in ski lifts (Fedosov et al. 2015) and cross- country skiing (Fedosov and Langheinrich 2015). Shiraishi et al., have demonstrated a wearable safety armor, to be used while skiing (Shiraishi et al. 2016). In addition, winter sports have been addressed in HCI research through virtual reality and games, where it has been pointed out that, for sports training, the feeling of realism is important (Jensen et al. 2015).

3 Exploring Interaction Design with Winter Sports

In this section, we provide examples of integrating technology into different winter sports, and describe our research on HCI design with each activity.

3.1 Illuminated Snowboard

Sports conducted in the mountains often involve high-end equipment, and activities such as mountaineering, skiing, and climbing typically adopt special clothing and tools which have been specifically designed to match the context. Despite the technicality of the gear, the equipment rarely includes interactive technology. We explored the integration of such technology, in the form of sensors and illumination elements to a snowboard (Colley and Häkkilä 2017; Colley et al. 2016). Interactive concepts including such light outputs can create enhanced experiences in dark winter contexts, emphasizing hedonic design drivers and creating, e.g., pleasurable, exciting, and surprising experiences. The concepts' outputs can be targeted both to the user themselves and to the surrounding people, e.g., friends skiing nearby or an audience standing next to the ski slope. Prior work on the topic has demonstrated an interactive snowboard concept visualizing the rider's weight distribution (Park and Lee 2016) (Fig. 1).

As our first prototype, we implemented a snowboard display showing the speed of the snowboarder. The implementation included a 3-axis accelerometer and, via a connected mobile phone, GPS information providing the board's location and speed. A mobile phone functioned as the user interface and memory for the system, and an Android-based mobile app was developed to enable setting a target speed and to record achieved speeds, enabling special lighting effects when previous best values were exceeded. The prototype implementation used a 1 m strip of 60 addressable RGB LEDs mounted on the front edge of the snowboard. The LEDs were driven by a small Arduino microcontroller board, which included an accelerometer and

Fig. 1 Prototype illuminated snowboard

Bluetooth. The setup was powered using a small 3.7 V rechargeable battery. The electronics were housed in a small box, slightly larger than a matchbox and attached to the board with a temporary mounting.

Our second illuminated snowboard prototype was again constructed around an Arduino microcontroller with an accelerometer and Bluetooth connectivity. In addition, a capacitive sensor driver was added, connected to copper tape touchstrips along the sides of the board. Based on the tilt of the board, its speed (via a Bluetooth connected smartphone GPS) and touching the touchstrips, various lighting effects could be triggered in a multicolored LED strip mounted around the perimeter of the snowboard. As initial effects, we chose to illuminate the side of the board that was either being grabbed with the hand (Fig. 1), or was edging into the snow—i.e., the edge which the board was tilted towards. Various thresholds and hysteresis were included in the algorithm to ensure the effects were stable and controllable. In addition, different colors were used to add to the range of effects the rider could activate.

3.2 Downhill Sports with VR In-the-Wild

Virtual Reality (VR) and Augmented Reality (AR) are nowadays finding increasing applications in a variety of use cases. Head-Mounted Displays (HMDs) are one of the main methods by which visual AR/VR experiences are delivered. Whereas the equipment has traditionally been primarily available only in laboratory environments, recent advances in commercial hardware such as the Oculus Rift and the Samsung Gear VR have enabled applications in less controlled in-the-wild environments. In our research, we decided to conduct experimental research on taking VR into a novel context of use, downhill winter sports (Colley et al. 2015). We aimed to create an immersive experience of skiing in a virtual reality ski resort, and explore the multisensory experience of blending VR and the physical world. Rather than attempting to artificially recreate the nonvisual sensory stimuli, such as sound, smell, and wind, in the virtual world, as, e.g., in the Birdly flying simulation (Rheiner 2014), we instead use the real-world context as the source of such inputs. Thus, the user experiences a blended virtual world, created from the combination of a virtual visual experience combined with the real (physical) world experience of the other senses.

We ran an in-the-wild experiment creating a Blended Virtuality on a skiing slope, where a skier and snowboarder wore an Oculus Rift HMD during the sport. To explore the concept, we created a simple virtual world environment in Unity 3D. The virtual environment was a snowy landscape that included gentle hills and trees. We then used an Oculus Rift DK1 HMD connected to a laptop PC located in a backpack worn by the skier. To enable precise tracking, we created a speed-over-ground sensor using a mechanical solution, 'the snow mouse'. The snow mouse consisted of a large plastic tub in which a standard Bluetooth mouse was located. The Bluetooth mouse was mounted in a position such that the scroll wheel of the mouse was in contact with the inner surface of the tub, and, as the plastic tub rotated, turned accordingly. After applying a calibration factor, this approach enabled accurate mapping of movement between physical and virtual worlds. Thus, as the skier moved, the virtual camera position in the virtual world was moved in parallel to their movement on the physical ski slope.

We trialed our prototype in-the-wild during one day on the beginners' slope of a downhill ski resort, with one skier and one snowboarder. Using the prototype included some risk of injury, as the VR HMD effectively blindfolds the skier from the real-world dangers. Hence, it was not possible to adopt members of the public as study participants, and both participants were members of the research team. During the study, other members of the research team ran or skied alongside the participant, shouting warnings of imminent collisions. The salient findings from the study related to the mismatch between visual and physical inputs, overall immersion, and multisensory experience. Both users reported it was somewhat difficult to balance while skiing/snowboarding. Based on the individual participant's perceived immersion level, the two testers reported somewhat opposite experiences. One being happy to ski in the virtual world and ignore the potential dangers of the real-world environment, while the other focused more closely on their other senses, particularly hearing, to detect the potential dangers or obstacles in the physical world (Fig. 2).

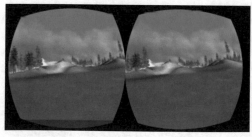 

Fig. 2 Skiing with a Head-Mounted Display and VR view. The Skier's view is shown in the left image

3.3   Cross-Country Skiing Integrated Displays

Cross-country skiing is an endurance sport, where the skier is exercising on nature trails, typically over distances of 10+ km in the cold and often dim light conditions of winter nature. The network of available ski tracks expands from tens to even hundreds of kilometers, although junctions are scarce compared to road networks, and the sport attracts both competitive, as well as recreational skiers. Hence, being somewhat comparable with hiking as a hobby. Solitude, silence, and nature landscapes are typical characteristics for skiing tracks. Cross-country skiing is an interesting design context as it contains both utilitarian and experience design drivers. The motivations for using technology relate to the (occasional) need for navigation information, and performance tracking information (e.g., distance, speed), but the use of mobile phone apps is difficult due to the cold weather, gloves, and ski pole bindings. On the other hand, being in nature can be a context where one wishes to leave technology behind (Sambasivan et al. 2009), and the technology design should be unobtrusive. In our research, we conducted a concept design for equipment-integrated pervasive displays, which would provide an unobtrusive frame to deliver information to the skier.

We created two concepts and designs for equipment-integrated information displays for cross-country skiers. As a preliminary step, a paper prototype and interview-based exploration on placing information display on different parts of the equipment, including skis and sticks was conducted. In the first concept, the information display was integrated on the ski, and the industrial design and ergonomics of the display were explored. A mobile phone UI was concepted to preset the variables visualized on the ski-display. However, the solution had usability challenges in readability, as the skis are not stable during the sport, and the information granularity should be designed accordingly, utilizing very simplistic graphics. As the next step, we explored attaching an information display to the cross-country ski shoe (Colley et al. 2018). Here, we attached LED strips to the ski shoe and used three different colors to indicate the speed of the skier. The skier preset the target value for the desired speed with a smartphone app, and the speed was detected through GPS tracking of the phone. A functional prototype was tested at a cross-country skiing track. With this approach, the ambient visualization technique provided a better match with the skiing context. However, an in-the-wild experiment revealed that, for a meaningful visualization, speed averaging should happen over a relatively long time window, as the momentary speed in cross-country skiing is subject to high variation. This is due to several factors, including the terrain changes, kick versus sliding phases of the movement, and the sliding characteristics of the skis and waxing. Based on the exploratory and design-oriented studies conducted, we conclude that there are both identified user needs and potential design solutions for pervasive display systems for cross-country skiing, but the area requires further work to find feasible and optimized solutions.

3.4 Sensor Concepts for Ice-Hockey and Skating

Skating is a classic example of a winter sport, carried out both outdoor and at indoor ice skating rinks. Although our HCI research on skating sports has been conducted at indoor rinks, we introduce it here as it inherently belongs to the family of winter sports. In our work, we have addressed both figure skating and ice-hockey, the two major sports conducted on skates (Fig. 3).

The ice-hockey playing youth was addressed in a study which explored a holistic mobile health application (Hakkila et al. 2016). The study explored the tracking of physical activity and training performance data using a wizard-of-Oz method to simulate equipment-integrated sensors, and charted the young athletes' opinions of a custom mobile health app design. As the salient findings, the teenage ice-hockey players had very positive opinions on getting both their own and their team's training and performance data. Integration of several different data sources, such as training and eating, under a single wellness app was wished for, in order to get a holistic view of factors affecting the athlete's performance.

We created an interactive skating dress, targeted to children training actively and competing in figure skating (Häkkilä et al. 2018). In this target user group, features to motivate the child to be physically active were not at the core of the concept. Rather the target was to design for features that would be esthetic and motivating in the context of training for children's competitive figure skating. We created a skating dress which detected the spinning movement of the skater, and where hem-integrated LEDs illuminated and changed color (from pink to green) with the speed of the spinning. Arduino-based electronics and a small battery were placed in a small pouch at the waist, under the hem. During the design process, two iterative prototypes were created. The target of the design was to provide the wearer and coach real-time feedback on the skater's performance. In addition, the changing illumination could serve as an esthetic addition to the skater's performance and as an inspiring element for the child skater.

Fig. 3 The interactive ice skating dress prototype. The illumination color depends on the skater's spinning speed

4 Discussion

In this section, we describe common themes and challenges associated with design and research on interactive systems for winter sports.

4.1 Contextual Conditions

The cold temperature creates many challenges when designing for the winter outdoors context. Hardware problems are usually encountered first, as batteries drain more quickly and electrical components and wiring become more fragile. Where rapidly-prototyped constructions have used adhesive tape, these typically do not hold well in the cold and the prototypes can begin to fall apart. Similarly, other equipments such as cameras (or smartphone cameras) needed to conduct evaluations outdoors, begin to have problems in winter conditions, such as reduced battery-life or even automatic low-temperature shutdown. The use of touchscreens in winter conditions is problematic as it requires removing gloves and is also adversely affected by snowflakes falling on the touchscreen (Ylipulli et al. 2014).

Working with winter sports typically requires traveling far from the research lab to access the required locations and infrastructure, such as skiing tracks or an ice skating rink. This brings additional logistical challenges, as the local infrastructure is often lacking in comparison to indoor studies. Especially, we highlight the lack of electricity mains power, e.g., for recharging batteries. In our studies, we have been lucky to have sufficient network coverage for a smartphone-based data connection, but we acknowledge that this may not be the case in all outdoor locations. The remote context also raises the threshold for the required maturity level of prototypes before they can be evaluated in context, as frequent travel between the lab and use context may not be feasible. Further, much of the fine-tuning and last minute adjustment that is typically needed with prototypes, e.g., changing a parameter in the code of an Arduino microcontroller and uploading it to the prototype, is not practical in an outdoor winter context. While the authors have performed such operations at −30 °C (−22 °F), they do not recommend it, as using a laptop keyboard in such conditions risks frostbite to the necessarily ungloved fingers. In our studies, the ski slope environments (Colley et al. 2015; Colley and Häkkilä 2017) were found to be particularly demanding contexts. In addition to the cold temperatures, such environments place physical demands on the researchers, e.g., repeatedly walking up and down ski slopes carrying equipment such as cameras, etc.

In-the-wild studies create a lot of hassle, but are deemed to be worth it Rogers et al. (2007). Without them, concepts cannot be reliably evaluated, especially as the outdoors context typically provides additional complexities which would be overlooked in lab studies.

4.2 Sports Skill Level

When designing for the sports domain, the researcher (or designer) needs to consider to which motivational and expertise level the design is targeted. This influences both the use cases and the functionality of the design and prototype. A vast amount of research exists addressing the challenge of how to motivate people to be physically more active (Consolvo et al. 2006), as well as persuasive design for facilitating behavior change (Hamari et al. 2014). In the case studies presented in this chapter, we have been more interested in targeting users who already are doing sports, and do not require any additional push to motivate them to start the activity. We have also targeted users of at least moderate skills level, and teaching the sports technique has not been the target of the introduced interactive systems. Tholander and Nylander (Tholander et al. 2015) have highlighted how technology in sports can have both an instrumental value in measuring and providing the user the knowledge of the performance, and experiential value in enhancing the experience with the sports. In our research, we have focused on the experiential side of the design and on recreational rather than professional level competitive sports. If high-level competitive scenarios were addressed, the use cases would concentrate more on the sports performance, and the tracking accuracy and unobtrusiveness of the design would play a stronger role. With experiential qualities in mind, our research links with the more general ideas of user experience research (Hassenzahl 2008; Hassenzahl and Tractinsky 2006), where hedonic and utilitarian aspects of the design form the holistic user experience with the interactive system. Whereas our case studies emphasize the hedonic design dimensions, such as visual effects, they also connect with utilitarian aspects, e.g., in providing feedback when more complex or challenging performance is achieved, as with the illuminated snowboard and the interactive skating dress.

The sports skill level needs to be considered not only from the viewpoint of the target user group, but also in regard to the researchers. The researchers need to understand the sport in order to be able to design for it. Moreover, testing and conducting user studies in-the-wild may require certain skills, e.g., to keep up with the sportsperson on the ski slope or ice rink. This is an important factor to take into account when planning the practicalities of studies and documentation in conducted the field.

5 Conclusion

In this chapter, we have addressed winter sports and introduced our research in the area covering several different sports. For HCI research, winter sports provide an interesting domain, which includes challenges both for the technical side and user experience design. The winter sports have common HCI design challenges, e.g., due to the cold temperature, and winter clothing. On the other hand, the sports differ from each other both for their equipment and special contextual requirements, e.g., prepared ski tracks, and each of them needs to be considered separately when designing for the specific sport. The winter outdoors sets specific challenges for running user studies and creating functional prototypes that can withstand the winter outdoor environment. Researchers should take extra care when designing the in-the-wild studies, and run a pilot study when possible to test the feasibility of the study procedure and durability of the research prototype. As winter sports is a relatively little investigated area among HCI research, it offers many possibilities for future researchers and designers.

References

Ahtinen A, Andrejeff E, Väänänen K (2016) Brainwolk: a mobile technology mediated walking meeting concept for wellbeing and creativity at work. In: Proceedings of the 15th international conference on mobile and ubiquitous multimedia. ACM, pp 307–309

Berglund ME, Duvall J, Dunne LE (2016) A survey of the historical scope and current trends of wearable technology applications. In: Proceedings of the 2016 ACM international symposium on wearable computers. ACM, pp 40–43

Choe EK, Lee NB, Lee B, Pratt W, Kientz JA (2014) Understanding quantified-selfers' practices in collecting and exploring personal data. In: Proceedings of the SIGCHI conference on human factors in computing systems. ACM, pp 1143–1152

Colley A, Häkkilä J (2017) Hedonic design for winter ubimount: illuminated snowboard in-the-wild. In: Proceedings of the 2017 ACM international joint conference on pervasive and ubiquitous computing and proceedings of the 2017 ACM international symposium on wearable computers, UbiComp '17. ACM, New York, NY, USA, pp 1027–1032. https://doi.org/10.1145/3123024.3124442. http://doi.acm.org/10.1145/3123024.3124442

Colley A, Häkkilä J, Lappalainen T (2016) Concept design for informative illumination on a snowboard. In: Proceedings of the 2016 ACM international joint conference on pervasive and ubiquitous computing: adjunct, UbiComp '16. ACM, New York, NY, USA, pp 872–876. https://doi.org/10.1145/2968219.2968540. http://doi.acm.org/10.1145/2968219.2968540

Colley A, Väyrynen J, Häkkilä J (2015) Skiing in a blended virtuality: an in-the-wild experiment. In: Proceedings of the 19th international academic Mindtrek conference, AcademicMindTrek '15. ACM, New York, NY, USA, pp 89–91. https://doi.org/10.1145/2818187.2818288. http://doi.acm.org/10.1145/2818187.2818288

Colley A, Woźniak PW, Kiss F, Häkkilä J (2018) Shoe integrated displays: a prototype sports shoe display and design space. In: Proceedings of the 10th Nordic conference on human-computer interaction. ACM, pp 39–46

Consolvo S, Everitt K, Smith I, Landay JA (2006) Design requirements for technologies that encourage physical activity. In: Proceedings of the SIGCHI conference on Human Factors in computing systems, pp 457–466

Daiber F, Jones M, Wiehr F, Cheverst K, Kosmalla F, Häkkilä J (2017a) Ubimount: 2nd workshop on ubiquitous computing in the mountains. In: Proceedings of the 2017 ACM international joint conference on pervasive and ubiquitous computing and proceedings of the 2017 ACM international symposium on wearable computers, pp 1022–1026

Daiber F, Kosmalla F, Wiehr F, Krüger A (2017b) Footstriker: a wearable ems-based foot strike assistant for running. In: Proceedings of the 2017 ACM international conference on interactive surfaces and spaces. ACM, pp 421–424

Edwards EA, Lumsden J, Rivas C, Steed L, Edwards L, Thiyagarajan A, Sohanpal R, Caton H, Griffiths C, Munafò M et al (2016) Gamification for health promotion: systematic review of behaviour change techniques in smartphone apps. BMJ Open 6(10):e012447

Fedosov A, Langheinrich M (2015) From start to finish: Understanding group sharing behavior in a backcountry skiing community. In: Proceedings of the 17th international conference on human-computer interaction with mobile devices and services adjunct. ACM, pp 758–765

Fedosov A, Niforatos E, Alt F, Elhart I (2015) Supporting interactivity on a ski lift. In: Adjunct proceedings of the 2015 ACM international joint conference on pervasive and ubiquitous computing and proceedings of the 2015 ACM international symposium on wearable computers. ACM, pp 767–770

Hakkila J, Alhonsuo M, Virtanen L, Rantakari J, Colley A, Koivumaki T (2016) Mydata approach for personal health–a service design case for young athletes. In: Proceedings of the 2016 49th Hawaii international conference on system sciences (HICSS), HICSS '16. IEEE Computer Society, Washington, DC, USA, pp 3493–3502. https://doi.org/10.1109/HICSS.2016.436. http://dx.doi.org/10.1109/HICSS.2016.436

Häkkilä J, Bidwell NJ, Cheverst K, Colley A, Kosmalla F, Robinson S, Schöning J (2018) Reflections on the naturechi workshop series: unobtrusive user experiences with technology in nature. Int J Mob Hum Comput Interact (IJMHCI) 10(3):1–9

Häkkilä J, Colley A, Inget V, Alhonsuo M, Rantakari J (2015) Exploring digital service concepts for healthy lifestyles. In: International conference of design, user experience, and usability. Springer, pp. 470–480

Häkkilä J, Helander V, Jamoido D, Colley A (2018) Designing an interactive ice skating dress for young athletes. In: Proceedings of the 2018 ACM international joint conference and 2018 international symposium on pervasive and ubiquitous computing and wearable computers, UbiComp '18. ACM, New York, NY, USA, pp 734–737. https://doi.org/10.1145/3267305.3267702. http://doi.acm.org/10.1145/3267305.3267702

Hamari J, Koivisto J, Pakkanen T (2014) Do persuasive technologies persuade?-a review of empirical studies. In: International conference on persuasive technology. Springer, pp 118–136

Hassenzahl M (2008) User experience (ux) towards an experiential perspective on product quality. In: Proceedings of the 20th conference on l'Interaction homme-machine, pp 11–15

Hassenzahl M, Tractinsky N (2006) User experience-a research agenda. Behav Inform Technol 25(2):91–97

Jensen MM, Rasmussen MK, Mueller FF, Grønbæk K (2015) Keepin'it real: challenges when designing sports-training games. In: Proceedings of the 33rd annual ACM conference on human factors in computing systems. ACM, pp 2003–2012

Jones MD, Anderson Z, Häkkilä J, Cheverst K, Daiber F (2018) Hci outdoors: understanding human-computer interaction in outdoor recreation. In: Extended abstracts of the 2018 CHI conference on human factors in computing systems. ACM, p W12

Kajastila R, Holsti L, Hämäläinen P (2016) The augmented climbing wall: high-exertion proximity interaction on a wall-sized interactive surface. In: Proceedings of the 2016 CHI conference on human factors in computing systems. ACM, pp 758–769

Mauriello M, Gubbels M, Froehlich JE (2014) Social fabric fitness: the design and evaluation of wearable e-textile displays to support group running. In: Proceedings of the SIGCHI conference on human factors in computing systems. ACM, pp 2833–2842

Mueller F, Edge D, Vetere F, Gibbs MR, Agamanolis S, Bongers B, Sheridan JG (2011) Designing sports: a framework for exertion games. In: Proceedings of the SIGCHI conference on human factors in computing systems. ACM, pp 2651–2660

Mueller F, Gibbs M (2006) A table tennis game for three players. In: Proceedings of the 18th Australia conference on computer-human interaction: design: activities, artefacts and environments. ACM, pp 321–324

Mueller F, Young D et al (2018) 10 lenses to design sports-hci. Found Trends® Hum Comput Interact 12(3):172–237

Muhar A, Schauppenlehner T, Brandenburg C, Arnberger A et al (2007) Alpine summer tourism: the mountaineers' perspective and consequences for tourism strategies in Austria. For Snow Landsc Res 81(7)

Nordbø I, Prebensen NK (2015) Hiking as mental and physical experience. In: Advances in hospitality and leisure. Emerald Group Publishing Limited, pp 169–186

Nylander S, Tholander J, Mueller F, Marshall J et al (2015) Hci and sports. In: Interactions, vol 22. Association for Computing Machinery (ACM), pp 30–31

Park HK, Lee W (2016) Motion echo snowboard: enhancing body movement perception in sport via visually augmented feedback. In: Proceedings of the 2016 ACM conference on designing interactive systems. ACM, pp 192–203

Posti M, Schöning J, Häkkilä J (2014) Unexpected journeys with the hobbit: the design and evaluation of an asocial hiking app. In: Proceedings of the 2014 conference on designing interactive systems. ACM, pp 637–646

Rheiner M (2014) Birdly an attempt to fly. In: ACM SIGGRAPH 2014 emerging technologies. ACM, p 3

Rogers Y, Connelly K, Tedesco L, Hazlewood W, Kurtz A, Hall RE, Hursey J, Toscos T (2007) Why it's worth the hassle: the value of in-situ studies when designing ubicomp. In: International conference on ubiquitous computing. Springer, pp 336–353

Sambasivan N, Ventä L, Mäntyjärvi J, Isomursu M, Häkkilä J (2009) Rhythms of non-use of device ensembles. In: CHI'09 extended abstracts on human factors in computing systems. ACM, pp 4531–4536

Schneegass S, Ogando S, Alt F (2016) Using on-body displays for extending the output of wearable devices. In: Proceedings of the 5th ACM international symposium on pervasive displays. ACM, pp 67–74

Shiraishi R, Fujita T, Inuzuka K, Takashima R, Sankai Y (2016) Augmentation of human protection functions using wearable and sensing system. In: Proceedings of the 7th augmented human international conference 2016. ACM, p 36

Taczanowska K, Brandenburg C, Muhar A, Hat-Pawlikowska K, Ziobrowski S, Chlipała B, Grocholski S, Krzeptowski J, Jodłowski M, Bielański M et al (2014) Who is hiking in the tatra national park, poland? a socio-demographic portrait of visitors. In: The 7th international conference on monitoring and management of visitors in recreational and protected areas, pp 27–29

Tholander J, Nylander S (2015) Snot, sweat, pain, mud, and snow: performance and experience in the use of sports watches. In: Proceedings of the 33rd annual ACM conference on human factors in computing systems. ACM, pp 2913–2922

Ylipulli J, Luusua A, Kukka H, Ojala T (2014) Winter is coming: introducing climate sensitive urban computing. In: Proceedings of the 2014 conference on designing interactive systems. ACM, pp 647–656

Creating a User-Controllable Skiing Experience for Individuals with Tetraplegia

Ahmad Alsaleem, Ross Imburgia, Andrew Merryweather, Jeffery Rosenbluth, Stephen Trapp, and Jason Wiese

Abstract Outdoor recreation improves the quality of life for individuals with tetraplegia, however, a range of barriers exist in accessing these sports. This chapter describes the iterative design and field evaluation of the Tetra-Ski, a novel power-assisted ski chair for individuals who use a power wheelchair. Users control the Tetra-Ski with a joystick or sip-and-puff controller either independently or collaboratively with a tethered skier through a Shared-Control scheme. A field study of the Tetra-Ski demonstrated the usability of the system. The chapter also reflects on the Shared-Control approach to controlling Tetra-Ski, which effectively supported the unique abilities of different users. These findings inform the future application of this Shared-Control approach for use with other assistive technology and less-dependent forms of outdoor recreation. Finally, we describe some of the challenges we have faced developing and deploying a sports activity (skiing) for individuals with tetraplegia.

A. Alsaleem (✉) · R. Imburgia · A. Merryweather · J. Rosenbluth · S. Trapp · J. Wiese
University of Utah, Salt Lake City, UT, USA
e-mail: ahmad.Alsaleem@utah.edu

R. Imburgia
e-mail: rimburgia@gmail.com

A. Merryweather
e-mail: a.merryweather@utah.edu

J. Rosenbluth
e-mail: jeffrey.rosenbluth@hsc.utah.edu

S. Trapp
e-mail: Stephen.Trapp@hsc.utah.edu

J. Wiese
e-mail: wiese@cs.utah.edu

© Springer Nature Switzerland AG 2020
D. S. McCrickard et al. (eds.), *HCI Outdoors: Theory, Design, Methods and Applications*, Human–Computer Interaction Series,
https://doi.org/10.1007/978-3-030-45289-6_15

1 Introduction

Physical medicine and rehabilitation is an interdisciplinary medical specialty that addresses the needs of individuals with disabilities or major health status changes. Adaptive recreation is an important aspect of adjusting to these changes and improving the overall quality of life. This is certainly true for individuals with tetraplegia (Slater and Meade 2004). Accordingly, there is a concerted effort to develop quality-of-life-enhancing opportunities, such as adaptive recreation, for this group (van Leeuwen et al. 2011). However, a range of barriers limit access to such activities, including technology availability, physical limitations, and limited resources (Kim et al. 2011; Scelza et al. 2005; Martin Ginis et al. 2010; Tasiemski and Osinska 2013). These barriers are especially common for individuals with complex medical conditions like tetraplegia.

To improve access, and thereby improve quality of life, we developed an adaptive alpine skiing platform (Tetra-Ski) that individuals with tetraplegia can control independently (see Fig. 1). Tetra-Ski features electrically powered actuators to manipulate skis using a joystick or mouth-controlled (sip-and-puff) system to enable an independent ski experience for individuals previously excluded from this activity. We developed Tetra-Ski through an iterative design process with the focus of providing

Fig. 1 Tetra-Ski in action

a safe, independent experience for individuals with tetraplegia (including complex disabilities) without compromising the performance.

The system uses a novel Shared-Control scheme to facilitate user control over a range of aspects of the ski experience, while delegating other aspects to a tethered ski instructor. We designed the Shared-Control scheme to improve safety and expand usability, while being considerate of important psychological variables like independence and autonomy. We developed Tetra-Ski over the past 5 years and continue to improve it iteratively through ongoing user testing with participants. Tetra-Ski is now available through the nonprofit Tetradapt.[1]

2 Tetraplegia

Tetraplegia, also known as quadriplegia, is paralysis caused by injury or disorder resulting in the partial or total loss of use of all four limbs and torso (Asia Classification 2020). Individuals with tetraplegia can lose sensation, muscle function, and movement below the site of the injury. As a result, a range of physical and socially imposed barriers exist to engage in physical activity.

Individuals with tetraplegia often experience limited control over their arms and trunk, as well as an impaired cardiovascular system function. Among other complications, individuals with this condition often have diminished thermoregulatory and respiratory capacity. Together, these functional limitations are significant challenges for them to participate in outdoor activities. In addition to medical barriers, they encounter notable social barriers (i.e., lack of support, few leisure opportunities and activities (Brown et al. 2002)) that further limit engagement in activities. Among a range of socially imposed barriers, the design of technology can facilitate or hinder participation (Barclay et al. 2016). Accordingly, the design of adaptive recreational experiences must not only be considerate of medical factors, but also incorporate best practices to overcome social and environmental barriers to participation.

2.1 Outdoor Activities for Individuals with Tetraplegia

A variety of outdoor activities exist for individuals with paraplegia; however, these become much more limited when the individual has medical needs that require greater assistance from rehabilitation technology (e.g., a power wheelchair), as it is the case with individuals with tetraplegia. Literature on accessible outdoor recreational activities these individuals is growing but remains quite limited. Often, outdoor experience offerings trade off between performance and independence. Recent work describes an independent sailing experience (Rojhani et al. 2016). This system uses a sip-and-puff controller for a binary command system (sip, puff) to enable some level of

---

[1] https://www.tetradapt.us/.

independent navigation of a watercraft (only offering steering control, but no thrust control).

Engaging in these experiences is challenging, and preparation and training can help to ensure a successful outdoor experience. Past work has explored virtual simulations as a means to prepare users for real-world adaptive recreation. One pilot study explored a virtual sailing simulation called VSail-Access (Recio et al. 2013). They found that VR preparation was linked to better performance of the assigned tasks in the real world. This study also indicated salutary mental health outcomes, like increased quality of life, associated with simulator use. However, access to such training platforms can also be limited and might require a substantial time investment before participating in real-world experience.

2.2 Benefits of Recreational Activities

Recreational activities have a number of positive biopsychosocial effects on individuals with tetraplegia. Global improvements in health-related quality of life are well-researched among individuals with tetraplegia who participate in recreational activities. Biological benefits include positive physical activity effects, such as improved cardiovascular functioning, as well as indirect influences on physical-health-related quality of life.

In addition to physical benefits, there is also ample evidence for positive impact on mental-health-related quality of life for individuals with tetraplgia (Slater and Meade 2004) as well as subjective well-being (Zabriskie et al. 2005). Participation has also been linked to positive changes in mood states including anger, depression, tension, and vigor (Lundberg et al. 2011). In addition to the effect on the individual participating in the activity, participation in adaptive recreation has positive effects on social functioning, such as quality of family life and social wellness (Zabriskie et al. 2005).

With regard to individuals with tetraplegia, Muraki and colleagues concluded "that sports activity can improve the psychological status, irrespective of tetraplegics and paraplegics, and that the psychological benefits are emphasized by sports activity at high frequency" (Muraki et al. 2000). Further, they described no significant differences in psychological measurements across sport types. This suggests that the important aspect of psychological benefits is not the kind of sports activity, but sports activity itself.

2.3 Challenges to Participate in Outdoor Recreational Activities

Unfortunately, access to and inclusion in outdoor recreation activities for individuals with tetraplegia have been limited, especially for winter sports. Barriers include medically related constraints to participation as well as practical barriers (i.e., transportation and lack of training) to access. Among many, some barriers that limit access include sport accessibility, complex and multifactorial physical considerations, and limited resources ranging from a systemic level to an individual level (Kim et al. 2011; Scelza et al. 2005; Martin Ginis et al. 2010; Tasiemski and Osinska 2013). Unfortunately these barriers are even more pronounced for individuals with complex medical conditions, like tetraplegia.

Adaptive skiing Adaptive alpine skiing is an extremely popular winter activity that has grown to accommodate almost all cognitive and physical disabilities. Its popularity has created opportunities to be sanctioned as an official Paralympic sport. However, it has gone largely unaddressed for individuals with diminished upper extremity functioning (tetraplegia, multiple sclerosis, neuromuscular disease), asymmetric strength (stroke, traumatic brain injury), and extensive limb loss. To the authors' knowledge, no prior adaptive skiing equipment existed to allow individuals with high-level tetraplegia to independently control speed or direction (Skiing & Snow Equipment-Disabled Sports USA 2020). Previously, those individuals could only ski through a completely piloted experience. For example, the Dualski[2] offers a fully dependent ski experience that is piloted by a tethered skier who controls all aspects of the turns and the direction for the adaptive skier.

2.4 Increasing Access Through Tetra-Ski

The **TRAILS (Technology Recreation Access Independence Lifestyle Sports)** program was established to increase access to recreational activities. TRAILS is a comprehensive outreach program based at the Rehabilitation Center at the University of Utah Health. The Rehabilitation Center is an interdisciplinary division devoted to medical care for individuals with rehabilitation conditions like tetraplegia among other diagnoses. TRAILS focuses on empowering individuals with disabilities through a range of programs and activities.

The TRAILS program runs an adaptive sport and adaptive technology development program in collaboration with a range of disciplines from the health sciences and engineering colleges at the university. Through this program, individuals get access to a variety of sporting activities, including downhill and cross-country skiing, sailing, tennis, basketball, cycling, recoil shooting, swimming, and other wellness activities. These activities are offered with the goal of supporting independence and flexible control through the patient's preferred assistive technology. This includes control systems like sip-and-puff or joystick controllers. In addition to offering direct access to recreation for individuals with disabilities, TRAILS is committed to bringing high-tech low-volume products to the marketplace, and has demonstrated success through the founding of a nonprofit organization and establishing a manufacturing system to widen access to its rehabilitation technology.

The Tetra-Ski is a ski system developed in conjunction with TRAILS through an interdisciplinary assistive technology initiative with rehabilitation professionals,

---

[2]http://www.dualski.com/en/.

Fig. 2 Shared-Control system in Tetra-Ski. The instructor is holding a remote control in his hand to adjust the Tetra-Ski user's turns. On the right is the remote control

mechanical engineers, and computer scientists. This device is a ski chair featuring electrically powered actuators on each of two skis, which can be controlled by either a joystick or a sip-and-puff mouth-controlled system (see Fig. 3) for independent control. A single tether to a traditional skier is used as an emergency brake but is not used for routine speed or directional control. A wireless remote control offers the instructor a way to demonstrate proper skiing technique and safely steer if assistance is needed. The Tetra-Ski offers an unprecedented level of independent control over a wide variety of terrains. At the University of Utah, it has completely replaced the dependant skiing paradigm previously used for individuals with high spinal cord injury and for other diagnoses with significant upper extremity impairments or asymmetry. Anyone that can independently operate a powered wheelchair will most likely be able to use Tetra-Ski after some training. A ski computer simulator has also been developed to specify customized control settings that can later be exported to the actual Tetra-Ski.

This technology is enhanced by a Shared-Control system (see Fig. 2). Shared-Control describes an approach where control of a device is shared between a user and another controlling entity, such as an instructor. This design scheme has been previously examined in wheelchair research (Demeester et al. 2008), but limited attention has been paid within adaptive recreation for individuals with tetraplegia. Shared-Control systems have recently been explored in outrigger canoe paddling with blind participants (Baldwin et al. 2019). The control system relies on two participants collaborating to control the paddling experience. The blind user controls everything in the paddling experience except for turning, which is controlled by another person using a wireless remote controller.

The Tetra-Ski implements a Shared-Control system in which the main user (individual with tetraplegia) collaborates with a control partner (ski instructor) to guide the ski apparatus. Tetra-Ski has enabled an unprecedented level of independent skiing for individuals previously excluded from controlling this activity for themselves. This technology has directly increased access both not only with local TRAILS programming, but also through a loan system in which the Tetra-Ski is used at multiple sites internationally.

Fig. 3 The Tetra-Ski has two input systems: a sip-and-puff controller (left) and a joystick controller (right)

3 Tetra-Ski Design

The Tetra-Ski was designed iteratively over a five-year period beginning in January 2014. The current iteration—as of May 2019—is presented in this book chapter. Our initial design goals were based on the overarching aim of enabling independent skiing for individuals with tetraplegia, and ongoing design sessions. The design goals included the following:

1. **Safety**. The safety of the skier is essential and is the most important criterion. The goal is to minimize additional risk beyond the baseline inherent risk in skiing.
2. **Independent piloting**. It should be possible for a user to operate Tetra-Ski completely independently and with as much autonomy as possible.
3. **Adaptability**. Maximizing adjustability to accommodate the diverse needs of users, their abilities, and their wide array of assistive technology.
4. **Diverse user controls**. Since individuals with tetraplegia use a range of control systems, we were committed to expanding control options from relying solely on hand-based controls.

3.1 Tetra-Ski Hardware

Tetra-Ski is an electrically powered adaptive alpine skiing device. This technology uses actuators to move the skis mounted below the seat. The actuators can be controlled using either a joystick or a mouth input device (sip-and-puff). Parts of the seating system were designed to support the arms, neck, feet, and legs of the skier to be adjusted into multiple positions. The goal was to provide the most comfortable seating for the skier and to avoid excess pressure on their body—thereby reducing the chance of pressure injuries due to the activity movement and seating position. This level of adjustability was also important due to the variability in the trunk and postural control capabilities of our target population. Accordingly, the customization allows the user to hold their body steady while they perform hard angle maneuvers with Tetra-Ski. Without this support, they would likely find these motions difficult or impossible.

3.2 Input System

The input system for the Tetra-Ski required special consideration and design innovation to create a usable system for individuals with tetraplegia. Multiple input systems were examined for use with the technology, including eye trackers, facial recognition systems, EMG wireless sensors, EEG sensors, and a tongue controller (Kim et al. 2013). We decided against these systems due to lack of access to the technology (tongue controller), poor outdoor performance (eye trackers, tongue controller, facial recognition systems), or limited accuracy/response time required for highly dynamic systems for activities like skiing (EMG sensors, EEG sensors). We also considered input control devices from the gaming community. One example is QuadJoy, an input device that combines a sip-and-puff controller and a joystick as one input module. A user can move the joystick part using his/her mouth and can easily sip or puff to perform additional commands (QuadJoy | Bridging Quality of Life for Handicap & Paralyzed 2020). QuadJoy is one example of an adaptive, customizable control system that enables individuals with tetraplegia to play mainstream video games independently. Similar technologies such as TetraMouse (2020) and Integra Mouse (Integramouse 2020) are designed to simulate the functionality of a mouse. These systems utilize innovative design concepts. Unfortunately, they are closed systems that have very specific purposes and are not tested for use in outdoor applications. Accordingly, we could not use these systems to further the aims of this project.

After review, joystick and sip-and-puff controllers were selected as the main control devices for Tetra-Ski. These two control systems are common inputs for power wheelchair users and offer many advantages in the design of the Tetra-Ski.

Joystick A joystick intrinsically maps to the LEFT, RIGHT, UP, and DOWN commands, making it a natural choice. However, mapping the commands from the joystick to control Tetra-Ski still required multiple iterative development cycles. We refined the actuators' response to the joystick to match the position of the joystick in relation to the user's body, joystick motion dead zones, and participant response time. Further, we specified a maximum rate of change for turning and adjusting the wedge of the ski to reduce the risk that the Tetra-Ski would flip due to overaggressive control input.

Sip-and-Puff The sip-and-puff control scheme presented a more difficult challenge for the research team and the engineers. Skiing is a physically demanding experience that requires continuous response and interaction by the user, and physical abilities associated with our target population bring additional challenges. Further, the respiratory capabilities (which sip-and-puff relies on) of a person with tetraplegia can be less than that of someone without tetraplegia. Accordingly, we made efforts to match the respiratory burden of engaging the sip-and-puff controller to the user's abilities.

We used the control scheme employed in power-assisted wheelchairs as a guide for the first iteration of the sip-and-puff control scheme (see Alsaleem et al. (2019)). However, participants found the control scheme was unusable for several reasons. First, the demand for our experience is much higher than the requirements for using a wheelchair system, which led to fatigue. Next, users would unintentionally trigger the wrong commands, probably because of situational factors. Finally, we found that this control scheme required continuous calibration on the slopes, which was not feasible. After experimenting with multiple sip-and-puff schemes (Alsaleem et al. 2019), we settled on continuous sipping and puffing for turning and defined a set of predetermined wedge angles that the user could cycle through by performing multiple sips or puffs. Even with these changes, there was still a learning curve for our users to overcome before they became comfortable using our new input system. However, time on the mountain is limited for a combination of practical reasons (amount of time in the cold, risk of pressure injuries, fatigue, and availability of equipment and instructors). To address this challenge, and in order to support our user to have a usable, enjoyable experience, we moved toward Shared Control.

3.3 Shared-Control System

We considered both independence and collaboration when developing the initial control system. However, we relaxed the constraint of full independence to explore new possibilities for an even more accessible design of the control system. Our intention was to maintain as much independence and control by the main user of the skiing experience as possible, while offering new functions and enhanced safety. Our control scheme was expanded based on an additional design goal:

5. **Shared Control**. The ski experience should accommodate a wide range of physical abilities and prior skiing experience. It should be possible for a skier to have a complete and successful experience while controlling most (but not necessarily all) aspects of the ski chair. Similarly, we should maintain as much autonomy and independence of use as possible, in spite of a collaborative control scheme.

The new system relies upon two users operating Tetra-Ski. The main skier (sitting in the Tetra-Ski) is responsible for the turning tasks and guiding the direction of Tetra-Ski. The tethered skier is responsible for ensuring the Tetra-Ski's skis are in the most optimal wedge (speed and turning speed) for the terrain, snow condition, and user performance.

The Shared-Control scheme was applied to both sip-and-puff as well as joystick controllers. For the joystick, the user can push the joystick left or right to turn, similar to the previous scheme. We created two modes for the joystick: (1) Joystick basic mode, where the users do not have control over the Up and Down commands and are only responsible for turning commands (left, right), and (2) joystick advanced mode, which is the same as described previously. For the sip-and-puff *basic mode*, a single Sip or single Puff will move the skis to left or right, an amount proportional to the amount of time the user sipped or puffed. Thus, the user has the option to continuously Sip or Puff for continuous turning.

The tethered skier is an experienced skier that is tethered to Tetra-Ski using a rope. The main responsibility for the tethered skier is to ensure the safety of the main skier. When in basic mode, they also have the job of determining the wedge for Tetra-Ski based on the terrain, snow conditions, and user performance. The tethered skier has a wireless remote controller designed to be used in a single hand for this purpose (see Fig. 2). The wireless remote controller consists of a joystick and a button. The joystick is used to

1. Refine user commands. For example, to complete a turn initiated by the main skier.
2. Take control in an emergency. Used to override main skier commands to avoid hazards or danger, including things that may not be visible to the main skier.

In addition to broadening the population of potential skiers, this Shared-Control scheme makes the Tetra-Ski experience more forgiving to a user's mistakes. This Shared-Control system is also designed with the physical abilities of our participants in mind. For example, it is not uncommon for physical fatigue to occur more frequently for individuals with tetraplegia. The Shared-Control system allows them to switch between advance mode and basic mode based on their energy level to maximize the time they spend engaged in the ski experience.

4   Tetra-Ski Deployment

During our deployment process (2017–2019), the team faced and overcame many practical challenges, including recruitment, customization and adaptation, instructor acceptance of Shared Control, and logistics. We describe these in further detail below.

4.1   Recruitment

Traditionally, a patient must be finished with acute rehabilitative care before they can participate in outdoor activities. Once the rehabilitation team indicates readiness to participate, information about sports and recreation are presented to the individual. Education is usually provided by a recreation, occupation, or physical therapist. Considering the injury characteristics, the individual may not be able to participate for a range of time—possibly up to 12 months. However, preparation for participation can occur much sooner. Readying someone for adaptive recreation not only includes education, but preparation for participation can be integrated into physical and occupational therapies.

The research team partnered with a rehabilitation team to identify appropriate candidates prior to deployment. This included the identification of participants and education about the opportunity for adaptive skiing with the Tetra-Ski. Because the research and development team are well integrated into the rehabilitation process at the primary site, recruitment was seamless. However, partnering sites required much more effort with regard to recruitment. From interviews with partnering sites, it was clear that the novelty of the activity and incomplete referral systems created barriers to recruitment. We attribute this to normative difficulties in developing partnerships related to new technology adoption. The partner sites were new to the Tetra-Ski, and this newness seemed to slow initial adoption. Adopting new technology is a challenge from a functional standpoint, however, the Tetra-Ski was also opening unexplored doors for participation of individuals with tetraplegia to ski independently. In many ways, an aspect of its novelty was the paradigm shift from the usual dependant skiing experience to one with far greater autonomy.

4.2 Customization and Adaptation

Although the Tetra-Ski can be deployed with a wide variety of individuals with tetraplegia, some items of adaptive sports equipment must be individualized for the participants. Reasons for this customization include differences in the skiing experience, as well as participant's level of impairment, trunk stability, mobility, body proportion, and alignment. This ensures a usable, safe, and enjoyable experience for our participants. For instance, participants often require small adjustments to the armrest to ensure control over the Tetra-Ski.

Customization of the controller is also common. Most of the sip-and-puff users requested to have their wheelchair input modality (often not sip-and-puff) as their primary input for Tetra-Ski. This request presents challenges in accommodating the range variation among input devices. For example, technology hardiness can be a constraint, because some input devices (i.e., head switch) were not meant to be used in an active, rough environment found in skiing. A goal of the design team is to identify input device(s) for Tetra-Ski that accommodate our users' needs and physical abilities as much as possible. This is an ongoing challenge.

4.3   Instructor–Skier Acceptance

The most unexpected challenge during the deployment period was overcoming perceived codependency issues between the main user and the instructor. Prior to the
Tetra-Ski, individuals with high tetraplegia (no upper extremity function) had a primarily dependent experience in adaptive ski equipment. Instructors either directly
steered the student's ski by holding on or by turning and slowing via multiple teth-
ers. It was found that most skiers preferred to ski as independently as possible.
Tetra-Skiers added much more independence to the overall ski experience. However,
greater autonomy included a steeper learning curve than what is required in a more
dependent ski apparatus. As a result, participants described mixed feelings about the
experience, since they had to slow down and learn how to ski as a beginner. This
was especially noted by individuals who had previously participated in a dependent
ski experience. Instructors also had mixed feelings as the need for traditional teth-
ering skills, which they had developed and perfected over a long period of time,
were no longer necessary. More recently, Tetra-Skiers and new instructors seemed
to develop a more mutual partnership where the skier was in charge of the skiing and
the instructor focused on teaching new skills—and ensuring a safe environment.

4.4   Logistical Costs

Skiing is an expensive sport (tickets and equipment) and Tetra-Skiers often require
the additional complexity of accessible transportation and caregiver support. Tetra-
Skiers also require two experienced instructors to provide a safe lesson. TRAILS
mitigates many of these expenses by providing free instruction, free equipment,
and free ski passes for the student and caregiver. TRAILS travels with equipment
to provide lessons at a preferred location for the client and limits overhead by not
owning or managing infrastructure at any of the ski areas. TRAILS' labor is provided
by the University of Utah Rehabilitation Center as part of its mission to enhance the
quality of life for individuals with disabilities. Grants from government agencies, not-
for-profit businesses, and individuals have helped TRAILS to expand programming
and contribute to program sustainability.

5   Participants' Reactions to Tetra-Ski

We conducted interviews with eight participants (P1–P8) after they had finished using
Tetra-Ski. This data helps illuminate their experiences and serves as an opportunity
to reflect on the current iteration of Tetra-Ski.

5.1 Participants Enjoyed Their Tetra-Ski Experience

Multiple participants reported positive reactions toward using Tetra-Ski: "Awesome! I will be happy to do it again." (P1), "It's awesome." (P2), "I would not change anything about this experience" (P6).

P7 reported that the Tetra-Ski experience provided him with the feeling of empowerment and autonomy:

> I would be interested in using the ski chair again because it gave me a sense of empowerment over my quadriplegia and control over my environment. ...... I like seeing beautiful things and going kind of fast ... [it was] fun being able to choose where I wanted to go.

Similar positive themes were reported across participants. Negative themes that arose from the interviews primarily included a need for greater access to other forms of adaptive outdoor experiences, including extreme sports activities. This indicates a need for more opportunities for adaptive recreation, especially in nontraditional domains.

5.2 Shared Control Helped Participants Feel Safe and Enabled Trainers to Adjust Their Support

Multiple participants reported that the Shared-Control system helped them feel safe during the experience. They were reassured knowing that the trainer could take control over Tetra-Ski if it was necessary to avoid a dangerous situation: "The [trainer] was always there to help out." (P1), "The [trainer] helped [me] not get in a lot of wrecks" (P3). The idea of Shared Control came so naturally that many of the participants did not even comment on it directly when they were queried about the control scheme.

5.3 Tetra-Ski Needs to Support More Input Devices

Joystick users overwhelmingly described Tetra-Ski as usable and that the control system was intuitive. The sip-and-puff users, however, had more varied feedback about usability. Participants who controlled Tetra-Ski using sip-and-puff reported that they would prefer using their current input device in their wheelchair as their primary input device for Tetra-Ski. We asked sip-and-puff participants how to improve sip-and-puff and they described a desire for a better calibration process and better positioning, but they still insisted on having more options for the input device.

5.4 Participants Asked for Minimum Adaption

Multiple reports from trainers indicated that participants resisted using sip-and-puff as their primary input device for Tetra-Ski even if they had limited hand motion and that sip-and-puff would be more usable (from the trainer perspective). Similarly, participants who had limited head motion or feet power asked for an input device to utilize that rather than using sip-and-puff.

6 Future Work

This work provided a number of insights into the next step design needs for the Tetra-Ski system. Pertinent next steps include designing next generation input devices for Tetra-Ski as well as a more sophisticated communication system for the users.

6.1 Next Generation Input Devices: A Need for Better Feedback on System State

Feedback from the trainers using the joystick control system consistently indicated that the users were not holding the joystick long enough to perform complete turns. This led to chaotic motions with the joystick in an attempt to make the skis turn faster. The problem seems to be that the position of the skis were not providing an in-the-moment, one-to-one match to the joystick movement. While it's possible to increase the response time from the skis to better match the movement of the joystick, it's inadvisable as it might lead to more tipping of Tetra-Ski and a potentially higher risk of accidents. A more feasible solution to be explored is to place a flag system on the tips of the skis to provide a visual cue for the users to see the current position of the skis. Another solution would be to provide haptic feedback for the user that would indicate the current location of the skis.

6.2 Better Communication System Between the Trainer and Tetra-Ski Users

Currently, the trainer relies on verbal communication to communicate instructions and guidance to Tetra-Ski users. Such communication can be obstructed by environmental conditions. Without an appropriate communication channel that can accommodate the noise of the surrounding environment, the trainer will likely need to interrupt the experience more frequently to ensure safety. Accordingly, these interruptions diminish the user's sense of autonomy. The next steps include developing a clear communication channel (i.e., radio communication) between the trainer and the main user. This step should be followed by an in-depth study of what types of communication should be provided and for what purposes. Verbal communication may not be the only answer for this goal, due to the nature of the experience that requires fast-paced communication and responses from both parties.

7 Conclusion

Designing an independently controllable ski experience for individuals with tetraplegia is an interdisciplinary effort that has both targeted and generalizable implications. Our findings can not only enhance the design of adaptive ski technology, but also inform the design of adaptive controls for other purposes. Aligned with the goals for enhancing autonomy and safety, the Shared-Control input scheme allowed individuals with tetraplegia to control their skiing experience safely with minimum training. This fostered independence and resulted in an enjoyable experience. Future directions include improving feedback and developing a communication system between the participant and the trainer. Addressing the complexities of the Shared-Control schemes in other contexts has the potential to further broaden access to user-controllable outdoor recreational activities for populations that have traditionally been excluded from them.

References

Alsaleem A, Imburgia R, Godinez M, Merryweather A, Altizer R, Denning T, Rosenbluth J, Trapp S, Wiese J (2019) Leveraging shared control to empower people with tetraplegia to participate in extreme sports. In: The 21st international ACM SIGACCESS conference on computers and accessibility. ACM, Pittsburgh, PA, USA, pp 470–481

Asia Classification http://www.scientificspine.com/spine-scores/asia-classification.html

Baldwin M, Hirano S, Derama R, Mankoff J, Hayes G (2019) Blind navigation on the water through shared assistive technology, Scotland, Glasgow

Barclay L, McDonald R, Lentin P, Bourke-Taylor H (2016) Facilitators and barriers to social and community participation following spinal cord injury. Aust Occup Ther J 63(1):19–28. https://doi.org/10.1111/1440-1630.12241, https://onlinelibrary.wiley.com/doi/abs/10.1111/1440-1630.12241

Brown M, Ma L, Gordon W, Spielman L (2002) Participation by individuals with spinal cord injury in social and recreational activity outside the home. Top Spinal Cord Inj Rehabil 7:83–100. https://doi.org/10.1310/7U35-GDQ4-FDV3-GVYV

Demeester E, Hüntemann A, Vanhooydonck D, Vanacker G, Van Brussel H, Nuttin M (2008) User-adapted plan recognition and user-adapted shared control: a Bayesian approach to semi-autonomous wheelchair driving. Auton Robot 24(2):193–211. https://doi.org/10.1007/s10514-007-9064-5, https://doi.org/10.1007/s10514-007-9064-5

Integramouse https://www.integramouse.com/startseite/

Kim IT, Mun JH, Jun PS, Kim GC, Sim YJ, Jeong HJ (2011) Leisure time physical activity of people with spinal cord injury: mainly with clubs of spinal cord injury patients in busankyeongnam, Korea. Ann Rehabil Med 35(5):613–626. https://doi.org/10.5535/arm.2011.35.5. 613, https://www.ncbi.nlm.nih.gov/pubmed/22506183

Kim J, Park H, Bruce J, Sutton E, Rowles D, Pucci D, Holbrook J, Minocha J, Nardone B, West D, Laumann A, Roth E, Jones M, Veledar E, Ghovanloo M (2013) The tongue enables computer and wheelchair control for people with spinal cord injury. Sci Trans Med 5(213):213ra166. https://doi.org/10.1126/scitranslmed.3006296.http://stm.sciencemag.org/content/5/213/213ra166.abstract

van Leeuwen C, Kraaijeveld S, Lindeman E, Post M (2011) Associations between psychological factors and quality of life ratings in persons with spinal cord injury: a systematic review. Spinal Cord 50:174. https://doi.org/10.1038/sc.2011.120

Lundberg N, Bennett J, Smith S (2011) Outcomes of adaptive sports and recreation participation among veterans returning from combat with acquired disability. Ther Recreat J 45(2):105–120

Martin Ginis KA, Latimer AE, Arbour-Nicitopoulos KP, Buchholz AC, Bray SR, Craven BC, Hayes KC, Hicks AL, McColl MA, Potter PJ, Smith K, Wolfe DL (2010) Leisure time physical activity in a population-based sample of people with spinal cord injury part i: demographic and injury-related correlates. Arch Phys Med Rehabil 91(5):722–728. https://doi.org/10.1016/j.apmr.2009.12.027

Muraki S, Tsunawake N, Hiramatsu S, Yamasaki M (2000) The effect of frequency and mode of sports activity on the psychological status in tetraplegics and paraplegics. Spinal Cord 38(5):309–314. https://doi.org/10.1038/sj.sc.3101002

QuadJoy | Bridging Quality of Life for Handicap & Paralyzed https://quadjoy.io/

Recio AC, Becker D, Morgan M, Saunders N, Schramm LP, McDonald JW (2013) Use of a virtual reality physical ride-on sailing simulator as a rehabilitation tool for recreational sports and community reintegration a pilot study, vol 92. https://doi.org/10.1097/PHM.0000000000000012

Rojhani S, Stiens S, Recio AC (2016) Independent sailing with high tetraplegia using sip and puff controls: integration into a community sailing center, 40. https://doi.org/10.1080/10790268.2016.1198548

Scelza WM, Kalpakjian CZ, Zemper ED, Tate DG (2005) Perceived barriers to exercise in people with spinal cord injury, 84. https://doi.org/10.1097/01.phm.0000171172.96290.67

Skiing & Snow Equipment-Disabled Sports USA https://www.disabledsportsusa.org/sports/adaptive-equipment/skiing-snow-equipment/

Slater D, Meade M (2004) Participation in recreation and sports for persons with spinal cord injury: review and recommendations. NeuroRehabilitation 19:121–129

Tasiemski T, Osinska M (2013) Sport in people with tetraplegia: review of recent literature

TetraMouse https://tetramouse.com/

Zabriskie R, Lundberg N, Groff D (2005) Quality of life and identity: the benefits of a community-based therapeutic recreation and adaptive sports program. Ther Recreat J 39:176–191

Zabriskie RB, Lundberg NR, Groff DG (2005) Quality of life and identity: the benefits of a community-based therapeutic recreation and adaptive sports program. Ther Recreat J39(3). https://js.sagamorepub.com/trj/article/view/971

Rethinking the Role of a Mobile Computing in Recreational Hiking

Zann Anderson and Michael Jones

Abstract Mobile computing devices, especially smartphones, are part of the recreational hiking experience in the United States. In our survey of over a thousand people in the United States in 2017, about 95% of respondents reported that they prefer to bring a smartphone when they go hiking. A smartphone used during hiking is simply a tool. That tool can improve or worsen the quality of a hiking experience. In this chapter, we propose a vision of interactive mobile computing design for hiking which may improve the quality of the hiking experience. Our vision of interactive computing and hiking is built on three principles: time spent outdoors is good for individuals, computing can play a positive role in outdoor recreation, and human–nature interaction is more important than human–computer interaction. We illustrate our approach using an extended scenario.

1 Introduction

Modern mobile computing technology is such that individuals carry small but remarkably capable computers with them nearly everywhere they go. This leads to computing's inclusion in activities and contexts where it was previously absent, changing these contexts and activities in both subtle and obvious ways. One such context is outdoor recreation, where the use of technology can be readily observed in many different forms.

Figures 1 and 2 illustrate computing technology use during outdoor recreation. Figure 1 shows a woman interacting with a smart watch outdoors. There are many reasons why she may choose to interact with her smart watch at this time. She could be checking her location or finding her bearings on a long hike or trail run. Perhaps, she

Z. Anderson
Utah Valley University, Orem, UT, USA
e-mail: zann.anderson@uvu.edu

M. Jones (✉)
Brigham Young University, Provo, UT, USA
e-mail: jones@cs.byu.edu

© Springer Nature Switzerland AG 2020   291
D. S. McCrickard et al. (eds.), *HCI Outdoors: Theory, Design, Methods and Applications*, Human–Computer Interaction Series,
https://doi.org/10.1007/978-3-030-45289-6_16

Fig. 1 A woman using a smart watch in the desert. The HCI community has the opportunity to investigate and explain this kind of interaction. This understanding will help us build interactive systems which enhance and enable outdoor recreation experiences (Photo credit: Blazej Lyjak, shutterstock.)

Fig. 2 A woman using a cell phone with a bare hand in a cold forest. Another opportunity facing the HCI community is designing and engineering systems which are comfortable for use in outdoor environments (Photo credit: Mila Drumeva, shutterstock.)

just received an important notification regarding an emergency back home. Looking at her watch for any one of these reasons could also result in getting sucked into reading interesting tweets from her notifications list. Therefore, her use of the smart watch could serve as a distraction from or an enabler for her outdoor activity. She likely has her own opinions of its place and purpose.

Like Toyama (2020), we see interactive computing as an *amplifier* of human intentions. In this view, computing provides leverage to give people more ability to realize their intention. While Toyama described this concept in the context of technology and poverty, we describe its application in the context of outdoor recreation. In outdoor recreation, people intend to experience *recreation* which includes a wide range of activities that are *not* work but which renew or refresh one's mind and body. Our vision of interactive computing in outdoor recreation is grounded in the belief that computing can amplify the intent to recreate.

2 Three Principles

We posit three principles as a framework for our vision of interactive computing in outdoor recreation. The three principles are

- Time spent outdoors is good for individuals and society;
- Computing can play a valuable role in enhancing, encouraging, and enabling time spent outdoors;
- In outdoor activities, human–nature interaction holds priority over human–computer interaction.

We use the term "principle" in the sense of "a comprehensive and fundamental law, doctrine or assumption".[1] In our usage, principles guide thinking and action but are not stated exclusively as laws based on empirical evidence. While there is some evidence to support the first two principles, each of the three principles could be properly thought of as an assumption.

After a brief summary of our vision, we will discuss each principle in turn and give some concrete design guidelines or suggestions which spring from the latter principles. These guidelines are intended to help navigate the tension between staying connected through technology and disconnecting from everyday pressures. We do so with the intent of allowing computing to fill meaningful roles while supporting the original motivation for engaging in outdoor recreation.

Our vision of interactive computing in outdoor recreation exists in a world in which computing is present but not obtrusive when we are outdoors. This world is similar to Weiser's version of the future (Weiser 1991) in which we allow computing to "fade into the background."

---

[1] See definition 1a of "principle" in the online edition of the Merriam-Webster dictionary www.merriam-webster.com. Accessed February 2020.

Fig. 3 A mountain bike
loaded for touring. Existing
technology already seeks to
augment such gear with
useful technology, and we
envision a future where
perhaps almost all of the
gears in this photo would be
computing-enabled

In the outdoors, computing can remain in the background to observe and respond in meaningful ways, all while remaining largely at the periphery of our experience. It will augment or be integrated into existing outdoor gear, neatly blending in with the physical world. It will not demand attention but will be available when needed. It will cater to individuals' human–computer interaction preferences while encouraging deeper human–nature interaction. We believe that computing which follows this vision can enhance, enable, and encourage outdoor recreation without detracting from human–nature interaction (Fig. 3).

Weiser concludes (Weiser 1991) by comparing information overload when using a computer to taking a walk in the woods:

> There is more information available at our fingertips during a walk in the woods than in any computer system, yet people find a walk among trees relaxing and computers frustrating. Machines that fit the human environment, instead of forcing humans to enter theirs, will make using a computer as refreshing as taking a walk in the woods.

A modern twist on Weiser's comparison is that people now take a computer (or two or three) with them when they take a walk in the woods. Our intent is to make taking a walk in the woods with a computer at least as refreshing as taking a walk in the woods without one.

3 Example Scenario

Throughout the remainder of this chapter, we illustrate our vision using an extended fictional scenario involving a person named Kerstin. Imagine that Kerstin is going backpacking for several days. Her goal is to disconnect for a time and to recuperate from grad school after her recent graduation. She is concerned about safety but is an experienced hiker and backpacker and knows the trail she is following well. She is carrying normal backpacking gear including a pack, tent, boots, and trekking poles, some of which are augmented by computing. She is also carrying food and water for her journey and knows where to source more along the way as necessary. She wants to spend time in reflection and finds that recording her experience helps her reflect more deeply while she is on the trail.

4 Principle 1: Time Spent Outdoors Is Good for Individuals and Society

Our society currently sees natural outdoor settings as valuable locations for recreation and restoration. This has not always been the case. Different cultures at different times place different values on wilderness. For example, upon arriving on the American coastline in 1620, William Bradford described the unspoilt natural scene as "a hideous and desolate wilderness" (Bradford 1650). Indeed, the American perception of wilderness has changed over the centuries (Nash 2014). Almost 200 years later in 1784, Jeremy Belknap wrote "these rugged and wild scenes" in New Hampshire are likely to "amaze, to soothe and to enrapture" (Belnap 1784). The appreciation of wilderness as a place for personal restoration was encoded into law by the Wilderness Act of 1964 which provides a way to set aside undisturbed wilderness for "the good of the whole people" to "use and enjoy" where "man himself is a visitor who does not remain".

Wilderness as considered in our vision of HCI in outdoor recreation is grounded in Muir and Marshall's preservation philosophies from the early twentieth century. Muir wrote:

> Climb the mountains and get their good tidings. Nature's peace will flow into you as sunshine flows into trees. The winds will blow their own freshness into you, and the storms their energy, while cares will drop off like autumn leaves. –Muir, *Our National Parks*. Muir (2018)

and Marshall wrote:

> In a world over-run with split second schedules, physical uncertainty and man-made superficiality … life's most splendid moments come in the opportunity to enjoy undefiled nature. Marshall (1934).

If "split-second schedules" and "man-made superficiality" created a need to "enjoy undefiled nature" in 1934, that need is no less urgent in a world of notifications and social media.

Appreciation of the natural world remains strong in the United States. The Outdoor Foundation reports that 44.9 million Americans participated in at least one hiking trip in 2017 (The Outdoor Foundation 2018). In comparison, 38.9 million people attended either Disneyland or Disney's Magic Kingdom in the same year (AECOM 2018).

A psychological theory also describes benefits from time in nature. Based on nearly 20 years of experimental study, Kaplan and Kaplan characterize reasons why time in nature has a restorative effect on people (Kaplan and Kaplan 1989). This effect restores a person's ability to maintain *directed attention*. Directed attention is a mental resource individuals expend when focusing on a task, particularly tasks that may not be intrinsically fascinating (James 1983). Eventually, directed attention becomes depleted, leading to directed attention fatigue. Directed attention fatigue leads to reduced inhibition, resulting in reduced executive function and increased irritability, impulsiveness, and irrationality.

In the Kaplans' model, time spent in a *restorative environment* restores directed attention. A restorative environment includes four factors:

- Being Away—the restorative environment must represent a break from one's typical environment, and in particular, from whatever activities deplete directed attention.
- Extent—the restorative environment must "be rich enough and coherent enough so that it constitutes a whole other world" (Kaplan 1995).
- Compatibility—the restorative environment should be compatible with one's goals and purposes.
- Soft Fascination—the restorative environment should be naturally fascinating, capturing one's attention without requiring effort.

The Kaplans conclude that "the natural environment seems to have some special relationship to each of the four factors that are important to a restorative experience" (Kaplan and Kaplan 1989, p. 195). A more recent review of research into the definition and impact of restorative environments finds that additional work is needed to characterize exactly what makes an environment "restorative" (Pearson and Craig 2014).

As we consider the role of interactive computing in outdoor recreation experiences, we can use the factors of a restorative environment as guidance. For example, how does smartphone use impact the feeling of "being away" from the daily routine or the sense of "soft fascination" in a new setting?

4.1   Scenario: Looking for Restoration

Kerstin's time in nature will give her a chance to be away from the pressures of daily routines. She's decided to backpack in the Needles District of Canyonlands National Park in Utah, United States, in the spring. This area is managed in a way that allows for recreational use while preserving the wilderness nature of the area.

Fig. 4 Typical scenes from the Needles District of Canyonlands National Park in Utah in the Spring. The Needles district is the setting for the fictitious example scenario that illustrates our vision of mobile computing in hiking

The weather is usually pleasant both night and day this time of year. Figure 4 shows typical scenes from this part of the Needles District. Trails wind through parks and sandstone fins spread out over a wide area. The rock formations fascinate her and capture her attention as she walks and rests.

Kerstin will have a more restorative experience if her smartphone does not interrupt her with reminders of her daily routine. Because her smartphone is out of place in this environment, tasks performed using the smartphone should not require getting the smartphone out at all. The smartphone should impact the experience in ways compatible with these goals.

This kind of terrain challenges her, but is not overwhelming at her skill level. She's picked this area because it is compatible with her goal to reflect on the transition between graduate school and the next phase of her life.

5 Principle 2: Computing Enhances, Enables, and Encourages Outdoor Recreation

Although computing itself is not a traditional part of outdoor recreation, technology defined more broadly is part of the experience. Outdoor recreationalists use a vast array of technology, including both computing and non-computing technology, from simple items such as boots or shoes to complex systems such as suspension linkages for mountain bikes or quick release bindings on alpine skis. Technology has a rich history of enhancing, enabling, and encouraging individuals to participate in outdoor activities. Mobile or ubiquitous computing technology allows computing to do the same by allowing individuals to bring computing systems outdoors.

5.1   Computing Is All Around Us in the Outdoors

Individuals already carry computers everywhere, including outdoors. This is clear from the results of our quantitative survey, in which 95% of respondents (n. 1002) indicated that they prefer to bring their cell phone when hiking (Anderson et al. 2017).

Computers continue to proliferate in all areas of modern life. Research and development efforts in the Internet of Things (IoT) and Body Area Networks (BANs) explore ways that computing can be leveraged in order to support and enhance daily life and health and wellness. Our philosophy embraces a similar notion; however, with much less collection and sharing of data than is typical of IoT (Gubbi et al. 2013; Atzori et al. 2010; Al-Fuqaha et al. 2015) and without the clinical health and wellness emphasis of BANs (Cavallari et al. 2014; Movassaghi et al. 2014).

We envision the quantity of outdoor computing devices, or compute-enabled pieces of gear, continuing to increase until computing is all around us in the outdoors. We hope that this does not mean individuals are staring at tiny screens on every surface. Rather, computing will fade into the background as it becomes part of existing gear in ways that augment their functionality, add new but congruent functionality, support other intents, and simplify interaction with technology.

Computing "all around us" outdoors refers to computing carried into—and back out of—the natural environment by the individual. The natural environment should be left as it is, rather than being littered with more man-made objects. However, it may prove useful to augment existing man-made structures and objects in the natural environment with computing in support of recreation. For instance, a map board at a trailhead could allow individuals to tap their phone on it and download a map via NFC.

5.2   Computers Observe and Act

Computing does not need user input in order to be useful. The computers embedded in a modern car are constantly working to maintain fuel efficiency, enable safe traction, lower emissions, and perform many other functions, all without any conscious input from the driver. The main thrust of IoT is to build embedded systems that work with little to no user input.

However, many of the interfaces on smartphones—the default computing device carried by individuals outdoors—are designed specifically to keep our attention. In fact, many apps and websites draw their revenue largely or entirely from advertising, which leads to interfaces which are designed to capture and keep users' attention (Krishna 2015). One goal of outdoor recreation is to spend time in a natural setting without distractions. Computing for outdoor recreation should observe and act with minimal screen time.

   This guideline expects devices, systems, and compute-enabled gear to gather data from the environment and from the user, to make judgments, and to execute actions in support of the user and their goals. This should all happen with little to no interaction from the user. This operates much like IoT and BAN systems; however, in our approach individuals' data should only be seen by the user's device, never shared with the wider world without permission. Furthermore, data should only be stored long enough to observe and act on it, and it should not be stored long-term either locally or in the cloud except as specifically requested by the user. This is a crucial difference from IoT and BAN approaches, where data collection, storage, and sharing are core tenets.

5.3 Smartphone as a Hub

Using the smartphone as a hub keeps computing in the background while bringing a powerful computing platform outdoors. A typical modern smartphone's capabilities include numerous sensors, multiple types of wireless connectivity, a camera, an LED light, and a speaker among others.

   Using the smartphone as a hub involves using the phone in Wi-Fi hub mode, allowing other systems and devices to connect. By doing this, connected devices and systems can easily communicate with not only the phone, but with other devices and systems as well. They may also take advantage of the phone's capabilities in support of their own roles. This also allows these peripheral devices and systems embedded in gear to be streamlined, relying on the phone for connectivity and other services, and incorporating only that functionality which is necessary to their particular roles.

   While leveraging the phone's capabilities, devices and systems can also interact with each other to increase functionality and/or usability. Inputs and outputs from different devices and systems, as well as data from the phone, can be paired in ways that create a better overall system.

5.4 Scenario: Phone Stays in the Pack but Remains Useful

Before she left home, Kerstin curated a selection of compute-enabled devices to bring. She brought only those items that support her goals for this trip. Because this is not a fitness training outing, she did not bring her heart rate monitor and will not record her walking pace for this trip. Those details would be a distraction. She decided to bring her smartphone, trekking poles, backpack, and a hat.

   Upon arriving at the trailhead near the Needles Outpost southeast of Moab, Utah, Kerstin gathers her gear and begins to prepare to hike. Because it is sunny, Kerstin puts on her hat. Although it looks like a normal hat, it includes a built-in camera. Before stepping onto the trail, Kerstin presses a button on her trekking pole, triggering her camera to take a picture of the rock formations visible from the trailhead and documenting the beginning of her journey.

A few miles down the trail, Kerstin enters a short, narrow slot canyon formed between two large sandstone walls. As she emerges in a park-like clearing surrounded by sandstone fins on the other side of the crack, she realizes that this is like her transition from University to career. She turns around to look at the crack and talks out loud about her transition. As she speaks, the camera recognizes her voice and begins to record video and audio. This recording is stored in the camera and uploaded to her smartphone in the background when the camera is not in use. This epiphany and location are now captured together for later reflection. When Kerstin stops for a breather, she sits on top of a rounded sandstone formation and takes her backpack off. Without her noticing, her backpack senses that she has set it down and sends an "OK" message to those observing her via her phone's app.

Stopping for the night, Kerstin sets up her tent. Removing the tent from her backpack triggers a "stopping for the night" message to be sent home, along with several photos she has taken during the day. Video she has recorded is not sent, as Kerstin has opted to keep these recordings for her own reflection. She sets her hat and trekking poles near her backpack, where they charge wirelessly from the built-in power bank, which has been charging during the day via a solar panel mounted on her pack.

6 Principle 3: Computing Respects the Primacy of Human–Nature Interaction

Individuals already carry and interact with computing devices during hiking and other outdoor activities. As outlined in the previous section, our vision involves even more computing devices and compute-enabled gear. However, this does not translate into more human–computer interaction. We envision computing which is designed to be increasingly hands-off and which allows individuals to focus on their recreation. In order to accomplish this goal, compute-enabled gear and devices should be designed to respect the primacy of human–nature interaction.

Human–nature interaction is the interaction between a person and the natural world. This could be as simple as watching the clouds go by while outside or looking through a window. It could be very immersive such as being outside on a mountainside during a torrential rainstorm. Human–nature interaction can be active and energetic such as skiing down a mountain at the edge of, but still within, one's skill level. Or it could be more passive such as watching the sunset on a beach over the ocean.

When a person is outside for recreation purposes, human–nature interaction is the primary purpose and human–computer interaction is secondary. This is because a hiker does not go on a hike in order to scroll through social media posts and a mountain biker does not go riding in order to check emails. Recreationalists go outdoors to do something other than interact with a computer. As stated in the second principle, interactive computing can *enhance or enable* the recreational experience. The third principle states that computing should be designed to be secondary to human–nature interaction.

6.1 Computing Fits the Physical Environment

In outdoor activities, selecting the right gear is very important. Individuals must consider weight, utility, safety, comfort, and other factors in deciding which gear to purchase. Activities requiring individuals to move quickly require a gear that is lightweight and not cumbersome, while activities involving greater distances or longer time outdoors require a gear which is somewhat heavier and more cumbersome as well as a greater variety of gear (Fig. 5).

Computing devices and systems need not become another decision point. Instead, computing should augment or be integrated with existing gear. We envision existing gear being augmented with computing in order to improve its efficacy, safety, durability, or usability. Devices and systems which do not integrate directly with existing gear can be designed to be placed as seamlessly as possible onto or into existing gear, thus providing input, output, and other functionality without becoming cumbersome, unwieldy, or intrusive.

The future of computing-enabled outdoor recreation gear should, on the surface, appear like a gear in use today. This provides an experience which is congruent with individuals' existing experience with human–nature interaction.

6.2 Computing Lives on the Periphery

With our guidelines *Smartphone As a Hub* and *Computing Fits the Physical Environment*, we have already specified computing's place as being very much out of sight and out of mind in outdoor recreation. This guideline is meant to expand on those. It concerns the physical placement of computing in outdoor recreation as well as the interactions users take with computing. Computing for outdoor recreation should not be placed in a way that demands attention. Placing computing within or making it easy to attach to existing gear will help ensure it remains physically peripheral.

While we envision devices and systems that require as little input and produce as little output as possible, some input/output (I/O) will still be necessary. It should, however, be done simply and unobtrusively. A touchscreen is not necessary when a button, knob, or other physical control will suffice. Audible or visible notifications are likely not necessary except in the most urgent cases, such as safety concerns. Rarely should computing in the outdoors demand an individual's attention through I/O.

Another consideration is the temporal placement of interactions. That is, if an interaction is necessary, particularly screen-based interaction, it should be placed

Fig. 5 A hiker enjoys a
mountain view.
Compute-enabled gear need
not add to the load he is
already carrying but should
fit in seamlessly and
augment existing gear

at the temporal periphery of an activity wherever possible. Apps or systems can be
initiated and halted at the trailhead or in the parking lot, allowing individuals to
benefit from their use without needing to interact with them during outdoor activity.

6.3 Computing Encourages More Human–Nature Interaction

Finally, computing should attempt, insofar as it is possible, to encourage individuals
to engage more and more deeply with nature. Much of this is accomplished with
our other guidelines which seek to avoid computing's intrusion on one's focus on

the natural world. However, we should also seek to actively encourage individuals to engage more with the natural world. This may take the form of disabling certain functionalities or apps on a smartphone when in "outdoors mode," alerting the individual to facets of the natural world they may have missed otherwise, or allowing for graceful transitions wherein frequent actions taken by the user are made to be less interaction-heavy and more natural, or possibly even automatic.

6.4 Scenario: No Human–Computer Interaction for a Few Days

Because she will be hiking in the desert for several days and water is scarce in the Needles District, Kirsten opts for lightweight gear to allow more capacity for carrying water. Her hat, poles, and backpack contain computing devices but the computing systems are cleverly concealed. None of the systems she has brought require input from her. There are no interfaces or notifications.

By the third day of the trip, Kirsten has forgotten that she has any computing equipment. Her devices continue to send updates to friends at home, but she has stopped recording video or voice memos. She has stopped using her computing systems because she is fully engaged in interacting with the natural environment around her.

On the final day, as she gets closer to her car at the parking lot. She realizes that her trip is rapidly coming to a close. When she is within sight of the parking lot, she speaks out loud to record a few final thoughts. The clarity obtained from a few days away from computing has given her a new perspective on the meaning of her career. She records those thoughts as the camera records the location. Once she returns to the car, the phone senses that it is back within the range of the car. As the car begins to move along the road, the phone sends a "hike is done, heading home" message to her friends so that they know when to expect her return.

7 Conclusion

We have outlined a vision of computing in outdoor recreation. The vision is based on three central principles, from which several guidelines follow. Given this philosophy and its guidelines, we hope to navigate the tension between the proliferation of computing devices on the trail and the many distractions that those devices bring with them. Ultimately, we believe that computing done well can enhance, encourage, and enable more outdoor recreation.

We do not discuss the technical and logistical challenges involved in building devices and systems for outdoor recreation. These include the lack of connectivity, the need for ruggedization, temperature, moisture, and other environmental challenges. While these are important considerations, we categorize them as engineering problems, separate from the design focus of our vision.

While our vision is carefully thought out and considers many sources, its value lies in practical application. We hope that our vision will provide inspiration and guidance to ourselves and others and look forward to apps, devices, and systems which are designed with these principles in mind. As our vision is applied to the process of designing and implementing gear and systems for the outdoors, we believe it will continue to be refined and strengthened. We also eagerly anticipate the accomplishment of our goal of allowing computing to enhance, enable, and encourage outdoor recreation.

References

AECOM (2018) Global attractions attendance report: theme index, museum index. https://www.aecom.com/content/wp-content/uploads/2018/05/2017-Theme-Museum-Index.pdf. Accessed 26 Oct 2018

Al-Fuqaha A, Guizani M, Mohammadi M, Aledhari M, Ayyash M (2015) Internet of things: a survey on enabling technologies, protocols, and applications. IEEE Commun Surv Tutor 17(4):2347–2376. https://doi.org/10.1109/COMST.2015.2444095

Anderson Z, Lusk C, Jones MD (2017) Towards understanding hikers' technology preferences. In: Proceedings of the 2017 ACM international joint conference on pervasive and ubiquitous computing and proceedings of the 2017 ACM international symposium on wearable computers, UbiComp '17. ACM, New York, NY, USA, pp 1–4. http://doi.acm.org/10.1145/3123024.3123089

Atzori L, Iera A, Morabito G (2010) The internet of things: a survey. Comput Netw 54(15):2787–2805. https://doi.org/10.1016/j.comnet.2010.05.010, http://www.sciencedirect.com/science/article/pii/S1389128610001568

Belnap J (1784) The history of new Hampshire

Bradford W (c. 1650) Of Plymouth plantation

Cavallari R, Martelli F, Rosini R, Buratti C, Verdone R (2014) A survey on wireless body area networks: technologies and design challenges. IEEE Commun Surv Tutor 16(3):1635–1657. https://doi.org/10.1109/SURV.2014.012214.00007

Gubbi J, Buyya R, Marusic S, Palaniswami M (2013) Internet of things (IoT): a vision, architectural elements, and future directions. Futur Gener Comput Syst 29(7):1645–1660. https://doi.org/10.1016/j.future.2013.01.010, http://www.sciencedirect.com/science/article/pii/S0167739X13000241

James W (1983) The principles of psychology, vols 1–2 (2 vols in 1). Harvard University Press. https://www.amazon.com/Principles-Psychology-Vols-1-2-Volumes/dp/0674706250?SubscriptionId=AKIAIOBINVZYXZQZ2U3A&tag=chimbori05-20&linkCode=xm2&camp=2025&creative=165953&creativeASIN=0674706250

Kaplan R, Kaplan S (1989) The experience of nature: a psychological perspective. CUP Archive

Kaplan S (1995) The restorative benefits of nature: toward an integrative framework. J Environ Psychol 15(3):169–182

Krishna G (2015) The best interface is no interface: the simple path to brilliant technology (Voices That Matter). New Riders. https://www.amazon.com/Best-Interface-No-brilliant-technology-ebook/dp/B00T0ER57I?SubscriptionId=0JYN1NVW651KCA56C102&tag=techkie-20&linkCode=xm2&camp=2025&creative=165953&creativeASIN=B00T0ER57I

Marshall R (1934) Letter to Harold Ickes

Movassaghi S, Abolhasan M, Lipman J, Smith D, Jamalipour A (2014) Wireless body area networks: a survey. IEEE Commun Surv Tutor 16(3):1658–1686. https://doi.org/10.1109/SURV.2013.121313.00064

Muir J (2018) Our national parks. Gibbs Smith

Nash R (2014) Wilderness and the American mind. Yale University Press

Pearson DG, Craig T (2014) The great outdoors? Exploring the mental health benefits of natural environments. Front Psychol 5:1178. https://doi.org/10.3389/fpsyg.2014.01178, https://www.frontiersin.org/article/10.3389/fpsyg.2014.01178

The outdoor foundation: outdoor participation report (2018). https://outdoorindustry.org/resource/2018-outdoor-participation-report/. Accessed 26 Oct 2018

Toyama K (2020) Technology is not the answer. The Atlantic

Weiser M (1991) The computer for the 21st century. Sci Am 265(3):94–104

Modeling Gaze-Guided Narratives for Outdoor Tourism

Peter Kiefer, Benjamin Adams, Tiffany C. K. Kwok, and Martin Raubal

Abstract Many outdoor spaces have hidden stories connected with them that can be used to enrich a tourist's experience. These stories are often related to environmental features which are far from the user and far apart from each other. Therefore, they are difficult to explore by locomotion, but can be visually explored from a vantage point. Telling a story from a vantage point is challenging since the system must ensure that the user can identify the relevant features in the environment. *Gaze-guided narratives* are an interaction concept that helps in such situations by telling a story dynamically depending on the user's current and previous gaze on a panorama. This chapter suggests a formal modeling approach for gaze-guided narratives, based on narrative mediation trees. The approach is illustrated with an example from the Swiss saga around 'Wilhelm Tell'.

1 Introduction

Outdoor spaces offer a variety of opportunities and experiences for tourists. On the one hand, they facilitate physical activities, such as hiking, skiing, or climbing. Previous HCI research has aimed at supporting these kinds of sports activities in a way that contributes to individuals' health, well-being, and safety (Bettini and Mascetti 2016; Wiehr et al. 2016). On the other hand, outdoor spaces also feature

P. Kiefer (✉) · T. C. K. Kwok · M. Raubal
Chair of Geoinformation Engineering, ETH Zurich, 8093 Zurich, Switzerland
e-mail: pekiefer@ethz.ch

T. C. K. Kwok
e-mail: ckwok@ethz.ch

M. Raubal
e-mail: mraubal@ethz.ch

B. Adams
Department of Computer Science and Software Engineering, University of Canterbury,
Christchurch 8020, New Zealand
e-mail: benjamin.adams@canterbury.ac.nz

© Springer Nature Switzerland AG 2020
D. S. McCrickard et al. (eds.), *HCI Outdoors: Theory, Design, Methods and Applications*, Human–Computer Interaction Series,
https://doi.org/10.1007/978-3-030-45289-6_17

unique opportunities for learning and entertainment (Sailer et al. 2016; Kiefer et al. 2006). For instance, there seems to be a widespread interest in knowing the names of environmental features in sight, as can be seen in the prevalence of augmented reality (AR) apps, such as PeakFinder.[1]

Many touristic outdoor spaces around the world have fascinating yet complex stories to tell, which are not easy to communicate through simple interaction approaches. Consider, for instance, the history and literary fiction connected with a Swiss mountain panorama (see Sect. 3 and Kiefer et al. 2014), Romantic poetry related to the English Lake District (Cheverst et al. 2016), or the formation history of geological phenomena in a US national park. The plot of such stories typically involves more than one environmental feature and has narrative ordering dependencies. Previous work on locative media has suggested to tell these stories by guiding users through a sequence of relevant places using positioning technology (Nisi et al. 2004; Cheverst et al. 2016) or through magic lens-based interaction with maps, such as in the WikEar system (Schöning et al. 2008). Often, however, a story involves environmental features which are far from the user and far apart from each other, but easy to explore visually from one (or a small set of) vantage point(s).

Here, we consider guides that tell stories to a tourist standing at a vantage point. A particular challenge is that the system must ensure the user can identify the relevant features in the environment. For such interaction scenarios, we have recently introduced *Gaze-Guided Narratives* (Kwok et al. 2019), a novel interaction concept which combines gaze guidance (Losing et al. 2014) with storytelling (Riedl and Bulitko 2012). While the benefits of the interaction concept were demonstrated with two user studies (Kwok et al. 2019), the creation of a gaze-guided narrative for a new panorama is cumbersome and laborious since the connection between panorama and audio content is currently defined by a developer on the source-code level. In order to support complex and large narrative structures and facilitate the inclusion of domain experts in the process, a formal modeling approach would be desirable that enables both, visual and automated model checking (e.g., for avoiding deadlocks and ensuring completeness).

This chapter proposes a formal modeling approach for gaze-guided narratives, which is based on narrative mediation trees. The approach allows us to model the state of an interactive narrative system such that we can differentiate between narrative-induced user actions (e.g., telling a user to look at a new landmark for the next part of the story) and user-directed changes in the narrative (changing the story because the user is focused on a new location). We illustrate the modeling approach with an example from the Swiss saga about 'Wilhelm Tell'.

The rest of the chapter is structured as follows: Sect. 2 discusses related work on storytelling, eye-based interaction, and reiterates on the gaze-guided narratives interaction concept (Sect. 2.3). In Sect. 3, the 'Wilhelm Tell' scenario is introduced. Gaze-guided narrative mediation trees are formally defined and illustrated with the 'Wilhelm Tell' scenario in Sect. 4. The chapter closes with a conclusion and outlook (Sect. 5).

---

[1] https://www.peakfinder.org/.

2 Related Work

2.1 Interactive Narratives

Interactive systems that tell narrative stories in virtual and real-world environments are now commonplace and are exemplified by computer games. But beyond entertainment, interactive narrative systems have been developed for education, similar to tourism guides (Webster 2019). With the increasing availability of location-based technologies, interactive narratives are being developed that unfold in the real world, including outdoors (Farman 2013). The degree of control that the user has to shape the narrative can vary from stories where the user is largely free to choose any path to the ones where the sequence of events in the narrative are highly controlled (Cavazza et al. 2002). Formally, this requires a graphical representation of the narrative state of the system and user, as well as the development of narrative planning algorithms, which are derived from general planning algorithms in artificial intelligence (Porteous et al. 2010; Young et al. 2013). Narrative intelligence research incorporates theory from narratology, where the narrative planning can be influenced by formal rules of how events, characters, goals, and themes combine to create an engaging and coherent story (Bal and Van Boheemen 2009; Riedl and Young 2010; Riedl and Bulitko 2012). In this work, we present an abstract graphical model for gaze-guided narratives which enables narrative planning, although it does not explicitly model all narrative elements, such as characters and themes. This is because in most cases, tourism guides do not have the same degree of narrative complexity as literary works, and the purpose of the storytelling is more informational than affectual. However, one could incorporate those elements in the choice of story plans that are available in the graph (see Sect. 4).

2.2 Outdoor Gaze-Based Interaction

Gaze-based interaction, as enabled by eye-tracking technology, can be used for implementing intuitive, natural, and unobtrusive ways of interacting with a computer system (Majaranta and Bulling 2014). While gaze-based interaction using stationary eye trackers has entered the consumer market, e.g., in gaze-based gaming (Turner et al. 2014), mobile gaze-based interaction is much less common and mostly at the stage of research prototypes (Bulling and Gellersen 2010). This applies even more to outdoor scenarios where eye tracking is often challenging due to interference with sunlight and higher mobility leading to degradation of calibration (Hansen and Pece 2005).

Despite these challenges, outdoor mobile eye tracking offers various opportunities for gaze-based interaction. For instance, by integrating gaze-based interaction with positioning, novel types of location-based services (LBS) become possible (Location-Aware Mobile Eye Tracking, Kiefer et al. 2012). Three types of spatial

Fig. 1 Demo of the gaze-based tourist guide for a panorama wall (exhibit at science fair)

Fig. 2 Gaze-based tourist guide for a city panorama

context can be used for this type of interaction (Giannopoulos et al. 2013): the space interacting in (i.e., the user's position), the space interacted with (i.e., the environmental object looked at), and the spatial information interacted with (e.g., a map used for orientation in wayfinding).

Here, we consider a stationary user interacting with static environmental features (e.g., mountains). A working prototype for these types of scenarios has been developed in the scope of the LAMETTA project (Location-Aware Mobile Eye Tracking For Tourist Assistance, http://www.geogaze.ethz.ch/lametta/) (Anagnostopoulos et al. 2017). Figure 1 shows the system at a science fair in Zurich (Scientifica, September 2017). The LAMETTA system has also been used outdoors for city panoramas (Fig. 2, Anagnostopoulos et al. 2017) and in a virtual CAVE (Cave Automatic Virtual Environment) environment (see next subsection).

Fig. 3 Gaze-Guided Narratives study carried out in the virtual CAVE environment

2.3 Gaze-Guided Narratives

We have recently introduced *Gaze-Guided Narratives* (Kwok et al. 2019), an inter-action concept that combines gaze guidance and narrative features. A prototype for demonstrating and testing the interaction concept was designed for the scenario of exploring a city panorama from a vantage point. First, we evaluated the system through an empirical controlled lab study in a virtual CAVE environment (Fig. 3) with 60 participants, and then the feasibility was demonstrated with a real-world out-door study with 16 tourists. Our results revealed that, compared to the system without the interaction concept, the system with *Gaze-Guided Narratives* could enhance user experience, lower cognitive load, and assist users in the acquisition of spatial knowl-edge in unfamiliar places.

Furthermore, *Gaze-Guided Narratives* are not only limited to tourism scenarios but can also be applied in other scenarios, such as mobile learning in outdoor space or the creation of dynamic story lines in location-based games (as suggested in a recent position paper, Kiefer 2019).

The work has demonstrated the benefits of using the *Gaze-Guided Narratives* interaction concept and it also showed the need for further development of a system-atic model which could support complex narrative structures.

3 Scenario: Swiss Mountain Panorama

We introduce the scenario of a tourist guide that builds a gaze-guided narrative around the Swiss saga of 'Wilhelm Tell', a drama written by Schiller in 1804 about the struggle for freedom in which the hero fights against the despotic authorities, represented by the character 'Hermann Gessler' (Schiller 2001). Figure 4 illustrates a number of places related to that story which can be seen from a vantage point on the Fronalpstock mountain.

Fig. 4 Story-related areas of interest for the Tell scenario (view from the Fronalpstock mountain looking toward Lake Lucerne). © Photo: Josef Schalch (http://mountainstamp.com/)

We consider the following requirements:

(R1) The system must not be visually distracting in order to enable full immersion and unobtrusive user experiences (Häkkilä et al. 2016).

(R2) The system should help the user correctly identify the places relevant for the story when they are mentioned.

(R3) The system should guide the user through the (not necessarily linear) story, but avoid being patronizing (e.g., not force the user to stare at one place for a long time).

(R4) The system should flexibly adapt to the user's interests (which are recognized from gaze).

Table 1 lists a possible gaze-guided narrative which evolves dynamically based on the user's gaze. The system provides information by audio, thus fostering a high degree of visual immersion contrary to displays (**R1**). Problems in visual search are detected and additional help is provided when necessary (**R2**, c, g). The system follows a predefined story line (**R3**, a, b, d, f), but inserts extra information based on the user's interest (**R4**, e). The user is free to explore the panorama during long explanations (**R3**, a, d, e), contributing to high immersion (**R1**).

The following section illustrates how the 'Wilhelm Tell' scenario can be modeled with *gaze-guided narrative mediation trees*, a formal modeling approach for gaze-guided narratives.

4 Gaze-Guided Narrative Mediation Trees

In this section, we introduce gaze-guided narrative mediation trees, which are trees of partial story plans for scenes, which are mediated by gaze-guided interaction. They are an adaptation of the *narrative mediation tree* formalization Riedl and Young

Table 1 Example for a gaze-guided narrative: the system guides the user and adapts its storytelling to her gaze

Alice is hiking in the Swiss Alps. She has reached a vantage point from where she can enjoy a view on Lake Lucerne (see Fig. 4). Her mobile phone vibrates and shows a notification that a gaze-guided narrative titled 'Wilhelm Tell's struggle for freedom' is available for her current position. She puts on her eye tracking-enabled goggles, plugs in the earphones and puts the phone back in her pocket

	System	Alice
a	Welcome to the story of Wilhelm Tell ... [introduction]	Alice freely explores the panorama while listening
b	The Tell story is tightly connected to the myth about the foundation of Switzerland which is supposed to have taken place at Rütliwiese, a small piece of grassland on the opposite side of the lake.	Alice looks at the wrong place
c	Let me help you find Rütliwiese... [more detailed description]	Alice searches and finds Rütliwiese
d	Yes, you found it. ... [starts story about Rütliwiese]	Alice listens and starts exploring the opposite hill
e	[interrupts story]. By the way, there is a beautiful hiking trail along the hill you are currently looking at. It starts at Rütliwiese. ... [continues story]	Alice further explores the hill and Rütliwiese
f	Now, let's start with the story of Tell. The story is about a conflict with Gessler, and it starts in Altdorf, a village at the left shore of the lake.	Alice searches
g	Actually, you have looked at Altdorf in the very beginning. Do you remember?	Alice looks at Altdorf
h	...	

(2006) developed for interactive stories in virtual settings, such as games, but where the user actions that drive the narrative are gaze-guided and story elements are associated with narrative regions within a visual scene. A gaze-guided narrative system can either intervene with a user action by redirecting the user's attention to enforce a particular linear sequence of story elements, or it can accommodate the user's action by branching the story. A gaze-guided narrative mediation tree provides a way of generating multiple story lines for a scene based on user interaction.

Definition 1 A **narrative region**, r, is a contiguous area in the scene with which narrative content is associated.

For scenes from a known, fixed vantage point, these can be defined as two-dimensional polygons within the scene. In other cases, regions within a scene can be derived from three-dimensional models of the physical environment surrounding the user (e.g., building models or topographical Viewshed data). A narrative region is geometrically defined and thus has no inherent semantics. However, when the regions are derived from features in geospatial data, the original features might have additional attributes, such as semantic types.

Definition 2 A **content node** is a tuple $< c, R >$, where c is an atomic unit of narrative content, such as a paragraph of audio text, and R is a set of narrative regions for which the content is relevant.

In many cases, R will be a singleton set, however, we leave open the possibility of content being related to more than one narrative region.

Definition 3 A **node transition** is a tuple $< n_1, \alpha, n_2 >$, where n_1, n_2 are content nodes and α is a directed gaze-guided action performed by the user (e.g., moving from one narrative region to the next).

Definition 4 A **partially ordered plan** is an ordered collection of node transitions that comprise a single (i.e., directed) spatial narrative for a given scene. It is defined as a tuple $< T, O >$, where T is a set of node transitions, and O is a set of ordering constraints $t_i < t_j$, where $t_i, t_j \in T$. The gaze-guided narrative mediation tree (defined below) has as an element, P, a set of partially ordered plans.

Definition 5 A **story branch** connects two partially ordered plans within the mediation tree, and is triggered by a user action that represents a user choice, such as looking at a new part of the scene. It is a tuple, $< p_1, C, \delta, p_2 >$, where $p_1, p_2 \in P$, δ is the user-directed gaze-based action, and C is a set of criteria that must be met for the branch to be made.

The criteria can be based on heuristics or classifiers utilizing different gaze-metrics that have been shown to be indicative for certain cognitive states, such as intent (Bednarik et al. 2012), interest (Krejtz et al. 2016), boredom (Kiefer et al. 2014), or internal thought (Huang et al. 2019). For instance, if the story is currently related to the narrative region r_1, but the user looks at a different narrative region r_2, the story branch may only be made if the following criterion is met: coefficient $\mathcal{K}$ indicates focal attention Krejtz et al. (2016). The criteria might also be informed by an additional user model, enabling personalized heuristics. In addition, the criteria $C(b)$ for a given branch b may be informed by the history of transitions executed up to that point in the narrative.

Definition 6 A **gaze-guided narrative mediation tree** represents the universe of narrative interactions that can be told for a scene. It is a tuple $< P, D, \Delta, B >$, where P is a set of partially ordered plans, B is a set of story branches, D is a set of user-directed gaze-based actions, and Δ is a library of gaze-guided actions, where $D \subseteq \Delta$.

A gaze-guided narrative system can use a mediation tree to maintain the state and interactively generate stories based on user interaction. Gaze-guided narrative mediation trees enable formalization of traditional (i.e., non-computationally delivered) narratives that have already been written for outdoor spaces. Spatial narratives

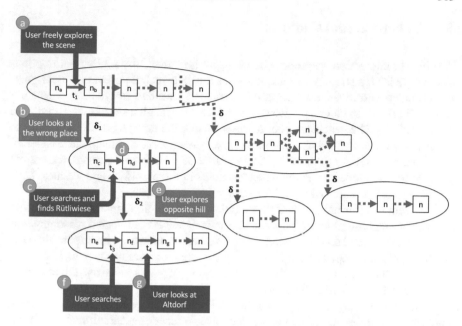

Fig. 5 This figure illustrates the gaze-guided meditation tree for the Wilhelm Tell example shown in Table 1, where each green-circled letter corresponds to a step shown in that table. The path taken by the user is highlighted by solid arrows in the tree, and alternative paths are indicated by dashed lines. The squares indicate content nodes that link narrative content and a region within the scene, and each oval indicates a partially ordered plan. The blue arrows indicate node transitions that are directed by the system within a single partially ordered plan. The orange arrows indicate story branches triggered by user actions, which changes the state to a new partially ordered plan

at existing touristic sites employ a variety of narrative strategies for guiding people through stories in space, including narratives at single points or places, narratives arranged in sequential paths (chronological or non-chronological) such as numbered tours, and narratives that consist of more complex spatial and temporal sequences that might be nonlinear and open-ended (Azaryahu and Foote 2008). In this model, a narrative at a single point is represented by a content node. A sequential, linear narrative is represented by a partially ordered plan. And spatial narratives with more complex sequences and multiple story lines are represented by a full mediation tree.

Figure 5 shows the path taken through a gaze-guided narrative mediation tree by the user in the example in Table 1. The user freely exploring the panorama is the first transition, t_1. Since there is no opportunity for the user to change the story at this point, this free exploration is not interpreted as a user-directed action. However, after n_b when the user looks at the wrong place, it is a user-directed action, δ_1, that causes a branch to a new partially ordered plan. Searching and finding Rütliwiese is another transition, t_2, because it is directed by the system. When the user starts exploring the hill, δ_2, another story branch occurs. Other possible paths through the tree are also sketched in Fig. 5, represented by the dashed lines.

5   Conclusion and Outlook

The type of interaction we propose in this paper is neither fully explicit nor implicit, and we envision a strategy that encompasses multiple techniques to reach our goal. Gaze-guided narratives are a form of interactive narrative storytelling where the storytelling process can be modeled as a trajectory through a state space (Riedl and Bulitko 2012). The gaze actions of the user dictate the ordering of the story and in some cases its outcome, but at the same time, it is important to maintain coherency in the narrative (Riedl et al. 2008). Story graphs as well as partially ordered scripts provide formal models to enforce dependencies in the narrative, and we have built on these to create a formal model for gaze-guided narratives.

Different to informal and less structured ways of specifying a narrative, such as drawing a graph on a whiteboard, our formalism enables automated reasoning and model checking, and can be applied to large narratives. However, in order to keep the modeling effort acceptable and feasible for non-computer scientists (e.g., historians or other domain experts), we envision that modeling of gaze-guided narratives should be supported by user-friendly tools.

Modeling user preferences based on gaze behavior in outdoor settings remains another open problem. We anticipate that bespoke user conceptual models will be necessary to create individuated gaze-guided narratives for different types of environments. Another key challenge is how to interpret gaze behavior as an indicator of user intent to make a shift in the story graph. We see these requisite components leading to a full program of future experimental research.

Acknowledgments   This work has been supported by ETH Zurich Research Grant ETH-38 14-2. We thank Lisa Stähli for helping with the content for the Tell scenario.

References

Anagnostopoulos VA, Havlena M, Kiefer P, Giannopoulos I, Schindler K, Raubal M (2017) Gaze-informed location based services. Int J Geogr Inf Sci 31(9):1770–1797. https://doi.org/10.1080/13658816.2017.1334896

Azaryahu M, Foote KE (2008) Historical space as narrative medium: on the configuration of spatial narratives of time at historical sites. Geo J 73(3):179–194. https://doi.org/10.1007/s10708-008-9202-4

Bal M, Van Boheemen C (2009) Narratology: introduction to the theory of narrative. University of Toronto Press

Bednarik R, Vrzakova H, Hradis M (2012) What do you want to do next: a novel approach for intent prediction in gaze-based interaction. In: Proceedings of the symposium on eye tracking research and applications. ACM, pp 83–90

Bettini C, Mascetti S (2016) Safetrekker: towards automatic recognition of critical situations in mountain excursions. In: (UbiMount) ubiquitous computing in the mountains (2016)

Bulling A, Gellersen H (2010) Toward mobile eye-based human-computer interaction. IEEE Pervasive Comput 9(4):8–12

Cavazza M, Charles F, Mead SJ (2002) Emergent situations in interactive storytelling. In: Proceedings of the 2002 ACM symposium on applied computing. ACM, pp 1080–1085

Cheverst, KWJ, Gregory IN, Turner H (2016) Encouraging visitor engagement and reflection with the landscape of the english lake district: exploring the potential of locative media. In: International workshop on 'Unobtrusive user experiences with technology in nature', pp 1–5

Farman J (2013) The mobile story: narrative practices with locative technologies. Routledge

Giannopoulos I, Kiefer P, Raubal M (2013) Mobile outdoor gaze-based GeoHCI. Geographic human-computer interaction. Workshop at CHI 2013. France, Paris, pp 12–13

Häkkilä J, Cheverst J, Schöning K, Bidwell J, Robinson NJS, Colley A (2016) NatureCHI: Unobtrusive user experiences with technology in nature. In: Proceedings of the 2016 CHI conference extended abstracts on human factors in computing systems, CHI EA '16. ACM, New York, NY, USA, pp 3574–3580. https://doi.org/10.1145/2851581.2856495

Hansen DW, Pece AE (2005) Eye tracking in the wild. Comput Vis Image Underst 98(1):155–181

Huang MX, Li J, Ngai G, Leong HV, Bulling A (2019) Moment-to-moment detection of internal thought during video viewing from eye vergence behavior. In: Proceedings of the ACM multimedia (MM) (2019). https://doi.org/10.1145/3343031.3350573

Kiefer P (2019) Gaze-based narratives for location-based games. In: Designing for outdoor play, workshop at CHI. https://doi.org/10.3929/ethz-b-000337913

Kiefer P, Giannopoulos I, Kremer D, Schlieder C, Raubal M (2014) Starting to get bored: an outdoor eye tracking study of tourists exploring a city panorama. In: Proceedings of the symposium on eye tracking research and applications, ETRA '14. ACM, New York, NY, USA, pp 315–318. https://doi.org/10.1145/2578153.2578216

Kiefer P, Matyas S, Schlieder C (2006) Learning about cultural heritage by playing Geogames. In: Harper R, Rauterberg M, Combetto M (eds) Entertainment computing—ICEC 2006, lecture notes in computer science, vol 4161. Springer, Berlin, Heidelberg, pp 217–228. https://doi.org/10.1007/11872320_26

Kiefer P, Raubal M, Probst T, Bär H (2014) Linear location-based services. In: Proceedings of the 11th international symposium on location-based services (LBS 2014), pp 239–243

Kiefer P, Straub F, Raubal M (2012) Towards location-aware mobile eye tracking. In: Proceedings of the symposium on eye tracking research and applications, ETRA '12. ACM, New York, NY, USA, pp 313–316. https://doi.org/10.1145/2168556.2168624

Krejtz K, Duchowski A, Krejtz I, Szarkowska A, Kopacz A (2016) Discerning ambient/focal attention with coefficient k. ACM Trans Appl Percept (TAP) 13(3):11

Kwok TC, Kiefer P, Schinazi V, Adams B, Raubal M (2019) Gaze-guided narratives: Adapting audio guide content to gaze in virtual and real environments. In: Proceedings of the 2019 CHI conference on human factors in computing systems, CHI '19. ACM, New York, NY, USA. https://doi.org/10.1145/3290605.3300721

Losing V, Rottkamp L, Zeunert M, Pfeiffer T (2014) Guiding visual search tasks using gaze-contingent auditory feedback. In: Proceedings of the 2014 ACM international joint conference on pervasive and ubiquitous computing: adjunct publication, UbiComp '14 adjunct. ACM, New York, NY, USA, pp 1093–1102. https://doi.org/10.1145/2638728.2641687

Majaranta P, Bulling A (2014) Eye tracking and eye-based human–computer interaction. In: Advances in physiological computing. Springer, pp 39–65

Nisi V, Wood A, Davenport G, Oakley I (2004) Hopstory: an interactive, location-based narrative distributed in space and time. In: International conference on technologies for interactive digital storytelling and entertainment. Springer, pp 132–141

Porteous J, Cavazza M, Charles F (2010) Applying planning to interactive storytelling: narrative control using state constraints. ACM Trans Intell Syst Technol (TIST) 1(2):10

Riedl MO, Bulitko V (2012) Interactive narrative: an intelligent systems approach. AI Mag 34(1):67

Riedl MO, Stern A, Dini D, Alderman J (2008) Dynamic experience management in virtual worlds for entertainment, education, and training. Int Trans Syst Sci Appl Spec Issue Agent Based Syst Hum Learn 4(2):23–42

Riedl MO, Young RM (2006) From linear story generation to branching story graphs. IEEE Comput Graph Appl 26(3):23–31

Riedl MO, Young RM (2010) Narrative planning: balancing plot and character. J Artif Intell Res 39:217–268

Sailer C, Kiefer P, Schito J, Raubal M (2016) Map-based visual analytics of moving learners. Int J Mob Hum Comput Interact 8(4). https://doi.org/10.4018/IJMHCI.2016100101

Schiller F (2001) Wilhelm Tell. Reclam

Schöning J, Hecht B, Starosielski N (2008) Evaluating automatically generated location-based stories for tourists. In: CHI'08 extended abstracts on human factors in computing systems. ACM, pp 2937–2942

Turner J, Velloso E, Gellersen H, Sundstedt V (2014) Eyeplay: applications for gaze in games. In: Proceedings of the first ACM SIGCHI annual symposium on computer-human interaction in play, CHI PLAY '14. ACM, New York, NY, USA, pp 465–468. https://doi.org/10.1145/2658537. 2659016

Webster A (2019) Assassin's creed origins new educational mode is a violence-free tour through ancient Egypt. https://www.theverge.com/2018/2/20/17033024/assassins-creed-origins-discovery-tour-educational-mode-release. Accessed 28 May 2019

Wiehr F, Kosmalla F, Daiber F, Krüger A (2016) Interfaces for assessing the rated perceived exertion (rpe) during high-intensity activities. In: Proceedings of the 2016 ACM international joint conference on pervasive and ubiquitous computing: adjunct, UbiComp '16. ACM, New York, NY, USA, pp 851–855. https://doi.org/10.1145/2968219.2968532

Young RM, Ware SG, Cassell BA, Robertson J (2013) Plans and planning in narrative genera-tion: a review of plan-based approaches to the generation of story, discourse and interactivity in narratives. Sprache und Datenverarb Spec Issue Form ComputMod Narrat 37(1–2):41–64

Conflict Between Trail Users Related to the Culture of Conservation

Abigail Bartolome

Abstract Hiking is a popular recreational activity for many—from tourists strolling through Yosemite Valley to thru-hikers dedicating months of their lives to their relationship with the trail; hiking is an activity that is widely accessible. Because of the diversity in motivations for hiking, there is inevitably a variety of hiking cultures. Exploring these different cultures and understanding how they relate to each other can help in engaging stakeholders of the trail. Understanding how different trail cultures relate to each other is an important step toward finding ways to encourage environmentally friendly outdoor recreation practices and developing hiker-approved (and environmentally conscious) technologies to use on the trail. In this chapter, we highlight the culture of conservation and how the values of conservancies conflict with their own missions. By studying tweets, we identify cultural differences between trail communities. We also identify the most significantly discussed forms of trail depreciation. Identifying the most significantly discussed forms of trail depreciation is helpful to conservation organizations so that they can more appropriately share which Leave No Trace practices hikers should place extra effort into practicing. In contrast, the lack of discussing conservation highlights the idea that preservation may not be a priority in hiking communities.

1 Introduction

In a memoir of her hike on the Pacific Crest Trail, *Wild*, Cheryl Strayed said to a reporter in an amused tone, "I'm not a hobo, I'm a long-distance hiker." Hiking is an activity that can be enjoyed by many, but some hikers have different definitions of what they expect out of a hike. Some hikers expect a leisurely stroll by their neighborhood pond; others expect to summit a 14,000-foot peak. Because it is an activity that is so versatile and accessible, it is difficult to make generalizations of hikers—what they value, what they look for in trails, etc.

A. Bartolome (✉)
Dartmouth College, Hanover 03755, USA
e-mail: abigail.bartolome.gr@dartmouth.edu

© Springer Nature Switzerland AG 2020
D. S. McCrickard et al. (eds.), *HCI Outdoors: Theory, Design, Methods and Applications*, Human–Computer Interaction Series,
https://doi.org/10.1007/978-3-030-45289-6_18

319

Fig. 1 "Heavy horse traffic has compacted and incised the main tread, which captures and retains water; subsequent hikers and horse riders seeking to avoid mudholes widen trails. Leave No Trace guidelines ask visitors to stay as close to the center of the tread as possible to avoid trail widening."— Marion et al. (2016)

This challenge of generalizing hikers poses a major problem for trail specialists. Every year, the number of northbound thru-hikers on the Appalachian Trail increase. Furthermore, as literature like Cheryl Strayed's *Wild* and Bill Bryson's *A Walk in the Woods* enter the mainstream culture, major hiking trails, such as the Appalachian Trail, are seeing increasing traffic each year. This increase in foot traffic has caused a strain in resources along these hiking trails, and it is imperative that conservation be a priority for all stakeholders of the trail Appalachian Trail Conservancy (2016). While trail experts are acutely aware of the need to consider the implications of foot traffic on the trail, it is not at the forefront of every hiker's mind. Figure 1 shows an example of hikers who are unaware that they are contributing to widening the trail by trying to circumvent the muddy areas of the trail. Forestry scientists and conservancy organizations are searching for ways to educate the public in ways to aid in the effort of preserving trails. Through the uses of Twitter and some deeper explorations of the communities and cultures on the trail, we can better understand the values and motivations of recreational hikers. By understanding the values of motivations of recreational hikers, we can help trail specialists in influencing hikers to adapt to hiking practices that are in line with the effort to conserve trail resources.

2 Cultures of the Triple Crown Trails

In *America's Greatest Hiking Trails*, Triple Crown veteran Karen Berger discussed each trail in a way that suggests that they each had a particular identity. She described the Appalachian Trail (AT) as "a Community in the Wilderness" because of its ability to attract hikers from a vast assortment of backgrounds and its remarkably large number of annual thru-hike attempts. She describes the Continental Divide Trail (CDT) as "the Wild Child," since those attempting to thru-hike the incomplete trail must often "make their own route, following the suggestions of those who have gone before, or improvising their own paths through trailless wetlands." She referred to the Pacific Crest Trail (PCT) as "the Soul of American Wilderness," because unlike the AT, which prides itself on being a community in the wilderness, and the CDT, which is known for its hikers conquering nature, the PCT is about "melding with the wilderness and sometimes submitting to it." Since she writes about each trail from her own personal knowledge and experience, the judgments that she made for assigning each trail an identity are personal to her. By aggregating the knowledge and experiences of a larger portion of each trail community, we can better understand that collective community's values and better define what the community of that trail values Berger (2014).

We studied the mission statements of each of the Triple Crown conservancy organizations to see whether an identity could be identified for each trail. Table 1 shows these mission statements. From the mission statements, it appeared that the Appalachian Trail's identity was focused on preserving "natural beauty and priceless cultural heritage." The Pacific Crest Trail Association's mission statement reflects an identity that values a "world-class experience" for those who use that trail. Meanwhile, the Continental Divide Trail Coalition's mission statement is centered around completing its construction and protecting its land. Alan Dix of the School of Computer Science at the University of Birmingham commented on the mission statements, stating that they were written by public relations and marketing experts who use flowery and generalized language to describe the trails. To put it succinctly, the mission statements were too innocuous to truly embody the spirit of the trails, because their mission statements were written in such a way to attract people to explore and protect their respective trails.

While the mission statements did not reflect an identity for the trails, they did reflect a collective conflict in trail conservation. All three mission statements demon-

Table 1 Mission statements of conservancy organizations and their respective trails

Conservancy organization	Trail	Mission statement
Appalachian trail conservancy	Appalachian trail	The Appalachian Trail Conservancy's mission is to **preserve and manage the Appalachian Trail**—ensuring that its vast natural beauty and priceless cultural heritage **can be shared and enjoyed today, tomorrow, and for centuries to come**. Appalachian Trail Conservancy (2018a)
Continental Divide Trail Coalition	Continental Divide Trial	The Continental Divide Trail Coalition's mission is to create a community **committed to constructing, promoting, and protecting, in perpetuity, the CDT**, which stretches from Canada to Mexico, through Montana, Idaho, Wyoming, Colorado, and New Mexico. Continental Divide Trail Coalition (2018)
Pacific Crest Trail Association	Pacific Crest Trail	The mission of the Pacific Crest Trail Association is to protect, **preserve, and promote** the Pacific Crest National Scenic Trail as a **world-class experience** for hikers and equestrians, and for all the values provided by **wild and scenic lands**. Pacific Crest Trail Association (2018)

strate the organizations' stewardship for the trails. Similarly, all three organizations state that their mission is to promote the trails. This creates a conflict in values because, as we will discuss later, increasing trail usage inevitably leads to trail degradation. Promoting trail use makes it difficult to preserve the trail because it inherently leads to an additional impact on the land, as well as adding a strain on the trail's resources.

3 The Conflict in Conservation Culture

In a position paper to the HCI Outdoors workshop at ACM CHI 2018, we discussed conservation as a trail culture Abigail et al. (2018).

The outdoor spaces that are so loved and coveted by trail enthusiasts are protected by hikers and conservancy organizations. One well known conservancy organization is the Leave No Trace Center for Outdoor Ethics. Practicing Leave No Trace is common in the conservation culture. Practices as common as "pack-it in, pack-it out" are part of Leave No Trace. Other less visible practices such as digging cat-holes (holes for solid human waste that are dug 4–6 inches in diameter and 6–8 inches in depth) 200 feet from the trail and water sources, or minimizing visible impact after camping in pristine areas, also are part of Leave No Trace, and thus conservation culture Marion (2014).

Our goal was to highlight a culture of stakeholders that take care of the trail because of how much they love and respect it. This culture is so passionate about caring for the outdoors that they consciously engage in practices that those outside of the zeitgeist might not even consider, such as cautiously disposing of used toothpaste by spitting toothpaste into rinse water and disposing of it far from a campsite or "broadcasting" their spit over a wide area. Leave No Trace (LNT) is a conservancy program that advocates for practicing low-impact outdoor skills Marion (2014). Further information on the details of this conservancy program can be found in *Leave No Trace in the Outdoors* Marion (2014), but the seven principles of Leave No Trace are as follows:

1. Plan Ahead and Prepare;
2. Travel and Camp on Durable Surfaces;
3. Dispose of Waste Properly;
4. Leave What You Find;
5. Minimize Campfire Impacts;
6. Respect Wildlife;
7. Be Considerate of Other Visitors.

This care for hiking trails extends all the way to planning the logistics of a hike. The Appalachian Trail Conservancy (ATC) has been concerned that the rise of hikers attempting to thru-hike the AT has led to overcrowding on trails. The ATC found that significantly more thru-hikers on the AT register as northbound hikers with a southern terminus start. Fewer hikers register as southbound hikers with a northern terminus start. Even fewer register as flip-floppers, where hikers start in the middle of the trail, hike toward one terminus and go back to where they started (by way of car, bus, flight, etc.) to hike toward the other terminus to finish. These options for starting an AT thru-hike can be found in Fig. 2 Appalachian Trail Conservancy (2018b). The exceptionally high demand for campsites along the Appalachian Trail can threaten its resources. The flip-flop itinerary for thru-hiking (start midway through the trail and hike in one direction, transport back to midway start point and hike in the opposite direction Appalachian Trail Conservancy (2018b)) evenly distributes the use of Appalachian Trail campsites and reduces the aggregate camping impact and crowding, thus alleviating stress on trail resources. For this reason, the ATC recommends flip-flopping for thru-hiking the AT. "The increase in flip-flop thru-hikes indicates that many hikers have recognized the benefits of non-traditional thru-hiking itineraries, both for themselves and the Trail" Appalachian Trail Conservancy (2016). While the rise in flip-flop thru-hikes is helpful in preserving the Appalachian Trail, there are

Northbound

Starting at Springer Mountain has long been the most popular place to start a thru-hike. But "popular" has led to "crowded" between March 1 and April 15. During this peak starting period, the southern end of the A.T. becomes a continuous stream of hikers during the day, with dozens of hikers clustered around campsites at night.

READ MORE

Flip Flop

Increasingly, hikers are choosing to start somewhere in the middle of the Trail. Generally, these alternative itineraries offer a gradual progression from easier to more difficult terrain and more frequent resupplies. You can also avoid crowds and the party atmosphere, follow favorable weather conditions and reduce crowding and minimize resource damage to the Trail.

READ MORE

Southbound

Maine has never been a popular place to start a thru-hike, and may never be. Katahdin is regarded as the most difficult mountain on the entire A.T. and the route through Maine is, in places, not so much a path as a climb or scramble over rocks and roots. It's no place for anyone who is inexperienced or out of shape to start a long-distance hike.

READ MORE

Fig. 2 Options for starting an Appalachian Trail thru-hike Appalachian Trail Conservancy (2018b)

still significantly more northbound thru-hikers and there is still a growing strain on trail resources.

The push for redistributing thru-hiking starting points demonstrates a conflict within the ATC's own values. Recall from Sect. 2 that the ATC's mission is to preserve the Appalachian Trail, while also ensuring that the beauty of the trail can be shared and enjoyed. With over three million visitors a year Appalachian Trail Conservancy (2020), it is clear the ATC has been able to share the beauty of the trail as expressed in their mission statement; however, it is clear that achieving their mission of sharing the trail is contradictory to preserving the trail.

The Appalachian Trail Conservancy also strives to protect the "trail experience." The Appalachian Trail Experience is defined to represent "the sum of opportunities that are available for those walking the Appalachian Trail to interact with the wild, scenic, pastoral, cultural, and natural elements of the environment of the Appalachian Trail, unfettered and unimpeded by competing sights or sounds and in as direct and intimate a manner as possible," Jeffrey (2018). In the July/August 1997 edition of the *Appalachian Trailway News*, the summary definition included the following opportunities ATC Board of Managers (1997):

- Opportunities for observation, contemplation, enjoyment, and exploration of the natural world.
- A sense of remoteness and detachment from civilization.
- Opportunities to experience solitude, freedom, personal accomplishment, self-reliance, and covery.
- A sense of being on the height of the land.

- Opportunities to experience the cultural, historical, and pastoral elements of the surrounding countryside.
- A feeling of being part of the natural environment.
- Opportunities for travel on foot, including opportunities for long-distance hiking.

In studying the Appalachian Trail Experience, we noted the phrase, "interact with the wild, scenic pastoral, cultural, and natural elements," and we associated that with the Appalachian Trail's mission statement in Table 1. We also note key words such as "observation," "contemplation," "self-discovery," "cultural," "historical," and "natural environment." Combined with the Appalachian Trail's mission statement and Karen Berger's characterization, we gather that the Appalachian Trail has a culture of hikers reflecting on themselves and experiencing self-realization from the heritage and natural beauty of the trail. The practice of Leave No Trace and other conservation-conscious practices is imperative to maintain this trail experience and sustain this culture. Here lies the heart of the conflict in AT conservation— the trail's mission of preserving its natural scenery fosters a trail experience that draws more visitors to the trail and consequently forms more wear and tear on the trail.

The Pacific Crest Trail Association also strives to protect the "trail experience." "Trail users seek the tangible and intangible benefits of wandering amongst the exceptionally scenic, wild, natural, and historic landscapes along the crest of the Pacific ranges of the United States. The Trail experience, as used in this context, represents the sum of experiences available to the traditional and intended user traveling along the PCT" Pacific Crest Trail Association (2015). The PCT experience is described to focus on "natural" and "undisturbed" landscapes, so the need to practice Leave No Trace is imperative. We noted that the PCT's mission statement also demonstrates the importance of maintaining a "world-class experience" and the value of maintaining "wild and scenic lands." In recalling Karen Berger's description of the Triple Crown trails, we realize that an important piece of the Pacific Crest Trail's culture is embracing the wilderness of the PCT and marveling at the drastic changes in terrain along the trail. The PCT's trail experience has a similar discrepancy to that of the AT's, where the PCTA promotes a world-class experience of undisturbed landscapes to attract visitors. If the visitors do not practice LNT, the world-class trail experience of undisturbed land will no longer exist.

4 Finding Trail Culture Using Twitter

Alan Dix's comment on the conservancy organization's mission statements motivated an effort to study the tweets by the Triple Crown trail communities in order to find each trail's unique identity. In order to find meaningful topics in the Triple Crown communities, we used latent Dirichlet allocation (LDA) to identify topics discussed in the AT community, PCT community, and CDT community. In this experiment, each corpus of tweets corresponded to its respective trail (e.g., tweets regarding the AT were in the AT community's corpus). The tweets from these experiments

Table 2 Details of tweet collection

Trail	Number of Tweets	Search queries
Appalachian Trail	24,954	"Appalachian Trail"
		"#appalachiantrail"
		"#at2017"
		@AT_Conservancy
Continental Divide Trail	2,508	"CDT"
		"#cdt"
		"#cdt2017"
		@CDNST1
		"#continentaldividetrail"
		"Continental Divide Trail"
Pacific Crest Trail	9,444	"Pacific Crest Trail"
		"#pacificcresttrail"
		"PCT"
		"#pct"
		"#pct2017"
		"@PCTAssociation"

were collected from January 2017–May 2017. Table 2 shows the number of tweets collected for each trail and the search queries used for data collection. After running LDA over 100 iterations, we found seven topics of seven-word distributions for each trail. The results of this experiment can be found in Fig. 3. Using rawgraphs.io, we were able to create visualizations for the Appalachian Trail topics and Pacific Crest Trail topics Michele et al. (2017). We created treemap visualizations, where each grouping of blocks of the same color is a topic, and the size of the block correlates to its term's probability of occurring in the topic, as shown in Figs. 3 and 4.

From Table 3, we can see that the Appalachian Trail community leans heavily toward discussing their in-the-moment experiences on the trail. AT Topic 1 refers to McAfee Knob—the most photographed site on the Appalachian Trail Roanoke Outside Foundation (2018). AT Topic 2 suggests the image of a hiker watching the sunrise over the Catawba Valley on a backpacking trip. AT Topic 5 describes a woman's hiking trip.

On the other hand, the Pacific Crest Trail tweets related more to planning the logistics of a hike. For example, PCT Topic 1 was about resupply tips in California, and PCT Topic 4 was about acquiring Danner boots at an Outdoor Research show. PCT Topic 6 is about hikers taking months off from their jobs for their PCT backpacking trips.

The Continental Divide Trail's datasets seemed to yield topics relating to bravery on the CDT and supporting the Continental Divide Trail Coalition (Twitter account: @cdnst1). The terms of the CDT's topics, however, were repeated through the seven topics. When looking at the datasets, the Appalachian Trail's corpus had 24,915

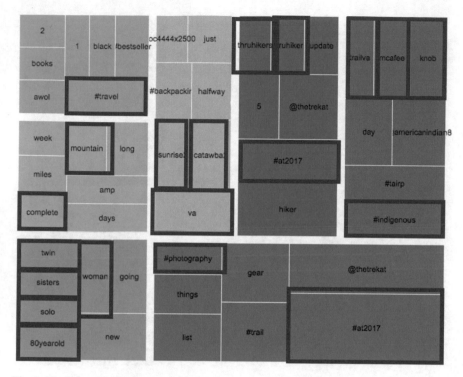

Fig. 3 TreeMap visualization of topic analysis on Appalachian Trail tweets

tweets and the Pacific Crest Trail's corpus had 8,547 tweets. On the other hand, the Continental Divide Trail's corpus had 2,457 tweets—fewer than 10% of the Appalachian Trail's and fewer than 35% of the Pacific Crest Trail's corpora.

We noticed that none of the topics reflected the mission statements of the Triple Crown conservancy organizations. These topics did not describe stewardship, preservation, or even depreciative behaviors. The United States National Park Service defines depreciative behaviors as "actions that degrade park resources or the experiences of others." Specific examples of depreciative behavior are National Park Service (2018)

- littering;
- feeding of wildlife;
- collection of greenwood for use in campfires;
- disfiguring trees and rocks;
- improper disposal of human waste in the backcountry;
- walking and hiking with pets that are not leashed;
- collection of specimens;
- construction of fire rings and ground fires in the backcountry;
- shortcutting on trail switchbacks.

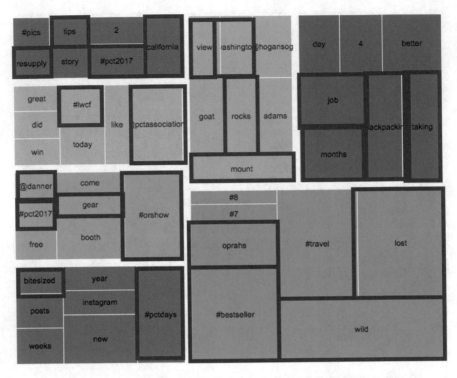

Fig. 4 TreeMap visualization of topic analysis on Pacific Crest Trail tweets

Littering seemed to be an obvious form of depreciative behavior as children are taught from a young age to not litter. Collecting specimens, such as rocks and flowers, and shortcutting on trail switchbacks, however, are less obvious forms of depreciative behavior, since their environmental impacts are less evident to those who do not spend much time on hiking trails. We decided that an interesting study might be to see which forms of depreciative behavior were most discussed on Twitter. Using a dataset of 1,592,059 tweets, we built a classifier to identify which tweets described a specific depreciative behavior. Table 4 provides details of this corpus.

Labeling training data is integral to building a classifier. In hand Labeling the training data for this classifier, we were able to intimately familiarize ourselves with tweets that mentioned depreciative behaviors. In the fall semester of 2017, Chon et al. built a tweet visualization tool for the CS 5604 class that made hand labeling the training data significantly easier, as it enabled them to search for key words relating to the depreciative behavior (e.g., searching for trash would correspond to littering) Jieun et al. (2017). As shown in Table 5, littering and walking with pets off-leash are the most tweeted about depreciative behaviors. Notice that there is a very small number of tweets related to depreciative behavior. There is not enough

Table 3 Results of topic analysis of tweets: January–May

Topic #	AT Topics	PCT Topics	CDT Topics
Topic 1	#indigenous, #tairp, #amerianindian8, day, knob, mcafee, trailva	California, #pct2017, 2, story, tips, resupply, #pics	help, #bravethecdt, #hikecdt, today, @cdnst1, vote, great
Topic 2	va, catawba, sunrise, halfway, #backpacking, just, oc4444x2400	@pctassociation, like, today, #lwcf, win, did, great	#bravethecdt, @cdnst1, #hikecdt, help, great, support, today
Topic 3	days, amp, long, mountain, complete, miles, week	mount, adams, goat, rocks, @hogansog, washington, view	#bravethecdt, help, today, @cdnst1, support, vote, great
Topic 4	#travel, #bestseller, black, 1, awol, books, 2	#orshow, booth, gear, come, free, #pct2017, @danner	#bravethecdt, help, today, great, @cdnst1, support, #hikecdt
Topic 5	new, going, woman, 80yearold, solo, sisters, twin	wild, lost, #travel #bestseller, oprahs, #7, #8	#bravethecdt, #hikecdt, @cdnst, support, help, great, today
Topic 6	hiker, #at2017, @thetrekat, 5, update, thruhiker, thruhikers	taking, #backpacking, months, job, better, 4, day	#hikecdt, #bravethecdt, @cdnst1, great, help, support, today
Topic 7	#at2017, @thetrekat #trail, gear, list, things, #photography	#pctdays, new, instagram, year, weeks, posts, bitesized	help, #bravethecdt, today, #votecdt, vote, 25k, @cdnst1

training data to train a good classifier, which shows just how a few people tweet about depreciative behaviors. The conflict of conservation cultures does not seem to be a priority in communities that tweet about hiking.

5 Conclusion

In this chapter, we have given examples of distinct trail cultures among the Triple Crown trails, and we have described conflicts within the trail culture of conservation. These conflicts can be identified and described by simply studying the mission statements of the trails' conservancy organizations, however, these conflicts do not appear to be publicly discussed on Twitter. More specifically, there is very limited discussion of trail depreciation culture on Twitter. The HCI community has demonstrated the power of Twitter and online communities (Gruzd et al. 2011; Zhao and Rosson 2009; Cristian et al. 2013; Stevie et al. 2018). By way of connecting with other hikers and sharing their hiking experiences, whether that means posting on the trail or later in a moment of reflection, members of the hiking community can

Table 4 Details of tweet collection—one year of collecting

Seed	Description	Number of Tweets
@AnishHikes	Tweets pulled from a Triple Crown veteran's Twitter account	3,082
Appalachian Trail	Search query for "Appalachian trail"	71,324
AT2017	Search query for "at2017"	711
@AT_Conservancy	Tweets pulled from Appalachian Trail Conservancy 's Twitter account	3,797
@CDNST1	Tweets pulled from Continental Divide Trail Coalition's Twitter account	2,291
CDT2017	Search query for "cdt2017"	17
Continental Divide Trail	Search query for "continental divide trail"	1,779
Hike	Search query for "hike"	1,477,708
@hikewithgravity	Tweets pulled from AT hiker who plans to hike PCT	543
@leavenotrace	Tweets pulled from the leave no trace Twitter account	3,266
Pacific Crest Trail	Search query for "pacific crest trail"	21,639
PCT2017	Search query for "pct2017"	378
@PCTAssociation	Tweets pulled from Pacific Crest Trail Association's Twitter account	878
@PCTNews	News posted by Halfmile PCT maps	1,261
@O_Cliff23	Tweets pulled from a Leave No Trace trainer who has hiked AT	213
@walkingthecdt	Tweets pulled from hikers who have hiked the CDT	172

develop bonds with each other and develop their values as a community. By creating a culture that represents the values of their members, it would be a strategic decision to use that influence to promote the idea of conservation and make it a priority for other hikers.

Table 5 Training data—breakdown of tweets for depreciative behaviors

Depreciative behavior	Number of Tweets
Littering	55
Walking and hiking with pets that are not leashed	54
Improper disposal of human waste in the backcountry	36
Disfiguring trees and rocks	28
Collection of specimens	10
Feeding of wildlife	8
Construction of fire rings and ground fires in the backcountry	4
Shortcutting on trail switchbacks	1
Collection of greenwood for use in campfires	0

Acknowledgments Thank you to Edward A. Fox, Scott McCrickard, Mike Jones, Tim Stelter, Jeffrey Marion, and the Digital Library Research Laboratory at Virginia Tech for supporting this research effort. Thank you to the National Science Foundation for funding the Integrated Digital Event Archiving and Library (IDEAL) (Grant IIS-1319578) and Global Event and Trend Archive Research (GETAR) (Grant IIS-1619028) projects which made this study possible.

References

Anatoliy G, Barry W, Yuri T (2011) Imagining Twitter as an imagined community. Am Behav Sci 55(10):1294–1318
Appalachian Trail Conservancy (2016) sees rise in ethical hiking practices among appalachian trail hikers. Accessed 12 Apr 2018
Appalachian Trail Conservancy (2018) Thru-Hiking, 2018. Accessed 12 Apr 2018
Appalachian Trail Conservancy (2018), Our mission, vision, and values. Accessed 12 Apr 2018
Appalachian Trail Conservancy (2020). Explore the Trail. Accessed 21 Jan 2020
ATC Board of Managers (1997) The Appalachian Trail experience, July/Aug 1997
Bartolome A, Fox EA, McCrickard DS (2018) Understanding trail cultures through various stakeholders of the trail. In ACM CHI Workshop on HCI Outdoors, Montreal, Canada, p 2018
Chancellor S, Hu A, De Choudhury M (2018) Norms matter: Contrasting social support around behavior change in online weight loss communities. In: Proceedings of the 2018 CHI conference on human factors in computing systems, CHI '18, New York. ACM, pp 666:1–666:14
Chon J, Wang H, Bian Y, Niu S (2017) CS5604: information and storage retrieval fall 2017-FE (Front-end team). http://hdl.handle.net/10919/81423
Continental Divide Trail Coalition (2018). CDTC background. Accessed 12 Apr 2018
Danescu-Niculescu-Mizil C, West R, Jurafsky D, Leskovec J, Potts C (2013) No country for old members: user lifecycle and linguistic change in online communities. In: Proceedings of the 22nd international conference on world wide web, WWW '13, New York. ACM, pp 307–318
Jeffrey M (2014) Leave no trace in the outdoors. Stackpole Books, Mechanicsburg, PA
Karen B (2014) America's great hiking trails. Rizzoli, New York, NY
Marion J (2018) The appalachian trail experience. Priv Commun

Marion Jeffrey L, Yu-Fai L, Holly E, Kaitlin B (2016) A review and synthesis of recreation ecology research findings on visitor impacts to wilderness and protected natural areas. J For 114(3):352–362

Mauri M, Elli T, Caviglia G, Uboldi G, Azzi M (2017) RAWGraphs: a visualisation platform to create open outputs. In: Proceedings of the 12th biannual conference on Italian SIGCHI chapter, CHItaly '17, New York. ACM, pp 28:1–28:5

National Park Service (2017). Depreciative visitor use, Dec 2017. Accessed Mar 2018

Pacific Crest Trail Association (2018) Our mission, vision and values. Accessed 12 Apr 2018

Pacific Crest Trail Association (2018). Pacific Crest Trail Association 2014—2017 strategic plan, July 2015. Accessed 12 Apr 2018

Roanoke Outside Foundation. Appalachian Trail hikes (2018). http://www.roanokeoutside.com/land/hiking/appalachian-trail-hikes/. Accessed 28 May 2018

Zhao D, Rosson MB (2009) How and why people Twitter: the role that micro-blogging plays in informal communication at work. In: Proceedings of the ACM 2009 international conference on supporting group work, GROUP '09, New York, NY, USA. ACM, pp 243–252

Printed in the United States
by Baker & Taylor Publisher Services